George Washington Sprott, Thomas Leishman

Book of Common Order of the Church of Scotland

commonly known as John Knox's liturg : and the Directory for public worship of God agreed upon by the Assembly of Divines at Westminster

George Washington Sprott, Thomas Leishman

Book of Common Order of the Church of Scotland
commonly known as John Knox's liturg : and the Directory for public worship of God agreed upon by the Assembly of Divines at Westminster

ISBN/EAN: 9783337290528

Printed in Europe, USA, Canada, Australia, Japan

Cover: Foto ©Lupo / pixelio.de

More available books at **www.hansebooks.com**

THE
BOOK OF COMMON ORDER

OF THE

CHURCH OF SCOTLAND

COMMONLY KNOWN AS JOHN KNOX'S LITURGY

AND

THE DIRECTORY

FOR THE PUBLIC WORSHIP OF GOD

AGREED UPON BY THE ASSEMBLY OF DIVINES AT WESTMINSTER

WITH

Historical Introductions & Illustrative Notes

BY THE

REV. GEORGE W. SPROTT, B.A., AND
REV. THOMAS LEISHMAN, M.A.

WILLIAM BLACKWOOD AND SONS
EDINBURGH AND LONDON
1868

PREFACE.

VARIOUS circumstances of late years have awakened a desire for information as to the worship of the Church of Scotland in former times. As the information has not hitherto been accessible in a compact form, we have endeavoured to supply the want by reprinting the old Scottish Liturgy, and the Westminster Directory, with Introductions and Notes, so as to furnish a continuous view of the worship of the Church since the Reformation.

Our object has been to search out and set forth the facts, in a spirit of fidelity to the truth and of loyalty to the Church.

It has long been the popular impression, that Knox's Liturgy, if used at all, was laid aside soon after the Reformation; that in 1637 the opposition to Laud's Book arose from the hostility of the people to read prayers; that any usages of a liturgical character that were retained after that time were the result of previous Prelatical influence; and that the mode of worship which became common some years after 1645 was the restoration of the Scottish service of an earlier time, before its simplicity had been corrupted by English innovations.

PREFACE.

Our investigations, it must be admitted, have not borne out the entire correctness of these views.

Whatever historical foundation there may be for them, it is plain that the further back we go towards the Reformation, the more does the worship of our Church resemble that of the Continental Reformed, and that some of the peculiarities of the later service were novelties in Scotland, countenanced neither by the Old Liturgy nor the Directory — novelties traceable originally to the Brownists, but mainly to the sectarian influence which was introduced into Scotland from the South at the time of Cromwell's invasion.

Those who, forgetful of the Reformed traditions of the Church, favoured the opinions and practices of the English sectaries, had at the time separated from the General Assembly, and their leaders were deposed. Yet the course of events was such, that some of their tendencies came to prevail. Novelties are very soon accepted as traditions of long standing, and hence innovations which, at their first appearance, were censured by the General Assembly, began, in course of time, to be regarded as the peculiarities of the Church. To defend them, was to maintain the cause for which our reformers and martyrs had suffered and died. The Protesterism of Cromwell's time was confounded with the second Reformation, and the names of Henderson, Dickson, Douglas, and Blair were quoted in support of opinions and practices to which, in their lifetime, they were hostile.

Indeed, the influx of English sectarianism into the Scottish Church has had the effect of blending with its old Reformed principles no little of the Independency of the seventeenth century.

This Southern influence has not only affected the worship of the Church, but to it we owe in a great measure the divisive spirit which has disintegrated Scottish society.

The Reformed Churches and the great Scottish Churchmen of former times never dreamt that separations were justifiable on such grounds as those on which they have since been defended. In America, at the present day, side by side, in the same circumstances, are to be seen the offshoots of the Continental and the Scottish Reformed Churches. The former, such as the Dutch Reformed Church, first planted in the New World, have completely preserved their unity. The latter is split into many "Presbyterian denominations."

It is now many years since a reaction set in against the departure from the old written regulations of the Church in the subject of worship. This reaction still continues, and there is no doubt some danger of its being carried too far; but there is little to be feared should its promoters seek merely the revival of the Reformed spirit in the Church, and the restoration of the state of things that prevailed before Cromwell's invasion and the schism in the Church of 1651—the first that had taken place since the Reformation.

Our hope is that the book which we now give to the public may be useful in affording information as to the past, and thereby to some extent in guiding opinion in the future.

We have to express our obligations to many kind friends

for the loan of books, and other assistance rendered to us in the prosecution of the work ; and, like most other inquirers in the same field for many years back, we have particularly to record our thanks to Mr David Laing of the Signet Library, Edinburgh.

THE EDITORS.

May 1868.

CONTENTS.

	PAGE
PREFACE,	v
INTRODUCTION TO THE BOOK OF COMMON ORDER,	xiii
BOOK OF COMMON ORDER.	
I. THE CALENDAR,	1
II. THE FAIRS,	4
III. THE CONFESSION OF THE CHRISTIAN FAITH,	5
IV. THE ORDER OF ELECTING MINISTERS, ELDERS, AND DEACONS, AND OF THEIR OFFICE AND DUTY,	11
V. THE WEEKLY ASSEMBLY OF THE MINISTERS,	15
VI. AN ORDER FOR INTERPRETATION OF THE SCRIPTURES AND ANSWERING OF DOUBTS,	17
VII. THE FORM AND ORDER OF ELECTING THE SUPERINTENDENT,	18
VIII. AN ORDER OF ECCLESIASTICAL DISCIPLINE,	27
IX. THE ORDER OF EXCOMMUNICATION AND OF PUBLIC REPENTANCE, WITH THE FORM OF ABSOLUTION,	31
X. THE VISITATION OF THE SICK, WITH A PRAYER FOR THE SICK,	71
XI. THE MANNER OF BURIAL,	78
XII. THE ORDER OF PUBLIC WORSHIP,	79
1. A Confession of Sins,	79
2. Another Confession used in the Church of Edinburgh,	80
3. A Confession of Sins to be used before Sermon,	83
4. A Confession used in the time of Extreme Trouble,	85

CONTENTS.

5. A Prayer after Sermon for the whole Estate of Christ's Church,	87
XIII. OTHER PUBLIC PRAYERS,	91
1. Another Manner of Prayer after the Sermon, used in the French Church of Geneva,	91
2. Another do. do.,	97
3. A Prayer used in the Churches of Scotland in the time of their Persecution by the Frenchmen, but principally when the Lord's Table is to be ministered,	103
4. A Thanksgiving unto God after our Deliverance from the Tyranny of the Frenchmen,	109
5. A Prayer used in the Assemblies of the Church,	110
6. A Prayer to be used when God threateneth His Judgments,	113
7. A Prayer in time of Affliction,	116
8. A Prayer for the King,	119
XIV. THE ADMINISTRATION OF THE LORD'S SUPPER,	121
XV. THE FORM OF MARRIAGE,	129
XVI. THE ORDER OF BAPTISM,	135
XVII. A TREATISE ON FASTING, WITH THE ORDER THEREOF,	150
XVIII. THE PSALMS OF DAVID,	195
XIX. CONCLUSIONS OR DOXOLOGIES,	201
XX. HYMNS,	203
1. The Ten Commandments,	203
2. The Lord's Prayer,	204
3. Veni Creator,	206
4. The Song of Simeon, called Nunc Dimittis,	208
5. The Twelve Articles of the Christian Faith,	209
6. The Song of Blessed Mary, called Magnificat,	212
XXI. CALVIN'S CATECHISM,	217
XXII. PRAYERS FOR PRIVATE HOUSES,	221
1. Morning Prayer,	221
2. Prayers before and after Meals,	223
3. Evening Prayer,	225
XXIII. OTHER PRAYERS,	227
1. A Complaint of the Tyranny used against the Saints of God, &c.,	227

CONTENTS.

2. A Godly Prayer to be said at all times, . 231
3. A Prayer to be said of the Child before he study his Lesson, ... 232
4. A Prayer to be said before a Man begin his Work, ... 233
5. A Prayer necessary for all Men, . . . 234

NOTES TO THE BOOK OF COMMON ORDER.

I. LIST OF EDITIONS, ... 237
II. STATEMENT ILLUSTRATING THE PEDIGREE OF THE BOOK OF COMMON ORDER, ... 240
II. CONTENTS OF THE BOOK, SOURCES FROM WHICH TAKEN, &C., ... 241

INTRODUCTION TO THE DIRECTORY, . . 257
DIRECTORY FOR THE PUBLIC WORSHIP OF GOD, ... 281
  THE ACT OF THE GENERAL ASSEMBLY, . . 284
  THE PREFACE, ... 287
    Notes, ... 325
  OF THE ASSEMBLING OF THE CONGREGATION, . 291
    Notes, ... 327
  OF PUBLIC READING OF THE HOLY SCRIPTURES, . 292
    Notes, ... 332
  OF PUBLIC PRAYER BEFORE THE SERMON, . . 293
    Notes, ... 335
  OF THE PREACHING OF THE WORD, . . . 299
    Notes, ... 336
  OF PRAYER AFTER THE SERMON, . . 303
    Notes, ... 339
  OF THE SACRAMENT OF BAPTISM, . . . 304
    Notes, ... 341
  OF THE SACRAMENT OF THE LORD'S SUPPER, . 308
    Notes, ... 346

CONTENTS.

OF THE SANCTIFICATION OF THE LORD'S DAY,
    Notes,
OF THE SOLEMNISATION OF MARRIAGE,
    Notes,
OF THE VISITATION OF THE SICK,
    Notes,
OF BURIAL OF THE DEAD,
    Notes,
OF PUBLIC SOLEMN FASTING,
    Notes,
OF THE OBSERVATION OF DAYS OF PUBLIC THANKS-GIVING,
    Notes,
OF SINGING OF PSALMS,
    Notes,
AN APPENDIX TOUCHING DAYS AND PLACES FOR PUBLIC WORSHIP,
    Notes,

INTRODUCTION

TO THE

BOOK OF COMMON ORDER.

As an introduction to the Book of Common Order, we purpose giving an account of the *law* and *usage* of the Church, as to worship, from the Reformation till 1645.

I. THE LAW.—In 1557, the Scottish Protestant Lords in Council resolved as follows, that "the Common Prayers be read weekly on Sunday, and other festival days, publicly in the parish kirks with the lessons of the Old and New Testaments, conform to the order of the Book of Common Prayers."* The Book of Common Prayers thus authorised, was the Second Book† of King Edward VI., and it was in use accordingly to some extent till superseded by the Book of Geneva.

In 1554, some English Protestants, flying from the persecutions under Queen Mary, took up their residence at Frankfort, and obtained from the Magistrates the use

---

* Knox's Works, Wodrow Society, vol. i. p. 275.
† Letter from Kircaldy of Grange, dated 1st July 1559. "As to parish churches, they cleanse them of images, and all other monuments of idolatry, and command that mass shall not be said in them; in place whereof the Book set forth by godly King Edward is read in the same churches." Sir William Cecil, writing 9th July 1559, says :—"The parish churches they deliver of altars and images, and have received the service of the Church of England, according to King Edward's Book." See Laing's Works of Knox, vol. vi. p. 34, 278 ; also M'Crie's Life of Knox, p. 354. The point was long discussed, but seems now to be regarded as settled.

of the French church there, with the condition that they should follow as nearly as possible the French Reformed Order of Worship.* This having been arranged. the Frankfort congregation sent letters to their exiled countrymen in other towns, inviting them to join them. The other exiles in reply objected to any departure from the English Liturgy, and a controversy began which was destined to last for centuries. The Frankfort congregation being itself divided, "after long debating" it was resolved that a new order of service should be drawn up by Whittingham,† Fox, Gilby, Cole, and John Knox, who had become one of their ministers. Their draft, which was afterwards printed, and known as the Book of Geneva, did not satisfy the advocates of King Edward's Book, and another order was agreed upon, to be observed till a certain date,—"some part taken forth of the English Book, and other things put to, as the state of that Church required."

Before the time agreed on had expired, Cox, who had been tutor to King Edward, and who was afterwards Bishop of Ely, arrived from England with some companions, and they at once began to interrupt the services by giving the responses, and repeating the Litany,—these parts of the Liturgy having been laid aside. Soon after, they contrived by intrigue to drive Knox away from Frankfort, and ere long Whittingham, with the greater part of the refugees, seeing no prospect of peace, removed to Geneva, and formed an English Church there in 1555. Knox was chosen one of its ministers, and the draft of the Liturgy prepared by him and others at Frankfort, was published at Geneva in 1556 for its use.

* See 'A Brief Discourse of the Troubles begun at Frankfort;' also Dyer's Life of Calvin, p. 422-433. Laing's Works of Knox, vol. iv. p. 9, *et seq.*

† Whittingham was afterwards ordained at Geneva, and subsequently became Dean of Durham.

THE BOOK OF COMMON ORDER.

Knox finally returned to Scotland in 1559, and after this, if not earlier, the Book of Geneva began to be used by some of the Reformed Congregations in this country. In the First Book of Discipline adopted by the Church in 1560, it is said to be "already used in some of our churches" and is called the 'Book of Our Common Order.' In 1562, the General Assembly enjoined its uniform use in "the administration of the sacraments and solemnisation of marriages, and burial of the dead,"* and it was reprinted in Edinburgh in that year, with some additions. . Between 1562 and 1564 it was modified and enlarged in this country, new prayers were added from Continental sources, others which had been used in Scotland previously were incorporated with it, and the Psalter completed. In this form it was printed in Edinburgh in 1564, and the Assembly of that year "ordained that every Minister, Exhorter, and Reader shall have one of the Psalm-books, lately printed in Edinburgh, and use the Order contained therein in Prayers, Marriage, and ministration of the Sacraments.†

The Book of Geneva thus remodelled is known as Knox's Liturgy, or 'Book of Common Order,' and it embodied the law of the Church as to worship from 1564 till 1645.

Before 1564 there was liberty to use the Common Prayers of King Edward's Liturgy, but after that date the use of the 'Book of Common Order' was enjoined in Prayers as well as in the special services. It was repeatedly printed (with some additions authorised by the Church) till 1644, and is frequently noticed in the Acts of Assembly. By order of the Church the Prayers were translated into Gaelic by Carswell, Superintendent of Argyle, and printed in 1567. In 1568 an edition was

---

* Book of the Universal Kirk, p. 13.
† Calderwood's History, Wod. Soc., vol. ii. p. 284.

published containing an immodest song, called *Welcome Fortune*, which the Assembly ordered to be deleted.* In 1579 the Parliament passed an Act requiring all gentlemen and yeomen, having property of a certain value, to possess copies. In the Assembly of 1601, a proposal having been made to alter some of the Prayers, it was resolved as follows:—" It is not thought good that the Prayers already contained in the Psalm-Book be altered, but if any brother would have any other Prayers added, which are meet for the time, ordains the same first to be tried, and allowed by the Assembly."†

The Acts of Assembly from 1560 to 1602 inclusive, are authoritative. The Assemblies of 1606, 1608, 1610, 1616, 1617, and 1618, were declared unlawful by the Church in 1638 and 1639; and their proceedings are to be "accounted as null, and of no effect."

In these Assemblies, attempts were made by the Court to set aside the 'Book of Common Order.' That which met at Aberdeen in 1616, acting under orders from King James, appointed a committee to revise the Liturgy, and to draw up a new form, to be strictly followed at all times of public worship both by Ministers and Readers.‡ The committee, some time after, prepared a draft, and submitted it to the King.§ It appears to have remained under consideration till the time of his death, when it fell into oblivion. There is a MS. copy of this draft in the British Museum, a transcript of which was published in the ' British Magazine' for 1845 and 1846. It is very much a compromise betwixt the English Liturgy and the 'Book of Common Order.' In 1618 the Assembly at Perth, acting under orders and threats from the King, agreed to five articles: the 1st enjoining Kneeling at the communion;

---

* Book of the Kirk, p. 100. † Ibid., p. 497. ‡ Ibid., p. 595.
§ Hall's Reliquiæ Liturgicæ, vol. i. p. xix.

the 2d, Private communion in cases of sickness; the 3d, Private baptism, "upon a great and reasonable cause;" the 4th, Episcopal confirmation; and the 5th, Permitting the observance of the five chief festival days. These Articles were ratified by Act of Parliament in 1621; but those who disregarded them were in the habit of urging, in addition to the unlawfulness of the Assembly, that some of them were only permissive, and that the former practices were not forbidden. Charles I., who succeeded his father in 1625, brought the question of a new Liturgy before the Scottish Prelates* in 1629. Coming to Scotland to be crowned in 1633, he revived the subject, and a committee was appointed to draw up a new form of service, after the model of the English Prayer-Book. Their draft having been revised and altered by Archbishop Laud, who is said to have disapproved of that one which was framed in King James's time, was printed; and in 1637 orders came from the Court enjoining its use in every church in the kingdom. It was introduced into St Giles's, Edinburgh, on the 23d of July of that year. No great change had hitherto taken place in the public worship of the Church, for though the English Liturgy had been read many years previously in the Chapel Royal, in the new college at St Andrews, and at St Giles's during the King's visit in 1633, these instances were exceptional. The previous interferences of

---

* At the Reformation the spiritual powers of the Prelates were abolished, but the temporal privileges, titles, and Parliamentary honours were maintained, and were enjoyed in some cases by laymen, in others by clergymen. In 1610, Prelates with English consecration were introduced, their consecration having taken place without authority from the Church. From 1610 to 1638 the office was kept up; but as many of the Prelates were parish Ministers, and seldom visited their dioceses, and as the Church was hostile, the exercise of their spiritual functions was very limited. The Assembly was still by law superior to the Prelates, and could try and depose them: and when it did so in 1638-39, the act was held to be constitutional, and not revolutionary. It was constantly maintained that "Episcopacy was never approved by any lawful Assembly in Scotland." It was only between 1610 and 1638 that Episcopacy affected the worship of the Church.

the Court had been endured, but the entire overthrow of the old Liturgy, and the substitution of another objectionable in its matter and form, without consent of Church or Parliament, was too much. The reading of Laud's book was the signal for riots in the churches of Edinburgh; soon the whole nation was roused, and all that the Court and Prelatic party had been doing for thirty years was, as Spottiswoode said, thrown down at once.

In the following year the General Assembly of Glasgow, which was virtually a national convention as well, abjured Laud's book and the Perth Articles, without regard to their civil sanction, and fell back upon the 'Book of Common Order,' to which, and the old Acts in its favour, it repeatedly appealed as containing the law of the Church on the subject of worship. This Assembly commented also on some verbal changes that Raban, the Aberdeen printer, had on his own authority made in an edition of the old Liturgy.* The Assembly of 1639 having agreed to waive all reference to that of the previous year, the lawfulness of which the King denied, abjured anew Laud's book and the Articles of Perth. It also ordained that no novation in worship should be suddenly enacted, but that "Synods, Presbyteries, and Kirks" should be advised with before the Assembly should authorise any change. In the Assemblies of 1640† and 1641 further Acts were passed

* Peterkin's Records of the Kirk, p. 169.

† The Act of the Assembly of 1640 against novations is not among the printed Acts. Principal Baillie tells us that in the Assembly of 1643, "a thorny business came in, which the Moderator by great wisdom got cannily convoyed. The brethren of Stirling and Perth had made great outcries that the Commission had authorised the clerk, in printing the Assembly Acts, to omit two Acts of Aberdeen, one anent the Sabbath, another about novations. In both these satisfaction was given; that our bounding the Sabbath from midnight to midnight might offend some neighbouring kirks. As for the other Act about novations, it was expressed as clearly in the printed Acts of the posterior Assembly."—Letters, vol. ii. p. 91. The Act seems to have referred chiefly to private conventicles. The author of 'Scots Affairs' says that it was "industriously concealed," and that it was " much quarrelled at by all that inclined towards the independent, or sectarian fanatic ways."— Gordon's

against innovations in public worship. The innovations referred to, however, were not now of a prelatic character, but had been introduced by those who were opposed altogether to liturgical forms and churchly usages. It appears also that the Assembly of 1640 summoned Raban the printer before it, and censured him for having curtailed one of the prayers in the 'Book of Common Order.'*

About this period, the plan of uniformity on an Episcopal basis, which had been so long prosecuted by King James and King Charles, was superseded by counter-proposals for uniformity between the Scottish Church and those favourable to Presbytery in the Church of England. In a letter from the Assembly of 1641 to some Ministers in England, a desire is expressed for one Directory for Public Worship common to both Churches. The Scottish Church was afraid of the "contagion" that might come from one Church to the other; and the idea entertained in the Assembly at this time was, that it should be beforehand in drawing up a new form, "wherein possibly England might agree." Henderson, then Moderator of the Assembly, was requested to undertake the work, but he did not prosecute it. Writing to Baillie on the subject in 1642, he says, "I did begin to put my hand to the task put upon me, but have ceased long since, because I had no time, . . . nor could I take upon me . . . to set down other forms of prayer than we have in our Psalm-Book, penned by our great and divine Reformers." He adds that they should wait "till we see what the Lord will do in England," and that "we are not to conceive that they

---

Scots Affairs, vol. iii. p. 223: Spal. Club. Among the unprinted Acts of the Assembly of 1643, there is an "Approbation of the Advice of the Commissioners of the late Assembly of St Andrews, for not printing two Acts of the last Assembly held at Aberdeen."—Records of the Kirk, p. 360. The unprinted Assembly papers of this period are understood to have been burnt in a great fire that took place early in last century.

* Scots Affairs, vol. iii. p. 238.

will embrace our form, but a new form must be set down for us all." *

A large Commission was appointed by the Assembly of 1642 in furtherance of the whole scheme of uniformity with England in doctrine, worship, and government on a Reformed Church basis. It appears also that the Commission of this Assembly wrote to some Presbyteries in the Synod of Glasgow and Ayr, to beware of innovations,—condemning those who scrupled at the usual ceremonies and forms of the Church as favourers of Brownism.† The following account of this letter is given in Bishop Burnet's Conferences:—" When some designers for popularity in the western parts of that Kirk did begin to disuse *the Lord's Prayer* in worship, and the singing the *Conclusion* or *Doxology* after the *Psalm*, and *the Minister's kneeling for private devotion* when he entered the pulpit, the *General Assembly* took this in very ill part, and in a letter they wrote to the presbyteries complained sadly, *Of a spirit of innovation was beginning to get into the Kirk, and to throw these laudable practices out of it, mentioning the three I named, which are commanded to be still practised; and such as refused obedience are appointed to be conferred with in order to the giving of them satisfaction; and if they continued untractable, the Presbyteries were to proceed against them, as they should be answerable to the next General Assembly.* This letter I can produce authentically attested." ‡

In the Assembly of 1643 it was ordained " that a Directory for Divine Worship . . . be framed and made ready in all the parts thereof against the next General Assembly,

---

* Baillie's Letters, vol. ii. p. 1, 2.

† Stevenson's History of the Church of Scotland, p. 504. Brownism, from the name of the founder of a somewhat fanatical sect of the period.

‡ Vindication of the . . . Church and State of Scotland in Four Conferences, p. 182. Glas. 1673. Burnet, who was nephew of Warriston, is supposed to have had access to his papers.

THE BOOK OF COMMON ORDER.

to be held in the year 1644. . . . And for preserving of peace and brotherly unity in the meanwhile, . . . the Assembly forbiddeth . . . all condemning one of another in such lawful things as have been universally received, and by perpetual custom practised, by the most faithful Ministers . . . in this Kirk since the first beginning of Reformation." The latter part of this Act was directed against the innovators referred to above.* At subsequent diets of the Assembly of 1643, the Solemn League and Covenant was approved of, and Commissioners were appointed to join the Divines met at Westminster, and to take part with them in drawing up a common Confession, Catechism, and Directory for the three kingdoms. In the Assembly of 1644 a letter was read from the Scottish Commissioners in London, in which they say, "The Common Directory for Public Worship in the Kirks of the three kingdoms is so begun . . . that we could not think upon any particular Directory for our own Kirk."†

The Westminster Directory was laid before the General Assembly in 1645, and an Act was passed approving the same, and ordering its use in every church in the kingdom. Some explanations were made with reference to the reading of Scripture and the administation of the two Sacraments; and it was also ruled that the adoption of the new Service should "be no prejudice to the order and practice of this Kirk in such particulars as are appointed by the Books of Discipline and Acts of General

---

* The resolution as to a Scottish Directory and the innovations is thus referred to by Baillie:—"We agreed to draw up some act for satisfying in some measure all. . . . I told Mr Henderson my mislike of some parts of it, as putting in too great an equality the novators and their opposites ; also my opinion that the Directory might serve for many good ends, but no ways for suppressing, but much increasing, the ill of novations. . . . Mr Henderson, Mr Calderwood, and Mr Dickson, were voiced to draw with diligence that Directory, wherein I wish them much better success than I expect."—Letters, vol. ii. p. 94.

† None of them, except Henderson, were on the committee charged with this work.

Assemblies, and are not otherwise ordered and appointed in the Directory."

There was no Act setting aside the 'Book of Common Order;'* proposals to this effect are said to have been rejected;† and there are parts of it which have never been superseded; still the Westminster Directory was henceforth of primary authority.

It thus appears, that from 1564 to 1645 the law of the Church enjoined the use of the 'Book of Common Order' in Prayers (*i. e.*, at the principal service on Sunday), Marriage, and Ministration of the Sacraments. The rubrics, as retained from the Book of Geneva, made provision for an extempore prayer before sermon, and allowed the Minister some latitude in the other two prayers. The forms for the special services were more strictly imposed, but liberty was also given to vary some of the prayers in them. The rubrics of the Scottish portions of the book are somewhat stricter, and, indeed, one or two of the Genevan rubrics were made more absolute in the Scottish emendations;

---

* Except a clause in the Act of the Commissioners of the Assembly for intimating the time when the practice of the Directory was to begin, be so interpreted. The time fixed by them was "forthwith" after the 17th of May 1645. In many parts of the country it was not introduced for a considerable time,—thus, by the Presbytery of Strathbogie, not till the 20th of September 1646.—Record, Spalding Club, p. 71.

† "That the use of the Lord's Prayer in public worship, as well as reading the old forms of prayer in the 'Book of Common Order,' continued till the 1638, I do not much question. The manner of their being left off between the 1638 and 1660, ¡I am told by old Ministers that it was not by any Assembly's Act, as Mr Edwards says, but by a gradual disuse, pretty much before the Assembly's Directory 1646, and generally after that. I have been told by Ministers who lived in those days, that an Act of Assembly was once proposed for laying aside the Lord's Prayer, the old forms of prayer, and probably the Doxology also; but Mr Calderwood, and some other old Ministers, opposed it—that is, the laying them aside by a formal Act; and so they were insensibly let fall into disuse."—Wodrow Correspondence, vol. iii. p. 494. A proposal to lay aside the Lord's Prayer enjoined by the Directory seems strange, and indeed the only foundation for this statement of Wodrow seems to have been a discussion in the Assembly as to laying aside the use of Gloria Patri. Wodrow mentions elsewhere that read forms of prayer were used in the kirks of Edinburgh till 1647, and the Lord's Prayer till 1649.—Analecta, vol. i. p. 274.

but no doubt the 'Book of Common Order' is best described as a discretionary Liturgy.

II. THE USAGE.—We shall now give some notices as to the Use of the book from the histories of the period, and some special Acts of Assembly not already referred to. We shall arrange these under the different services.

First of all, however, it is necessary to notice *the office of Reader*. The 'First Book of Discipline' directed that in all parishes "where no Ministers can be had presently," the most suitable persons should be selected " to read the Common Prayers and the Scriptures." This was at once put in force, and for some years it was usual for one Minister to have charge of several parishes, with Readers under him, one resident in each. Thus in 1567 there were about 289 Ministers and 715 Readers in the Church. Many of the first Readers had been ordained Priests,[*] and were Probationers for the Reformed pastorate. It seems probable that in many a country parish the old Priest became Reader to his old flock; and, indeed, the new arrangement of Minister and Readers was somewhat analogous to that which preceded, when each parish had its own Priest to read the Missal and Breviary, with an occasional visit and sermon from a preaching Friar. Afterwards the Readers were of two classes, one class consisting of aspirants to the Ministry, the other of Schoolmasters and Catechists not looking forward to promotion in the Church. The Assembly of 1581, hoping that all parishes would soon be supplied with Clergymen, forbade the farther appointment of Readers, but the Act was very much a dead letter. We find the Presbytery of Edinburgh in 1583 appointing a Reader as before, and

---

[*] Some of the early Session Records, as St Andrews, mention the reception of many conforming Priests.

other Presbyteries universally till 1645. Though not quite on its old footing, it was an ordinary office in the Church till that time, and it is worthy of note that it received the sanction of the Glasgow Assembly of 1638.* In country parishes where no separate person was appointed, the Schoolmaster was required to discharge the duties of the office; if indeed it is not more correct to say, that the Reader in such cases acted as Schoolmaster. The Reader assisted the Clergyman in various parts of his work, and particularly in the reading of the Prayers and Scriptures in Public Worship. The Reader's service was universal in cities and burghs, and as Schoolmasters, Expectants,† and apparently Precentors in some cases, "read in kirks," it seems to have been very general in country parishes.

To return, we shall give some notices as to

THE USE OF THE COMMON PRAYERS AND THE ORDER OF PUBLIC WORSHIP.

James Melville, in his Autobiography, speaks of "the prayers in the kirk every morning"‡ at St Andrews in 1572, and says that the order of the College of Glasgow, to which he went afterwards, was, "that every Regent, his week about, convoyed the scholars to a kirk hard adjacent, where the people convened; and that Regent read the Common Prayers, with a chapter or two."§ In 1595 the Kirk-Session of Glasgow ordered "that prayers be read in the High Kirk at seven in the morning, and at five at even in the New Church."‖ Calderwood mentions that Robert Bruce, the famous leader of the Anti-Prelatic party in the Church, during his banishment at Inverness, where

---

* Records of the Kirk, p. 34, 37.
† Act of Assembly 1640—"If any expectant shall refuse to subscribe the Covenant, he shall be declared uncapable of . . . reading at a kirk."
‡ Autobiog. Wod. Soc., p. 27.   § Ibid., p. 55.
‖ Life of Weems, p. 22. Maitland Club.

he remained four years, from 1605 to 1609, taught "every Sabbath before noon, and every Wednesday, and read the prayers every other night at even."* As regards his own practice, Calderwood elsewhere writes as follows :—" During the whole thirteen years" (that is, from 1604 till 1617) "in which I discharged the functions of the Ministry, whether in administering the Sacraments or in celebrating other sacred rites, I never used the exhortations or prayers which are extant in our Agenda. So also many others."†

Cowper, Bishop of Galloway, in his 'Seven Days' Conference between a Catholic Christian and a Catholic Roman,' has given an account of the Public Worship of the Church in his day, written between 1613 and 1619, when his death took place. The conference goes on as follows :—

R. What is this the people are going to do?

C. They bow themselves before the Lord, to make an humble confession of their sins, and supplications for mercy; which you will hear openly read out by the public Reader. Now, when it is done, what think you of the prayer?

R. Truly, I think there is nothing in it, but that whereunto every

---

* Calderwood's History, vol. vi. p. 291, 292.

†. Altare Damascenum, p. 613: published in Holland in 1623, during the author's banishment. We add some extracts as to his opinions on the subject. " Sic etiam alii complures; et omnibus etiam liberum est idem facere. Et puerile est, ut mihi videtur, aliter facere. . . . Non mihi placet, dicam ingenuè quod sentio quòd Minister adstringat se verbis praescriptis in publicis precibus, aut exhortationibus ceu admonitionibus in sacris celebrandis, etiam si à veris doctis et piis conceptae sint, praesertim recitando è libro; nam attentio ad verba recitanda e libro et magis impediunt (*sic*), affectuum impetus, et correspondentes gestus corporis exteriores, quam si quis memoriae ita infixerit, ut affectui accommodata sint cumque quasi sequantur. De re ista tamen litem nemini moveo, nec propterea à sacris hoc modo celebratis, si non aliae accesserint corruptelae quae secessionem merentur, abstinendum judico." "Probamus praescriptum ordinem . . . etiam illa orationum et admonitionum exemplaria, quae habentur in liturgiis nostris, dummodo tradantur ut exemplaria, non ut praescripta quibus praecepto adstringendus Minister, et rectius facere censeo, qui non haeret in formulis verborum, ubi non determinavit scriptura quam qui ne γρυ quidem addere vult, etiamsi liberum illi sit, et nullo obligetur praecepto ad conceptas verborum formulas. In Anglicana igitur liturgia primum quod damnamus est, praescripta in omnibus liturgiae partibus praecepta, et imperata non leviori quàm suspensionis, excommunicationis, depositionis, et deprivationis poena."—P. 613-616.

good Christian should say, Amen: and it hath done me much good to see the people, with humble reverence, sighing and groaning, accompanying the prayer up to God. But what go they now to do?

C. Every one is preparing (as you see) their Psalm-Book, that all of them, with one heart and mouth, may sing unto the Lord. . . .

R. . . . What doth the Reader now—is he making another prayer?

C. No. Yonder book, which now he opens, is the Bible. . . . These are the three exercises which are used in all our congregations every Sabbath, one hour before the Preacher come in; first Prayer, then Psalms, then reading of Holy Scripture; and by these the hearts of the people are prepared the more reverently to hear the Word, and you see all is done with great quietness, devotion, and reverence. . . .

R. But what are they doing now?

C. You hear the third bell ringing, and in this space the reading ceaseth, and at the end of the bell ringing the Preacher will come. . . .

R. . . . There comes the Preacher. And now (I pray you), tell me how I should behave myself.

C. Trouble you not, do as you see others beside you: for, first, he will *conceive* a prayer, at the which the people humble themselves; thereafter he reads his text of Holy Scripture: this the people hear with reverence; then he falls to the preaching, which some hear with their heads covered, some otherwise (in that you may do as your health requires). The preaching being ended, he concludes all with a Thanksgiving; after which there is a Psalm sung by the whole congregation, and then the Minister blesseth the people in the name of the Lord, and so dimits them: you will see no other thing else." *

All this is in strict conformity with the 'Book of Common Order.' The prayer after sermon is perhaps called a Thanksgiving, because the Catholic Christian is showing the similarity betwixt the order observed in Scotland, and that practised in the days of Justyn Martyr. In 1619, Hog, who appeared before Spottiswood and the High Commission, on a charge of preaching against the Articles of Perth, was asked why he prayed "after sermon against Bishops as bellygods and hirelings?" He admitted that he prayed against "bellygods and hirelings," but "alleged

* Cowper's Works, p. 639.

that his prayer was conform to the Common Prayer." The Archbishop said that it made no "mention of bellygods, but of hirelings only." Hog answered that "the hirelings mentioned in that prayer were bellygods." The Archbishop said that "in short space that Book of Discipline shall be discharged; and Ministers shall be tied to set prayers, and shall not be suffered to conceive prayers as they please themselves."*

In 1619, the Kirk-Session Records of Glasgow mention two Readers, one "to read daily as well the morning as the evening prayers from April to October, at seven morning and five evening, and the other part at eight and six;"† and similar notices occur in all the Burgh and chief Session Records of the country. In 1625, the Synod of Fife "appointed that ordinary Readers in all congregations shall be tied to read in the public audience of the people only such prayers as are printed in the Psalm-Book, and ordained by the Kirk of Scotland to be read publicly."‡ In 1631, one of the reasons given by the Anti-Prelatic party against receiving King James's version of the Psalms was, "If it should happen, which God forbid, that our book of Psalms in metre . . . were removed, it might then be justly feared . . . that the Common Prayers" (with this the other heads of the 'Book of Common Order' are mentioned) . . . "would all be suppressed, to the great hindrance of public and private uses."§ In 1637, Patrick Henderson, who was set aside for refusing to read Laud's book, had been in the habit of reading Knox's Liturgy every morning, on week day as well as Sunday, in St Giles's Church. He had read it there as usual at eight o'clock on the morning of the riot, and when he finished, he said,

---

* Cald. Hist., vol. vii. p. 368, 369.
† Life of Weems, p. 22. Mait. Club.
‡ Records of the Synod of Fife, p. 103. Abbotsford Club.
§ Ban. Miscel., vol. i. p. 234.

"Adieu, good people; for I think this is the last time of my reading prayers in this place."* After the "Maid's Commotion" in Edinburgh, the Prelates directed that there "should be a surcease of the Service-Book;" that "in the whole churches of this city sermon shall be made at the accustomed times by regular and obedient Ministers; and that a prayer shall be made before and after sermon; and that neither the old service nor the new established service be used in this interim."† The daily service was for a time discontinued. There were no "prayers read morning or evening as the custom was; yea, for five or six months after this, Mr Patrick Henderson read not the prayers." ‡ In consequence of this, one of the charges brought against the Prelates at the Glasgow Assembly, and mentioned among the reasons for their deposition, was the "interdicting morning and evening prayers,"—that is, the daily reading of the 'Book of Common Order' in church. The petitions sent in against Laud's book at the time refer to the old Liturgy as containing the form of worship received at the Reformation, and universally practised since. § The

* Quoted by M'Crie, jun., and Russell. No reference given.
† Baillie's Letters, vol. i. p. 448.
‡ Row's History, p. 410.
  The Bishops "did inhibit the ordinary morning and evening prayers, customable in Edinburgh since the Reformation." The people of Edinburgh, "with cries and tears, desired the . . . keeping away the Service-Book and restoring their own." —Rothes's Relation, p. 4 and 15.

§ Forty-six of these petitions, from burghs, parishes, and presbyteries, are preserved in the Register House, Edinburgh. We subjoin a few extracts from them, showing the terms in which they are couched :—" Which books we find to vary much from the public form of religion and worship which, according to the laws of this realm, both ecclesiastical and civil, we have ever had and practised since our happy reformation from Popery."—" We having for the form of worship according to God's own Word, established among us, Acts of Parliament and General Assemblies yet standing, and found the sensible blessing of God in the exercise thereof so long enjoyed, to our great comfort and edification."—" Far different from that Book of Common Prayer which we have enjoyed many years." In none of them have we observed any reference to the question of a Liturgy as such, whether discretionary or prescribed, though they all complain of the imposition of Laud's book as the only form of public worship in the kingdom.

Ministers declared "that they were ready to alter everything that could be made appear . . . unsound . . . in the Liturgy which they had received from their ancestors."*
It appears, also, that it was the understanding of some of the leading clergy who were disposed to receive Laud's book, that it was to be read by the Readers, as Knox's book had been before, and not ordinarily by themselves.† In a small tract of 1638, attributed to George Gillespie, ‡ giving reasons for the refusal of the Service-Book, it is said, "Though a prescript form of Liturgy were lawful, yet there is no warrant for imposing of one; for might not able Ministers at least make a prescript form to themselves, which would fit them and their people best? But if it were lawful to impose one, then there is one in this country already. Ought not that rather to be imposed than any other, seeing it is already established by Parliament now of a long time? But now, if a new one ought to be imposed, then it ought to come in by a lawful manner." One of the animadversions upon Laud's book by a Committee of the Glasgow Assembly was, that "it abolishes a lawful and long-used external form of divine service, and in its place substitutes another."§ In the King's Declaration (Dr Balcanquhal) it is stated, that King James's reason for wishing to introduce a new service into Scotland immediately after he succeeded to the English throne was, "the deformity which was used in Scotland, where no set or public form of prayer was used, but Preachers, or Readers, and ignorant Schoolmasters prayed in the Church, sometimes so ignorantly as it was a shame to all religion

---

* Stevenson's History, p. 172. Spang's Historia Motuum, p. 32.
† Stev. Hist., p. 171. Records of the Kirk, p. 53.
‡ "Ye have here . . . some reasons against the service in print. . . . I am informed . . . that they came from Mr George Gillespie."—Baillie to Spang, Letters, vol. i. p. 90. The reasons are given, though not verbatim, in Row's Hist., p. 405, 406. They are opposed to all strictly prescribed forms.
§ Historia Motuum, p. 204.

to have the majesty of God so barbarously spoken unto, sometimes so seditiously that their prayers were plain libels."* The Assembly of 1639, however, selected this among other statements for condemnation and denial.†

Gordon, Parson of Rothiemay, who lived at the time, says, that those who tried "to justle out" the "prayers and form of service used before in the Church of Scotland," tacitly condemned the French Church, "from whom that model was mostly borrowed;" that admitting there were defects in the old Liturgy, "the medicine was worse than the disease;" that "this Service-Book did put the patient out of one sickness into another worse than the former, which was *that Ministers prayed extempore.*" ‡ He tells us also that about 1640 "set forms of prayer in public began to be dishaunted by all, and such as used them were looked upon as not spiritual enough." §

In Henderson's 'Government and Order of the Church of Scotland,' || first published in 1641, we have an account of the manner in which Divine service was then conducted. It was written to correct misconceptions that prevailed in

* King's Declaration, p. 16.
† Records of the Kirk, p. 266.
‡ Scots Affairs, vol. ii. p. 80. For Gordon's statement as to the source of the prayers, see Notes after the reprint. Among our other obligations, we are indebted to the French Church for suggesting the emblem of the burning bush. At the first Synod of Vitre, held in 1583, in the castle of the Earl of Laval, it adopted for a seal the burning bush, in the midst *Jehovah* in Hebrew letters, and round the circle *Flagror, non consumor.*—Quick's Syn., vol. i. p. 146. Quick elsewhere speaks of the motto as *Comburo, non consumor*, and says, that with this seal "those venerable Councils sealed all their letters and despatches." The heraldic authorities in Scotland do not trace the use of the burning bush in this country further than the time of William of Orange. The Irish offshoot of the Church uses the same emblem, with *Ardens sed virens* for motto.
§ Ibid., vol. iii. p. 250.
|| Though anonymous, and written as if by an Englishman, there can be no doubt that Henderson was the author. Baillie speaks of Henderson writing such a work at the time. It was republished in London "by authority" in 1644, with a new title, the omission of the preface, and some verbal changes. Apparently the Scottish Commissioners had revised and adopted it. In a pamphlet of 1659 it is referred to as Henderson's.

THE BOOK OF COMMON ORDER. xxxi

England, one of which was that the Scots "had no certain rule or direction for their public worship, but that every man, following his extemporary fancy, did preach or pray what seemed good in his own eyes." "Against this," Henderson says, "the form of prayers, administration of the sacraments, admission of Ministers, excommunication, solemnising of marriage, visitation of the sick, &c., which are set down before their Psalm-Book, and to which the Ministers are to conform themselves, is a sufficient witness: for although they be not tied to set forms and words, yet are they not left at random; but for testifying their consent, and keeping unity, they have their Directory and prescribed Order." He describes the order of public worship as follows:—"When so many of all sorts, men and women, masters and servants, young and old, as shall meet together are assembled, the public worship beginneth with prayer and reading some portion of Holy Scripture, both of the Old and New Testament, which the people hear with attention and reverence; and after reading, the whole Congregation joineth in singing some Psalm.* This reading and singing do continue till the preaching begin; at which time the Minister, having prefaced a little for quickening and lifting up the hearts of the people, first maketh a prayer for remission of sin, sanctification, and all things needful, joining also confession of sins and thanksgiving with special relation to the hearers. After which, in the forenoon, is another Psalm, and after the Psalm a prayer for a blessing upon the preaching of the Word." Then follows the sermon. "After sermon he praiseth God, and prayeth again for a blessing, joining earnest petitions for the Church universal, and for the

---

* Down to this point we have the Reader's service, which is only indicated by the Minister's service being called the preaching. Hence the later use of the terms, *the preaching*, and *the preachings*.

coming of the kingdom of Christ, for all the afflicted Churches, for the Churches in his Majesty's dominions, for the Church of Scotland, ministry and people, for the King, the Queen, the Prince, and their whole royal progeny, for all the members of that particular Congregation, as well absent in their lawful affairs as present, for all that are afflicted among them, in body, mind, or means. The prayer ended, a Psalm is sung, and the people dismissed with a blessing." The prayers given with Henderson's Sermons,* preached after the Swearing of the Covenant in 1638, and before the Glasgow Assembly, are in accordance with this description, except that the Lord's Prayer always ends the prayer before sermon, and the first or Reader's prayer is omitted, as not being part of the Minister's service. In addition to these contemporary notices, we add two from later times. Sage, writing in 1695, says that Knox's Liturgy "continued to be in use even after the beginning of the horrid revolution in the days of King Charles I., and many old people yet alive remember well to have seen it used indifferently both by Presbyterians and Prelatists." † And Wodrow: "I hear that the Lord's Prayer was generally used in the kirks of Edinburgh till the year 1649, and read forms of prayer till the 1647." ‡ Knox's book was necessarily the common Church book for some years after 1645, as the new Psalter was not then introduced.

As many writers of the period state that there was uniformity in the worship of the Church till the passing of the

---

* There can be little doubt that these Sermons, which have been recently published, are genuine, though not verbally accurate, as the MS. was probably written out from notes by some shorthand writer who heard Henderson deliver them. A MS. copy of Leighton's Sermons, preached at Newbattle, formerly in the Queensbery Library, now in the possession of the Rev. J. Elder Cumming, Edinburgh, differs considerably from the printed editions.

† Sage's Works, Spot. Soc., vol. i. p. 351.
‡ Analecta, vol. i. p. 274.

THE BOOK OF COMMON ORDER. xxxiii

Perth Articles in 1618, it seems clear, from the notices we have quoted, that from the Reformation till that time divine service was usually conducted in close accordance with the Book of Common Order.

The bell having been rung an hour before, was rung the second time at 8 o'clock for the Reader's Service. The congregation then assembled,* and engaged for a little in private devotion.† The Reader took his place at the "lectern," read the Common Prayers, and in some churches the Decalogue and Creed.‡ He then gave out large portions of the Psalter, the singing of which was concluded with Gloria Patri, and next read chapters of Scripture§ from the Old and New Testaments, going through in order any book that was begun, as required by the First Book of Discipline. After an hour thus spent, the bell rang the third time, and the Minister entered the pulpit, and "knelt for private devotion." He then began with a "conceived" prayer, chiefly for "illumination," as in other Reformed Churches. He next preached the sermon, and then read or repeated one of the Prayers in

* In 1600 and later the Session of Monifieth ordered the "catalogue to be read" every Sunday in church to mark absentees.—Rec. See Christian Instruc. for Dec. 1839. In 1643 the Presbytery of Strathbogie ordained that such as were not present at the Reader's Service were to be "punished as absents from the kirk."—Rec., p. 37, Spal. Club.

† Sage says that till 1645 and later it was the custom for people entering church "to uncover their heads," and to "put up a short prayer to God, some kneeling, some standing. This custom was so universal that the vestiges of it may be even yet observed amongst old people . . . who continue to retain it."—Works, vol. i. p. 360, Spot. Soc.

‡ In 1504 the Aberdeen Session ordered the Reader "to repeat at the ending of the Prayers both on Sunday in the morning and on the week-days the 10 Commands, as well as the Belief."—Selections, Spal. Club, p. 38.

§ King James's version, first published in 1611, was not cordially received in Scotland, and was little used before 1645. The Genevan Bible was in common use. The Westminster Directory mentions no particular version, as it was the intention of the Assembly Divines to bring out a new translation. The present version came gradually into use; but, "till within the last 40 years, a Bible of Geneva translation was used in the Church of Crail" in Fife. So wrote Principal Lee in 1824.—Memorial for Bible Soc., p. 112, 113.

the Liturgy for all conditions of men, or extemporised one "conform" to it, concluding with the Lord's Prayer and the Creed. After this there followed a Psalm and the Benediction. Between 1618 and 1638 the usage continued, with these differences—that in some parts of the country, the Minister's salutation was lengthened into a preface; there was an additional Prayer and Psalm before Sermon at the morning service,* and the Lord's Prayer was used at the end of the Prayer before Sermon; the recital of the Creed was omitted by many of the Clergy;† and the practice of their not reading any part of the Prayers, which was not unusual in the time of Calderwood's first incumbency, became common among those who opposed the Court policy. Between 1638 or 1640 and 1645, the reading of prayers by the Clergy, which had still continued to be the rule in some parts of the country, was given up, and was henceforth confined to the Reader's Service. During these seven years, the Church was also troubled with innovations of a Brownist tendency, but these were exceptional.

The afternoon service was for many years catechetical. The First Book of Discipline enjoined, that on Sunday afternoon the children should be publicly examined in the Catechism, in the audience of the people, according to the order indicated in the Catechism itself. Calvin's Catechism, which is referred to, is divided into portions for successive Sundays; and after the children were examined, the Minister was to give a short discourse to the people on the doctrine of the day. Melville mentions

---

* Baillie speaks of two prayers before sermon as the custom. It is not easy to say whether he refers to the two of the Liturgy or to the second and third of the three mentioned by Henderson.

† In an unpublished paper of the Wodrow MSS. fol. 44, No. 24', containing a few notes on the Book of Common Order unfavourable to its liturgical use, it is said, "The rehearsal of the Belief had been disused for many years, till now, of late, the formalists have revived it, because there is an intention to bring in the English service." The date of the MS. is probably about 1637.

that he repeated the Catechism in this way on Sunday afternoons in presence of the people. The other great Catechism of the Reformed, the Heidelberg, was also of public authority in the Church of Scotland, was bound with some editions of the Liturgy, and used in catechising. It is also divided into portions for the Sundays of the year. The First Book of Discipline prescribes that there should be prayers (*i.e.*, the reading of the Common Prayers) on Sunday afternoons, where there was neither preaching nor catechising.

Daily service on week-days was very general from the time of the Reformation. In towns the Readers read the Common Prayers, with portions of Scripture, every morning and evening through the year, and the trades provided lights for this purpose during the winter. There was daily service even in country villages. Thus in 1661 the Earl of Callender desired of the Synod of Lothian and Tweeddale "that reading of Scripture and Prayers be publicly used in towns and villages every morning and evening on the week-days, according to that former laudable practice of this Church." * Henderson says that "week-day Sermons . . . in cities and towns use to be at least two days every week;" and this had been the practice from the Reformation till his time.† At these Sermons

---

* Records of Synod. The following extract from the Session Records of St Andrews, of-date Aug. 14, 1597, quoted by Principal Lee, Lectures, vol. i. p. 211, gives an idea of what the Reader's service usually was:—"Mr Robert Zuill ordained to read every day morn and even except the days of public teaching a chapter of the New Testament and another of the Old before noon, beginning at Genesis and Matthew, with a prayer before and after; and evening, some Psalms, with a prayer before and after." It is also worthy of note, that in large towns one of the churches was kept open all day for private prayers. In 1619 "the Glasgow Session appoints the New Kirk door to be opened at 5 in the morning and closed at 9 at night for the summer half-year, and for the winter from 7 in the morning till 5 in the evening. "This," adds Wodrow, "like the Old Kirk at Edinburgh, was for particular persons praying in the kirk."—Life of Weems, p. 22.

† The Session Records of St Andrews, Glasgow, and other towns, show that till 1600, the week-day sermons were preached on the old Church-days, Wednes-

the First Book of Discipline recommends that the Common Prayers which it enjoined on other week-days should not be read, lest the people should "think them no prayers which be made before and after sermons." This seems to imply that at first the people were disposed to regard extempore prayers as no prayers at all, just as at the end of the period we are considering there were those who began to take a similar view of read prayers.

BAPTISM.

The rubrics in the Baptismal Service make no mention of the Minister having liberty to depart from the form given. In the Book of Geneva, one of them stood thus— "*The Minister exhorting the people to pray, saith in this manner, or such like, kneeling.*" But this is changed in the Scottish book to, "*Then followeth this prayer.*" No doubt, however, there was diversity of practice. The long exposition of the Creed is not in the Geneva Book, and is omitted in the later editions of the Book of Common Order. It was probably not used at the service, but the parent or godfather always rehearsed the Belief as prescribed. After 1638 some of the innovators omitted it, but they were condemned by the Church for so doing; and in 1645 the Scottish Commissioners wished its insertion in the Westminster Baptismal Directory. Baillie, speaking of his wish to have all the Scottish usages retained, says, "As for the changes in our Church, I had laboured with my colleagues to have eschewed them all, and found Mr Henderson not much from my mind; but others were passionate for them, and at last carried Mr Henderson, then me, to their mind. The Belief in Baptism was never said

---

days and Fridays. After that date, the King directed the service to be changed to the Tuesdays [and Thursdays], to commemorate his escape from the Gowrie conspiracy.

in England, and they would not undergo that yoke. . . . We got the Assembly to equivalent interrogatories, much against the mind of the Independents, and we were assured to have the Creed a part of the Catechism."*

Henderson says, "He that presenteth the child maketh confession of the faith into which the child is to be baptised, and promiseth to bring up the child in that faith, and in the fear of God." In his account the baptismal formula is stated thus—"*Into the name of the Father, Son, and Holy Ghost.*" The Assembly of 1582 strictly forbade baptism in private houses. The Assembly of 1602 allowed it in church on other than preaching days; that of 1618 permitted it in private in cases of sickness. This was again disallowed in 1638; and Henderson says, "It is never ministered in private houses." It usually took place as soon as possible after the child was born, and generally after the sermon.

The child was to be presented for baptism accompanied with the father and godfather. One of Knox's sons had for godfather Whittingham, the other Coverdale, formerly Bishop of Exeter. James Melville also mentions that the Earl of Mar was his godfather. Opposition to this custom, which was common to all the Reformed Churches, was one of the points of the Brownists at their first appearance in Scotland in 1584. Brown "made shew, after an arrogant manner, before the Session of the Kirk of Edinburgh, that he would maintain that witnesses at baptism was not a thing indifferent, but simply evil. But he failed in his probation."† In Aberdeen it became the fashion for every "servile man in the town" to invite "twelve or sixteen persons to be his gossips and godfathers to his

---

* Letters, vol. ii. p. 258. "The Belief not said in England"—*i.e.*, not by the sponsors.
† Cald. Hist., vol. iv. p. 1.

bairn," till the session in 1622 forbade any more than "four at the most."*

In later times, while some continued to regard godfathers as additional sponsors, others looked upon them merely as witnesses.

All who sought baptism for children were required to be able to repeat the Lord's Prayer, Belief, and Ten Commandments, and it was the duty of the Reader to instruct those who were ignorant.

THE LORD'S SUPPER.

A suitable prayer is given in the Liturgy, to be used on days of Holy Communion before the sacramental service itself. The rubrics give permission to the Minister to vary the Prayer before Distribution. The form given is entirely eucharistic, and is wanting in that invocation of the Holy Spirit which has generally been considered so important a part of the Communion Service.† Apparently this omission was urged by some, who were averse to being tied to set forms, in their arguments with those who adhered to the precise words of the book. Thus Row, relating how, in 1622, through kneeling at a Communion, the table was overturned and the cup spilled, says, "Mr Patrick Galloway having kneeled and prayed, I would say having read the prayers of consecration, wherein there is not one word of Lord bless the elements or action." ‡

---

* Records, p. 109. There is a similar notice in the Glasgow Session Records as late as 1646, ordering those who had children baptised on Sunday to have no more gossips than six. In 1647, at Glasgow, those seeking baptism were still required to give an account of the Lord's Prayer, Creed, and Ten Commandments.—Life of Weems.

† The invocation was omitted at the Reformation from the fear of its being misapprehended. "The English, yea, no Reformed Liturgy, had any forms of consecration."—Baillie's Parallel of the Liturgy and Mass-Book, p. 44. In reality, the Roman Catholics attribute the consecration to the repetition of the words of institution, and their Mass is held to be invalid by the Greeks because it has no formal invocation of the Holy Spirit. ‡ Hist., p. 331.

Scrimgeour, who was a decided anti-prelatist, and who in 1620 was charged before the High Commission with disregarding the Perth Articles, read in his defence as follows :—" Neither is there any warrantable form directed nor approven by the Kirk beside that which is in print before the Psalm-Book, according to the which, like as I have always done, so now I minister that sacrament." *

From the description of a Communion at Perth in 1580,† it appears that the choir of the church, where the altar had stood, was occupied with tables and seats; that this was railed off; that the communicants entered by two doors in the rails, giving their tokens and alms to the deacons as they entered; and that there were two ministrations, the first at five, and the second at half-past nine A.M. ‡

In 1623 Calderwood describes a Scottish Communion as follows :—

"Among us, the Minister, when the sermon is finished, reads the words of institution, gives a short exhortation and admonition, then blesses. The blessing or thanksgiving ended, he says, 'Our Lord, on that night on which He was betrayed, took bread, and gave thanks, as we have already done, and brake, as I also now break, and gave to His Disciples, saying (then he hands it to those nearest on the right and the left), This is my body,' &c. He adds nothing to the words of Christ, changes nothing, omits nothing. Then those next break a particle off the larger fragment § or part, and hand what is left to those sitting nearest, so long as there is any portion of the fragment over. Then those who serve the tables, when one fragment

---

* Cald. Hist., vol. vii. p. 422.
† Scott's History of the Reformers, p. 191.
‡ At Glasgow, in 1586 and 1587, the time of convening on Communion Sundays was at four in the morning, and at eight in the morning.—Wod., Life of Weems, p. 25. In the Canongate, Edinburgh, in 1613, there was no "morning service" on the Communion Sunday, but preaching began at eight o'clock.—Principal Lee's Lectures, vol. i. p. 398.
§ In Aberdeenshire, the bread is cut into *dice*; and within the recollection of many, some of the old people received the Communion fasting, and many of the older clergy used the mixed cup.

is done, offer the paten, from which another in like manner takes a similar larger fragment or κλασμα, and breaking, hands to the next, and so on. In like manner the Minister delivers the cup to those nearest, repeating the words of Christ, without addition, mixture, change, or omission, and they hand it to those sitting beside them ; and when the wine is done, those who serve fill it anew. As soon as he has delivered both elements to those sitting nearest him, using only the words of Christ, whilst they distribute amongst themselves the bread and the cup, the Minister, as long as the action of eating and drinking lasts, addresses those at the table. . . . Whilst they are rising from the table, and others are taking their place, the Minister is silent, and those leaving and those approaching the table, together with the whole Congregation, either sing, or the Reader reads the history of the Passion. But when the Minister is speaking, and when the communicants hand to one another the elements, neither is the history of the Passion read nor Psalms sung, as it is not expedient. . . . If the whole communicants could sit at one time at the tables, it would be more agreeable and advantageous, as they could thus all together eat, drink, meditate, sing, and hear the Minister's address. . . . In this form our Church has now for sixty years celebrated the Holy Supper." *

In Henderson's description of the Communion, it is said, "After sermon, immediately the Pastor useth an exhortation, and debarreth from the table all ignorant, profane, and scandalous persons." Then, going to the table, "he first readeth and shortly expoundeth the words of institution ; . . . next he useth a prayer wherein he both giveth thanks . . . and prayeth earnestly to God for His powerful presence, and effectual working to accompany His own ordinance. . . . The elements thus being sanctified by the Word and prayer, the Minister sacramentally breaketh the bread, taketh and eateth himself, and delivereth to the people . . . saying, *Take ye, eat ye; this is the Body of the Lord, which is broken for you: Do it in remembrance of Him.* After all at the table have taken and eaten, the Minister taketh the cup, and, drinking first

* Altare Damascenum, p. 777, 778.

THE BOOK OF COMMON ORDER.

himself, he giveth it to the nearest, saying, *This cup*, &c. . . . The Minister, . . . after the giving of the elements, doth either by his own speech stir up the communicants to spiritual meditations, . . . or causeth be read the history of the Passion. . . . After all at the table have received the cup, they rise from the table . . . (and) another company cometh, . . . during which time of removing . . . the whole congregation singeth some part of a Psalm, as Ps. 22 or 103. After the last company hath received, the Minister . . . goeth to the pulpit, where, after a short speech, tending to thanksgiving, he doth again solemnly give thanks unto God, . . . and prayeth as on other Sabbaths. The prayer ended, all join in singing a Psalm of praise, suitable to the occasion, and are dismissed with the blessing, before which none are to depart unless in case of necessity."*

At first, separate ministrations on the same day, and often on two or three successive Sundays, were common, but it is probable that a succession of *tables* was also practised in some churches from the time of the Reformation. The table addresses, given sometimes instead of the reading of the history of the Passion, one to each company, were quite short, only lasting till all had received the elements.

At a communion in 1619, the "tickets" or tokens are spoken of as being taken "at the doors."† In 1618 the Aberdeen session enjoined that the alms of the communicants should be taken up at their rising from the table,

---

* There are some interesting points of difference between this account and Calderwood's, showing the changes that had taken place in twenty years, and the departure from the order of Knox's book. In this and other parts of Henderson's work, many expressions, and almost whole sentences, are to be found, which were afterwards embodied in the Westminster Directory.

† Cald. Hist., vol. vii. p. 357. The use of tokens is mentioned in 1572.—Lee's Lectures, vol. i. p. 392.

xliv INTRODUCTION TO

MARRIAGE.

In the Form of Marriage, the rubrics allow the Minister latitude in the prayer or blessing, but not in the exhortations or vows.* The Assembly of 1570 ordained anew that all marriages should be solemnised "according to the order published." At first the Church required the ceremony to be performed in all cases at the morning service on Sundays, but after 1579 it was allowed on week-days, provided a sufficient number were present and "preaching joined thereto." The old practice of marrying on Sunday in face of the congregation was, however, long common, †

Ministers who will not imitate their irregular courses ; . . . observers do perceive a clear design in all this to set up themselves as the only pious and zealous people."
—Rise and Progress of Present Divisions in the Church of Scotland, 1653. Dr John Erskine says, "It is not improbable that the practice of the Ministers of the counties of Down and Antrim about 1626, many of whom afterwards came over to Scotland, might contribute to multiply sermons . . . before and after communion."
—IV. Disser., p. 311. Livingston, after his return from Ireland, preached his famous sermon at Shotts on the Monday after a Communion, in 1630; but the Monday service did not take root till much later. Dr Erskine, along with the Synod of Glasgow and Ayr, of which he was at the time a member, moved, last century, for quarterly communions, with one week-day service.

It may here be stated that no form is given in the Book of Common Order for admission to the Lord's Supper. Such forms were wanting in all the Reformed Liturgies at first, but they have since beeñ supplied. The First Book of Discipline says that "none are to be admitted to this mystery who cannot formally say the Lord's Prayer, the Articles of the Belief, nor declare the sum of the law." Calvin's Little Catechism, and, after 1592, Craig's Catechism, was used for the instruction of young communicants. It was the practice to admit the young to the Lord's table at an early age—*e.g.*, James Melville at 12. Bishopping or prelatic confirmation was enjoined in 1618, but the practice was never introduced to any considerable extent. Henderson says, "None are admitted . . . but such as, upon examination, are found to have a competent measure of knowledge in the grounds of Christian religion and the doctrine of the Sacraments, and are able . . . and profess themselves willing to examine themselves, and to renew their covenant made with God in Baptism, promising to walk as beseemeth Christians, and to submit themselves to all the ordinances of Christ."

* Many who have been most hostile to set forms have yet held that in all cases where professions of faith and solemn engagements are imposed, the questions should be fixed 'as in our present Ordination Service', and the Minister not allowed to extemporise or vary them.

† Sir Thomas Hope mentions the marriage of his son in 1638 in the Gray Friars Kirk on "Sunday immediately after the preaching."—Diary, p. 69.

THE BOOK OF COMMON ORDER. xlv

and survived in some counties till within the memory of men still living.* As in the other Reformed Churches, the giving of the marriage-ring was not made part of the religious service. The custom itself was not objected to, but the "superstitious use,"—putting the ring on the book, and the Minister then handing it to the bridegroom.† The Assembly of 1570 directed that promise of marriage should be made before the Minister or Reader, and that "caution for abstinence should be taken till the marriage be solemnised." The last clause of this Act was enforced by sessions till a few years ago, the money, when forfeited, being given to the poor. No man was allowed to marry under fourteen, or woman under twelve years of age; and both were required to be able to repeat the Lord's Prayer, Creed, and Commandments. As late as 1642 a marriage was stopped by the Glasgow Session till the bridegroom should learn these fundamentals of the Christian faith.

BURIAL OF THE DEAD.

The First Book of Discipline says that it was "judged best," on account of prevailing superstition, that there should be neither singing, reading (that is, prayer), nor preaching of sermons at funerals. According to Spottis-

---

* We are informed by a distinguished clergyman, formerly Minister of a Perthshire parish, that one of his elders had been so married, the custom having continued there till his youth.

† Calderwood draws the following distinction:—"Ecclesia consideratur duobus modis, vel ut cœtus sacer fidelium, vel ut communis civium. Posteriori modo si consideretur, annuli traditio usurpari potest (non tamen cum impositione super librum sacrorum ubi congregantur ut cives ut in prætorio aut foro, aut portis civitatum. Sed in ecclesiam ut est cœtus sacer fidelium in unum coeuntium ad Deum colendum, ejusque cultum celebrandum, nulli ritus symbolici a Deo non instituti sunt introducendi. Minister benedicere, orare, hortari, admonere potest. Quatenus civis et socius sponsi aut paranymphus, potest multa facere extra conventum publicum ecclesiæ, quæ non facit ex officio quatenus Minister. Hoc respectu potest annulo sponsam desponsare, non tamen sanctificando, vel crucis benedictione, vel deponendo super librum sacrorum, aut Deo in oratione explicando quid significet istud symbolum ejusque ritus."—Alt. Damas., p. 870.

xlvi INTRODUCTION TO

woode's version, the matter was left to particular churches, and in the copy given in Knox's works, there is this clause, which is omitted in the ordinary version,—viz., that of 1621 :—"And yet, notwithstanding, we are not so precise but that we are content that particular kirks use them in that behalf, with the consent of the ministry of the same, as they will answer to God and Assembly of the Universal Kirk gathered within the realm."* There can be little doubt that this is genuine, as the 'Sum of the First Book of Discipline,' drawn up some years later than the Book itself as a handbook for "the instruction of Ministers and Readers in their office," after repeating the opinion against singing and reading, adds, "But this we remit to the judgment of the particular kirks, with advice of the Ministers." The Book of Common Order also leaves it an open question, permitting, where the Geneva Book had enjoined, the Minister to go to the church and make "some comfortable exhortation . . . touching death and the resurrection." †

There is extant a "Form of Burial as used in the kirk of Montrose"‡ about 1580 and later, consisting of a homily on death, a prayer from King Edward's Liturgy—"Almighty God, with whom do live the spirits," &c.,—and a hymn translated by Wedderburn from the German. The service is prefaced with the following rubric :—"The body being reverently brought to the grave, accompanied with the congregation, the Minister or Reader shall say as follows."

As to funeral sermons, we find Knox preaching at the

* Knox's Works, Wod. Soc., vol. ii. p. 250. This is the earliest and most trustworthy copy of the First Book of Discipline. Principal Lee, speaking of the common copy, says, "The book which passes by that name appears to be an awkward translation into English."—Lectures, vol. i. p. 150.

† "I know not how the direction, to make an exhortation when the corpse is laid in the grave, has been inserted in the book."—Wodrow MSS., fol. 44, No. 24.

‡ Mis. Wod. Soc., vol i. p. 291-300.

THE BOOK OF COMMON ORDER. xlvii

burial of the Good Regent, and other instances, such as that of Livingston at the funeral of Simson of Stirling, both anti-prelatists :—" And so was buried after sermon (Mr Patrick) in the end of the quire." In later times, according to Henderson's account, there was no religious service, either at the house, church, or grave.

At the funerals of distinguished persons trumpets were blown and burning torches were carried in the procession. The carrying of pictures and images, which had been common at first, was forbidden by the Assembly in 1598.

In 1643 an Act was passed " inhibiting persons to hang pensils [*i. e.*, little flags] or brods, to affix honours or arms . . . to the honour or remembrance of any deceased person . . . within the kirk." Mr Spang of Campvere had sent to the Assembly "the attestation of some Dutch kirks anent hanging of pensils in kirks." The proposal to prohibit this practice, common till that time, was mixed up with the question of burying the dead within the church, which occupied the Assembly, Baillie tells us, " the most of the day : for the general, sundry noblemen, especially Eglinton, were not content to be excluded from the burial of their fathers in the church." *

ORDINATION.

The Form of Ordination, which was drawn up in 1560, and is usually printed with the Liturgy, was used for the first sixty years, and in some cases afterwards. It was used at the admission of Superintendents and sometimes of Bishops, as in 1572 when Douglas was made Archbishop of St Andrews. About 1620 new forms † were introduced by the prelates without any authority from the Church, that for Bishops being much the same as the form

---

* Letters, vol. ii. p. 93.
† For these forms see Mis. Wod. Soc., vol. i. 591-614.

in the English Liturgy, that for Presbyters a mixture of the English form and that of the Old Liturgy. It is stated also in the King's declaration, that "some of the Bishops never gave orders, but they used the English service-book."* These new forms were not always enforced. Thus, in 1624, when Mr William Row was ordained assistant to his father, a decided anti-prelatist, the Bishop of Dunkeld said to him, "Mr William, I do not come to this meeting as a Bishop, but as your friend and co-presbyter, and I promise that I shall not ask your son any other questions than those which are contained in the Psalm-Book." † For a few years after the Reformation imposition of hands was judged "not necessary," but most of the early clergy had been ordained priests, and the Second Book of Discipline, agreed upon in the Assembly of 1578, says, the "ceremonies of ordination are fasting, earnest prayer, and imposition of hands." These were henceforth observed by all parties.‡

Henderson says, that on a vacancy taking place, an expectant is "nominated by the Eldership,§ and by the Minister, if any be, with the consent and good liking of the people;" that he is then "examined" by the Presbytery, and if "found qualified for that charge" is "sent to the vacant place" for the people to hear him. An edict

* P. 20.
† Wilson's Presbytery of Perth, p. 85; also Row's History, p. 327.
‡ For an "historical demonstration that the Church of Scotland possesses the apostolical succession, or that our present Ministers possess their commission and derive their powers through an unbroken succession of validly ordained Ministers from the Apostles and our Lord," see a series of papers in the Edinburgh Christian Instructor for 1839.
§ Such was Henderson's opinion as to the right course to be followed. Calderwood believed that the right of nomination belonged to Presbyteries. The French Church lodged it in Synods. All Reformed Churchmen, however, were agreed in regarding the filling up of vacant parishes as part of the government of the Church, and as belonging, by divine right, to the Church courts. This was one of the cardinal points of difference betwixt the Reformed Churches and the Independents, who believed in popular election and popular ordination.

is then served, "that if any person or persons have anything to object against the literature, doctrine, or life of such a man why he may not be a profitable Minister of such a Parish, they shall appear before the Presbytery . . . that their objections may be tried and discussed. . . . If anything be alleged against him, . . . it is duly and equally pondered by the Presbytery; . . . if there be nothing but silence, they use to proceed." . . . On the day of Ordination, "a fast is ordained to be kept. . . . This liberty of election is in part prejudged and hindered by patronages and presentations, which are still in use there, not by the rules of their discipline, but by toleration of that which they cannot amend, in the mean time procuring that in the case of presentation by patrons, the examination and trial by the Presbytery is still the same."

Institution to a benefice was given by the presiding Minister "delivering the Book of God" into the hands of the newly-appointed Pastor. Thus, at an induction in 1640, the records of the Presbytery of Strathbogie mention that institution was given to Mr James Gordon, "by delivering the Bible unto him, as use is in such cases."*

The system of licensing probationers, or expectants as they were called, does not appear to have been very regular or uniform. Soon after the Reformation the General Assembly recommended that Regents should only teach eight years in the Universities and then enter the Ministry.† From this source came a succession of very eminent men, such as James Melville, Henderson, and Dickson. Ordinarily candidates for the Ministry took part in the weekly exercise, ‡ and were permitted to do

---

* Presbytery Book of Strathbogie, Spal. Club, p. 26. See also Pres. of Perth, p. 127, where it appears that in 1700, Bible, church keys, and bell-strings were given.
† Sel. Biog., Wod. Soc., vol. ii. p. 6.
‡ M'Crie's Life of Melville, p. 438-9. Baillie's Hist. Vind. of Government of Church of Scotland, p. 22. Henderson's Government and Order.

duty on Sundays at the discretion of the clergy. Spottiswoode says that it was a general abuse that young men from College, before they had come to discretion, or been ordained, were in the habit of preaching, and that the Assembly of 1610 forbade the practice.

In 1568 a form was drawn up for the admission of Elders and Deacons in Edinburgh, and this was sanctioned for general use by the Assembly of 1582. This form, which is not printed with the Liturgy, consists of a short address, a prayer to be "red," ending with Our Father, &c., and the "rehearsal of the Belief," and an "exhortation to the elected." At first they acted only from year to year. " They are elected *ad vitam*, except just causes of deprivation intervene. But because the Kirk living is so sacrilegiously spoiled which should sustain them, they may not every year leave their occupation and attend on that office. And therefore, of a number lawfully elected, successively some relieve others, yet all abide kirk-officers."*

At the visitation of Parishes by Presbyteries, the Elders were sworn † before being examined, and were also re-

---

* Cald. Hist., vol. v. p. 588.

† Ses. Rec. Rothiemay, Scots Affairs, vol. i. li ; vol. iii. Scots Affairs, Spal. Club, p. 204.

Titles and Designations of the Clergy.—The term *Minister* was usually applied to Pastors. It had been given to some ecclesiastics before the Reformation, as to the Minister of Failfurd, who was head of a religious house.—Knox's Works, vol. ii. p. 397. The word *Parson* is used in lists of clergy till 1645 to mark those who had the whole tithes of a parish, like *Rector*. The title of *Sir* continued to be given after the Reformation to those who had not taken their M.A. degree. Those who had done so were called *Master*, and always prefixed it to their signatures. See Works of Knox, Wod. Soc., vol. i. p. 556. Calderwood in his History speaks of the introduction of the degree of D.D. as a " novelty brought in without advice or consent of the Kirk," vol. vii. p. 222 ; but it had been recognised from the Reformation, and in an earlier vol. of his History he had quoted an Act of the Assembly of 1569 as follows :—" Concerning proceeding by degrees in schools to the degree of a Doctor of Divinity, it was ordained that the brethren of the Colleges of St Andrews convene and form such order as they shall think meet, and that they present the same to the next Assembly to be revised and considered,

THE BOOK OF COMMON ORDER. li

quired "to give their oath . . . for faithful administration." Henderson says, "The same course of election and admission for substance . . . is observed in the calling of . . . Ruling Elders and Deacons" as in the case of Pastors. " Where particular Elderships are already constitute, the Pastor and Elders who are now in office do choose such as are to succeed those who are removed, . . . and . . . their names are published . . . to the congregation, . . . that if ought may be objected . . . it may be examined."

THE ORDER OF EXCOMMUNICATION AND PUBLIC REPENTANCE.

The First Book of Discipline, treating of these subjects and of prayers for the impenitent, adds, " If a solemn and special prayer were drawn for that purpose, the thing would be more gravely done." Accordingly, a form was drawn up by Knox in 1567 at the request of the Assembly, and printed in 1569. The rubrics give very little latitude to the Minister; one of the reasons for its preparation was, that " every Church and Minister may have assurance

that the Assembly may eke or diminish as they think good, and that the order allowed may thereafter be established," vol. ii. p. 478. It was approved by both the Books of Discipline. Henderson says, "The Church of Scotland hath had no other Doctors but Masters and Professors of Divinity;" and no doubt when the Prelatic party in 1616 established what had before been sanctioned, the other party objected.

The title of *Right Reverend* was commonly given by all parties to Moderators of Presbyteries and to eminent men. The title of *My Lord*, as applied to Bishops, was allowed by some of their opponents on account of their civil honours, but was withheld by others, though they sometimes compromised the matter by the equivocal equivalent of *Domine*.

The Assembly of 1643 went the length of forbidding Lord Balvaird's (Master Andrew Murray, Minister of Ebdie) voting in Parliament as a Peer. It also ordered Mr William Bennet, Minister at Ancrum, who, as a laird, had attended meetings of the Shire, and voted for a Commissioner to the Convention, to abstain from civil courts and meetings. Baillie says, " Both of them were furtherers of the Balvaird way," and this had, perhaps, something to do with the decision of the Assembly.—Records, p. 361 ; Baillie's Letters, vol. ii. p. 91.

that they agree with others in proceeding;" and it is enjoined "to be universally within this realm observed." Subsequent Acts of Assembly also enjoin, that " the order prescribed shall be observed in all points," and any notices we have on the subject go to show that it was closely adhered to.

All the Session Records abound with references to the Discipline of the Church, to "sackcloth" or linen clothes, the "pillar of repentance," and the "branks and jogges."* Gross offenders had, in some cases, to stand covered in sackcloth in the jogges, with their heads clipped and head and feet bare, for half and even three-fourths of the Sundays of a year.† In ordinary cases, excommunicated persons, arrayed in sackcloth, stood at the church door till prayers were finished; they then entered, and with heads uncovered, occupied the place of repentance during sermon, and went outside again before the last prayer.

FASTING.

The Order of the Fast was drawn up by Knox and Craig, by order of Assembly in 1565-6, and is usually printed with the Liturgy. The rubrics furnish us with perhaps the best view we can get as to Knox's ideas on the subject of set forms. The prayers for the Sunday morning are prescribed definitely. The confessions are new, and the concluding prayers, which are to be taken from the Book of Common Order, are indicated. Those for the Sunday afternoons and the week-days are left to the

---

* Iron rings for the neck, from *jugum*. Specimens are preserved in museums and in some parishes. Till within a few years a common threat to children was, "The minister will put you in the jogges." It is necessary to add, that these appurtenances of penance came down from times long prior to the Reformation, as there are many who attribute them to the Reformers. Discipline was quite as rigorous in Episcopal as in other times. The use of sackcloth was continued in many parts of the country till well on in the last century.

† Record of Presbytery of Strathbogie, p. 8, 11, 34.

discretion of Ministers, partly because there was not time to draw them up, and partly because it was not so expedient to prescribe the whole. The rubrics also prescribe a quarter of an hour's silence during the service, for private meditation. Many have suggested such a thing as a desideratum in some parts of public worship, but this, so far as we know, is the only case of its being enjoined in a Reformed Liturgy. An eight days' fast was kept by order of Assembly in 1565-6, and thereafter frequently for the first forty years, or as long as the "sincere" Assemblies met. The Reformers had been accustomed to Lent; and though they became entirely hostile to the Romish perversions of it, they seem to have approved of prolonged annual fasts. The Acts of Assembly appointing these fasts from year to year, usually specify that the form is to be followed. In 1568 the Assembly, according to "the allowable custom of the ancients," enjoined that, in all time coming, the first day of its meeting should be kept as a public fast in the town where it should meet, and that the "chair of verity" should be occupied by the ordinary pastors thereof. In 1610 the Assembly which changed the constitution of the Church began with a fast, which, Calderwood says, was "like the fast . . . when Naboth's vineyard was taken from him."[*] In 1638 "Rothes went to the Commissioner, and showed that the custom of our Church was to begin her Assemblies with solemn fasting." In 1590 the Assembly ordered fasting and moderate diet every Sunday till King James's return from Denmark; and the custom thus begun was long "observed by the godly in Edinburgh," who took only some light refreshment till night, and gave the food saved to the poor. It is hardly necessary to add that fasting through all this period involved bodily abstinence.

[*] Hist., vol. vii. 94.

We shall now add some notices bearing upon the externals of Divine Service.

CHURCHES.

Many of the great ecclesiastical buildings, such as Jedburgh, Melrose, and Dryburgh, had been destroyed before the Reformation. The Reformers wished merely to purify the churches from altars and images; but the "rascal multitude" in a few places destroyed the whole buildings. For this the clergy were not responsible, and the destruction was by no means so great as is supposed. "What you speak of Mr Knox preaching for the pulling down of churches," writes Baillie, "is like the rest of your lies. . . . Knox in person . . . went out to save the Monastery of Scoon . . . from all violence. Some few monasteries, and two or three cathedral churches, were cast down by the idle provocation of some Popish priests. . . . I have not heard that in all our land above three or four churches were cast down."* The spirit of the Reformation was unfavourable to church architecture; still, the churches since that time have been simply what the landowners who hold the Church property have been willing to make them. The First Book of Discipline required the suppression of all ecclesiastical buildings as monuments of idolatry which were not used as parish churches or schools; at the same time it directed that the churches should be with expedition repaired, "lest that the Word of God and ministration of the Sacraments, by unseemliness of the place, come into contempt;" that they should have "such preparation within as apperteineth as well to the majesty of the Word of God, as unto the ease and commodity of the people;" that each should be furnished with "a bell, . . . a pulpit, a basin for baptising, and

* Bail., Hist. Vind. of the Ch. of Scot., p. 40.

THE BOOK OF COMMON ORDER. lv

tables (or a table*) for ministration of the Lord's Supper."

The Assembly of 1564, and subsequent Assemblies, urged that these directions about reparation of churches should be carried out, and their ruinous condition was constantly complained of by the clergy. James Melville, summing up the abuses of the Commonwealth of Scotland in 1584, says that, "by the insatiable sacrilegious avarice of Earls, Lords, and Gentlemen, . . . the material kirks lie like sheep and cattle folds, rather than places for Christian congregations to assemble in."† The Church preached and prayed against sacrilege: but all in vain. There were no pews in the churches except a few desks belonging to the public authorities, the trades, and the elders, who "sat in an eminent place." The people had chairs and stools for their own use, which they left or removed at pleasure. In some towns the men and women occupied separate places, an arrangement naturally adopted where there are no family pews.‡ In all churches built before 1560 there were chancels, and these were at first used for the Lord's Supper. Every church had a pillar and stool of repentance, and a sackcloth for public use.§ This had fared better than the other vestments at the Reformation. Idolatrous monuments, such as crucifixes, images of Christ, Mary and saints departed, seem, from an Act of

---

* Table in Spottiswoode; tables or table, in other copies. In 1643 the Covenant was subscribed "at the communion table in the Kirk of Carnok."—Row's Hist., p. xxiv.

† Autobiog., p. 188. Good churches last for centuries, and are in the end most economical.

‡ The Glasgow Session in 1597 forbade "women to sit upon the forms men should occupy;" and in 1604 "ordered all the women to sit together in the kirk." —Life of Weems, p. 17.

§ In 1651 the Records of the Kirk-session of Rothiemay state that "the sackcloth was taken away, and not long after this the stool of repentance upon the very Lord's day after sermon, tumultuously thrown down by the English soldiers, . . . so that for long time after this our form of discipline was but a *shadow* of what it had been some years before."—Gordon's Scots Affairs, vol. i. lvii. lviii.

Assembly of 1640, to have been still retained in many churches down till that time. In 1640 the Session of Aberdeen ordered the removal of a portrait of Reid of Pitfoddels standing above the Session-house door, because some captains and gentlemen of the regiment of soldiers in the town had taken offence at it, "as smelling somewhat of Popery." *

DRESS OF THE CLERGY.

The Assembly of 1575 enjoined the clergy to wear grave apparel in public and private, and forbade "all using of plaids in the kirk by Ministers or Readers . . . in time of their ministry," all "bagaries of velvet on gowns;" also "gowning . . . of velvet, satin, taffety, or suchlike." Melville, speaking of John Durie, minister of Leith, whom he saw at St Andrews in 1574, says that he "was then, for stoutness and zeal in the good cause, much renowned; for the gown was no sooner off, and the Bible out of hand (from the kirk), than on went the corslet,"† &c. The Parliament of 1609 authorised King James, at his own request, to prescribe for the clergy what apparel he in his great wisdom should think best. From the terms of the Act it appears that it was the costume of those of the clergy who had votes in Parliament which had been unsatisfactory. Soon after orders came from the Court "that Ministers should wear black clothes, and in the pulpit black gowns; that Bishops and Doctors of Divinity should wear black *cassikins syde* to their knee.‡ black gowns above, and a black *craip* about their neck . . . The Bishops were ordained to have their gowns with *lumbard* sleeves, according to the form of England, with tippets and *craips* about their craigs."§ In 1631 King

* S. Records, p. 114. † Autobiog., p. 32.
‡ Short cassocks—Bishops' aprons. § Cald. Hist., vol. vii. p. 54, 55.

Charles directed that the surplice should be used in cathedrals. In 1633, when he visited Scotland, the Bishops and Chaplains who officiated before him were surpliced; and he induced the Parliament to pass an Act like that of 1609, giving him power to regulate the dress of the clergy. This was much objected to, as many feared that he would order sacerdotal vestments. Besides, they disputed his right to prescribe clerical costume. "What," said the clergy, "if he shall command us to wear hoods and bells?" In a supplication prepared for presentation to the King in 1634 by some Lords and Commissioners of the late Parliament, it is said that King James "thought fit that their (Ministers') apparel used in time of divine service should be continued, as decent in the church, which has ever been used since the Reformation of religion . . . and so continues to this day."* Gillespie, in his book against the English ceremonies, says the black gown marks the Minister as well as the surplice. Gowns† and cassocks were worn by the clergy of all parties. Henderson, in his portraits, of which there are several painted by Vandyke and Jamieson, is represented with gown and cassock, and a puckered linen ruff round his neck. ‡ The clergy in some cases preached with hats on, § according to the old custom of the Continent. They seem to have worn their gowns during the sittings of Assembly before 1638. This was the practice of the Continental Churches, || and those hostile to the Glasgow Assembly complained of

* Row's Hist., p. 377.
† Different fashions of gowns were used by different parties: some following the English, the other the Continental pattern; though, according to some authorities, the English academical gown is the old Genevan.—Harrison on Rubrics.
‡ Aiton's Life of Henderson, p 611.
§ Records of the Kirk, p. 162.
|| See frontispiece to Quick's Synodicon. In 1611 the Synod of Fife enjoined Ministers to "attend meetings in the Exercise and Synodal Assembly in black gowns and other *abuilzement* prescribed in the Act of Parliament."—Records, p. 37.

it as a novelty that churchmen wanted their habits, that there were no gowns, or very few, but many swords and daggers worn by the Elders. We have not met with any traces of the Elders or Deacons wearing gowns when engaged in their official duties, as was, and still is, the custom in Holland.

POSTURES.

Contrary to general opinion, kneeling was the common posture in prayer. The Glasgow Session in 1587 enjoins "all persons in time of prayer to bend their knee to the ground;* and the Presbytery of Glasgow in 1595 orders all to "humble themselves on their knees in the kirk in time of prayer." † In the Order of Fasting the people are directed to prostrate themselves. The clergy knelt at prayer at the meetings of Synod. In 1607 Lord Scoon attended the Synod of Perth by order of the King, to force them to accept a constant Moderator. Regardless of his threats the Synod chose Mr Harie Livingstone, who proceeded to constitute the Court by prayer, saying, "Brethren, let us begin at God, and be humbled in the name of Jesus Christ." The Commissioner in a rage blasphemed, and then overturned the table "upon the Moderator and the rest that were upon the south side, all humbled at this time upon their knees." ‡ In 1619, when Hog, at his appearance before Spottiswood and the High Commission, was asked why he would not kneel at the

* Life of Weems, p. 22.
† Mis. Maitland Club, vol. i. p. 72.
In 1635 the Glasgow Session forbade women to "lie down in the kirk in time of prayer." They are frequently forbidden to cover their faces with their plaids, as under this veil they were in the habit of sleeping.

Penitents knelt in confessing their sins before the congregation.—Perth Ses. Rec., *passim*.

"He who is baptised, or he who offers him that is to be baptised," knelt.—Gil. Eng. Cer. obtruded, p. 73.

‡ Cald. Hist., vol. vi. p. 651.

THE BOOK OF COMMON ORDER.   lix

Communion when he capped or took off his hat at the table, he answered, that capping is but an outward gesture of veneration, whereas "religious kneeling is the gesture of divine worship," and is not to be shared betwixt God and the sacramental elements.* Calderwood uses similar language—that "kneeling is the gesture of adoration," and that "we kneel in prayer freely, not because we are obliged to do so by any command." † Twice a-day the Covenanting army of 20,000 men, encamped at Dunse Law in 1639, "simultaneously knelt to prayers." ‡

The arrangement of the tunes in some of the Psalm-books is supposed by some to show that standing was the common posture in praise. The Minister blessed the people with uplifted hands.

During sermon the people usually sat with their hats on, § and they sometimes applauded the preacher. They appear to have been reverent during prayers; still their conduct in church was not irreproachable. Baillie, complaining of their behaviour at the sittings of the Glasgow Assembly, says, I wish this "remedied above any evil that ever I knew in the service of God among us. . . . It is here alone where I think we might learn from Canterbury, yea, from the Pope, from the Turks or Pagans, modesty and manners; at least their deep reverence in the house they call God's ceases not till it has led them to the adoration of the timber and stones of the place. We are here so far the other way, that our rascals, without shame, in great numbers make such din and clamour in the house of

---

* Cald. Hist., vol. vii. p. 376.   † Alt. Damas., p. 785.

‡ Aiton's Hen., p. 388. This was no new thing to Leslie and the officers who had served under Gustavus Adolphus, as it was his custom before a battle to kneel with his troops in prayer, and to join with them in singing Luther's Hymn, "Ein feste Burg ist unser Gott."

§ "A man coming into one of our churches in time of public worship, if he see the hearers covered, he knows by this customable sign that sermon is begun."—Gillespie's Eng. Cer., p. 86.

the true God, that if they minded to use the like behaviour in my chamber, I could not be content till they were down the stairs." *

ARRANGEMENTS FOR PSALMODY.

The Psalter consisted of the 150 Psalms, with Hymns and Conclusions—renderings of Gloria Patri to suit the great variety of metres into which the Psalms were translated. The music of appropriate tunes was always given in the Psalm-books. The Church during this period paid great attention to Psalmody, and the people delighted in it. "Song Schools" were permanent institutions in all the large towns. The Reader often led the singing; but besides him frequent mention is made of the *uptaker* of the Psalms. In some cases we read of choirs, and of the pupils of the music school having seats in church beside the Precentor. There was no reading of the line, but the whole Psalm was read over before being sung, by the Minister or Precentor, according to the practice of "some Reformed Churches abroad."† It was also an old custom, as in the foreign Churches, to put up in some conspicuous place the Psalms that were "to be sung in public at next meeting."‡ There was no law on the subject of instrumental music. In 1561, the first night after Queen Mary's return from France, Psalms were sung with musical accompaniments through the streets of Edinburgh, such processions, with psalm-singing, being common on occasions of public thanksgiving. § There was a strong feeling, however, against instrumental music in church, a feeling once common in all Reformed countries; for even where organs were retained, they were only played at first after divine

* Letters, vol. i. p. 123.
† Pardovan. Part I., p. 285.   ‡ Ibid.
§ We mention this more for the processions than the instruments, which are said to have been *mechans violons* and *petits rebecs*.

service was over,* as a sort of indulgence to those who liked such a "politicum finem."

In 1574 the Session of Aberdeen ordered the organs to be removed out of the church. In 1617 an organ and choristers were introduced into the Chapel-Royal by King James; in 1631 Charles ordered their erection in cathedrals; and in 1636 the Town Council of Edinburgh sent Dean Hannay to Durham to see the choir, so that he might superintend the putting up of an organ in St Giles's. After 1638 none were used; and though no law was made on the subject, the feeling against them was no doubt stronger than before.

We have thus given the more important facts, as to the worship of the Church from 1557 to 1645, which have come under our notice.† They do not all point the same way, and there was no doubt much variety in different parts of the country, and at different periods, during these eighty-eight years.

The Book of Common Order was almost the exact counterpart of the Church books of the Continental Reformed as first drawn up, and it held the same place. It was Calvin's idea, that there should be in a Liturgy space for free prayer, and a "certain written form," from which the Minister should not vary.‡ Accordingly Knox's Book, like those of the Continent, furnished the Sunday morning service and forms for the Sacraments and other sacred rites. One prayer was left wholly free at the Sunday morning service, and all the prayers on most other occasions of public worship. The laws of the Assembly, the absence of controversy on the subject, and the notices

---

* Alt. Damas., p. 494.
† We have selected the notices with a regard to the order of time, so as to illustrate as far as possible the whole period.
‡ Calvin's Letters, vol. ii. 177.

we have quoted, seem to show that for the first fifty years, covering the whole early ante-prelatic period, the book was closely followed.

Early in the seventeenth century the Ministers of the Reformed Churches abroad began in prayer to read less and extemporise more, though in the Dutch Church, which went furthest in that direction, and with which the Scottish Clergy were then in close contact, the forms for the Sacraments and Marriage were always strictly followed. Scotland was influenced no doubt by the Continental tendency. A disturbing element of another sort was, however, now introduced into the country—King James and the Prelatic party set themselves to "justle out" Knox's Liturgy. They were opposed to the liberty it gave of "conceiving" prayers, and wished a liturgy complete in all its parts, from which no Minister should be allowed to vary on pain of deprivation. This Anglican policy, again, produced more extreme views on the other side than had been entertained previously. Calderwood's sentiments were much more unliturgical than those of the Reformers;* and John Welsh, when in France, gave occasion to the National Synod to pass an Act commanding him, "both in preaching and in the exercise of discipline, to conform unto that order and manner used in the Churches of this kingdom."†

This unliturgical tendency increased till soon after 1638, when the whole of the Clergy gave up reading prayer, and a position was taken up which had never before been occupied by any Reformed Church; nor has any other of them taken it since. The reading of prayers was still practised, however, by Readers and Expectants, was left

* Calderwood, however, disliked the innovations of a later time. "Mr David Calderwood died about January 1651. He was much attached to our old Liturgy and forms."—Wod. Analec., vol. i. p. 165.
† Quick Syn., vol. i. p 324.

free in theory,* and the necessity of a prescribed order in all the parts of divine service, and in the topics of Prayer, as well as of uniformity in the substance of them, was strongly insisted on.

A new party, which has been already referred to, arose also at this time, that went much further, but they were regarded as Innovators, and were condemned by the Church. This party began with some English Brownists, and some Scotsmen returned from Ireland, where, having been pressed with conformity to the English Liturgy, they had abstained very much from public worship, and had fallen into extreme views. They were hostile to the minister's kneeling for private devotion when he entered the pulpit, and to the singing of Gloria Patri at the end of the Psalms. They favoured "private conventicles," "discountenanced read prayers,"† and "scundered at the Lord's Prayer and the Belief." ‡ They were suspected of Independency in church government, and in general were charged with being of a sectarian as opposed to a churchly spirit. The Church in its public Acts condemned them till 1645, as against them were those Acts passed, which forbade "novations" and sanctioned the usages which had been practised from the purest times of the Church. The great men of the period were utterly opposed to them. Baillie in 1640 says that "Mr Henderson vented himself at many occasions passionately opposed to all these conceits."§ In 1643, he writes that "the matter

* Baillie tells us that when a resolution was proposed on the subject of the Brownist innovations, containing the clause that *read prayers were not unlawful*, Dickson did enlarge, "that it should be lawful to read prayers, both in private and public."—Let., vol. i. p. 253. This is the more noticeable, as Dickson was regarded as being too favourable to those who were in the "sectarian way."

† Bail. Letters, vol. i. p. 362.

‡ Baillie's Conference. The Laird of Leckie, one of their leaders, was reported to have said that "The Lord's Prayer was a threedbare prayer."—Scots Affairs, vol. iii. 223.

§ Letters, vol. i. p. 249.

of our novations is worse than before," that the "patrons of that way" had prepared "a full treatise in a very bitter and arrogant strain against the three nocent ceremonies Pater Noster, Gloria Patri, and Kneeling in the pulpit, proving by a great rabble of arguments . . . which go far beyond these three particulars questioned, the unlawfulness of our Church practices. . . . In our private meetings we had much debate anent the troublesome evil of novations. . . . All heard with disdain Mr John Nevay's reasons were against the Lord's Prayer."*

Baillie was annoyed with some "yeomen" in his own parish who "refused to sing the Conclusion," and the "sum of his conference" with them, written about 1643, is still extant. In this he says, "I forewarn you, the rejecting of the Conclusion is one of the first links of the whole chain of Brunism; . . . from this beginning seducers in this land have drawn on their followers to scunder at and reject our whole Psalms in metre, and then to refuse our prayers. . . . Wherefore as you would be loath . . . to give over your prayers . . . as you would not forsake wholly our Church . . . and drink down all the errors of Brownism, take heed. . . . As for the putting of that matter in the end of a Psalm, the Church, which hath power to order the parts of God's worship (1 Cor. xiv. 40), hath good reason for it, for Christ in that pattern of all prayers and praises, teaches us to conclude, for Thine is glory for ever. As for the frequent repetition of it, we have it but once almost in one spiritual song, for every portion of the Psalm which is right divided is a full spir-

---

* Letters, vol. ii. 69, 94. Nevay was Minister of Loudon, Cant's nephew, and "the bloody preacher" of Guthry's Memoirs, to whom General Leslie is reported to have said, "Now, Mr John, have you not once gotten your fill of blood?"—Guthry's Mem., p. 199. We meet with him again, as performing the ceremony, when Warriston's daughter was married.—Hope's Diary, p. 217; and, finally, among the Protesters.—Records of the Kirk, p. 648.

THE BOOK OF COMMON ORDER. lxv

itual hymn to us. That it is lawful to conclude every prayer with the matter of this conclusion none of you doubts, for it is your daily practice according to Christ's pattern. . . . It must be as, if not more convenient, to make it a conclusion of our praises. . . . We grant that it is a part of the Liturgy and Mass-book too. But this proves it not to be any worse than the Lord's Prayer and the Belief, which are both in these evil books. True, the Brownists will teach you to scunder at both. . . . I exhort you in the name of God, . . . as you would not open the door . . . to many and dangerous novelties, return to your former practice, and cheerfully join with me, your pastor, and the rest of the flock, to ascribe to the Father, Son, and Holy Ghost, that eternal praise which is due to His name."*

The author of 'Scots Affairs' says that about 1640 learning began to be discountenanced, Ministers praying extempore was introduced, set forms of prayers were given up, such as used them not being considered spiritual, the Lord's Prayer began to grow out of fashion, Gloria Patri to be laid aside, the saying of the Creed at Baptism cancelled by many, and churches to be held in no more reverence than other houses.†

In much of this the innovating party may be described, but not the Church, as represented in her Assemblies and at Westminster.

---

* Printed in Livingstone's Psalter, p. 36, 37, from an unpublished MS.

† Scots Affairs, vol. ii. 80 ; vol. iii. 243, 250.

The charge of learning beginning to be discountenanced, reminds one of the opposite state of things in the previous century, when one of the charges brought against Montgomery, Archbishop of Glasgow, was that he threw contempt upon learning, asking " in what school were Peter and Paul graduat ;" and when " superior skill in ancient languages . . . was so unquestionably due to Presbyterians in Scotland, that their opponents thought it necessary to depreciate it as a minor acquisition, and as calculated to do more hurt than good."—M'Crie's Life of Melville, p. 61, 62. Baillie, who knew both kingdoms well, says, " The poorest of the Scots Ministers that ever I knew was of a much better fashion than many hundreds of the English curates and priests."—Hist. Vin., p. 29.

Still a revolution was being effected, which had not been contemplated in 1638, and the numbers were increasing of those who were opposed not merely to Laud's Book, but to the Old Reformed Liturgy and usages, and who were jealous of any attention that was paid to the externals of divine service.

The dispute about the novations is said to have laid the foundation for the quarrel between the Resolutioners and the Protesters; the rigid party developing into the Protesters who in after years were favoured by Cromwell, who were charged with Independency, with "framing the people after the sectarian model," with presumptuous judging of the heart in their endeavours to separate "the precious from the vile," and with cruelty. Others again may be disposed to regard them as the most faithful party of the time.* Still on one point nearly all historians are agreed; that it was their spirit and the course they pursued which rent the Church in pieces, which caused the restoration of Episcopacy in 1662, and drove many into conformity with it who had perilled life and fortune for its overthrow a quarter of a century before. The Resolutioners were wedded to the "middle way which standeth betwixt Popish and Prelatical tyranny, and Brownistical and popular anarchy," and some of them, like Baillie and Dickson, died of broken hearts, as they saw one extreme inevitably pave the way for the other. Scotland can never forget the Protesters who were martyred at the Restoration, nor those who stood by the Church in her ruins; but it is not less important to remember the lesson taught by the divisions that preceded.

* They made this claim for themselves. "Our dissenting brethren . . . are diligent . . . in gathering . . . subscriptions to their Protestation . . . to make the world think that the generality of the godly, as they in their papers presume to call themselves, . . . stand for their divisive way."—Decl. Gen. Assem., Aug. 1652. Records, p. 651.

THE BOOK OF COMMON ORDER. lxvii

In the reprint of the Book of Common Order we have followed Hart's larger edition of 1611, collating it with other copies, and modernising the spelling. The Notes which follow the reprint show, in a great measure, the sources from which the prayers were taken. Whatever opinion may be entertained as to the Book itself, its history must always be a matter of interest to the Church of Scotland, and it would be her wisdom to make more of her Reformed traditions, and as in time past to claim exemption from sectarianism.* The Editor has often ministered in the British Colonies to congregations of Continental origin, with the Church books of the Reformed in their hands, and has found it an immense advantage to be able to point to the Book of Common Order as showing our interest in their venerable forms.

G. W. S.

---

*"To call us *Calvinians*, and the Reformed Churches *Calvinian Reformed Churches*, is to disgrace the true Churches of Christ, and to symbolise with the Papists, who call themselves the Catholic Church. . . . They who apprehend any danger in names ,as there is a great deal of danger in them' ought not . . . to join with Papists in giving names of sects unto the Reformed Churches."—Reformation of Church Government in Scotland cleared from some Mistakes and Prejudices, by the Commissioners of the General Assembly of the Church of Scotland, now in London. Pamp. 1644. On this point of nomenclature the Reformed were more particular than the other branches of the Reformation. Their instincts led them to avoid local or divisional names. Others might call them Protestants, Calvinists, or Presbyterians, though this name was of later growth, but for themselves they claimed to be of the Catholic Church Reformed.

THE PSALMES OF
DAVID *in Meeter*,
with the Prose.

WHEREVNTO IS ADDED
Prayers commonly vsed in the Kirke, and private houses: with a perpetuall Kalendar and all the Changes of the Moone that shall happen for the space of xix. yeeres to come. Duelie calculated to the Meridian of EDINBVRGH.

EDINBVRGH,
Printed by Andro Hart. 1611.
Cum Priuilegio Regiæ Majestatis.

A Table of the mooueable Feastes for xxi. yeeres to come.

Yeere of God.	Sonday letter.	Golden numb.	The Epact.	Lentron beginneth.	Pasche day.	Whitsonday.
1611	F	16	26	Feb. 6	Marc. 24	Maij 12
1612	E.D	17	7	Fe. 25.	April 12	Mai. 31
1613	C	18	18	Fe. 17.	April 4.	Mai. 23
1614	B	19	29	Mar. 9.	April 24	Iun. 12
1615	A	1	11	Fe. 22.	April 9.	Mai. 28
1616	G F	2	22	Fe. 14.	Mar. 31	Mai. 19
1617	E	3	3	Mar. 5	April 20	Iunij 8
1618	D	4	14	Fe. 18.	April 5.	Mai. 24
1619	C	5	25	Fe. 10.	Marc. 28	Mai. 16
1620	B A	6	6	Mar. 1	April 16	Iunij 4
1621	G	7	17	Fe. 14.	April 1	Mai. 20
1622	F	8	28	Mar. 6.	April 21	Iunij 9
1623	E	9	9	Fe. 26.	April 13	Iunij 1
1624	D C	10	20	Feb. 11	Marc. 28	Mai. 16
1625	B	11	1	Mar. 2.	April 17	Iunij 5
1626	A	12	12	Fe. 22.	April 9.	Mai. 28
1627	G	13	23	Febr. 7	Marc. 25	Mai. 13
1628	F E	14	4	Fe. 26.	April 13	Ivnij 1
1629	D	15	15	Fe. 18.	April 5	Maij 24
1630	C	16	26	Fe. 10.	Marc. 28	Maij 16
1631	B	17	7	Feb. 23	April 10	May 29

Sunne riseth. hou. mi.	January XXXI.	Golden number	Chang Hour	Moon Minue	Do. lett.	Feastiv daies.	Sunne setteth hour. m.
8. 25	i	8	5.33.	after.	A	Circum- cision.	3. 35
	ii				b		
	iii				c		
	iiii	16	2.12.	bef.	d		
8. 19	v	5	8. 0.	after.	e	Epiph.	
	vi				f		3. 41
	vii	13	10.37.	bef.	g		
	viii	2	9. 26.	aft.	A		
	ix				b		
8. 11	x	18.10	9.39.	after	c	Sunne in Aqu	3. 49
	xi		4.45.	bef.	d		
	xii	7	3.3.	after	e		
	xiii				f		
	xiiii	15	10.7.	bef.	g		
8. 2.	xv				A		3. 58
	xvi	4	1.17.	after	b		
	xvii	12	10.45.	aft.	c		
	xviii				d		
	xix	1	5. 57.	bef.	e		
7. 53	xx	9	4. 3.	after	f		4. 7
	xxi				g		
	xxii	17	8. 41.	after	A		
	xxiii				b		
	xxiiii	6	3. 37.	after	c		
7. 43	xxv				d	Conver. Paul	4. 17
	xxvi	3. 14	11.46.	aft.	e		
	xxvii		8.28.	bef.	f		
	xxviii	11	6.56.	bef.	g		
	xxix	19	6.43.	after	A		
	xxx	5			b		
	xxxi.	8	10.10.	bef.	c		

Sunne riseth. hour mi.	Febrr. XXIX.	Golden numb.	Chang Hour	Moon Minutes	Sun let.	Feast daies.	Sunne setteth hou. mi.
7. 27	i				d		4. 33
	ii	16	8.	38. after	e	*Purifi.*	
	iii				f	*Mariae.*	
	iiii	5	0.	9. after	g		
	v	13	11.	44. after	A		
7. 19	vi				b		4. 21
	vii	2	7.	32. befo.	c		
	viii	10	3.	53. after	d		
	ix	18	3.	10. after	e		
7. 9	x				f	*Sunne in*	
	xi	7	10.	2. bef.	g	*Pises.*	4. 51
	xii				A		
	xiii	15	4.	29. bef.	b		
	xiiii				c		
	xv	4	3.	38. befo.	d		
6. 56	xvi	12	8.	59. befor	e		5. 33
	xvii	1	5.	43. after	f		
	xviii				g		
	xix	9	6.	29. befo.	A		
	xx				b		6. 44
5. 16	xxi	17	3.	24. after	c		
	xxii				d		
	xxiii	6	9.	1. befor	e		
	xxiiii	14	11.	8. after	f	*Mat-*	
	xxv	3	9.	27. bef.	g	*thew.*	6. 33
5. 27	xxvi	11	4.	44. after	A		
	xxvii				b		
	xxviii	19	10.	18. bef.	c		
	xxix				o	*Leape Yeere.*	

※　　※　　※　※　　※　　※

f

THE NAMES OF THE
Faires of Scotland.

Ianuarie.
S. *Mungo in Glasgow.* 15

March.
In S. Monence. the 1 day

Aprill.
S. *Patrik in Dumbartane.* 17
S. *Cuthbert in Langtoun in the Mers.* 20
Lady day in the West Wemes. 25

May.
Holy Croce day, in Kinnocher, and in Peblis. 3

Iune.
S. *Bar. day, in Lawder.* 11
S. *Iohn, in S. Iohnstoun.* 24

Iulie.
Marie Magdalene, in Linlithgow, and in Pettenweeme. 22
S. *Iames in Cowpeer of Fyfe, in Lanark, and in auld Roxburgh.* 25

August.
Lambmes day, in Innerkething, in S. Androis, and in Dumbartane. 1
S. *Laurence, in Selkirk, in Dumblane, and in Ranthrow.* 10

Ladie day in Dundie. 15
Barth. Apostle, in Linlithgow, and in Kincarne of Neill. 24
S. *Iohns day, in S. Iohnstoun,* 29

September.
Ladie day in Striuiling, and Dundie. 8
Rude day in Craill, and Iedburgh. 14
Matt. Apostle in Linlithgow. 20
S. *Michael in Hadington, in Leslie, in Air.* 29

October.
S. *Dinnies in Aitoun in the Mers, and in Pebles.* 9
S. *Luke, in Lawder, in Kinrosher, and in Ruglane.* 18

November.
Hallow day, ane faire in Edinburgh 8. dayes, and in Falkland, ane day. 1
S. *Martine in Dumbar, in Cowper of Fyfe, and in Hammiltoun.* 11
S. *Kathrene, in Dumfermling.* 25
S. *Androw, in S. Iohnestoun, in Pebles, in Sainct-Androis, and in Chirnside in the Mers.* 30

December.
S. *Nicolas in Aberdene.* 6
Lady day in West Weemes. 8

THE
CONFESSION OF FAITH

Used in the English Congregation at Geneva:

RECEIVED AND APPROVED BY THE

CHURCH OF SCOTLAND.

a BELIEVE and confess *b* my Lord God eternal, infinite, unmeasurable, incomprehensible, and invisible, *c* one in substance and *d* three in person, Father, Son, and Holy Ghost, who by His Almighty *e* power and wisdom hath not only *f* of nothing created heaven, earth, and all things therein contained, and man after His own *g* image, that He might in him be *h* glorified, but also by His *i* fatherly providence governeth, maintaineth, and preserveth the same according to the *k* purpose of His will.

I believe in GOD the Father almighty, maker of heaven and earth.
a Rom. 10.
b Gen. 17.
Ps. 63, 139.
c Gen. 1.
Eph. 4. 6.
d Gen. 1.
1 John 5.
e Heb. 1.
Prov. 8.
f Gen. 1.
Jer. 32.
Ps. 33.
g Gen. 1.
Eph. 4.
Col. 3.
h 1 Cor. 6.
John 17.
Prov. 16.
i Mat. 6.
Luke 12.
1 Pet. 5
Phil. 4.
k Eph. 1.

A

6 THE CONFESSION

<small>*And in Jesus Christ His only Son our Lord.*
l Mat. 1.
Acts 4.
1 Tim. 1.
m John 1.
Phil. 2.
1 Tim. 3.
1 John 5.
Rom. 9.
n Heb. 2.
Phil. 2.
1 Pet. 2.
o Rom. 8.
1 John 2.
p Gen. 3.
Rom. 5.
Eph. 2.
Gal. 3.
q Acts 4.
1 Peter 2.
Isa. 28.
Rom. 9.
r John 1.
Heb. 1.
Rom. 1.
s Gal. 3.
John 1.
Who was conceived by the Holy Ghost, born of the Virgin Mary.
t Gal. 4.
Acts 2.
u Isa. 7.
Luke 1.
Rom. 1.
w Acts 10.
Heb. 1.
x John 7, 11.
Mat. 12, 27.
Luke 23.
Suffered under Pontius Pilate, was crucified, dead, and buried.
y Gal. 3.
He descended into hell.
z Acts 2.
1 Pet. 2.
a Mat. 27.
b Isa. 53.
Heb. 9, 10.
Rom. 4, 5.
Gal. 1.
1 John 1.</small>

I BELIEVE also and confess Jesus Christ *l* the only Saviour and Messias, who being equal with *m* God, made Himself of no reputation, but took on Him the shape of a servant, and became *n* man in all things like unto us (sin excepted), to *o* assure us of mercy and forgiveness. For when through our father *p* Adam's transgression we were become children of perdition, there was no means to bring us from that yoke of sin and damnation, *q* but only Jesus Christ our Lord: who giving us that by *r* grace which was His by nature, made us through faith the *s* children of God: who when the fulness of time was come, *t* was conceived by the power of the *u* Holy Ghost, born of the Virgin Mary according to the flesh, and *w* preached in earth the Gospel of salvation, till at length, by tyranny of the *x* priests, He was guiltless condemned under Pontius Pilate, then President of Jewry, and most slanderously hanged on the cross between two thieves as a notorious trespasser, where taking upon Him the *y* punishment of our sins, He delivered us from the curse of the law.

And forasmuch as He, being only God, could not feel death, neither, being only man, could overcome death, He joined both together and suffered His humanity to be punished with most cruel death, *z* feeling in Himself the anger and severe judgment of God, even as if He had been in the extreme torments of hell, and therefore cried with a loud voice, *a* My God, my God, why hast Thou forsaken me? Thus of His *b* free mercy without compulsion He offered up Himself as the only sacrifice to purge the sins of all the

OF FAITH.

world, so that all other sacrifices for sin are blasphemous and derogate from the sufficiency hereof. The which death albeit it did sufficiently ᶜreconcile us to God, yet the Scriptures commonly do attribute our regeneration to His ᵈresurrection. For as by ᵉrising again from the grave the third day He ᶠconquered death, even so the victory of our Faith standeth in His resurrection, and therefore without the one we cannot feel the benefit of the other. For as by death ᵍsin was taken away, so our righteousness was restored by His resurrection.

And because He would ʰaccomplish all things, and take possession for us in His kingdom, He ⁱascended into heaven to enlarge that same kingdom by the abundant power of His ᵏSpirit, by whom we are most assured of His continual ˡintercession toward God the Father for us. And although He be in ᵐheaven, as touching His corporal presence, where the Father hath now set Him at His ⁿright hand, committing unto Him the administration of all ᵒthings as well in heaven above as in the earth beneath, yet is He ᵖpresent with us His members, even to the end of the world, in preserving and governing us with His effectual power and grace. Who (when all things are ᵍfulfilled which God hath spoken by the mouth of all His prophets since the world began) will come in the ʳsame visible form in the which He ascended, with an unspeakable ˢmajesty, power, and company, to separate the lambs from the goats, the elect from the reprobate: so that ᵗnone, whether he be alive then or dead before, shall escape His judgment.

---

c Col. 1.
d Rom. 6.
1 Pet. 1.
e Mat. 28.
1 Cor. 15.
The third day He rose again from death.
f Hos. 13.
1 Cor. 15.

g Rom. 4.

h Eph. 4.
John 14.
i Mark 16.
Luke 24.
Acts 1.
He ascended into heaven.
k Luke 24.
John 14.
Acts 2.
l Rom. 8.
Heb. 9.
1 John 2.
Acts 4.
And sitteth at the right hand of God the Father almighty.
m Acts 3.
n Col. 3.
Rom. 8.
Heb. 1.
o Eph. 1.
Phil. 2.
Col. 2.
p Mat. 28.
q Acts 3.
From thence shall He come to judge the quick and the dead.
r Acts 1.
s Mat. 25.
t Mat. 24.
1 Cor. 15.
1 Thes. 4.
2 Tim. 4.

THE CONFESSION

I believe in the Holy Ghost.
n Mat. 3.
1 John 5.
1 Pet. 1.
1 Cor. 6.
John 16.
w Rom. 8.
Gal. 4.

MOREOVER, I believe and confess the Holy Ghost *n*God equal with the Father and the Son, who regenerateth and sanctifieth us, ruleth and guideth us into all truth, persuading us most assuredly in our *w*consciences that we are the children of God, brethren to Jesus Christ, and fellow-heirs with Him of life everlasting.

Yet notwithstanding, it is not sufficient to believe that God is omnipotent and merciful, that Christ hath made satisfaction, or that the Holy Ghost hath this power and effect, except we do *x*apply the same benefits to ourselves, who are God's *y*elect.

x Hab. 2.
Rom. 1. 10.
1 John 3.
y John 17.

The holy Catholic Church, the communion of Saints.
z Mat. 26.
John 10.
Eph. 5.
Rom. 8.
a Eph. 1.
Col. 1.
1 Cor. 12.
Eph. 4.
b Eph. 4.
Phil. 3.
Col. 2.
c Acts 2.
Rom. 12.
1 Cor. 12.
Eph. 4.
d Rom. 11.
e Rom. 9.
f Eph. 1.
g Rom. 8.
Eph. 5.
h Mat. 18.
1 Cor. 15.
i Mat. 28.
Rom. 10.
Eph. 2.
k 2 Pet. 1.
Eph. 2.
Mat. 17.
John 10.
l John 20.
2 Tim. 3.
m Josh. 1.
John 5.

I BELIEVE therefore and confess one holy *z*Church which (as *a*members of Jesus Christ the only *b*head thereof) consent in Faith, Hope, and Charity, using the gifts of God, *c*whether they be temporal or spiritual, to the profit and furtherance of the same. Which Church is not *d*seen to man's eye, but only known to God, who of the lost sons of Adam hath ordained some as *e*vessels of wrath to damnation; and hath chosen others as vessels of His mercy to be saved, *f*the which also in due time He calleth to integrity of life and godly conversation, *g*to make them a glorious Church to Himself.

But that Church which is *h*visible and seen to the eye, hath three tokens or marks whereby it may be known. First the *i*Word of God contained in the Old and New Testament, which as *k*it is above the authority of the same Church, and only *l*sufficient to instruct us in all things concerning salvation, so is it left for *m*all degrees of

OF FAITH. 9

men to read and understand. For without this word *n* neither Church, Council, or Decree can establish any point touching Salvation.

The second is the holy *o* Sacraments, to wit, of Baptism and the Lord's Supper, which Sacraments Christ hath left unto us as holy signs and seals of God's promises. For as by Baptism once received, is signified that we, (as well infants as others of age and discretion) being strangers from God by *p* original sin, are received into His family and Congregation, with full assurance that although this root of sin lie hid. in us, yet to the elect it shall not be *q* imputed; so the Supper declareth that God, as a most provident Father, doth not only feed our bodies, but also spiritually nourish our souls with the graces and benefits of Jesus Christ, (which the Scripture calleth *r* eating of His flesh and drinking of His blood). Neither must we in the administration of these Sacraments follow man's fancy, but as Christ Himself hath ordained so must they be ministered, and by such as by *s* ordinary vocation are thereunto called. Therefore whosoever reserveth and worshippeth these Sacraments, or contrariwise contemneth them in time and place, procureth to himself damnation.

The third mark of this Church is Ecclesiastical Discipline, which standeth in admonition and correction of faults: the final end whereof is excommunication, by the consent of the Church *t* determined, if the offender be obstinate. And besides this Ecclesiastical Discipline I acknowledge to belong to the Church a politic Magistrate, who ministereth to every man justice, defending the good, and punishing the evil, to whom *u* we must

n Mat. 15.
Eph. 5.

o Mat. 26, 28.
Rom. 4.

p Rom. 6.
Gal. 3.
Col. 2.
Tit. 3.

q Rom. 4.
Ps. 32.

r 1 Cor. 11.
John 6.

s Heb. 5.
John 3.

t Mat. 18.
Luke 17.
Lev. 19.
Ecclus. 19.
1 Cor. 5.

u Rom. 13.
Wisdom 6.
Tit. 3.
1 Pet. 2.

THE CONFESSION.

^w Acts 5.
^x Exod. 32.
2 Kings 18, 23.
2 Chr. 29, 30.
^y 2 Tim. 4.
Mat. 15.
Isa. 29.
Heb. 9.
Acts 10.
1 John 2.
Rom. 7.
Gal. 5.
Col. 2.
Rom. 14.
1 Tim. 4.
Mat. 19.
1 Cor. 7.
1 Cor. 10.
2 Cor. 6.
Luke 17.
Rom. 3.
1 Cor. 3.

The forgiveness of sins.
^z Isa. 33.
Mat. 18.
John 20.
Rom. 1, 10.
2 Cor. 5.
Eph. 2.

^a 2 Pet. 2.
Jude.
Rom. 9.
^b Acts 24.
1 Cor. 15.
Phil. 3.
1 Thes. 4.
The resurrection of the body.
^c 2 Thes. 1.
2 John 1.
Isa. 30.
John 5.
^d Mat. 25.
^e 1 Thes. 4.
Isa. 26.
And life everlasting.

^f 1 Cor. 13.
1 John 3.
Jer. 31.

render honour and obedience in all things which are not ^wcontrary to the word of God.

And as ^xMoses, Hezekiah, Josiah, and other godly Rulers purged the Church of God from superstition and idolatry; so the defence of Christ's Church appertaineth to the Christian Magistrates, against all idolaters and heretics, as Papists, Anabaptists, with suchlike limbs of Antichrist, to root out all ^ydoctrine of devils and men, as the mass, purgatory, *Limbus Patrum,* prayers to saints and for the dead, free-will, distinction of meats, apparel, and days, vows of single life, presence at idol-service, man's merits, with suchlike; which draw us from the society of Christ's Church, wherein standeth only remission of ^zsins purchased by Christ's blood, to all them that believe, whether they be Jews or Gentiles, and lead us to vain confidence in creatures, and trust in our own imaginations. The punishment whereof, although God oftentimes ^adeferreth in this life, yet after the general ^bresurrection, when our souls and bodies shall rise again to immortality, they shall be ^cdamned to unquenchable fire: and then we, who have forsaken all men's wisdom to cleave unto Christ, shall hear the joyful voice, ^dCome, ye blessed of my Father, inherit ye the kingdom prepared for you from the beginning of the world, and so shall go triumphing with Him in ^ebody and soul, to remain everlastingly in glory, where we shall see God face to face, and shall no more need one to instruct another; ^ffor we shall all know Him from the highest to the lowest. To Whom, with the Son, and the Holy Ghost, be all praise, honour, and glory, now and ever. So be it.

OF THE MINISTERS

AND THEIR ELECTION.

What things are chiefly required in the Ministers.

LET the ^aChurch first diligently consider, that the Minister who is to be chosen, be not found ^bculpable of any such faults, which St Paul reprehendeth in a man of that vocation; but, contrariwise, endued with such virtues, that he may be able to undertake his charge, and diligently execute the same. Secondly, that he ^cdistribute faithfully the Word of God, and minister the Sacraments sincerely; ever careful, not only to teach his flock publicly, but also privately to ^dadmonish them; remembering always that if anything ^eperish through his default, the Lord will require it at his hands.

a Acts 1, 13, 14.

b 1 Tim. 3.
2 Tim. 2, 4.
Ezek. 33.
Jer. 3.
John 21.
Isa. 62.
1 Cor. 9.

c 2 Tim. 2.
1 Cor. 4.
Mat. 26.
1 Cor. 1.

d Acts 20.
2 Tim. 4.
e Ezek. 3.
1 Cor. 9.

Of their Office and Duty.

BECAUSE the charge of the Word of God is of greater ^fimportance than that any man is able to dispense therewith, and St Paul exhorteth to ^gesteem them as Ministers of Christ, and disposers of God's mysteries, not ^hLords or Rulers, as St Peter saith, over the flock; therefore the Pastor's or Minister's chief office standeth

f 1 Cor. 9.
Acts 6.
Luke 12.

g 1 Cor. 4.
2 Cor. 4.
h 1 Pet. 5.
2 Cor. 1.
Mat. 20.

OF MINISTERS.

j Mat. 26, 28. Mal. 2. 1 Pet. 4. Acts 3. 16. 1 Cor. 1, 15.

k Acts 20. 1 Cor. 4.

l 1 Cor. 5.

m 1 Cor. 14.

in *j* preaching the Word of God, and ministering the Sacraments; so that in consultations, judgments, elections, and other political affairs, his *k* counsel, rather than authority, taketh place. And if so be the Congregation upon just cause agree to excommunicate, then it belongeth to the Minister, according to their *l* general determination, to pronounce the sentence, to the end that all things may be done *m* orderly, and without confusion.

The manner of electing the Pastors or Ministers.

n Acts 14. Tit. 1.

THE Ministers and Elders, at such times as there wanteth a Minister, *n* assemble the whole Congregation, exhorting them to advise and consider who may best serve in that room and office; and if there be choice, the Church appoint two or three upon some certain day to be examined by the Ministers and Elders.

o 1 Tim. 3. Tit. 1.

First, as touching their *o* doctrine, whether he that should be Minister have good and sound knowledge in the Holy Scriptures, and fit and apt gifts to communicate the same to the edification of the people: for the trial whereof, they propose him a theme or text, to be treated privately, whereby his ability may the more manifestly appear unto them.

Secondly, they inquire of his life and conversation, if he have in times past lived without slander, and governed himself in such sort as the Word of God hath not *p* heard evil † or been slandered through his occasion; which being severally done, they signify unto the Congregation whose gifts they found most meet and profitable for that Min-

p Rom. 2. James 1. 1 Sam. 2. 1 Tim. 5. † *Been evil heard* in some copies.

OF ELDERS.   13

istry: appointing also by a general consent eight days at the least, that every man may diligently inquire of his life and manners.

At the which time, the Minister exhorteth them to humble themselves to God by *q* fasting and prayer, that both their election may be agreeable to His will, and also profitable to the Church. *q* Acts 13, 14.

And if in the mean season anything be brought against him, whereby he may be found unworthy by lawful probations, then is he dismissed, and some other presented. If nothing be alleged, upon some certain day, one of the Ministers, at the morning sermon, presenteth him again to the Church, framing his sermon, or some part thereof, to the setting forth of his duty.

Then, at afternoon, the Sermon ended, the Minister exhorteth them to the election, with the *r* invocation of God's name, directing his prayer as God shall move his heart. In like manner after the election, the *s* Minister giveth thanks to God, with request of such things as shall be necessary for his office. After that he is appointed Minister, the people sing a psalm, and depart.

r 1 Cor. 10.
Col. 3.
Mat. 9.

s 1 Thes. 5.
Col. 4.
Ephes. 5.
Phil. 1.

OF THE ELDERS,

And as touching their Office and Election.

THE *t* Elders must be men of good life and godly conversation; without blame and all suspicion; careful for the flock, wise, and above all things fearing God. Whose office standeth in governing with the rest of the Ministers; in consulting, admonishing, correcting, and ordering all

t Num. 11.
Acts 14. 16.
Rom. 12.
Ephes. 4.
1 Cor. 12.
James 5.
1 Pet. 5.

things appertaining to the state of the Congregation. And they differ from the Minister in that they preach not the Word, nor minister the Sacraments. In assembling the people, neither they without the Ministers, nor the Ministers without them, may attempt anything. And if any of the just number want, the Minister, by the consent of the rest, warneth the people thereof, and finally admonisheth them to observe the same order which was used in choosing the Ministers, as far forth as their vocation requireth.

OF THE DEACONS,
And their Office and Election.

u Acts 6.
1 Tim. 3.

THE *u*Deacons must be men of good estimation and report, discreet, of good conscience, charitable, wise, and, finally, endued with such virtues as St Paul requireth in them. Their office is to gather the Alms diligently, and faithfully to *w*distribute it, with the consent of the Ministers and Elders: also to *x*provide for the sick and impotent persons, having ever a diligent care that the charity of godly men be not wasted upon loiterers and idle vagabonds. Their election is, as hath been before rehearsed, in the Ministers and Elders.

w Rom. 12.
x 2 Thes. 3.

WE are not ignorant that the Scriptures make mention of a fourth kind of Ministers left to the Church of Christ, which also are very profitable, where time and place do permit.

y Ephes. 4.
1 Cor. 12.

These Ministers are called ^y Teachers, or Doctors, whose office is to instruct and teach the faithful in *sound doctrine, providing with all diligence that the purity of the Gospel be not corrupted, either through ignorance or evil opinions. Notwithstanding, considering the present state of things, we comprehend under this title such means as God hath in His Church, that it should not be left desolate, nor yet His doctrine decay for default of Ministers thereof.*

Therefore, to term it by a word more usual in these our days, we may call it the order of Schools, wherein the highest degree, and most annexed to the Ministry and government of the Church, is the exposition of God's Word contained in the Old and New Testaments.

But because men cannot so well profit in that knowledge, except they be first instructed in the tongues and humane sciences (for now God worketh not commonly by miracles), it is necessary that seed be sown for the time to come, to the intent that the Church be not left barren and waste to our posterity, and that Schools also be erected and Colleges maintained with just and sufficient stipends, wherein youth may be trained in the knowledge and fear of God, that in their ripe age they may prove worthy members of our Lord Jesus Christ, whether it be to rule in civil policy, or to serve in the spiritual Ministry, or else to live in godly reverence and subjection.

THE WEEKLY ASSEMBLY
Of the Ministers, Elders, and Deacons.

TO the intent that the Ministry of God's Word may be had in reverence, and not brought to contempt through the evil [z] conversation of such

[z] Rom. 2.
Ezek. 36.
Isa. 52.

as are called thereunto, and also that faults and vices may not by long sufferance ^agrow at length to extreme inconveniences: it is ordained, that every Thursday the Ministers and Elders, in their Assembly or Consistory, diligently ^bexamine all such faults and suspicions as may be espied, not only among others, but chiefly among themselves, lest they seem to be culpable of that which our Saviour Christ ^creproved in the Pharisees, who could espy a mote in another man's eye, and could not see a beam in their own.

And because the ^deye ought to be more clear than the rest of the body, the Minister may not be spotted with any vice, but† to the great slander of God's Word, whose message he beareth. Therefore it is to be understood that there be certain faults, which, if they be deprehended in a Minister, he ought to be deposed—as heresy, papistry, schism, blasphemy, perjury, fornication, theft, drunkenness, usury, fighting, unlawful games, with suchlike.

Others are more tolerable, if so be that after brotherly admonitions he amend his fault, as strange and unprofitable fashion in preaching the Scriptures, curiosity in seeking vain questions, negligence as well in his sermons and in studying the Scriptures, as in all other things concerning his vocation, scurrility, flattering, lying, backbiting, wanton words, deceit, covetousness, taunting, dissolution in apparel, gesture, and other his doings; which vices, as they be odious in all men, so in him that ought to be as an ^eexample to others of perfection, in no wise are to be suffered: especially if so be that, according to God's ^frule,

Marginal notes:
- a 2 Tim. 2.
- b 1 Cor. 5.
- c Mat. 7. Luke 6. Rom. 2.
- d Mat. 6. Luke 11.
- † *but* omitted in later copies.
- e Mat. 5. Mark 9.
- f Mat. 18. Luke 17. James 5.

being brotherly advertised, he acknowledge not his fault and amend.

INTERPRETATION OF THE SCRIPTURES.

EVERY week once the Congregation assemble to hear some place of the Scriptures orderly ᵍexpounded. At the which time it is lawful for every man to speak or inquire, as God shall move his heart and the text minister occasion, so it be without pertinacity or disdain, as one that rather seeketh to profit than to contend. And if so be any contention rise, then such as are appointed Moderators either satisfy the party, or else, if he seem to cavil, exhort him to keep silence, referring the judgment thereof to the Ministers and Elders, to be determined in their assembly beforementioned.

ᵍ 1 Cor. 14.
1 Thes. 5.
Ephes. 4.
1 Cor. 12.

THE FORM AND ORDER

OF THE

ELECTION OF THE SUPERINTENDENT,

WHICH MAY SERVE IN ELECTION OF
ALL OTHER MINISTERS.

At Edinburgh, the 9th of March, anno 1560.
John Knox being Minister.†

† *Moderator* in some copies.

FIRST was made a Sermon, in the which these heads were intreated: First, the necessity of Ministers and Superintendents. 2. The crimes and vices that might unable them of the Ministry. 3. The virtues required in them. 4. And last, whether such as, by public consent of the Church, were called to such office, might refuse the same.

The Sermon finished, it was declared by the same Minister, maker thereof, that the Lords of Secret Council had given charge and power to the Churches of Lothian to choose M. John Spotswood Superintendent, and that sufficient warning was made by public edict to the Churches of Edinburgh, Linlithgow, Stirling, Tranent, Haddington, and Dunbar, as also to Earls, Lords, Barons, Gentlemen, or others, that have, or that might claim to have, voice in election, to be present that day at that same hour.

THE SUPERINTENDENT.

And therefore inquisition was made who were present and who were absent, after was called the said M. John, who answering, the Minister demanded if any man knew any crime or offence to the said M. John that might unable him to be called to that office. And that he demanded thrice. Secondarily, question was moved to the whole multitude, if there was any other whom they would put in election with the said M. John. The people were asked if they would have the said M. John Superindentent? If they would honour and obey him as Christ's Minister, and comfort and assist him in everything pertaining to his charge?

They answered.

We will, and we do promise unto him such obedience as becometh the sheep to give unto their Pastor, so long as he remaineth faithful in his office.

The answers of the people and their consent received, these questions were proposed to him that was to be elected.

Seeing that ye hear the trust and desire of this people, do ye not think yourself bound in conscience before God to support them that so earnestly call for your comfort, and for the fruit of your labours? | Question.

If anything were in me able to satisfy their desire, I acknowledge myself bound to obey God calling by them. | *Answer.*

Do ye seek to be promoted to this office and charge for any respect of worldly commodity, riches, or glory? | Question.

ELECTION OF

Answer. God knoweth the contrary.

Question. Believe ye not that the doctrine of the Prophets and Apostles contained in the books of the New and Old Testaments is the only true and most absolute foundation of the universal Church of Christ Jesus, insomuch that in the same Scriptures are contained all things necessary to be believed for the salvation of mankind?

Answer. I verily believe the same, and do abhor and utterly refuse all doctrine alleged necessary to salvation, that is not expressedly contained in the same.

Question. Is not Christ Jesus, man of man according to the flesh, to wit the Son of David, the seed of Abraham, conceived of the Holy Ghost, born of the Virgin His mother, the only Head and Mediator of His Church?

Answer. He is, and without Him there is neither salvation to man, nor life to angel.

Question. Is not the same Lord Jesus the only true God, the Eternal Son of the Eternal Father, in whom all that shall be saved were elected before the foundation of the world was laid?

Answer. I acknowledge and confess Him in the unity of His Godhead to be God above all things, blessed for ever.

Question. Shall not they whom God, in His eternal counsel, hath elected, be called to the knowledge of His Son, our Lord Jesus? and shall not they who of purpose are called in this life be justified? and where justification and free remission of sins is obtained in this life by free grace, shall not the glory of the sons of God follow in the general resurrection, when the Son of God shall appear in His glorious majesty?

THE SUPERINTENDENT.

Answer. This I acknowledge to be the doctrine of the Apostles, and the most singular comfort of God's children.

Question. Will ye not then contain yourself in all doctrine within the bounds of this foundation? Will ye not study to promote the same, as well by your life as by your doctrine? Will ye not, according to the graces and utterance that God shall grant unto you, profess, instruct, and maintain the purity of the doctrine contained in the sacred Word of God? And to the uttermost of your power will ye not gainstand, and convince the gainsayers, and the teachers of men's inventions?

Answer. That do I promise in the presence of God, and of His congregation here assembled.

Question. Know ye not that the excellency of this office to the which God hath called you, requireth that your conversation and behaviour be such as that ye may be irreprehensible, yea, even in the eyes of the ungodly?

Answer. I unfeignedly acknowledge, and humbly desire the Church of God to pray with me, that my life be not slanderous to the glorious Evangel of Christ Jesus.

Question. Because ye are a man compassed with infirmities, will ye not charitably, and with lowliness of spirit, receive admonition of your brethren? And if ye shall happen to slide, or offend in any point, will ye not be subject to the discipline of the Church, as the rest of your brethren?

The answer of the Superintendent or Minister to be elected.

Answer. I acknowledge myself a man subject to infirmity,

and one that hath need of correction and admonition, and, therefore, I most willingly subject myself to the wholesome discipline of the Church, yea, to the discipline of the same Church by the which I am now called to this office and charge; and here, in God's presence and yours, do promise obedience to all admonitions secretly or publicly given: unto the which if I be found inobedient, I confess myself most worthy to be ejected, not only from this honour, but also from the society of the faithful, in case of my stubbornness. For the vocation of God to bear charge within His Church maketh not men tyrants nor lords, but appointeth them servants, watchmen, and pastors to the flock.

This ended, question must be asked again of the multitude.

Question. Require ye any farther of this your Superintendent?

If no man answer, let the Minister proceed.

Will ye not acknowledge this your brother for the Minister of Christ Jesus? Will ye not reverence the word of God that proceedeth from his mouth? Will ye not receive of him the Sermon of exhortation with patience; not refusing the wholesome medicine of your souls, although it be bitter and unpleasing to the flesh? Will ye not finally maintain and comfort him in his ministry against all such as wickedly would rebel against God, and His holy ordinances?

The People answer.

Answer. We will, as we shall answer to the Lord Jesus,

THE SUPERINTENDENT.

who hath commanded His Ministers to be had in reverence, as His Ambassadors, and as men that carefully watch for the salvation of our souls.

Let the Nobility be urged with this.

Ye have heard the duty and profession of this our brother, by your consents appointed to this charge, as also the duty and obedience which God requireth of us towards him here in his Ministry: But because that neither of both are able to perform anything without the especial grace of our God in Christ Jesus, who hath promised to be with us present even to the consummation of the world, with unfeigned hearts let us crave of Him His benediction and assistance in this work begun to His glory, and for the comfort of His Church.

The Prayer.

O Lord, to whom all power is given in heaven and in earth, Thou that art the Eternal Son of the Eternal Father, who hast not only so loved Thy Church that, for the redemption and purgation of the same, Thou hast humbled Thyself to the death of the cross, and thereupon hast shed Thy most innocent blood to prepare to Thyself a spouse without spot, but also, to retain this Thy most excellent benefit in recent memory, hast appointed in Thy Church Teachers, Pastors, and Apostles, to instruct, comfort, and admonish the same: look upon us mercifully, O Lord, Thou that only art King, Teacher, and High Priest to Thy own flock: and send unto this our brother, whom, in Thy name, we have charged with the chief care of Thy Church, within the bounds of L., such portion of Thy Holy Spirit, as thereby he may rightly divide Thy Word, to the instruction of Thy flock, and to the confutation of pernicious errors and damnable superstitions. Give unto him, good Lord, a mouth and wisdom, whereby the enemies of Thy truth may be confounded, the wolves expelled and driven from Thy fold, Thy sheep may be fed in the wholesome pastures of Thy most holy Word, the blind and ignorant may be illuminated with Thy true knowledge: finally, that, the dregs of superstition and idolatry which yet resteth within this Realm being purged and removed, we may all not only have occasion to glorify Thee our only Lord and Saviour, but also daily to grow in godliness and obedience of Thy most holy will, to the destruction of the body of sin, and to the restitution of that image to the which we were once created, and to the which, after our fall and defection, we are renewed by participation of Thy holy Spirit, whom, by true faith in Thee, we do profess as the blessed of Thy Father, of whom the perpetual increase of Thy graces we crave, as by Thee our Lord, King, and only Bishop we are taught to pray, *Our Father, &c.*

The prayer ended, the rest of the Ministers and Elders of that Church, if any be present, in sign of their consent, shall take the elected by the hand.

The chief Minister shall give the benediction as followeth:—

God, the Father of our Lord Jesus Christ, who hath commanded His Gospel to be preached to the comfort of His elect, and hath called thee to

THE SUPERINTENDENT. 25

the office of a watchman over His people, multiply His graces with thee, illuminate thee with His Holy Spirit, comfort and strengthen thee in all virtue, govern and guide thy ministry to the praise of His holy name, to the propagation of Christ's kingdom, to the comfort of His Church, and, finally, to the plain discharge and assurance of thy own conscience, in the day of the Lord Jesus: to whom, with the Father, and with the Holy Ghost, be all honour, praise, and glory, now and ever: So be it.

The last Exhortation to the Elected.

Take heed to thyself, and unto the flock committed to thy charge: feed the same carefully, not as it were by compulsion, but of very love, which thou bearest to the Lord Jesus: walk in simplicity and pureness of life, as it becometh the true servant and the ambassador of the Lord Jesus. Usurp not dominion, nor tyrannical authority over thy brethren: be not discouraged in adversity, but lay before thyself the example of the Prophets, Apostles, and the Lord Jesus, who in their ministry sustained contradiction, contempt, persecution, and death: fear not to rebuke the world of sin, justice, and judgment. If anything succeed prosperously in thy vocation, be not puffed up with pride, neither yet flatter thyself as that the good success proceeded from thy virtue, industry, or care. But let ever that sentence of the Apostle remain in thy heart, *What hast thou which thou hast not received? If thou hast received, why gloriest thou?* Comfort the afflicted, support the poor, exhort others to support them. Be not solicited † for things of

† So in the best editions.

this life, but be fervent in prayer to God for the increase of His Holy Spirit. And finally, behave thyself in this holy vocation with such sobriety as God may be glorified in thy ministry. And so shalt thou shortly obtain the victory, and shalt receive the crown promised, when the Lord Jesus shall appear in His glory, whose omnipotent Spirit assist thee and us to the end.—Amen.

Sing the 23d Psalm.

THE ORDER

OF THE

ECCLESIASTICAL DISCIPLINE.

AS no city, town, house, or family can maintain their estate and prosper without policy and governance, even so the Church of God, which requireth more purely to be governed than any city or family, cannot, without spiritual policy and Ecclesiastical Discipline, continue, increase and flourish. And as the *a* Word of God is the life and soul of this Church, so this godly order and discipline is, as it were, sinews in the body, which knit and join the members together with decent order and comeliness. It is a bridle to stay the wicked from their mischiefs. It is a spur to prick forward such as be slow and negligent, yea, and for all men it is the Father's rod, ever in readiness to chastise gently the faults committed, and to cause them afterward to live in more godly fear and reverence. Finally, it is an order left by God unto His Church, whereby men learn to frame their wills and doings according to the law of God, by instructing and admonishing one another, yea, and by correcting and punish-

_{The necessity of discipline.}

_{*a* Eph. 5.}

_{What discipline is.}

ing all obstinate rebels and contemners of the same.

For what cause it ought to be used.

There are three causes chiefly which move the Church of God to the executing of Discipline. First, That men of evil conversation be not numbered among God's children, to their Father's *b* reproach, as if the Church of God were a sanctuary for naughty and vile persons. The second respect is that the good be not infected with accompanying the evil: which thing St Paul foresaw, when he commanded the Corinthians to banish from among them the incestuous adulterer, saying, *c* A little leaven maketh sour the whole lump of dough. The third cause is, that a man thus corrected or excommunicated might be ashamed of his fault, and so through repentance come to amendment, the which thing the Apostle calleth *d* delivering to Satan, that his soul may be saved in the day of the Lord, meaning that he might be punished with excommunication, to the intent his soul should not perish for ever.

b Eph. 5.

c 1 Cor. 5.
Gal. 5.

d 2 Thes. 3.
1 Cor. 5.

The order of proceeding in private discipline.

First, therefore, it is to be noted that this censure, correction, or discipline, is either private or public: private, as if a man commit either in manners or doctrine [any fault] against thee, to admonish him brotherly *e* between him and thee: if so be he stubbornly resist thy charitable advertisements, or else by continuance in his fault declareth that he amendeth not, then, after he hath been the second time warned in presence of two or three witnesses, and continueth obstinately in his error, he ought, as our Saviour Christ commandeth, to be disclosed and uttered to the Church, so that, according to public discipline, he

e Mat. 18.
Luke 17.
James 5.
Lev. 19.
2 Thes. 3.

DISCIPLINE.

either may be received through repentance, or else be punished, as his fault requireth. *(Public discipline.)*

And here, as touching private discipline, three things are to be noted. First, that our admonitions proceed of a godly zeal and conscience, rather seeking to win our brother than to slander him. Next, that we be assured that his fault be reprovable by God's Word. And finally, that we use such modesty and wisdom, that if we somewhat doubt of the matter whereof we admonish him, yet, with godly exhortations, he may be brought to the knowledge of his fault. Or if the fault appertain to many, or be known of divers, that our admonition be done in presence of some of them. *(What things are to be observed in private discipline.)*

Briefly, if it concern the whole Church, in such sort that the concealing thereof might procure some danger to the same, that then it be uttered to the Ministers and Seniors, to whom the policy of the Church doth appertain.

Also, in public discipline, it is to be observed that the Ministry pretermit nothing at any time unchastised with one kind of punishment or other, if they perceive anything in the Congregation, either evil in example, slanderous in manners, or not beseeming their profession: as if there be any covetous person, any adulterer, or fornicator, forsworn, thief, briber, false-witness-bearer, blasphemer, drunkard, slanderer, usurer, any person disobedient, seditious, or dissolute, any heresy or sect, as Papistical, Anabaptistical, and suchlike: briefly, whatsoever it be that might *f*spot the Christian congregation: yea, rather, whatsoever is not to edification, ought not to escape either admonition or punishment. *(Of public discipline, and of the end thereof. f Eph. 5.)*

Excommunication is the last remedy.

And because it cometh to pass some time in the Church of Christ, that when other remedies assayed profit nothing, they must proceed to the Apostolical rod and correction, as unto excommunication (which is the greatest and last punishment belonging to the spiritual Ministry), it is ordained that nothing be attempted in that behalf without the determination of the whole Church:

Rigour in punishment ought to be avoided.

wherein also they must beware, and take good heed, that they seem not more ready to expel from the Congregation, than to receive again those in whom they perceive worthy fruits of repentance to appear; neither yet to forbid him the hearing of Sermons, who is excluded from the Sacraments and other duties of the Church, that he may have liberty and occasion to repent.

God's Word is the rule of discipline.

Finally, that all punishments, corrections, censures and admonitions, stretch no further than God's Word, with mercy, may lawfully bear.

MATTH. XVIII.

If any refuse to hear the Congregation, let him be to thee as a heathen and as a publican.

THE ORDER

OF

EXCOMMUNICATION

AND OF

PUBLIC REPENTANCE

Used in the Church of Scotland, and commanded to be Printed by the General Assembly of the same, in the month of June 1571.

TO THE READER.

*A*LBEIT *that in the Book of Discipline the causes, as well of Public Repentance as of Excommunication, are sufficiently expressed, yet, because the form and order are not so set forth, that every Church and Minister may have assurance that they agree with others in proceeding, it is thought expedient to draw that order which, universally within this Realm, shall be observed.*

And, first, we must understand what crimes be worthy of Excommunication, and what of Public Repentance.

IN the first, it is to be noted, that all crimes that by the law of God deserve death, deserve also excommunication from the society of

Christ's Church, whether the offender be Papist or Protestant: for it is no reason that, under pretence of diversity of religion, open impiety should be suffered in the visible body of Christ Jesus. And, therefore, wilful murderers, adulterers (lawfully convict), sorcerers, witches, conjurors, charmers, and givers of drinks to destroy children, and open blasphemers (as if any renounce God, deny the truth and the authority of His holy Word, railing against His blessed Sacraments), such, we say, ought to be excommunicate from the society of Christ's Church, that their impiety may be holden in greater horror, and that they may be the more deeply wounded, perceiving themselves abhorred of the godly. Against such open malefactors the process may be summoned, for, the crime being known, advertisement ought to be given to the Superintendent of the Diocese, either by the Minister, or by such as can best give information of that fact, except in reformed towns and other places where the Ministry is planted with Minister and Elders, according to the Act of the General Assembly made the 26th of December 1568. And if there be no Superintendent where the crime is committed, then ought the information to pass from such as are offended to the next Superintendent, who, with expedition, ought to direct his letters of summons to the parish Church where the offender hath his residence, if the Ministry be there planted, and if it be not, or if the offender have no certain dwelling-place, then ought the summons to be directed to the chief town, and best reformed Church in that Diocese where the crime was committed, appointing to the

OF EXCOMMUNICATION.

offender a certain day, time, and place, where and when he shall appear before the Superintendent and his assessors, to hear that crime tried, as touching the truth of it, and to answer himself why the sentence of excommunication should not be pronounced publicly against him. If the offender, lawfully warned, appear not, inquisition being taken of the crime, charge may be given by the Superintendent to the Ministers, so many as shall be thought necessary for publication of that sentence, to pronounce the same the next Sunday, the form whereof shall after be declared. But and if the offender appear, and allege for himself any reasonable defence—to wit, that he will not be fugitive from the law, but will abide the censure thereof for that offence—then may the sentence of excommunication be suspended, till that the Magistrate be required to try that cause; wherein, if the Magistrates be negligent, then ought the Church from secret inquisition to proceed to public admonition, that the Magistrates may be vigilant in that cause of blood, which crieth vengeance upon the whole land where it is shed without punishment. If no remedy by them can be found, then justly may the Church pronounce the offender excommunicate, as one suspect, besides his crime, to have corrupted the judges, revengers of the blood: and so ought the Church to proceed to excommunication, whether the offender be fugitive from the law, or if he procure pardon, or elude the severity of justice by means whatsoever, besides the trial of his innocency.

If the offender abide an assize, and by the same be absolved, then may not the Church pronounce excommunication, but justly may exhort the man by whose hand the blood was shed to enter into consideration with himself how precious is the life of man before God, and how severely God commandeth blood (howsoever it be shed, except it be by the sword of the Magistrate) to be punished: and so may enjoin unto him such satisfactions to be made publicly to the Church, as may bear testification of his obedience and unfeigned repentance. If the offender be convict, and execution follow according to the crime, then, upon the humble suit of him that is to suffer, may the Elders and Ministers of the Church not only give unto him consolation, but also pronounce the sentence of absolution, and his sin to be remitted, according to his repentance and faith. And thus much for excommunication of public offenders.

And yet further, we must consider, that if the offender be fugitive from the law, so that punishment cannot be executed against him, in that case the Church ought to delay no time; but upon the notice of his crime, and that he is fled from the presence of the judge, it ought to pronounce him excommunicated publicly, and so continually to repute him, until such time that the Magistrate be satisfied. And so, whether the offender be convict in judgment, or be fugitive from the law, the Church ought to proceed to the sentence of excommunication: The form whereof followeth:—

OF EXCOMMUNICATION.

The Minister, in public audience of the People, shall say:—

IT is clearly known unto us that N., sometime baptised in the name of the Father, and of the Son, and of the Holy Ghost, and so reputed and counted for a Christian, hath fearfully fallen from the society of Christ's body, by committing of cruel and wilful murder (or by committing filthy adultery, &c.), which crime, by the law of God, deserveth death. And because the civil sword is in the hand of God's Magistrate, who, notwithstanding, oft winks at such crimes, We, having place in the Ministry, with grief and dolour of our hearts, are compelled to draw the sword granted by God to His Church; that is, to excommunicate from the society of Christ Jesus, from His body the Church, from participation of sacraments and prayers with the same, the said N.

AND, THEREFORE, IN THE NAME AND AUTHORITY OF THE ETERNAL GOD, AND OF HIS SON JESUS CHRIST, We pronounce the said N. excommunicate and accursed in that his wicked fact; and charge all that favour the Lord Jesus so to repute and hold him (or her), until such time as that either the Magistrate have punished the offender as God's law commands, or that the same offender be reconciled to the Church again by public repentance: and, in the mean time, we earnestly desire all the faithful to call upon God to move the hearts of the upper powers so to punish such horrible crimes that malefactors may fear to offend, even for fear of punishment; and also so to touch the heart of the offender, that he may deeply consider how fearful it is to fall into the hands of the Eternal God, that by unfeigned repentance he may apprehend mercy in Jesus Christ, and so avoid eternal condemnation.

THE sentence of excommunication once pronounced, the Church may not suddenly admit the murderer, or convict adulterer, to repentance and society of the faithful, albeit that pardon be purchased of the Magistrate: but first ought inquisition to be taken, if the murderer have satisfied the party offended, that is, the kin and friends of the man slain. Which if he hath not done, neither is understood willingly so to do, the Church in no wise may hear him. But and if he be willing to satisfy, and the friends exceed measure, and the possibility of him that hath committed the crime, then ought the Church to put moderation to the unreasonable, in case the civil Magistrate hath not so done before; and so proceed with him that offereth repentance, that the wilfulness of the indiscreet be not hindrance to the reconciliation of him that earnestly craveth the benefit and society of the Church.

And yet may not the Church receive any excommunicate at his first request; but in such grievous crimes as before are expressed (of others shall be after spoken), forty days at the least after his first offer may be appointed to try whether the signs of repentance appear in the offender or not. And yet, in the mean time, the Church may comfort him by wholesome admonitions, assuring him of God's mercy, if he be verily penitent: he may also be admitted to the hearing of the Word, but in no wise to participation of prayers, neither before nor after Sermon. This first forty days expired, upon his new suit, the Superintendent or Session may enjoin such pains as may try whether he be penitent or not: the least are, the murderer must stand three several Sundays in a public place before the Church door, barefooted and bareheaded, clothed in base and abject apparel, having the same weapon which he used in the murder, or the like, bloody, in his hand, and in conceived words shall say to such as shall enter into the Church:—

The Confession of the Penitent.

SO far hath Satan gotten victory over me, that cruelly I have shed innocent blood, for the which I have deserved death corporal and eternal; and so I grant myself unworthy of the common light, or yet of the company of men. And yet, because in God there is mercy that passeth all measure, and because the Magistrate hath not taken from me this wretched life, I most earnestly desire to be reconciled again with the Church of Christ Jesus, from the society whereof mine iniquity hath caused me to be excommunicated. And, therefore, in the bowels of Christ Jesus, I crave of you to pray with me unto God, that my grievous crime may be of Him remitted; and also that ye will be suppliants with me to the Church, that I abide not thus excommunicate unto the end.

At the last of the three Sundays, certain of the Elders shall receive him into the Church, and present him before the preaching place, and shall declare unto the Minister, that all that was enjoined to that offender was obediently fulfilled by him. Then shall the Minister recite unto him, as well the grievousness of his sin, as the mercies of God, if he be penitent; and thereafter shall require of the Church, if that they desire any further satisfaction. And if no answer be given, then shall the Minister pronounce his sin to be remitted according to his repentance; and shall exhort the Church to embrace him as a brother, after that prayer and thanksgiving be given to God, as after shall be described.

And thus far to be observed for the order in receiving of them that have committed capital crimes, be it murder, adultery, incest, witchcraft, or others before expressed.

Resteth yet one other kind of offenders that deserve excommunication, albeit not so summarily; to wit, such as have been partakers with us in doctrine and Sacraments, and have returned back again to the Papistry, or have given their presence to any part of their abomination, or yet that of any long continuance withdraw themselves from the society of Christ's body, and from the participation of the Sacraments, when they are publicly ministered. Such, no doubt, declare themselves worthy of excommunication. But first, they must be called, either before the Superintendent with some joined with him, or else before the Elders and Session of the best and next reformed Church, where the offenders have their residence, who must accuse their defection, exhort

PUBLIC REPENTANCE. 39

them to repentance, and declare to them the danger wherein they stand.

Whom, if the offender heareth, the Session or Superintendent may appoint him a day to satisfy the Church publicly, whom by his defection he had offended. But if he continue stubborn, then may the Session or Superintendent command the Minister or Ministers to declare, the next Sunday, the defection of such a person, and his obstinate contempt. And this advertisement given two Sundays, the third may the sentence of excommunication be pronounced.

OFFENCES THAT DESERVE PUBLIC REPENTANCE, AND ORDER TO PROCEED THEREIN.

SUCH offences as fall not under the civil sword, and yet are slanderous and offensive in the Church, deserve public repentance, and of these some are more heinous than others; fornication, drunkenness used, swearing, cursed speaking, chiding, fighting, brawling, and common contempt of the order of the Church, breaking of the Sabbath, and suchlike, ought to be in no person suffered. But the slander being known, the offender should be called before the Ministry, his crime proved, accused, rebuked, and he commanded publicly to satisfy the Church: which if the offender refuse, they may proceed to excommunication, as after shall be declared. If the offender appear not, summons ought to pass to the third time. And then, in case he appear not, the Church may decern the sentence to be pronounced.

Other, if it be less heinous, and yet deserve admonition : as wanton and vain words, uncomely gestures, negligence in hearing the preaching, or abstaining from the Lord's Table when it is publicly ministered, suspicion of avarice or of pride, superfluity or riotousness in cheer or raiment : these, we say, and such others that of the world are not regarded, deserve admonition among the members of Christ's body. First, secretly, by one or two of those that first espy the offence. Which if the person suspected hear, and give declaration of amendment, then there needeth no further process. But if he contemn and despise the admonition, then should the former admonishers take to themselves two or three faithful and honest witnesses, in whose presence the suspected offender should be admonished, and the causes of their suspicion declared. To whom, if then he give signification of repentance, and promise of amendment, they may cut of all further accusation. But and if he obstinately contemn both the said admonitions, then ought the first and second brethren signify the matter to the Minister and Elders in their Session, who ought to call the offender, and before the complainers accuse him, as well of the crime, as of the contempt of the admonition : if then he acknowledge his offence, and be willing to satisfy the brethren before offended, and the Session then present, there needeth no farther publication of that offence. But if he declare himself inobedient to the Session, then, without delay, the next Sunday ought the crime, and the order of admonitions passed before, be publicly declared to the Church, and the person (without specification of his name) be admonished to satisfy in public that which he refused to do in secret; and that for the first. If he offer himself to the Church before the next Sunday, the discretion of the Ministry may take such order, as may satisfy as well the private persons that first were offended, as the Church, declaring the repentance and submission of that brother that before appeared stubborn and incorrigible. But and if he abide the second admonition public, when that his name shall be expressed, and his offences and stubbornness declared, then can no satisfaction be received but in public: yea, it may not be received before that he have humbly required the same of the Ministry and Session of the Church, in their appointed assembly.

If he continue stubborn, then the third Sunday ought he to be charged publicly to satisfy the Church for his offence and contempt, under the pain of excommunication. The order whereof shall after be declared.

And thus a small offence or slander may justly deserve excommunication, by reason of the contempt and disobedience of the offender. If the offender show himself penitent between the first admonition and the second, and satisfy the Ministry of the Church, and the brethren that before were offended in their assembly, then it may suffice that the Minister, at commandment of the Session, declare the next Sunday (without compearing or expressing of the person) his repentance and submission in these or other words:—

THE ORDER OF

IT was signified unto you before, dearly beloved, that one certain brother [or brethren] was noted, or at least suspected, of some offence, whereof he being admonished by one or two, appeared lightly to regard the same. And therefore was he and his offence notified unto the Ministry, in their assembly, who, according to their duty and charge, accused him of the same: And not finding in him such obedience as the profession of a Christian requireth, fearing that such offences and stubbornness should engender contempt, and infect others, they were compelled to notify unto you the crime, and the proceeding of the Session, minding to have sought the uttermost remedy in case the offender had continued obstinate. But seeing that it hath pleased God to mollify the heart of our brother, whose name we need not to express, so that he hath not only acknowledged his offence, but also hath fully satisfied the brethren that first were offended, and us the Ministry, and hath promised to abstain from all appearance of such evil as whereof he was suspected and admonished, we have no just cause to proceed to any farther extremity, but rather to glorify God for the submission of our brother, and unfeignedly pray unto Him that in the like case we, and every one of us, may give the like obedience.

THE FORM AND ORDER OF PUBLIC REPENTANCE.

IT is first to be observed, that none may be admitted to public repentance except that first they be admitted thereto by the Session and Assembly of the Ministers and Elders; in the which they ought sharply to be examined, what fear and terror they have of God's judgments, what hatred of sin, and dolour for the same, and what sense and feeling they have of God's mercies; in the which if they be ignorant, they ought diligently to be instructed: for it is but a mocking to present such to public repentance as neither understand what sin is, what repentance is, what grace is, nor by whom God's favour and mercy are purchased. After, then, that the offender shall be in the assembly instructed, so that he have some taste of God's judgments, but chiefly of God's mercies in Christ Jesus, he may be presented before the public Church, upon a Sunday after the sermon, and before the prayers and psalm; and then the Minister shall say:—

Beloved and dearest brethren, we, by reason of our charge and Ministry, present before you this brother, that by the infirmity of flesh and craft of Satan hath fearfully fallen from the obedience of his God, by committing N. of a crime, &c. [let the sin be expressed], by the which he hath not only offended against the Majesty of God, but also by the same hath given great slander and offence to His holy Congregation: and, therefore, doth to his own confusion (but to the glory of God, and our great comfort) present himself here before you, to witness and declare his unfeigned repentance, the thirst and the care that he hath to be reconciled with God through Jesus Christ, and with you, his brethren, whom he hath offended. And, therefore, it is requisite that ye and he understand what assurance we have to require such public satisfaction of him, what profit we ought to learn in the same, and what profit and utility redound to both of this his humiliation.

That public repentance is the institution of God, and not man's invention, may be plainly gathered of the words of our Master, commanding that if any have offended his brother, in what sort soever it be, that he shall go to him, and be reconciled unto his brother. If the offence committed against one brother requireth reconciliation, the offence committed against many brethren requireth the same. And if a man be charged by Christ Jesus to go to a man whom he hath offended, and there, by confessing of his offence, require reconciliation, much more is he bound to seek a whole multitude whom he hath offended, and before them with all humility require the same. For that woe which our Master, Christ Jesus, pronounceth against every man that hath offended the least one within His Church, remaineth upon every public offender, until such time as he declare himself willing to remove the same: which he can never do until such time as he let the multitude whom he hath offended understand his unfeigned repentance. But because that all men of upright judgment agree in this, that public offences require public repentance, we pass to the second head, which is, what it is that we have to consider in the fall and sin of this our brother: if we consider his fall and sin in him only, without having consideration of ourselves and of our own corruption, we shall profit nothing, for so shall we but despise our brother and flatter ourselves. But if we shall earnestly consider what nature we bear, what cor-

PUBLIC REPENTANCE. 45

ruption lurketh in it, how prone and ready every one of us is to such and greater impiety, then shall we, in the sin of this our brother, accuse and condemn our own sins, in his fall shall we consider and lament our sinful nature, also shall we join our repentance, tears, and prayers with him and his, knowing that no flesh can be justified before God's presence, if judgment proceed without mercy. The profit which this our brother and we have of this his humiliation is, that we and he may be assured that more ready is our God to receive us to mercy through Jesus Christ His only Son, than we are to crave it. It is not sin, be it never so grievous, that shall separate us from His favour, if we seek to His mercy: for as all have sinned, and are by themselves destitute of God's grace, so is He ready to show mercy unto all that unfeignedly call for the same. Yea, He doth not only receive such as come, but He, by the mouth of His dear Son, calleth upon such as be burdened and laden with sin, and solemnly promiseth that He will refresh them.

We have, besides, another commodity, to wit, that if we shall hereafter fall in the like, or greater (for we stand not by our own power, but by grace only), that we be not ashamed in this same sort to humble ourselves, and confess our offence. Now therefore, brother, as we all praise God in this your humiliation, beseeching Him that it be without hypocrisy, so it becometh you earnestly to consider of what mind, and with what heart, ye present yourself here before this assembly. It is not your sin that shall separate you from your God, nor from His mercy in Jesus Christ, if you repent the same: but hypocrisy and impenitence, which God remove from you and us, are nowise tolerable before His presence.

The offender ought to protest before God that he is sorry for his sin, and unfeignedly desireth God to be merciful unto him, and that for the obedience of His dear Son, our Lord Jesus Christ.

The Minister.

WE can only see that which is without, and according to your confession judge, leaving the secrets of the heart to God, who only can try and search the same. But because unfeigned repentance for sin, and simple confession of the same, are the mere gifts of God, we will join our prayers with yours, that the one and the other may be granted to you and us.

The Prayer.

ETERNAL and everliving God, Father of our Lord Jesus Christ, Thou that by the mouth of Thy holy Prophets and Apostles hast plainly pronounced that Thou desirest not the death of a sinner, but rather that he may convert and live; who also hast sent Thy only Son to suffer the cruel death of the Cross, not for the just, but for such as find themselves oppressed with the burden of sin, that by Him and His advocation they may have access to the throne of Thy grace, being assured that before Thee they shall find favour and mercy: we are assembled, O Lord, in Thy presence, and that in the name of this same our Lord Jesus, Thy dear Son, to accuse before Thee our sins, and before the feet of Thy Majesty to crave

PUBLIC REPENTANCE. 47

mercy for the same. We most humbly beseech Thee, O Father of mercies, first that Thou wilt touch and move our hearts by the power of Thy Holy Spirit, in such sort that we may come to a true knowledge of our sins. But chiefly, O Lord, [that] it will please Thee to move the heart of this our brother, N., &c., who, as he hath offended Thy Majesty, and a great number of this Thy holy Congregation, by his grievous and public sin, so doth he not refuse publicly to acknowledge and confess the same, as that this his humiliation, given to the glory of Thy name, presently doth witness. But because, O Lord, the external confession, without the dolour of the heart, availeth nothing in Thy presence, we most humbly beseech Thee that Thou wilt so effectually move his heart and ours also, that he and we without hypocrisy, damning that which Thy Law pronounceth unjust, may attain to some sense and feeling of Thy mercy, which Thou hast abundantly showed unto mankind in Jesus Christ our Lord. Grant, O Lord, unto this our brother the repentance of the heart, and sincere confession of his mouth, to the praise of Thy name, to the comfort of Thy Church, and to the confusion of Satan. And unto us grant, O Lord, that albeit we cannot live altogether clean of sin, yet that we fall not in horrible crimes, to the dishonour of Thy holy name, to the slander of our brethren, and infamy of Thy holy Evangel which we profess. Let Thy godly power, O Lord, so strengthen our weakness, that neither the craft of Satan, nor the tyranny of sin, draw us utterly from Thy obedience. Give us grace, O Lord, that by holiness and innocence of life, we may declare to this wicked generation what difference there is between the sons of light and the sons of darkness, that men, seeing our good works, may glorify Thee, and Thy Son Jesus Christ, our only Saviour and Redeemer: to Whom, with Thee and the Holy Spirit, be all honour, praise and glory, now and ever. Amen.

The prayer finished, the Minister shall turn him to the penitent brother, and in full audience shall say:—

YE have heard, brother, what is your duty towards the Church which ye have offended; to wit, that willingly ye confess that crime that ye have committed, asking God mercy for the same, and so that ye may reconcile yourself to the Church which ye have offended. Ye have heard also the affection and care of the Church towards you, their penitent brother, notwithstanding your grievous fall, to wit, that we all here present join our sins with your sin, we all repute and esteem your fall to be our own: we accuse ourselves no less than we accuse you: now, finally, we join our prayers with yours, that we and you may obtain mercy, and that by the means of our Lord Jesus Christ. Let us, therefore, brother, have this comfort of you, that ye will openly and simply confess your crime, and give to us attestation of your unfeigned repentance.

The penitent shall then openly confess the crime, whatsoever it be, and shall desire God's mercy, and pray the Church to call to God for mercy with him, and unfeignedly desire that he may be joined again to their society and number.

PUBLIC REPENTANCE.   49

IF the penitent be confounded with shame, or such one as cannot distinctly speak to the comfort and instruction of the Church, the Minister shall make repetition, that every head may be understood by itself, and thereafter shall ask the penitent if that be his confession, and if so he believeth. His answer affirmative being received, the Minister shall ask the Congregation if they judge any further to be required for their satisfaction and reconciliation of that brother. No contradiction being made, the Minister shall say to the penitent :—

We have heard, dear brother, your confession, for the which we from our hearts praise God, for in it the Spirit of Jesus Christ hath confounded the Devil, and broken down his head and power, in that, that ye to the glory of God have openly damned yourself and your impiety, imploring grace and mercy, for Christ Jesus His Son's sake. This strength, submission, and obedience cannot proceed from flesh and blood, but is the singular gift of the Holy Ghost. Acknowledge, therefore, it to be given unto you by Jesus Christ our Lord, and now take heed, lest at any time ye be unmindful of this great benefit, which no doubt Satan doth envy, and will assail by all means possible, that you may abuse it. He will not cease to tempt you to fall again in such, or crimes more horrible. But resist the Devil, and he shall flee from you. Live in sobriety, be instant in prayer, commend yourself unfeignedly to God, who, as He is faithful, so shall He give to us victory over sin, death, and Satan, and that by the means of our Head and Sovereign Champion Jesus Christ, to whom be all praise, glory, and honour, now and ever. Amen.

An Admonition to the Church.

IT is your duty, brethren, to take example of this our penitent brother: first, that ye be unfeignedly displeased in your own hearts for your sins; secondarily, that with this our brother ye accuse them in the sight of God, imploring grace and mercy for your offences committed; and last, if any of you shall after this publicly offend, that ye refuse not with the like reverence to satisfy the Church of God, offended in you. Now only resteth that ye remit and forget all offences which ye have conceived heretofore, by the sin and fall of this our brother: accept and embrace him as a member of Christ's body: let none take upon him to reproach or accuse him for any offences, that before this hour he hath committed. And that he may have the better assurance of your good will and reconciliation, prostrate yourselves before God, and render Him thanks for the conversion and repentance of this our brother.

The Thanksgiving.

HEAVENLY Father, Fountain of all mercy and consolation, we confess ourselves unworthy to be counted amongst Thy children, if Thou have respect to the corruption of our nature. But seeing it hath pleased Thy Fatherly goodness, not only freely to choose us in Thy dear Son, our Lord Jesus Christ, by His death to redeem us, by His Evangel to call us, and by His Holy Spirit (which both are Thine) to illuminate us; but also, that Thou hast commanded Thy Word and holy Evangel to be preached, to the end that the penitent shall have an assurance of the remission of their sins, not only for a time, but even so oft as men from sorrowful hearts shall call for Thy grace and mercy. In consideration of this Thy Fatherly adoption and ineffable clemency shown upon us, we cannot but praise and magnify Thy Fatherly mercy: a testimony whereof we not only feel in ourselves, but also see the same evidently in the conversion of this our brother, whom Satan for a time held in bondage, but now is set at freedom by the power of our Lord Jesus Christ, and is returned again to the society of Thy body. Grant unto us, heavenly Father, that he and we may more and more be displeased for our sins, and proceed in all manner of good works, to the praise of Thy holy name, and edification of Thy Church, by Jesus Christ our Lord and only Saviour. So be it.

The Thanksgiving finished, the Minister shall require of the Penitent, if that he will be subject to the discipline of the Church, in case he after offend, who, answering that he will, the Minister shall say in manner of absolution:—

If thou unfeignedly repent thy former iniquity, and believe in the Lord Jesus, then I, in His name, pronounce and affirm that thy sins are forgiven, not only on earth, but also in heaven, according to the promises annexed with the preaching of His Word, and to the power put in the Ministry of His Church.

Then shall the Elders and Deacons, with Min-

THE FORM OF

isters (if any be), in the name of the whole Church, take the reconciled brother by the hand, and embrace him, in sign of full reconciliation. Then after, shall the Church sing the 103*d Psalm, so much as they think expedient. And so shall the assembly with the benediction be dismissed.*

THE FORM OF EXCOMMUNICATION.

AFTER that all admonitions, both private and public, be past, as before is said, then must the Church proceed to excommunication if the offender remain obstinate. The Sunday, therefore, after the third public admonition, the Minister, being before charged by the Session or Elders, shall thus signify unto the Church after Sermon:—

It is not known unto you with what lenity and carefulness the Ministry and the whole Church, by private and public admonitions, hath sought N., &c., to satisfy the Church, and to declare himself penitent for his grievous crimes and rebellion, by the which he hath offended God's majesty, blasphemed His holy name, and offended His Church, in whom to this day we find nothing but stubbornness. We cannot, therefore, of conscience wink any longer at the disobedience of the said N.; lest that his example infect and hurt others. We are compelled, therefore, in the fear of God, to give the said N. into the hands and power of the Devil, to the destruction of the flesh, if that by that mean he may be brought to the consideration of himself, and so repent, and avoid that fearful condemnation that shall fall on all inobedient in the day of the Lord Jesus. And lest that any shall think that we do this of manly [human] presumption, without the assurance of the Scripture, ye shall shortly hear what commandment and authority we have so to do.

First, we have the commandment of our Master and Saviour, Jesus Christ, to hold such for ethnicks and publicans, as will not hear the voice of the Church. But plain it is, that this obstinate N. hath contemptuously refused all wholesome admonitions, and therefore we, not one or two, but the whole Church, must hold him as a publican, that is, as one cut off from the body of Jesus Christ, and unworthy of any society with Him, or with the benefits of His Church, till his new conversion, and his receiving again.

Secondarily, we have the command of the Apostle St Paul, and the fearful sentence which he, being absent, did notwithstanding pronounce against the incest, with his sharp rebuke to the Corinthians, because that with greater zeal and expedition they expelled not from among them that wicked man. And if any think that the offence of this forenamed obstinate is not so heinous as that of the incest, let such understand that mercy and favour may rather be granted to any other sin than to the contempt of wholesome admonitions, and of the just and lawful ordinances of the Church. For other sins, how heinous soever they be (so be it that they deserve not death), as by unfeigned repentance they are remitted before God, so, upon the same humbly offered unto the Church, order may be taken that the offender may be comforted, and at length restored to the society of the Church again. But such as proudly contemn the admonition of the Church, private or public, declare themselves stubborn, rebellious, and altogether impenitent, and therefore most justly ought they to be excommunicate.

The precept of God given under the law, to expel from the midst of God's people such as were leprous (without exception of person), is to us an assurance that we ought to expel from the society of Christ's body such as be stricken with spiritual leprosy; for the one is no less infective and dangerous than is the other. Now, seeing that we know excommunication is God's ordinance, let us, in few words, understand the utility and use of the same.

By it, first, the Church is purged of open wicked doers, which is no small commodity, considering that we fight in the midst and eyes of this wicked generation, which seeketh in us nothing more than occasion of slander. Secondarily, by it is the Church, and every member of the same, retained in obedience and fear, whereof all have need, if the frailty of our flesh shall be rightly considered. Thirdly, by it we exercise a singular work of charity, while that we declare ourselves careful to keep the flock of Christ in purity of manners, and without danger to be infected. For, as it were a work both uncharitable and cruel to join together in one bed, persons infected with pestilent or other contagious and infective sores with tender children, or with such as are whole, so it is no less cruelty to suffer among the flock of Jesus Christ such obstinate rebels. For true is that sentence of the Apostle, A little leaven corrupteth the whole mass. But lest that we should seem to usurp power over the Church, or to do anything without the knowledge and consent of the whole body, for this present we delay the sentence, willing such as have anything to object in the contrary to propone [propound] the same the next session day, or else to signify the same to some of the Ministers or Elders, that answer may be given thereto, and, in the mean time, we will call to God for the conversion of the impenitent.

The Prayer for the Obstinate.

ETERNAL and ever-living God, Father of our Lord Jesus Christ, whose very property is to show mercy, and to restore life, even when to man's judgment death hath gotten dominion over Thy creatures: for Thou hast first sought, called, accused, and convicted our father Adam, after his transgression, and being so dead in sin, and thrall to Satan, that he could neither confess his offence, nor yet ask mercy for the same, Thou, by Thy free promises of mercy and grace, gavest unto him a new life and strength to repent. The same order must Thou keep, O Lord, with all Thy chosen children of his posterity; for in man's corrupt nature there can be no obedience until that Thou, by operation of Thy Holy Spirit, work the same. And therefore we most humbly beseech Thee, for Jesus Christ Thy Son's sake, pitifully to look upon this Thy creature, who once was baptised in Thy name, and hath professed himself subject to Thy religion, and unto the discipline of Thy Church, whom Satan, alas! now so blindeth, that obstinately he contemneth the one and the other. We have followed, O Lord, the rule prescribed unto us by Thy dear Son, our Lord Jesus Christ, in admonishing and threatening him, but hitherto have profited nothing concerning him and his humiliation.

But, O Lord, as Thou alone knowest, so mayest Thou alone change and mollify the hearts of the proud and impenitent. Thou, by the voice of Thy prophet Nathan, wakenedst David from his deadly security. Thou, without any prophet, didst beat down the pride of Manasseh in the prison, after he had shed the blood of Thy servants, and had replenished Jerusalem with all kind of impiety. Thou turnedst the heart of Peter at the look of Thy dear Son, our Lord Jesus Christ, after that fearfully, with horrible imprecations, he had thrice openly denied Him.

O Lord, Thy mercies without measure endure for ever, to the which we, after long travail, do remit this obstinate and impenitent [person]; earnestly desiring Thee, O Father of mercies, first so to pierce his heart with the fear of Thy severe judgments, that he may begin to understand, that thus contemning all wholesome admonitions, he provoketh Thy wrath and indignation against himself. Open his eyes, that he may see how fearful and terrible a thing it is to fall into Thy hands: and, therefore, mollify and anoint his heart by the unction of Thy Holy Spirit, that he may unfeignedly convert unto Thee, and give unto Thee that honour and obedience that Thou requirest in Thy holy Word, and so to our comfort, that now mourn for his rebellion, that he may subject himself to the just ordinance of Thy Church, and avoid that fearful vengeance that most assuredly shall fall

EXCOMMUNICATION. 57

upon all the inobedient. These Thy graces, heavenly Father, and farther, as Thou knowest to be expedient for us, and for Thy Church universal, we call, according as we be taught to pray by our Sovereign Master, Christ Jesus, saying, *Our Father, &c.*

THE second Sunday, after sermon and public prayers, the Minister shall, in audience of the whole Church, ask the Elders and Deacons, who must sit in an eminent and proper place, that their answer may be heard.

The Minister.

HATH he, whom the last day we admonished, under the pain of excommunication, to satisfy the Church for his public slander and contempt of the Ministry, by himself or by any other, offered his obedience unto you?

They shall answer, as the truth is, Yea, *or* Nay.

If he hath sought the favour of any within the Ministry, with promise of obedience, then shall further process be delayed, and he commanded to appear before the Session in their next assembly, where order may be taken for his public repentance, as in the former head is expressed. If he have not laboured to satisfy the Church, then shall the Minister proceed, and say:—

It cannot be but dolorous to the body that any one member thereof should be cut off and perish: and yet, it ought to be more fearful to the member than to the body, for the member cut off can do nothing but putrefy and perish, and yet the body may retain life and strength. But the rebellion of this obstinate may proceed, in one part, from ignorance; for it may be that he understandeth not what excommunication is, and what is the danger of the same. I shall, therefore, in few words, open the one and the other.

Lawful excommunication (for the thunderings of that Roman Antichrist are but vanity and wind) is the cutting off from the body of Jesus Christ, from participation of His holy Sacraments, and from public prayers with His Church, by public and solemned [solemn] sentence, all obstinate and impenitent persons, after due admonitions, which sentence, lawfully pronounced on earth, is ratified in heaven, by binding of the same sins that they bind on earth. The danger hereof is greater than man can suddenly espy: for seeing that without the body of Jesus Christ there abideth nothing but death and damnation to mankind, in what estate shall we judge them to stand that justly are cut off from the same?

Yea, what horrible vengeance hangeth upon them and their posterity, notable and severe punishments may instruct us. Cain, the murderer, was not accursed within his own person only, but that same malediction ran in his posterity, and upon all that joined therewith, till that all mankind was destroyed by water (eight persons reserved). Cham likewise was accursed in his son Canaan, the severity whereof proceeded even to the rooting out of that whole race and nation. The simple word of our Master, Jesus Christ, caused the fig-tree suddenly to wither. At the voice of Peter, Ananias and Sapphira were stricken to death. The same God and Lord Jesus, with

EXCOMMUNICATION.

the power of His Holy Spirit, that then was potent and just, worketh even now in the Ministry of His Church, the contempt whereof He will in no wise suffer unpunished. And, therefore, ye that have acquaintance or familiarity with the forenamed obstinate, declare unto him these dangers, and will him not to tempt the uttermost. And thus, yet again let us pray to God for his conversion.

Let the former Prayer be publicly said.

THE third Sunday let the first question be proponed by the Minister to the Elders and Deacons, concerning the submission of the obstinate so oft admonished, as was proponed the second. If repentance be offered, let order be taken, as is before said, with one charge to the Church, to praise God for the conversion of that brother. If repentance be not offered, then shall the Minister expone [expound] wherein the person that is to be excommunicate hath offended; how oft, and by whom he hath been admonished, as well privately as publicly; and shall demand of the Elders and Deacons, if it be not so, whose answer received, the Minister shall ask the whole Church if they think that such contempt should be suffered among them: and if then no man make intercession for the obstinate, the Minister shall proceed and say :—

Of very conscience we are compelled to do that which to our hearts is most dolorous; to wit, to give over to the hands of the devil this forenamed obstinate contemner, N., whom once we esteemed a member of our body, and that not only for the crime which he hath committed, but much rather for his proud contempt and intolerable rebellion, lest that our sufferance of him in this his impiety should not only be imputed unto us, but also that he should infect others with the same pestilence. And, therefore, we must use the last remedy, how grievous soever it be unto us. And yet I desire you, for more ample declaration of your Christian charity towards him, [that] ye pray with me unto God now, for the last, for his conversion.

The last Prayer before the Excommunication.

OMNIPOTENT, Eternal, and merciful Father, who, for that good will that Thou bearest unto us in Jesus Christ, Thy dear Son, wilt not the death and destruction of a sinner, but rather that he, by inspiration and moving of Thy Holy Spirit, convert and live: who also dost witness the virtue and strength of Thy Word to be such, that it causeth the mountains to shake, the rocks [to] tremble, and the floods to dry up: Behold, we Thy children and people here prostrate before Thee, most humbly beseech Thee, in the name of Thy dear Son, our Lord Jesus Christ, that Thou wilt move and pierce the heart of our impenitent brother, whom Satan so long hath indured and hardened: let it please Thy Majesty, by the virtue of Thy Holy Spirit, that Thou wilt mollify the same: expel his darkness, and, by the light of Thy grace, that Thou wilt so illuminate him, that now at length he may feel, first, how grievously he hath offended against Thy Majesty; and, secondarily, against Thy holy Church and assembly. Give him Thy grace to acknowledge, accuse, and damn [condemn], as well before us whom he hath offended, as before Thy presence, this his proud contempt, lest that we, by the same provoked, be compelled with all our griefs to cut him off from Thy mystical body, whom we, O Lord, unfeignedly desire to retain within Thy Church, as a lively member of Thy dear Son, our Lord Jesus. Hear us, merciful Father, call back again this our impenitent brother that now tendeth to eternal destruction; that we all, who, before Thy presence, even for his rebellion, do mourn, may receive him again with gladness and joy, and so render praise and honour to Thee before this Thy holy congregation.

We grant ourselves, O Lord, unworthy whom Thou shouldst hear, because we cease not to offend Thee by our continual transgressing of Thy holy precepts. Look not upon us, merciful Father, in this our corrupt nature, but look Thou to Thy dear Son, whom Thou of Thy mere mercy hast appointed our Head, great Bishop, Advocate, Mediator, and only Propitiator. In Him, and in the merits of His death, we humbly beseech Thee mercifully to behold us, and suffer not the most innocent blood of Thy dear Son shed for us, and for this our impenitent brother, to be profaned by the tyranny and slight of Satan. But by the virtue of the same, let this our impenitent brother be brought to unfeigned repentance, that so he may escape that fearful condemnation in the which he appeareth to fall. This we ask of Thee, O heavenly Father, in the boldness of our Head and Mediator, Jesus Christ, praying, as He hath taught us, *Our Father which art, &c.*

If, after this prayer, the obstinate appear not to

THE FORM OF

offer his repentance, then shall the Minister proceed and say :—

BRETHREN, seeing that, as ye have heard, this obstinate and impenitent person, N., hath so grievously offended against God, and against this His holy congregation, who by no means (as ye may perceive) can be brought to repentance; whereof it is evident by the Word of God, that he is fallen from the kingdom of Heaven, and from the blessed society of the Lord Jesus. And we (albeit with dolour of our hearts) may now execute that which the commandment of Jesus Christ, and the practice of His Apostle, showeth that of our office we ought to do; to wit, that we shall publicly declare and pronounce such to have no society with us, as declare themselves obstinate and rebellious against all wholesome admonitions, and the blessed ordinances of His Church. And that we may do the same, not of our own authority, but in the name and power of our Lord Jesus Christ, before whom all knees are compelled to bow, let us humbly fall down before Him, and on this manner pray, and pronounce this sentence.

The Invocation of the Name of Jesus Christ to excommunicate the impenitent, together with the Sentence of Excommunication.

O LORD JESUS CHRIST, the only and eternal King of all the chosen children of Thy heavenly Father, the Head and Lawgiver of thy Church; who by Thy own mouth hast commanded that such offenders as proudly contemn the admonitions of Thy Church, shall be cast out from the

EXCOMMUNICATION. 63

society of the same, and shall be reputed of Thy professors as profane ethnicks: we, willing to obey this Thy precept, which also we have received by institution of Thy Apostle, are here presently convened, in Thy name, to excommunicate, and cast forth from the society of Thy holy body, and from all participation with Thy Church in sacraments or prayers, N. Which thing we do at Thy commandment, and in Thy power and authority, to the glory of Thy holy name, to the conservation and edification of this Thy Church, in the which it hath pleased Thee to place us Ministers, and to the extreme remedy of the stubborn obstinacy of the forenamed impenitent. And because Thou hast promised Thyself ever to be with us, but specially with such as uprightly travel in the Ministry of Thy Church, whom also Thou hast promised to instruct and guide by the dictament of Thy Holy Spirit, we most humbly beseech Thee so to govern and assist us in the execution of this our charge, that whatsoever we in Thy name do here pronounce on earth, that Thou wilt ratify the same in heaven. Our assurance, O Lord, is Thy expressed Word. And, therefore, in boldness of the same, *Here I* [*we*], *in Thy name*, and at the commandment of this Thy present congregation, cut off, seclude, and excommunicate from Thy body, and from our society, N., as a person slanderous, proud, contemner, and a member for this present, altogether corrupted, and pernicious to the body. And this his sin (albeit with sorrow of heart) by virtue of our Ministry we bind, and pronounce the same to be bound in heaven and earth. We farther give over in [to] the hands and power of the devil the said N., to the destruction of his flesh; straitly charging all that profess the Lord Jesus, to whose knowledge this our sentence shall come, to repute and to hold the said N. accursed, and unworthy of the familiar society of Christians: declaring unto all men that such as hereafter, before his repentance, shall haunt, or familiarly accompany him, are partakers of his impiety, and subject to the like condemnation. This our sentence, O Lord Jesus, pronounced in Thy name, and at Thy commandment, we humbly desire Thee to ratify, according to Thy promise. And yet, Lord, Thou that camest to save that which was lost, look upon him with the eyes of Thy mercy, if Thy good pleasure be; and so pierce Thou his heart, that he may feel in his breast the terrors of Thy judgment, that by Thy grace he fruitfully may be converted to Thee; and so damning his own impiety, he may be with the like solemnity received within the bosom of Thy Church, from the which this day (with grief and dolour of our hearts) he is ejected.

Lord, in Thy presence we protest that our own affections move us not to this severity, but only the hatred of sin, and obedience that we give to Thy own commandment. And, therefore, O heavenly Father, we crave the perpetual assistance of Thy Holy Spirit, not only to bridle our corrupt affections, but also so to conduct us in all the course of our whole life, that we never fall to the like impiety and contempt; but that continually we may be subject to the voice of Thy Church, and unto the Ministers of the same, who truly offer to us the Word of Life, the blessed Evangel

ABSOLUTION. 65

of Thy only beloved Son Jesus Christ: to Whom, with Thee and the Holy Spirit, be all praise, glory and honour, now and ever. So be it.

The Sentence pronounced, and the Prayer ended,

THE Minister shall admonish the Church that all the faithful do hold the excommunicate as an ethnick, as before is said, that no man use his familiar company: and yet that no man accuse him of any other crime than of such as he is convicted of, and for the which he is excommunicate; but that every man shall secretly call to God for grace to be granted to the excommunicate. Such as have office in the Ministry may, upon licence required of the Church, speak with the excommunicate, so long as hope resteth of his conversion. But if he continue obstinate, then ought all the faithful utterly to abhor his presence and communication. And yet ought they more earnestly to call to God that Satan in the end may be confounded, and the creature of God freed from his snares by the power of the Lord Jesus. And with the accustomed benediction, the assembly shall be dismissed, after they have sung the 101st Psalm, or one portion thereof, as it shall please the congregation.

THE ORDER TO RECEIVE THE EXCOMMUNI-
CATE AGAIN TO THE SOCIETY
OF THE CHURCH.

FIRST, we must observe, that such as deserve death for that crime committed, never be admitted to the society of the Church, until such time as either the Magistrate punish according to the law, or else pardon the crime, as before we have said. But such as for other offences, and for their contempt, are excommunicate, may be received when they shall earnestly seek the favours of the Church. They must begin at the Ministry, the Elders, and the Deacons, who must expone [declare] their repentance to the Minister or Ministers in their assembly; a day may be appointed to the excommunicate to present himself before them. The signs of his repentance ought to be diligently inquired; as, What hath been his behaviour since the time of his excommunication, what he will offer for his satisfaction to the Church, and unto whom he hath exponed the grief and dolour of his heart? If the excommunicate be found penitent, and obedient in all things, the Minister, the next Sunday, may give advertisement to the whole Church of his humiliation, and command them to call to God for increase of the same. The next Session day, the Minister may appoint to the excommunicate such satisfaction as they think most expedient; to the which if the excommunicate fully agree, then may the said Ministry appoint unto him a certain day when he shall fulfil the same.

For this is principally to be observed, that no excommunicate person may be received to the society of the Church again, until such time as he hath stood at the Church door, at the least more Sundays than one: which days being expired, and the whole satisfaction complete, some of the Elders shall pass to the excommunicate, after that the former prayer of the Minister in the pulpit be

ABSOLUTION.

ended, and shall present him to a certain place appointed for the penitents; where he shall stand in the same habit in the which he made satisfaction, until the sermon be ended. And then shall the same Elders that brought him into the church present him to the Minister, with these or the like words :—

This creature of God, N., that for his wickedness and obstinate rebellion hath been excommunicate from the body of Jesus Christ, but now, by the power of the Spirit of God, is called back again by repentance, so far as the judgment of man can perceive, for he hath not only craved the favours of the Ministry, that he might be received into the body of the Church again, but also most obediently hath subjected himself to all that we have commanded, for trial of his humiliation. And, therefore, we present him before you to be examined; and if his repentance be sufficient, to be received again to the body of the Church.

Then shall the Minister render thanks, first to God, for that part of his humiliation, and also desire the Church of God to do the same with him. Thereafter he shall address him to the person excommunicate; and, first, shall lay before him his sin; then after, the admonitions that were given unto him, to satisfy the Church for the same; and, last, his proud contempt and long obstinacy, for the which he was excommunicate. And of every one he shall require his peculiar confession, with accusation of himself and detestation of his impiety. Which being received, he shall render thanks to God as followeth :—

We thank the mercy and goodness of God,

through Jesus Christ our Lord, for this thy conversion, N., into the which [wherein] thou hast not so much ashamed thyself, as that thou hast confounded and overcome Satan, by whose venomous and deceivable enticements, thou hitherto hast been rebellious to the wholesome admonitions of the Church. And yet, because we can but only see that which is external, we will join our prayers with thine, that thy humiliation may proceed from the heart.

Let the prayers appointed to be said in the receiving of the penitent be said also here; which ended, let the Church and the penitent be admonished, as is expressed, except that the crime of his Excommunication must ever be alleged and mentioned.

The Prayer containing his receiving to the Church.

LORD JESUS CHRIST, King, Teacher, and our eternal Priest, who, with the preaching of Thy blessed Evangel, hast joined the power to bind and loose the sins of men; who hast also pronounced that whatsoever by Thy Ministers is bound on earth shall be bound in the heaven, and also that whatsoever is loosed by the same shall be loosed and absolved with Thee in the heaven: look, O Lord, mercifully upon this Thy creature, N., &c., whom Satan of long time hath holden in bondage, so that not only he drew him to iniquity, but also that he so hardened his heart that he despised all admonitions, for the which his sin and contempt we were compelled to excommunicate him from our body. But now, O Lord, seeing that the Spirit of our Lord Jesus Christ hath so far prevailed in him that he is returned to our society, it will [let it] please Thee, for the obedience of our Lord Jesus, so to accept him, that his former inobedience be never laid to his charge; but that he may increase in all godliness, till that Satan finally be trodden under his feet and ours, by the power of our Lord Jesus Christ: to Whom, with Thee and with the Holy Spirit, be all honour and glory, now and ever. So be it.

The Form of Absolution.

IN the name and authority of Jesus Christ, I, the minister of His blessed Evangel, with consent of the whole Ministry and Church, absolve thee, N., from the sentence of Excommunication, from the sin by thee committed, and from all censures laid against thee for the same before, according to thy repentance; and pronounce thy sin to be loosed in heaven, and thee to be received again to the society of Jesus Christ, to His body the Church, to the participation of His Sacraments, and, finally, to the fruition of all His benefits: IN THE NAME OF THE FATHER, THE SON, AND THE HOLY SPIRIT. SO BE IT.

The absolution pronounced, the Minister shall then call him Brother, and give him admonition to watch and pray that he fall not in the like temptation; that he be thankful for the mercy shown unto him, and that he show the fruits of his conversion in life and conversation.

Thereafter the whole Ministry shall embrace him, and such others of the Church as be next unto him, and then shall a Psalm of thanksgiving be sung.

70 THE FORM OF ABSOLUTION.

This order may be enlarged or contracted, as the wisdom of the discreet Minister shall think expedient; for we rather show the way to the ignorant, than prescribe order to the learned, that cannot be amended.

A Prayer.

PRESERVE the public face of Thy Church within this Realm, O Lord: Dilate the kingdom of Thy Son, Jesus Christ, universally: And so farther disclose and break down the tyranny of that Roman Antichrist, by the power of Thy Son, our Lord Jesus Christ. So be it. 1567.

a Rom. 16.   *a Soli sapienti Deo per Jesum Christum gloria in perpetuum. Amen.*

THIS BOOK is thought necessary and profitable for the Church, and commanded to be printed by the General Assembly. Set forth by John Knox, Minister: And sighted by us whose names follow, as we were appointed by the said General Assembly.

John Willok.   *David Lindesay.*
M. John Craig.   *Gulielmus Chris-*
Robert Pont.   *tesonus.*
John Row.   *James Craig, &c.*

THE
VISITATION OF THE SICK.

BECAUSE the visitation of the sick is a thing very necessary, and yet, notwithstanding, it is hard to prescribe all rules appertaining thereunto, we refer it to the discretion of the godly and prudent Minister, who, according as he seeth the patient afflicted, either may lift him up with the sweet promises of God's mercy through Christ, if he perceive him much afraid of God's threatenings: or contrariwise, if he be not touched with the feeling of his sins, may beat him down with God's justice; evermore, like a skilful physician, framing his medicine according as the disease requireth. And if he perceive him to want any necessaries, he not only relieveth him according to his ability, but also provideth by others, that he may be furnished sufficiently. Moreover, the party that is visited may at all times for his comfort send for the minister, who doth not only make prayers for him there presently, but also, if it so require, commendeth him in the public prayers to the Congregation.

A Prayer to be said in Visiting of the Sick.

O OUR good God, Lord and Father, the Creator and Conserver of all things, the fountain of all goodness and benignity; like as

THE VISITATION

(among other Thine infinite benefits, which Thou of Thy great goodness and grace dost distribute ordinarily unto all men) Thou givest them health of body, to the end that they should the better know Thy great liberality, so that they might be the more ready to serve and glorify Thee with the same: so, contrariwise, when we have evil-behaved ourselves, in offending Thy Majesty, Thou hast accustomed to admonish us, and call us unto Thee, by diverse and sundry chastisements, through the which it hath pleased Thy goodness to subdue and tame our frail flesh: but specially by the grievous plagues of sickness and diseases; using the same as a mean to awake and stir up the great dulness and negligence that is in us all, and advertising us of our evil life by such infirmities and dangers, especially when, as they threaten the very death, which (as assured messengers of the same) are all to the flesh full of extreme anguish and torments, although they be, notwithstanding, to the spirit of the Elect, as medicines both good and wholesome. For by them Thou dost move us to return unto Thee for our salvation, and to call upon Thee in our afflictions, to have Thine help who art our dear and loving Father.

In consideration whereof, we most earnestly pray unto Thee, our good God, that it would please Thine infinite goodness to have pity upon this Thy poor creature whom Thou hast, as it were, bound and tied to the bed by most grievous sickness, and brought to great extremity by the heaviness of Thine hand. O Lord, enter not into account with him, to render the reward due unto his works; but through Thine infinite mercy remit all his

OF THE SICK. 73

faults, for the which Thou hast chastised him so gently; and behold rather the obedience which Thy dear Son, Jesus Christ our Lord, hath rendered unto Thee—to wit, the sacrifice which it pleased Thee to accept as a full recompense for all the iniquities of them that receive Him for their justice and satisfaction, yea, for their only Saviour.

Let it please Thee, O God, to give him a true zeal and affection to receive and acknowledge Him for his only Redeemer: to the end also that Thou mayest receive this sick person to Thy mercy, qualifying all the troubles which his sins, the horror of death, and dreadful fear of the same, may bring to his weak conscience: Neither suffer Thou, O Lord, the assaults of the mighty adversary to prevail, or to take from him the comfortable hope of salvation which Thou givest to Thy dearly beloved children.

And, forasmuch as we are all subject to the like state and condition, and to be visited with like battle, when it shall please Thee to call us unto the same, we beseech Thee most humbly, O Lord, with this Thy poor creature, whom Thou now presently chastisest, that Thou wilt not extend Thy rigorous judgment against him; but that Thou wouldst vouchsafe to show him Thy mercy, for the love of Thy dear Son, Jesus Christ our Lord, who, having suffered the most shameful and extreme death of the cross, bore willingly the fault of this poor patient, to the end that Thou mightest acknowledge him as one redeemed with His precious blood, and received into the communion of His body, to be participant of eternal felicity, in the company of Thy blessed angels. Wherefore, O Lord, dispose and move his heart to receive, by Thy grace, with all meekness, this gentle and fatherly correction, which Thou hast laid upon him; that he may endure it patiently, and with willing obedience; submitting himself with heart and mind to Thy blessed will and favourable mercy, wherein Thou now visitest him after this sort, for his profit and salvation. It may [let it] please Thy goodness, O Lord, to assist him in all his anguishes and troubles. And although the tongue and voice be not able to execute their office, in this behalf, to set forth Thy glory, that yet at least Thou wilt stir up his heart to aspire unto Thee only, who art the only fountain of goodness; and that Thou fast root and settle in his heart the sweet promises which Thou hast made unto us in Christ Jesus, Thy Son, our Saviour, to the intent he may remain constant against all the assaults and tumults which the enemy of our salvation may raise up to trouble his conscience.

And seeing it hath pleased Thee, that by the death of Thy dear Son, life eternal should be communicated unto us, and by the shedding of His blood the washing of our sins should be declared; and that by His resurrection also, both justice and immortality should be given us; may it please Thee to apply this holy and wholesome medicine to this Thy poor creature, in such extremity, taking from him all trembling and dreadful fear, and to give him a stout courage in the midst of all his present adversities.

And forasmuch as all things, O heavenly

OF THE SICK. 75

Father, be known unto Thee, and Thou canst, according to Thy good pleasure, minister unto him all such things as shall be necessary and expedient, let it please Thee, O Lord, so to satisfy him by Thy grace as may seem most meet unto Thy divine Majesty. Receive him, Lord, into Thy protection, for he hath his recourse and access to Thee alone; and make him constant and firm in Thy commandments and promises: and also pardon all his sins, both secret and those which are manifest, by the which he hath most grievously provoked Thy wrath and severe judgments against him; so as, in place of death (the which both he and all we have justly merited), Thou wilt grant unto him that blessed life which we also attend and look for, by Thy grace and mercy. Nevertheless, O heavenly Father, if Thy good pleasure be that he shall yet live longer in this world, may it then please Thee to augment in him Thy graces, so as the same may serve unto Thy glory; yea, Lord, to the intent he may conform himself the more diligently, and with more carefulness, to the example of Thy Son, Christ Jesus; and that in renouncing himself, he may cleave fully unto Him, who, to give consolation and hope to all sinners to obtain remission of all their sins and offences, hath carried with Him into the heavens the thief who was crucified with Him upon the cross.

But if the time, by Thee appointed, be come that he shall depart from us unto Thee, make him to feel in his conscience, O Lord, the fruit and strength of Thy grace, that thereby he may have a new taste of Thy Fatherly care over him from the beginning of his life unto the very end of the same, for the love of Thy dear Son, Jesus Christ our Lord.

Give him Thy grace, that, with a good heart and full assurance of faith, he may receive to his consolation so great and excellent a treasure, to wit, the remission of his sins in Christ Jesus Thy Son, who now presenteth Him [self] to this poor person in distress, by the virtue of Thy promises revealed unto him by Thy Word, which he hath exercised with us in Thy Church and congregation, and also in using the Sacraments which Thou therein hast established, for confirmation of all their faith that trust in Thee unfeignedly.

Let true faith, O Lord, be unto him as a most sure buckler, thereby to avoid the assaults of death, and more boldly walk for the advancement of eternal life, to the end that he, having a most lively apprehension thereof, may rejoice with Thee in the heavens eternally.

Let him be under Thy protection and governance, O heavenly Father. And although he be sick, yet canst Thou heal him: he is cast down, but Thou canst lift him up: he is sore troubled, but Thou canst send redress: he is weak, but Thou canst send strength: he acknowledgeth his uncleanness, his spots, his filthiness, and iniquities, but Thou canst wash him, and make him clean: he is wounded, but Thou canst minister most sovereign salves; he is fearful and trembling, but Thou canst give him good courage and boldness. To be short, he is, as it were, utterly lost, and a strayed sheep, but Thou canst call him home to Thee again. Wherefore, O Lord, seeing that this poor creature (Thine own workmanship)

OF THE SICK.

resigneth him [self] wholly into Thy hands, receive him into Thy merciful protection. Also, we poor miserable creatures, who are, as it were, in the field, ready to fight till Thou withdraw us from the same, vouchsafe to strengthen us by Thine Holy Spirit, that we may obtain the victory, in Thy name, against our deadly and mortal enemy: And, furthermore, that the affliction and the combat of this Thy poor creature in most grievous torments, may move us to humble ourselves with all reverent fear and trembling under Thy mighty hand, knowing that we must [all] appear before Thy judgment-seat, when it shall please Thee so to appoint. But, O Lord, the corruption of our frail nature is such that we are utterly destitute of any means to appear before Thee, except it please Thee to make us such as Thou Thyself requirest us to be; and further, that Thou give us the spirit of meekness and humility, to rest and stay wholly on those things which Thou only commandest.

But forasmuch as we be altogether unworthy to enjoy such benefits, we beseech Thee to receive us, in the name of Thy dear Son our Lord and Master, in whose death and satisfaction standeth wholly the hope of our salvation.

May it also please Thee, O Father of comfort and consolation, to strengthen with Thy grace those who employ their travel and diligence to the aiding of this sick person, that they faint not by overmuch and continual labour, but rather to go heartily and cheerfully forward in doing their endeavours towards him: and if Thou take him from them, then of Thy goodness to comfort them, so as they may patiently bear such departing, and praise Thy name in all things. Also, O heavenly Father, vouchsafe to have pity on all other sick persons, and such as be by any other ways or means afflicted; and also on those who as yet are ignorant of Thy truth, and appertain nevertheless unto Thy kingdom; in like manner on those that suffer persecution, [are] tormented in prisons, or otherwise troubled by the enemies of the Verity, for bearing testimony to the same; finally, on all the necessities of Thy people, and upon all the ruins or decays which Satan hath brought upon Thy Church. O Father of mercy, spread forth Thy goodness upon all those that be Thine, that we, forsaking ourselves, may be the more inflamed and confirmed to rest only upon Thee alone. Grant these our requests, O our dear Father, for the love of Thy dear Son, our Saviour Jesus Christ, Who liveth and reigneth with Thee in unity of the Holy Ghost, true God for evermore. So be it.

THE BURIAL.

THE corpse is reverently brought to the grave, accompanied with the Congregation, without any further ceremonies: which being buried, the Minister if he be present, and required, goeth to the Church, if it be not far off, and maketh some comfortable exhortation to the people, touching death and [the] resurrection.

[*Then blesseth the people, and so dismisseth them.*[a]]

[a] In some copies.

THE ORDER OF PUBLIC WORSHIP.

When the Congregation is assembled at the hour appointed, the Minister useth this confession, or like in effect, exhorting the people diligently to examine themselves, following in their hearts the tenor of his words.

THE CONFESSION OF OUR SINS.

O ETERNAL GOD and most merciful Father, we confess and acknowledge here before Thy Divine Majesty, that we are miserable sinners, conceived and born in sin and iniquity, so that in us there is no goodness;[a] for the flesh evermore rebelleth against the Spirit, whereby we continually transgress Thy holy precepts and commandments,[b] and so do purchase to ourselves, through Thy just judgment, death and damnation.[c] Notwithstanding, O heavenly Father, forasmuch as we are displeased with ourselves for the sins that we have committed against Thee, and do unfeignedly repent us of the same,[d] we most humbly beseech Thee, for Jesus Christ's sake, to show Thy mercy upon us, to forgive us all our sins,[e] and to increase Thy Holy Spirit in us, that we, acknowledging from the bottom of our hearts our own unrighte-

a Rom. 3, Psa. 14, 51.

b Gal. 5. Rom. 7.
c Rom. 2, 5.

d Jer. 3.

e Rom. 5.

ousness, may from henceforth not only mortify our sinful lusts and affections, but also bring forth such fruits as may be agreeable to Thy most blessed will,*f* not for the worthiness thereof, but for the merits of Thy dearly beloved Son Jesus Christ our only Saviour, whom Thou hast already given, an oblation and offering for our sins,*g* and for whose sake we are certainly persuaded that Thou wilt deny us nothing that we shall ask in His name according to Thy will.*h* For Thy Spirit doth assure our consciences that Thou art our merciful Father,*i* and so lovest us Thy children through Him, that nothing is able to remove Thy heavenly grace and favour from us.*k* To Thee, therefore, O Father, with the Son and the Holy Ghost, be all honour and glory, world without end. So be it.

f Col. 3.
Eph. 6.
1 Pet. 2.

g Rom. 5.
Eph. 2.
Heb. 9.

h John 14.
Mat. 7.
James 1.

i John 3.
Rom. 8.

k Rom. 8.

Another Confession and Prayer commonly used in the Church of Edinburgh on the day of Common Prayer.

O DREADFUL and most mighty God, Thou that from the beginning hast declared Thyself a consuming fire against the contemners of Thy most holy precepts, and yet to the penitent sinners hast always showed Thyself a favourable Father, and a God full of mercy: we Thy creatures and workmanship of Thine own hands, confess ourselves most unworthy to open our eyes unto the heavens, but far less to appear in Thy presence. For our consciences accuse us, and our manifold iniquities have borne witness against us, that we have declined from Thee. We have been polluted with idolatry; we have given Thy glory to creatures;

PUBLIC WORSHIP. 81

we have sought support where it was not to be found, and have lightlied[l] Thy most wholesome admonitions. The manifest corruption of our lives in all estates evidently proveth that we have not rightly regarded Thy statutes, laws, and holy ordinances; and this was not only done, O Lord, in the time of our blindness; but even now, when of Thy mercy Thou hast opened unto us an entrance to Thy heavenly kingdom, by the preaching of Thy holy Evangel, the whole body of this miserable realm still continueth in their former impiety. For the most part, alas! following the footsteps of the blind and obstinate Princess,[m] utterly despise the light of Thy Gospel, and delight in ignorance and idolatry; others live as a people without God, and without all fear of Thy terrible judgments. And some, O Lord, that in mouth profess Thy blessed Evangel, by their slanderous life blaspheme the same. We are not ignorant, O Lord, that Thou art a righteous judge, that can not suffer iniquity long to be unpunished upon the obstinate transgressors; especially, O Lord, when that, after so long blindness and horrible defection from Thee, so lovingly Thou callest us again to Thy favour and fellowship, and that yet we do obstinately rebel. We have, O Lord, in our extreme misery, called unto Thee; yea, even when we appeared utterly to have been consumed in the fury of our enemies, and then didst Thou mercifully incline Thine ears unto us. Thou foughtest for us even by Thine own power, when in us there was neither wisdom nor force. Thou alone brakest the yoke from our necks, and set us at liberty, when we by our foolishness

[l] Lightly esteemed.

[m] Later copies have blind and obstinate Princes.

had made ourselves slaves unto strangers, and mercifully unto this day hast continued with us the light of Thine Evangel, and so ceasest not to heap upon us benefits both spiritual and temporal. But yet, alas! O Lord, we clearly see that our great ingratitude craveth further punishment at Thy hands, the signs whereof are evident before our eyes. [For the whispering of sedition, the contempt of Thy graces offered, and the maintenance of idolatry, are assured signs of Thy further plagues to fall upon us in particular for our grievous offences. And this unmeasurable intemperateness of the air doth also threaten Thine accustomed plague of famine, which commonly followeth riotous excess and contempt of the poor, wherewith, alas! the whole earth is replenished.] We have nothing, O Lord, that we may lay betwixt us and Thy judgment but Thine only mercy freely offered to us in Thy dear Son, our Lord Jesus Christ, purchased to us by His death and passion. For if Thou wilt enter into judgment with Thy creatures, and keep in mind our grievous sins and offences, then can there no flesh escape condemnation. And therefore we most humbly beseech Thee, O Father of mercies, for Christ Jesus Thy Son's sake, to take from us these stony hearts, who so long have heard as well Thy mercies as severe judgments, and yet have not been effectually moved with the same; and give unto us hearts mollified by Thy Spirit, that may both conceive and keep in mind the reverence which is due unto Thy Majesty. Look, O Lord, unto Thy chosen children, labouring under the imperfection of the flesh, and grant unto us that

These clauses included within this [ ] may be used, or any one of them, as occasion serveth.

victory that Thou hast promised unto us by Jesus Christ Thy Son, our only Saviour, Mediator, and Lawgiver: to Whom, with Thee and the Holy Ghost, be all honour and praise, now and ever. Amen.

A Confession of Sins, to be used before Sermon.

TRUTH it is, O Lord, that we are unworthy to come to Thy godly presence, by reason of our manifold sins and wickedness, much less are we worthy to receive any grace or mercy at Thy hands, if Thou shouldst deal with us according to our deservings, for we have sinned, O Lord, against Thee, and we have offended Thy godly and divine Majesty. If Thou shouldst begin to reckon with us, even from our first conception in our mother's womb, Thou canst find nothing at all in us, but occasion of death and eternal condemnation. For truth it is, that first we were conceived in sin, and in iniquity was every one of us born of our mother; all the days of our life we have so still continued in sin and wickedness, that rather we have given ourselves to follow the corruption of this our fleshly nature, than otherwise, with that earnest care and diligence to serve and worship Thee our God, as it becometh us; and, therefore, if Thou shouldst enter into judgment with us, just occasion hast Thou, not only to punish these our wretched and mortal bodies, but also to punish us both in body and soul eternally, if Thou shouldst handle us according to the rigour of Thy justice. But yet, O Lord, as on the one part we acknowledge our own sins and offences, together with the fearful judgment of

Thee our God, that justly by reason thereof Thou mayest pour upon us; so also on the other part we acknowledge Thee to be a merciful God, a loving and a favourable Father to all them that unfeignedly turn unto Thee. Wherefore, O Lord, we Thy people, and the workmanship of Thine own hands, most humbly beseech Thee, for Christ Thy Son's sake, to show Thy mercy upon us, and forgive us all our offences; impute not unto us the sins of our youth, neither yet receive Thou a reckoning of us for the iniquity of our old age, but as Thou hast showed Thyself merciful to all them that have truly called unto Thee, so show the like mercy and the like favour unto us Thy poor servants. Indue our hearts, O God, with such a true and perfect acknowledging of our sins, that we may pour forth before Thee the unfeigned sighs and sobs of our troubled hearts and afflicted consciences, for our offences committed against Thee. Inflame our hearts with such a zeal and fervency towards Thy glory, that all the days of our life our only study, travail, and labour, may be to serve and worship Thee our God in spirit, in truth and verity, as Thou requirest of us. And that this may be the better performed in us, preserve us from all impediments and stays that in anywise may hinder or stop us in the same; but in special, O Lord, preserve us from the craft of Satan, from the snares of the world, and from the naughty lusts and affections of the flesh. Make Thy Spirit, O God, once to take such full possession and dwelling in our hearts, that not only all the actions of our life, but also all the words of our mouth, and the least thought and cogitation of our minds, may be guided and ruled thereby.

And finally, grant that all the time of our life may be so spent in Thy true fear and obedience, that altogether we may end the same in the sanctification and honouring of Thy blessed name, through Jesus Christ our Lord, to Whom, with Thee and the Holy Ghost, be all honour and glory, for now and for ever. So be it.

A Confession of Sins, and Petitions made unto God in the time of our extreme Troubles, and yet commonly used in the Churches of Scotland, before the Sermon.

ETERNAL and everlasting God, Father of our Lord Jesus Christ, Thou that showest mercy and keepest covenant with them that love, and in reverence keep Thy commandments, even when Thou pourest forth Thy hot displeasure and just judgments upon the obstinate and disobedient; we here prostrate ourselves before the throne of Thy Majesty, from our hearts confessing that justly Thou hast punished us by the tyranny of strangers, and that more justly Thou mayest bring upon us again the bondage and yoke which of Thy mercy for a season Thou hast removed. Our Kings, Princes, and People, in blindness, have refused the Word of Thy eternal verity, and in so doing we have refused the league of Thy mercy offered to us in Jesus Christ Thy Son; which albeit Thou now of Thy mere mercy hast offered to us again in such abundance, that none can be excused by reason of ignorance, yet nevertheless, to the judgment of men, impiety overfloweth the whole face of this Realm.

For the great multitude delight themselves in ignorance and idolatry: and such, alas! as appear to reverence and embrace Thy Word, do not express the fruits of repentance as it becometh the people to whom Thou hast showed Thyself so merciful and favourable. These are Thy just judgments, O Lord, whereby Thou punishest sin by sin, and man by his own iniquity; so that there can be no end of sin except Thou prevent us with Thy undeserved grace. Convert us, therefore, O Lord, and we shall be converted; suffer not our unthankfulness to procure of Thy most just judgments that strangers again reign over us; neither yet that the light of Thy Gospel be taken from us. But howsoever it be that the great multitude be altogether rebellious, and also that in us there remain perpetual imperfections, yet for the glory of Thine own name, and for the glory of Thine only beloved Son Jesus Christ, whose verity and Evangel Thou of Thy mere mercy hast manifested among us: let it please Thee to take us into Thy protection and defence, that all the world may know, that as of Thy mere mercy Thou hast begun this work of our salvation amongst us, so of this same mercy Thou wilt continue the same. Grant us this, O merciful Father, for Christ Jesus Thy Son's sake.—Amen.

This done, the people sing a Psalm all together, in a plain tune: which ended, the Minister prayeth for the assistance of God's Holy Spirit, as the same shall move his heart, and so proceedeth to the Sermon; using after the Sermon this Prayer following, or suchlike.

A PRAYER FOR THE WHOLE ESTATE OF CHRIST'S CHURCH.

ALMIGHTY GOD, and most merciful Father, we humbly submit ourselves,[a] and fall down before thy Majesty,[b] beseeching Thee, from the bottom of our hearts, that this seed of Thy Word now sown among us may take such deep root, that neither the burning heat of persecution cause it to wither, neither the thorny cares of this life do choke it, but that, as seed sown in good ground, it may bring forth thirty, sixty, and an hundred fold,[c] as Thy heavenly wisdom hath appointed. And because we have need continually to crave many things at Thy hands, we humbly beseech Thee, O heavenly Father, to grant us Thine Holy Spirit to direct our petitions,[d] that they may proceed from such a fervent mind as may be agreeable to Thy most blessed will.

And seeing that our infirmity is able to do nothing without Thy help,[e] and that Thou art not ignorant with how many and great temptations we poor wretches are on every side enclosed and compassed,[f] let Thy strength, O Lord, sustain our weakness, that we, being defended with the force of Thy grace, may be safely preserved against all assaults of Satan, who goeth about continually like a roaring lion, seeking to devour us.[g] Increase our faith,[h] O merciful Father, that we do not swerve at any time from Thy heavenly Word, but augment in us hope and love with a careful keeping of all Thy commandments, that no hardness of heart,[i] no hypocrisy, no concupiscence

[a] 1 Pet. 5.
[b] Num. 16. Deut. 9. Josh. 7.
[c] Mat. 13.
[d] Luke 11. Rom. 8, 12. James 5. 1 John 5. Wisd. 9.
[e] 2 Cor. 3. John 15. Phil. 2.
[f] Ps. 40. 1 Pet. 1.
[g] 1 Pet. 5.
[h] Luke 17.
[i] Ps. 95. Heb. 3, 4.

of the eyes, nor enticements of the world, do draw us away from Thy obedience.*k* And seeing we live now in these most perilous times, let Thy fatherly providence defend us against the violence of all our enemies, which do everywhere pursue us; but chiefly against the wicked rage and furious uproars of that Romish idol, enemy to Thy Christ.*l*

Furthermore, forasmuch as by Thy holy Apostle we are taught to make our prayers and supplications for all men,*m* we pray not only for ourselves here present, but beseech Thee also to reduce all such as be yet ignorant from the miserable captivity of blindness and error to the pure understanding of Thy heavenly truth, that we all with one consent and unity of minds may worship Thee our only God and Saviour:*n* and that all Pastors, Shepherds, and Ministers to whom Thou hast committed the dispensation of Thy holy Word, and charge of Thy chosen people,*o* may both in their life and doctrine be found faithful, setting only before their eyes Thy glory, and that by them all poor sheep, which wander and go astray, may be gathered and brought home to Thy fold.

Moreover, because the hearts of rulers are in Thy hands,*p* we beseech Thee to direct and govern the hearts of all Kings, Princes, and Magistrates, to whom Thou hast committed the sword;*q* especially, O Lord, according to our bounden duty, we beseech Thee to maintain and increase the noble estate of the King's Majesty, and his honourable Council, with all the estate and whole body of the Commonwealth. Let thy fatherly favour

PUBLIC WORSHIP. 89

so preserve him, and Thy Holy Spirit so govern his heart, that he may in such sort execute his office, that Thy religion may be purely maintained, manners reformed, and sin punished,[r] according to the precise rule of Thy holy Word.

    r 1 Tim. 2.
    1 Pet. 2.

And for that we be all members of the mystical body of Christ Jesus,[s] we make our requests unto Thee, O heavenly Father, for all such as are afflicted with any kind of cross or tribulation,[t] as war, plague, famine, sickness, poverty, imprisonment, persecution, banishment, or any other kind of Thy rods, whether it be grief of body or unquietness of mind; that it would please Thee to give them patience and constancy till Thou send them full deliverance [out] of all their troubles.[u]

    s Rom. xii.
    1 Cor. 12.
    t James 5.
    u 2 Cor. 1.
    Heb. 13.

And finally, O Lord God, most merciful Father, we most humbly beseech Thee to show Thy great mercy upon our brethren who are persecuted, cast in prison, and daily condemned to death for the testimony of Thy truth:[w] And though they be utterly destitute of all man's aid,[x] yet let Thy sweet comfort never depart from them, but so inflame their hearts with Thy Holy Spirit, that they may boldly and cheerfully abide such trial[y] as Thy godly wisdom shall appoint;[z] so that at length, as well by their death as by their life,[a] the kingdom of Thy Son Jesus Christ may increase and shine through all the world: In whose name we make our humble petitions unto Thee, as He hath taught us, saying, *Our Father, &c.*

    w Rom. 8.
    Ps. 44.
    Heb. 13.
    x John 16.
    y 1 Pet. 1.
    z Acts 2.
    Mat. 10.
    Luke 21.
    a Rom. 14.

ALMIGHTY and everliving God, vouchsafe, we beseech Thee, to grant us perfect continuance in Thy* lively faith, augmenting the same

    * Or *the.*

in us daily,[b] till we grow to the full measure of our perfection in Christ,[c] whereof we make our Confession, saying, *I believe in God the Father Almighty, &c.*

[b] Luke 17.
[c] Eph. 4.

Then the people sing a Psalm, which ended, the Minister pronounceth one of these blessings, and so the Congregation departeth.

THE Lord bless us and save us, the Lord make His face to shine upon us, and be merciful unto us; the Lord turn His countenance towards us, and grant us His peace.[d]

[d] Num. 6.

THE grace of our Lord Jesus Christ, the love of God, and the communion of the Holy Ghost, be with us all.[e] So be it.

[e] 2 Cor. 13.

It shall not be necessary for the Minister daily to repeat all these things before mentioned, but, beginning with some manner of confession, to proceed to the Sermon, which ended, he either useth the Prayer for all Estates *before mentioned, or else prayeth, as the Spirit of God shall move his heart, framing the same according to the time and matter which he hath entreated of. And if there shall be at any time any present plague, famine, pestilence, war, or suchlike, which be evident tokens of God's wrath, as it is our part to acknowledge our sins to be the occasion thereof, so are we appointed by the Scriptures to give ourselves to mourning, fasting, and prayer, as the means to turn away God's heavy displeasure.[f] Therefore it shall be convenient, that the Minister at such time do not only admonish the people thereof, but also use*

[f] Deut. 30.
2 Sam. 24.
1 Kings 8.
Ezra 9.
Neh. 9.
Dan. 9.

PUBLIC PRAYERS. 91

some Form of Prayer, according as the present necessity requireth, to the which he may appoint, by a common consent, some several day after the Sermon, weekly to be observed.

These [two] prayers following are used in the French Church of Geneva. The first serveth for Sunday after the Sermon, and the other that followeth is said upon Wednesday, which is the day of Common Prayer.

Another Manner of Prayer after the Sermon.

ALMIGHTY GOD and heavenly Father, since Thou hast promised to grant our requests, which we shall make unto Thee in the name of our Lord Jesus Christ, Thy well-beloved Son; and we are also taught by Him and His Apostle to assemble ourselves in His name, promising that He will be amongst us, and make intercession for us unto Thee, for the obtaining of all such things, as we shall agree upon here on earth : we therefore (having first Thy commandment to pray for such as Thou hast appointed rulers and governors over us, and also for all things needful, both for Thy people and for all sorts of men ; forasmuch as our faith is grounded on Thy holy Word and promises, and that we are here gathered together before Thy face, and in the name of Thy Son our Lord Jesus), we, I say, make our earnest supplication unto Thee our most merciful God and bountiful Father, that for Jesus Christ's sake, our only Saviour and Mediator, it would please Thee, of Thine infinite mercy, freely to pardon our offences, and in such sort to draw and lift up our hearts and affections towards Thee, that our requests may both proceed of a fervent mind, and also be agreeable unto Thy most blessed will and pleasure, which is only to be accepted.

(.) We beseech Thee, therefore, O heavenly Father, as touching all Princes and Rulers, unto whom Thou hast committed the administration of [Thy] justice, and namely, as touching the excellent estate of the King's* Majesty, and all his honourable Council, with the rest of the Magistrates and Commons of the Realm; that it would please Thee to grant him Thy Holy Spirit, and increase the same from time to time in him, that he may with a pure faith acknowledge Jesus Christ Thine only Son our Lord, to be King of all kings and Governor of all governors, even as Thou hast given all power unto Him both in heaven and on earth; and so give himself wholly to serve Him, and to advance His Kingdom in his dominions (ruling by Thy Word his subjects, who are Thy creatures and the sheep of Thy pasture), that we, being maintained in peace and tranquillity, both here and everywhere, may serve Thee in all holiness and virtue; and finally, being delivered from all fear of enemies, may render thanks unto Thee all the days of our life.

We beseech Thee also, most dear Father and Saviour, for all such as Thou hast appointed Ministers unto Thy faithful people, and to whom Thou hast committed the charge of souls, and the ministry of Thy holy Gospel, that it would please Thee so to guide them with Thy Holy Spirit, that they

* The name of the reigning sovereign is mentioned in some editions.

may be found faithful and zealous of Thy glory, directing always their whole study unto this end, that the poor sheep which be gone astray out of the flock may be sought out and brought again unto the Lord Jesus, who is the Chief Shepherd and Head of all Bishops, to the intent they may from day to day grow and increase in Him unto all righteousness and holiness: and on the other part, that it would please Thee to deliver all Thy Churches from the danger of ravening wolves, and from hirelings, who seek their own ambition and profit, and not the setting forth of Thy glory only, and the safeguard of Thy flock.

Moreover, we make our prayers unto Thee, O Lord God, most merciful Father, for all men in general, that as Thou wilt be known to be the Saviour of all the world, by the redemption purchased by Thine only Son Jesus Christ, even so that such as have been hitherto held captive in darkness and ignorance for lack of the knowledge of Thy Gospel, may, through the preaching thereof, and the clear light of Thy Holy Spirit, be brought into the right way of salvation, which is to know that Thou art only very God, and that He whom Thou hast sent is Jesus Christ: likewise, that they whom Thou hast already endued with Thy grace, and illuminated their hearts with the knowledge of Thy Word, may continually increase in godliness, and be plenteously enriched with spiritual benefits, so that we may altogether worship Thee, both with heart and mouth, and render due honour and service unto Christ our Master, King, and Lawgiver.

In like manner, O Lord of all true comfort, we

commend unto Thee in our prayers all such persons as Thou hast visited and chastised by Thy Cross and tribulation, all such people as Thou hast punished with pestilence, war, or famine, and all other persons afflicted with poverty, imprisonment, sickness, banishment, or any like bodily adversity, or hast otherwise troubled and afflicted in spirit: that it would please Thee to make them perceive Thy fatherly affection toward them—that is, that these crosses be chastisings for their amendment, to the intent that they should unfeignedly turn unto Thee, and so, by cleaving unto Thee, might receive full comfort, and be delivered from all manner of evil. But especially, we commend unto Thy divine protection all such who are under the tyranny of Antichrist, and both lack this food of life, and have not liberty to call upon Thy name in open assembly, chiefly our poor brethren who are imprisoned and persecuted by the enemies of Thy Gospel, that it would please Thee, O Father of consolations, to strengthen them by the power of Thy Holy Spirit, in such sort as they never shrink back, but that they may constantly persevere in Thy holy vocation, and so to succour and assist them as Thou knowest to be most expedient, comforting them in their afflictions, maintaining them in Thy safeguard against the rage of wolves, and increasing in them the gifts of Thy Spirit, that they may glorify Thee their Lord God, both in their life and in their death.

Finally, O Lord God, most dear Father, we beseech Thee to grant unto us also, who are here gathered together in the name of Thy Son Jesus, to hear His Word preached,* that we may acknowledge truly and without hypocrisy, in how miserable a state of perdition we are by nature, and how worthily we procure unto ourselves everlasting damnation, heaping up from time to time Thy grievous punishments toward us, through our wicked and sinful life, to the end, that (seeing there remaineth no spark of goodness in our nature, and that there is nothing in us, as touching our first creation, and that which we receive of our parents, meet to enjoy the heritage of God's kingdom) we may wholly render up ourselves with all our hearts, with an assured confidence unto Thy dearly beloved Son Jesus, our Lord, our only Saviour and Redeemer, to the intent that He, dwelling in us, may mortify our old man, that is to say, our sinful affections; and that we may be renewed unto a more godly life, whereby Thy holy name (as it is worthy of all honour) may be advanced and magnified throughout the world, and in all places: likewise, that Thou mayest have the tuition and governance over us, and that we may learn daily more and more to humble and submit ourselves unto Thy Majesty, in such sort that Thou mayest be counted King and Governor over all, guiding Thy people with the sceptre of Thy Word, and by the virtue of Thy Holy Spirit, to the confusion of Thine enemies, through the might of Thy truth and righteousness; so that by this means, all power and height which withstand Thy glory may be continually thrown down and abolished, until such time as the full and perfect face of Thy Kingdom shall appear, when Thou shalt show Thyself in judgment in the person of

* If the Lord's Supper be administered, there is here added this clause, *And to celebrate His holy Supper.*

Hallowed be Thy name.

Thy Kingdom come.

Thy Son: whereby also we, with the rest of Thy creatures, may render unto Thee perfect and true obedience, even as Thy heavenly angels do apply themselves only to the performing of Thy com- mandments, so that Thine only will may be ful- filled without any contradiction, and that every man may bend himself to serve and please Thee, renouncing their own wills, with all the affections and desires of the flesh. Grant us also, good Lord, that we, thus walking in the love and dread of Thy holy name, may be nourished through Thy goodness, and that we may receive at Thy hands all things expedient and necessary for us, and so use Thy gifts peaceably and quietly, to this end, that when we see that Thou hast care of us, we may the more effectuously acknowledge Thee to be our Father, looking for all good gifts at Thine hand, and by withdrawing and pulling back all our vain confidence from creatures, may set it wholly upon Thee, and so rest only in Thy most bounti- ful mercy. And forasmuch as while we continue here in this transitory life, we are so miserable, so frail, and so much inclined unto sin, that we fall continually and swerve from the right way of Thy commandments; we beseech Thee, pardon us our innumerable offences, whereby we are in danger of Thy judgment and condemnation, and forgive us so freely, that death and sin may hereafter have no title against us, neither lay unto our charge the wicked root of sin which doth evermore remain in us, but grant that by Thy commandment we may forget the wrongs which others do unto us, and instead of seeking vengeance, may procure the wealth of our enemies. And forasmuch as of our-

Marginal notes:
Thy will be done in earth, as it is in heaven.
Give us this day our daily bread.
And forgive us our tres- passes, as we forgive them that trespass against us.

PUBLIC PRAYERS. 97

selves we are so weak, that we are not able to stand upright one minute of an hour, and also that we are so belaid and assaulted evermore with such a multitude of so dangerous enemies, that the devil, the world, sin, and our own concupiscences, do never leave off to fight against us: let it be Thy good pleasure to strengthen us with Thy Holy Spirit, and to arm us with Thy grace, that thereby we may be able constantly to withstand all temptations, and to persevere in this spiritual battle against sin, until such time as we shall obtain the full victory, and so at length may triumphantly rejoice in Thy Kingdom, with our Captain and Governor Jesus Christ our Lord.

And lead us not into temptation, but deliver us from evil.

This prayer following is used to be said after the Sermon on the day which is appointed for Common Prayer: and it is very proper for our estate and time, to move us to true repentance, and to turn back God's sharp rods which yet threaten us.

Another Prayer.

GOD ALMIGHTY, and heavenly Father, we acknowledge in our consciences and confess, as the truth is, that we are not worthy to lift up our eyes unto heaven, much less meet to come into Thy presence, and to be bold to think that Thou wilt hear our prayers, if Thou have respect to that which is in us; for our consciences accuse us, and our own sins do bear witness against us; yea, and we know that Thou art a righteous Judge, who dost not count sinners righteous, but punishest the faults of such as transgress Thy commandments. Therefore, O Lord, when we consider our whole life, we are confounded in our own hearts, and cannot choose but be beaten down, and, as it were, despair, even as though we were already swallowed up in the deep gulf of death. Notwithstanding, most merciful Lord, since it hath pleased Thee of Thine infinite mercy, to command us to call upon Thee for help, even from the deep bottom of hell; and that the more lack and default we feel in ourselves, so much the rather we should have recourse unto Thy Sovereign bounty: since also Thou hast promised to hear and accept our requests and supplications, without having any respect to our worthiness, but only in the name and for the merits of our Lord Jesus Christ, whom alone Thou hast appointed to be our Intercessor and Advocate; we humble ourselves before Thee, renouncing all vain confidence in man's help, and cleave only to Thy mercy, and with full confidence call upon Thine holy name, to obtain pardon for our sins.

First, O Lord, besides the innumerable benefits which Thou dost universally bestow upon all men on earth, Thou hast given us such special graces, that it is not possible for us to rehearse them, no, nor sufficiently to conceive them in our minds. As, namely, it hath pleased Thee to call us to the knowledge of Thine holy Gospel, drawing us out of the miserable bondage of the devil, whose slaves we were, and delivering us from most cursed idolatry and wicked superstition, wherein we were plunged, to bring us into the light of Thy truth.

Notwithstanding, such is our obstinacy and unkindness, that not only we forget those Thy benefits, which we have received at Thy bountiful hands, but have gone astray from Thee, and have turned ourselves from Thy Law, to go after our own concupiscences and lusts, and neither have given worthy honour and due obedience to Thine holy Word, neither have advanced Thy glory as our duty required. And although Thou hast not ceased continually to admonish us most faithfully by Thy Word, yet we have not given ear to Thy fatherly admonition. Wherefore, O Lord, we have sinned and have grievously offended against Thee, so that shame and confusion appertaineth unto us: and we acknowledge that we are altogether guilty before Thy judgment, and that if Thou wouldest entreat us according to our demerits, we could look for none other than death and everlasting damnation. For although we would go about to clear and excuse ourselves, yet our own conscience would accuse us, and our wickedness would appear before Thee to condemn us. And in very deed, O Lord, we see by the corrections which Thou hast already used towards us, that we have given Thee great occasion to be displeased with us; for seeing that Thou art a just and upright Judge, it cannot be without cause that Thou punishest Thy people, wherefore forasmuch as we have felt Thy stripes, we acknowledge that we have justly stirred up Thy displeasure against us, yea, and yet we see Thine hand lifted up to beat us afresh: for the rods and weapons wherewith Thou art accustomed to execute Thy vengeance are already in Thine hand, and the threatenings of

Thy wrath, which Thou usest against the wicked sinners, be in full readiness.

Now, though Thou shouldest punish us much more grievously than Thou hast hitherto done, and that whereas we have received one stripe, Thou wouldest give us an hundred; yea, if Thou wouldest make the curses of Thine Old Testament which came then upon Thy people Israel to fall upon us, we confess that Thou shouldest do therein very righteously, and we cannot deny but we have fully deserved the same.

Yet, Lord, forsomuch as Thou art our Father, and we be but earth and slime: seeing Thou art our Maker, and we the workmanship of Thine hands: since Thou art our Pastor and we Thy flock: seeing also that Thou art our Redeemer, and we are the people whom Thou hast bought: finally, because Thou art our God, and we Thy chosen heritage; suffer not Thine anger so to kindle against us, that Thou shouldest punish us in Thy wrath, neither remember our wickedness, to the end to take vengeance thereof, but rather chastise us gently, according to Thy mercy.

Truth it is, O Lord, that our misdeeds have inflamed Thy wrath against us, yet, considering that we call upon Thy name, and bear Thy mark and badge, maintain rather the work that Thou hast begun in us by Thy free grace, to the end that all the world may know that Thou art our God and Saviour. Thou knowest that such as be dead in grave, and whom Thou hast destroyed and brought to confusion, will not set forth Thy praise, but the heavy souls, and comfortless, the humble hearts, the consciences oppressed and laden with the grievous burden of their sins, and therefore thirst after Thy grace, they shall set forth Thy glory and praise.

Thy people of Israel oftentimes provoked Thee to anger through their wickedness, whereupon Thou didst, as right required, punish them; but so soon as they acknowledged their offences and returned to Thee, Thou didst receive them always to mercy; and were their enormities and sins never so grievous, yet for Thy covenant's sake, which Thou hadst made with Thy servants Abraham, Isaac, and Jacob, Thou hast always withdrawn from them the rods and curses which were prepared for them, in such sort that Thou didst never refuse to hear their prayers.

We have obtained, by Thy goodness, a far more excellent covenant which we may allege; that is, the covenant which Thou first madest and establishest by the hand of Jesus Christ our Saviour, and was also by Thy divine providence written with His blood, and sealed with His death and passion.

Therefore, O Lord, we, renouncing ourselves and all vain confidence in man's help, have our only refuge to this Thy most blessed covenant, whereby our Lord Jesus, through the offering up of His body in sacrifice, hath reconciled us unto Thee. Behold [us] therefore, O Lord, in the face of Thy Christ, and not in us, that by His intercession Thy wrath may be appeased, and that the bright beams of Thy countenance may shine upon us to our great comfort and assured salvation; and from this time forward vouchsafe to receive us under Thy holy tuition, and govern us with Thy holy

Spirit, whereby we may be regenerate anew unto a far better life.

So that Thy name may be sanctified: Thy Kingdom come: Thy will be done on earth, as it is in heaven: Give us this day our daily bread: And forgive us our debts, even as we forgive our debtors: And lead us not into temptation, but deliver us from evil: For Thine is the kingdom, and the power, and the glory, for ever and ever. Amen.

And albeit we are most unworthy in our own selves to open our mouths, and to entreat Thee in our necessities, yet forasmuch as it hath pleased Thee to command us to pray one for another, we make our humble prayers unto Thee, for our poor brethren and members, whom Thou dost visit and chastise with Thy rods and corrections, most instantly desiring Thee to turn away Thine anger from them. Remember, O Lord, we beseech Thee, that they are Thy children, as we are: and though they have offended Thy Majesty, yet that it would please Thee not to cease to proceed in Thine accustomed bounty and mercy, which Thou hast promised should evermore continue towards all Thine Elect. Vouchsafe therefore, good Lord, to extend Thy pity upon all Thy Churches, and towards all Thy people, whom Thou dost now chastise either with pestilence or war or suchlike Thine accustomed rods, whether it be by sickness, prison, or poverty, or any other affliction of conscience and mind: that it would please Thee to comfort them as Thou knowest to be most expedient for them, so that Thy rods may be instructions for them to assure them of Thy favour, and for their amendment, when Thou shalt give them

PUBLIC PRAYERS. 103

constancy and patience; and also assuage and stay Thy corrections, and so at length, by delivering them from all their troubles, give them most ample occasion to rejoice in Thy mercy, and to praise Thy holy name: chiefly that Thou wouldest, O Lord, have compassion as well on all, as on every one of them, that employ themselves for the maintenance of Thy truth: strengthen them, O Lord, with an invincible constancy: defend them, and assist them in all things and everywhere, overthrow the crafty practices and conspiracies of their enemies and Thine: bridle their rage, and let their bold enterprises which they undertake against Thee and the members of Thy Son, turn to their own confusion: and suffer not Thy kingdom of Christians to be utterly desolate, neither permit that the remembrance of Thy holy name be clean abolished in earth, nor that they among whom it hath pleased Thee to have Thy praises celebrated, be destroyed and brought to nought, and that the Turks, Pagans, Papists, and other Infidels might boast themselves thereby, and blaspheme Thy name.*

> * To this the Minister addeth that part which is in the former prayer marked thus (.), p. 92.

A Prayer used in the Churches of Scotland, in the time of their Persecution by the Frenchmen: but principally when the Lord's Table was [or is] to be ministered.

ETERNAL and ever-living God, Father of our Lord Jesus Christ, we Thy creatures and the workmanship of Thine own hands, sometime dead by sin, and thrall to Satan by means of the same, but now of Thy mere mercy called to liberty and life by the preaching of Thy Gospel, do take upon us this boldness (not of ourselves, but of the commandment of Thy dear Son, our Lord Jesus Christ) to pour forth before Thee the petitions and complaints of our troubled hearts, oppressed with fear and wounded with sorrow. True it is, O Lord, that we are not worthy to appear in Thy presence, by the reason of our manifold offences, neither yet are we worthy to obtain any comfort at Thy hands, for any righteousness that is in us. But seeing, O Lord, that to turn back from Thee, and not to call for Thy support in the time of our trouble, it is the entrance to death, and the plain way to desperation : we therefore, confounded in ourselves (as the people that on all sides are assaulted with sorrows), do present ourselves before Thy Majesty, as our Sovereign Captain and only Redeemer Jesus Christ hath commanded us, in whose name and for whose obedience we humbly crave of Thee remission of our former iniquities, as well committed in matters of religion, as in our lives and conversation. The examples of others that have called unto Thee in their like necessities, give unto us hope that Thou wilt not reject us, neither yet suffer us for ever to be confounded. ' Thy people Israel did oftentimes decline from Thy laws, and did follow the vanity of superstition and idolatry, and oftentimes didst Thou correct and sharply punish them, but Thou didst never utterly despise them, when in their miseries unfeignedly they turned unto Thee. Thy Church of the Jews were sinners, O Lord, and the most part of the same did consent unto the death of Thy dear Son our Lord Jesus Christ; and yet didst not Thou despise their prayers, when in the time of their grievous persecution they called for Thy support. O Lord, Thou hast promised no less to us than Thou hast performed to them, and therefore take we boldness at Thine own commandment, and by the promise of our Lord Jesus Christ, most humbly to crave of Thee, that as it hath pleased Thy mercy, partly to remove our ignorance and blindness by the light of Thy blessed Evangel, that so it may please Thee to continue the same light with us, till that Thou deliver us from all calamity and trouble. And for this purpose, O Lord, let it please Thee to thrust out faithful workmen in this Thy harvest, within this Realm of Scotland, to the which, after so long darkness of Papistry and superstition, Thou hast offered the truth of Thine Evangel in all pureness and simplicity: continue this Thy grace with us, O Lord, and purge this Realm from all false teachers, from dumb dogs, dissembling hypocrites, cruel wolves, and all such as show themselves enemies to Thy true religion.*(.)

But now, O Lord, the dangers which appear, and the trouble which increaseth by the cruel tyranny of forsworn strangers, compelleth us to complain before the throne of Thy mercy, and to crave of Thee protection and defence against their most unjust persecution. That nation, O Lord, for whose pleasure, and for defence of whom we have offended Thy Majesty and violated our faith, oft breaking the leagues of unity and concord which our Kings and Governors have contracted with our neighbours; that nation, O Lord, for whose alliance our fathers and predecessors have

* Here may be added the prayers for Magistrates as before, p. 92. These prayers following were first used when both the Kings of France were living.

shed their blood, and we (whom by tyranny they oppress) have oft sustained the hazard of battle; that nation, finally, to whom always we have been faithful, now, after their long-practised deceit, by manifest tyranny do seek our destruction. Worthily and justly mayest Thou, O Lord, give us to be slaves unto such tyrants, because for the maintenance of their friendship we have not feared to break our solemn oaths made unto others, to the great dishonour of Thy holy name: and therefore justly mayest Thou punish us by the same nation, for whose pleasure we feared not to offend Thy divine Majesty. In Thy presence, O Lord, we lay for ourselves no kind of excuse, but for Thy dear Son Jesus Christ's sake we cry for mercy, pardon and grace. Thou knowest, O Lord, that their crafty wits in many things have abused our simplicity: for under pretence of the maintenance of our liberty, they have sought and have found the way (unless Thou alone confound their counsels) to bring us in [to] their perpetual bondage. And now the rather, O Lord, do they seek our destruction, because we have refused that Roman Antichrist, whose kingdom they defend in daily shedding the blood of Thy saints. In us, O Lord, there is no strength, no wisdom, no number nor judgment to withstand their force, their craft, their multitude, and diligence: and therefore look Thou upon us, O Lord, according to Thy mercy.

Behold how mercifully God hath broken the yoke of our servitude.

Behold the tyranny used against our poor brethren and sisters, and have Thou respect to that despiteful blasphemy which incessantly They spue forth against Thine eternal truth. Thou hast assisted Thy Church even from the beginning, and for the deliverance of the same Thou hast plagued the cruel persecutors from time to time.

Thy hand drowned Pharaoh: Thy sword devoured Amalek: Thy power repulsed the pride of Sennacherib: And Thine angel so plagued Herod, that worms and lice were punishers of his pride. O Lord, Thou remainest one for ever, Thy nature is unchangeable, Thou canst not but hate cruelty, pride, oppression, and murder, which now the men whom we never offended pretend against us: Yea further, by all means they seek to banish from this Realm Thy dear Son our Lord Jesus Christ, the true preaching of His Word, and faithful ministers of the same, and by tyranny they pretend to maintain most abominable idolatry, and the pomp of that Roman Antichrist. Look Thou, therefore, upon us, O Lord, in the multitude of Thy mercies, stretch out Thine arm and declare Thyself protector of Thy truth, repress the pride, and daunt Thou the fury of these cruel persecutors: suffer them never so to prevail against us, that the brightness of Thy Word be extinguished within this Realm; but whatsoever Thou hast appointed in Thine eternal counsel to become of our bodies, yet we most humbly beseech Thee for Jesus Christ Thy Son's sake, so to maintain the purity of Thy Gospel within this Realm, that we and our posterity may enjoy the fruition thereof, to the praise and glory of Thy holy name, and to our everlasting comfort. And this we most effectuously desire of Thy mercy, by the merits and intercession of our Lord Jesus Christ: To Whom, with Thee and the Holy Ghost, be all honour, glory, praise, and benediction, now and ever. Amen.

PUBLIC PRAYERS.

This is added so oft as the Lord's Table is ministered.

Now last, O Lord, we that be here assembled to celebrate the Supper of Thy dear Son our Lord Jesus Christ, who did not only once offer His body and shed His blood upon the cross for our full redemption, but also, to keep us in recent memory of that His so great a benefit, provided that His body and blood should be given to us to the nourishment of our souls; we, I say, that presently are assembled to be partakers of that His most holy Table, most humbly do beseech Thee to grant us grace, that in sincerity of heart, in true faith, and with ardent and unfeigned zeal, we may receive of Him so great a benefit; to wit, that fruitfully we may possess His body and His blood, yea Jesus Christ Himself, very God and very Man, who is that heavenly bread which giveth life unto the world. Give us grace, O Father, so to eat His flesh and so to drink His blood, that hereafter we live no more in ourselves, and according to our corrupt nature, but that He may live in us, to conduct and guide us to that most blessed life that abideth for ever. Grant unto us, O heavenly Father, so to celebrate this day the blessed memory of Thy dear Son, that we may be assured of Thy favour and grace towards us. Let our faith be so exercised, that not only we may feel the increase of the same, but also that the clear confession thereof, with the good works proceeding of it, may appear before men to the praise and glory of Thy holy name, who art God everlasting, blessed for ever. So be it.

A THANKSGIVING UNTO GOD

After our Deliverance from the Tyranny of the Frenchmen, with Prayers made for the Continuance of the Peace betwixt the Realms of England and Scotland.

NOW, Lord, seeing that we enjoy comfort both in body and spirit, by reason of this quietness of Thy mercy granted unto us, after our most desperate troubles, in the which we appeared uttrely to have been overwhelmed, we praise and glorify Thy mercy and goodness, who piteously looked upon us when we in our own selves were utterly confounded. But seeing, O Lord, that to receive benefits at Thy hands, and not to be thankful for the same, is nothing else but a seal against us in the day of judgment, we most humbly beseech Thee to grant us hearts so mindful of the calamities past, that we continually may fear to provoke Thy justice to punish us with the like or worse plagues. And seeing that when we by our own power were altogether unable to have freed ourselves from the tyranny of strangers, and from the bondage and thraldom pretended against us, Thou of Thine especial goodness didst move the hearts of our neighbours (of whom we had deserved no such favour) to take upon them the common burden with us, and for our deliverance not only to spend the lives of many, but also to hazard the estate and tranquillity of their Realm and Commonwealth: grant unto us, O Lord, that with such reverence we may remember Thy benefits received, that after this in our default, we never enter into hostility against the Realm and nation of England. Suffer us never, O Lord, to fall to that ingratitude and detestable unthankfulness, that we should seek the destruction and death of those whom Thou hast made instruments to deliver us from the tyranny of merciless strangers. Dissipate Thou the counsels of such as deceitfully travail to stir the hearts of the inhabitants of either Realm against the other. Let their malicious practices be their own confusion; and grant Thou of Thy mercy, that love, concord, and tranquillity may continue and increase amongst the inhabitants of this Isle, even to the coming of our Lord Jesus Christ, by whose glorious Gospel Thou of Thy mercy dost call us both to unity, peace, and Christian concord, the full perfection whereof we shall possess in the fulness of thy Kingdom, when all offences shall be removed, iniquity shall be suppressed, and Thy chosen children be fully endued with that perfect glory, in the which now our Lord Jesus reigneth: To Whom, with Thee and the Holy Ghost, be all honour, praise, and glory, now and ever. So be it.

A Prayer used in the Assemblies of the Church as well Particular as General.

ETERNAL and ever-living God, Father of our Lord Jesus Christ, Thou that of Thine infinite goodness hast chosen to Thyself a Church, unto the which ever from the fall of man Thou hast manifested Thyself, first, by Thine own voice to Adam; next to Abraham and his seed, then to all Israel, by the publication of Thy holy law; and last by sending of Thine only Son our Lord Jesus Christ, the great Angel of Thy counsel, into this world, and clad with our nature, to teach unto us Thy holy will, and to put an end to all revelations and prophecies, who also elected to Himself Apostles, to whom, after His resurrection, He gave commandment to publish and preach His Evangel to all Realms and nations, promising to be with them even to the end of the world; yea, and moreover, that wheresoever two or three were gathered together in His name, that He would be there in the midst of them, not only to instruct and teach them, but also to ratify and confirm such things as they shall pronounce or decree by Thy Word. Seeing, O Lord, that this hath been Thy love and Fatherly care towards Thy Church, that not only Thou plantest it, rulest and guidest the chosen in the same by Thy holy Spirit and blessed Word, but also, that when the external face of the same is polluted, and the visible body falleth to corruption, then Thou of Thy mercies providest that it may be purged and restored again to the former purity, as well in doctrine as in manners: whereof Thou hast given sufficient document from age to age, but especially now, O Lord, after this public defection from Thy truth and blessed ordinance, which our fathers and we have seen in that Roman Antichrist, and in his usurped authority. Now I mean, O Lord, Thou hast revealed Thyself and Thy beloved Son Jesus Christ clearly to the world again, by the true preaching of Thy blessed Evangel, which also of

Thy mercy is offered unto us within this Realm of Scotland, and of the same Thy mercy hast made us ministers, and burdened us with a charge within Thy Church. But, O Lord, when we consider the multitude of enemies that oppose themselves unto Thy truth, the practices of Satan, and the power of those that resist Thy kingdom, together with our own weakness, few in number, and manifold imperfections, we cannot but fear the sudden taking away of this Thy great benefit: and therefore, destitute of all worldly comfort, we have refuge to Thine only mercy and grace, most humbly beseeching Thee, for Christ Jesus Thy Son's sake, to oppose Thine own power to the pride of our enemies, who cease not to blaspheme Thine eternal truth.

Give unto us, O Lord, that presently are assembled in Thy name, such abundance of Thy Holy Spirit, that we may see those things that shall be expedient for the advancement of Thy glory, in the midst of this perverse and stubborn generation. Give us grace, O Lord, that, universally amongst ourselves, we may agree in the unity of true doctrine. Preserve us from damnable errors, and grant unto us such purity and cleanness of life that we be not slanderous to Thy blessed Gospel. Bless Thou so our weak labours, that the fruits of the same may redound to the praise of Thy holy name, to the profit of this present generation, and of the posterity to come, through Jesus Christ our Lord, to Whom, with Thee and the Holy Ghost, be all honour and praise, now and ever. Amen.

A Prayer to be used when God threateneth His Judgment.

O LORD our God, Father everlasting and full of compassion, hear from the heavens our prayers and supplications, which from our sorrowful hearts and wounded consciences we pour forth presently before Thy Majesty. Thou hast, O Lord, in the multitude of Thy mercies, not only created us reasonable creatures, but also, of Thine inestimable goodness, hast sent the great Angel of the Covenant, our Lord Jesus Christ, to redeem us, by whom Thy wrath is taken away, the law is satisfied, and the power of death, of hell, and of Satan is broken. Moreover when, as we lay in the shadow of death, and the fearful darkness of the soul, which was brought in by that man of perdition, the Antichrist and his supporters, conspired enemies to Thy Son our Lord Jesus, Thou madest the light of Thy Gospel to shine amongst us in such abundance, that no nation or country hath the lamp of Thy truth, showing the way to life everlasting, so clearly shining amongst them. With these benefits spiritual, it pleaseth Thee of the same goodness to continue temporal blessings: for whose eyes have not seen Thy mighty arm fighting for us? whose heart is so blinded that it cannot perceive in all our afflictions Thy wonderful deliverance? who cannot but confess that always we were covered under Thy shadow? Thou wast our hope, our fortress, and our God, Thou coveredst us under Thy wings, and we were sure under Thy feathers. But, alas, O Lord, the consideration of Thy benefits is a matter of sorrow to our wounded consciences: for the multitude of Thy blessings convict us of the more fearful unthankfulness. In such a light, what is among us but works of darkness? and so this Thy great and inestimable kindness, with unkindness have we recompensed again. Thou gently hast called us, and yet dost call on us, but who did hear? Thou threatenedst, but who did tremble? Thou punishedst, but we would not receive correction. A fire appeareth presently to be kindled in Thy wrath, but where is the repentance amongst us to slacken it? O Lord, we know the dumb and insensible elements of the world admonish us of our great unthankfulness, the heavy face of the heavens, the unnatural dealings on the earth, the contagion and infection of the air, threaten Thy judgments. Those creatures Thou hast formed for man's comfort, but mighty art Thou, who turnest that to the discomfort and hurt of them who repine against Thee, which otherwise should have been comfortable. Besides all these things, we clearly see the enemies of Thy truth raging against Thy Church, to the judgment of man like to prevail. Yea, further, Lord, Satan taking upon him the shape of an angel of light, is in this corrupt age most busy to shake the foundation of all true religion, that he may involve again the blind world in fearful darkness. These Thy judgments, O Thou righteous Judge of the world, are hid from the eyes of them whom the god of this world hath darkened. But, O Lord, when we consider them we must tremble, and when we behold them we must stoop and confess that we have offended Thy Majesty. O Lord, we dare not be bold altogether to crave that Thou wilt not correct; for we understand that by external afflictions and corrections, as certain means and bitter medicine, Thou healest the wounds and sores of the inward man. Yet, Lord, correct us in Thy mercy, and not in Thy fierce wrath, lest peradventure we be bruised into powder: when as the fire departeth from Thy presence, and is kindled in Thine indignation, separate us from the number of those above whose heads Thy righteous judgments do hang, and the sword of Thy vengeance threateneth eternal destruction: And to this end and purpose create in us new hearts, give unto us the spirit of unfeigned repentance, work in us a sorrowing for our sins, a detestation and hatred of the same, together with a love unto righteousness, that we, being not conformable to the wicked world, but making Thy revealed will a rule to lead our life by, may offer ourselves up in a lively sacrifice unto Thee, consecrating unto Thy glory body and soul, and all the actions of the same. Preserve us, good Lord, from the fearful thraldom of conscience and bondage of idolatry: continue the light of Thy glorious Gospel amongst us: repress the pride of them who seek to have the candlestick removed and the shining light extinguished. Purge this country, by such means as Thou knowest to serve best for Thine own glory, of murder, fornication, adultery, incest, oppression, sacrilege, and such other like abominations, which have defiled Thine inheritance. Grant us thankful hearts for Thy benefits and manifold blessings poured upon us, for the which also open our mouths to sound Thy praises, and offer the sacrifice of thanksgiving, wherein Thou dost delight. Arm us with Thy power to strive against Satan, against the flesh, against the world, and against all those things which drive us away from Thine obedience; that, walking in Thy paths, and obeying Thy blessed ordinances, we may so end our lives in the sanctification of Thy name, that at last we may attain to that blessed immortality, and that crown of glory prepared for Thine elect in Jesus Christ the King of glory and God of immortality, in whose name we crave most humbly these Thy graces to be poured upon us most miserable sinners; and further, as Thy wisdom knoweth to be necessary for us, and for Thy Church universal dispersed upon the face of the whole earth, praying unto Thee with all humility and submission of minds, as we are taught and commanded to pray, saying, *Our Father which art in heaven, &c.*

A Prayer in time of Affliction.

JUST and righteous art Thou, O dreadful and most high God, holy in all Thy works and most just in all Thy judgments, yea even then when as Thou punishest in greatest severity. We have before, O Lord, felt Thy heavy hand upon us: and when we cried upon Thee in our calamities and afflictions most mercifully Thou inclinedst Thine ears unto us. But, alas, O Lord, we have not answered in our lives, glorifying Thy holy name, as Thou answeredst us when we called in our distress, but did return unto our wonted sin, and so provoked Thee through our misdeeds unto displeasure: And therefore hast Thou most justly turned Thyself to punish us again in bringing amongst us this noisome and destroying plague, according to the threatening of Thy law, because we have not made our fruit of Thy former corrections. Our repentance, O Lord, hath been like the dew that suddenly vanisheth away: yea, the great multitude abide darkened in their hearts through their own pride, and walking in the lusts of their own hearts, securely contemning Thy blessed ordinances: for who hath mourned for the universal corruption of this blind age? or ceased the murderer from his murder? the oppressor from his oppression? the deceitful man from his deceit? the contemner of Thy word from his contempt? and the licentious liver from his licentiousness? Yea, Lord, where could the man be found that sought not himself, albeit with the hurt of others and defacing of Thy glory? So universally did and presently doth that root of all evil, covetousness, reign throughout this whole country. Yea, Lord, they to whom Thou grantest worldly blessings in greatest abundance, have been and are possessed with this unclean spirit of avarice: the more Thou gavest, the more insatiably thirsted they to have, and ceased not till they did spoil Thee of Thine own patrimony: and yet in this matter they will not know themselves to sin and offend Thy majesty. Therefore cannot Thy justice longer spare, but it must punish and strike, as Thou threatenest in Thy holy law. Now we know, Lord, that Thy judgments commonly begin at Thine own house, and therefore hast Thou begun for to correct us, albeit yet in Thy mercy, and not in greatest severity. Wherefore, good Lord, either in the multitude of Thy mercies remove this bitter cup away from us, or else grant us Thy grace patiently and obediently so to drink the same, as given out of Thine own hand for our amendment. We acknowledge, O Lord, that afflictions are molestuous, noisome, and hard to be borne with of frail flesh, but Christ Jesus hath suffered heavier torments for us, and we have deserved more than we sustain, who so oft have merited the very hells. If it please Thy majesty to continue our punishment, and double our stripes, then let it please Thee in like manner to enlarge our patience, and make our corporal afflictions serve to our humiliation, invocation of Thy name, and obedience to Thy holy ordinances. Or if of a fatherly pity it shall please Thee to be content with this gentle correction, let the calm appear after this present tempest, that in respect of both the one and the other we may glorify Thee, in that first Thou hast corrected to amendment, lest we should have slept in sin to our destruction; and, secondly, that Thou hast taken away the bitterness of our affliction with the sweetness of Thy comfortable deliverance, in the first having respect to the necessity, and in the last to our infirmity. But, Lord, again we know, albeit Thy judgments thus begin at Thine own house, and they of Thy family appear only to be beaten of Thee, yet the wicked shall not escape, but they shall drink the dregs of the cup of Thine indignation: let it be they escape the famine, the pestilence shall apprehend them; if they escape the pestilence, the sword shall devour them; if they shall not fall by the edge of the sword, Thou art able to make any of Thy smallest and least creatures to be a stumblingblock before their feet, whereat, albeit they reach their heads above the clouds, they shall fall most fearfully. But, O Lord, now it is Thine own inheritance for the which we sigh and groan before Thy Majesty: look upon it therefore from the heavens, and be merciful to Thy people: let Thine anger and Thy wrath be turned away from us, and make Thy face to shine lovingly upon Thine own sanctuary. O Lord, hear: O Lord, forgive: O Lord, consider; grant our requests for Thine own sake, O our God, and that in the name of Thine only begotten Son, Jesus Christ, our only Saviour and Mediator, in whose name we pray unto Thee as we are taught, saying, *Our Father, &c.*

A Prayer for the King.

O LORD JESUS CHRIST, most high, most mighty, King of kings, Lord of lords, the only Ruler of princes, the very Son of God, on whose right hand sitting, dost from Thy throne behold all the dwellers upon earth: with most lowly hearts we beseech Thee, vouchsafe with favourable regard to behold our most gracious Sovereign Lord, King JAMES the Sixth,* and so replenish him with the grace of Thy Holy Spirit, that he always may incline to Thy will, and walk in Thy way. Keep him far off from ignorance, but through Thy gift let prudence and knowledge

* Later copies have "CHARLES, by Thy grace, our King's Majesty, together with his Queen, and their happy offspring."

always abound in his royal heart. So instruct him, O Lord Jesus, reigning over us on earth, that his humane Majesty always may obey Thy Divine Majesty in fear and dread. Indue him plentifully with heavenly gifts : grant him in health and wealth long to live : heap glory and honour upon him : glad him with the joy of Thy countenance : so strengthen him that he may vanquish and overcome all his and our foes, and be dread and feared of all the enemies of this his Realm. Amen.

THE MANNER

OF THE

ADMINISTRATION

OF

THE LORD'S SUPPER.

The day when the Lord's Supper is ministered, which is commonly used once a-month, or so oft as the Congregation shall think expedient, the Minister useth to say as follows:—

LET us mark, dear brethren, and consider how Jesus Christ did ordain unto us His holy Supper, according as St Paul maketh rehearsal in the eleventh chapter of the First Epistle to the Corinthians, saying, "I have received of the Lord that which I have delivered unto you, to wit, That the Lord Jesus, the same night that He was betrayed, took bread; and when He had given thanks, He brake it, saying, Take ye, eat ye; this is my body, which is broken for you: do ye this in remembrance of Me. Likewise after Supper, He took the cup, saying, This cup is the New Testament, or Covenant, in my blood; do ye this, so oft as ye shall drink thereof, in remembrance of Me:

For as oft as ye shall eat this bread, and drink of this cup, ye shall declare the Lord's death until His coming. Therefore, whosoever shall eat this bread, and drink of the cup of the Lord, unworthily, he shall be guilty of the body and blood of the Lord. Then see that every man prove and try himself, and so let him eat of this bread, and drink of this cup; for whosoever eateth or drinketh unworthily, he eateth and drinketh his own damnation, for not having due regard and consideration of the Lord's body."

This done, the Minister proceedeth to the Exhortation.

DEARLY beloved in the Lord, forasmuch as we be now assembled to celebrate the Holy Communion of the body and blood of our Saviour Christ, let us consider these words of St Paul, how he exhorteth all persons diligently to try and examine themselves before they presume to eat of that bread, and to drink of that cup; for as the benefit is great, if, with a true penitent heart and lively faith, we receive that holy Sacrament (for then we spiritually eat the flesh of Christ and drink His blood, then we dwell in Christ, and Christ in us, we be one with Christ, and Christ with us*a*), so is the danger great if we receive the same unworthily, for then we be guilty of the body and blood of Christ our Saviour, we eat and drink our own damnation, not considering the Lord's body, we kindle God's wrath against us, and provoke Him to plague us with divers diseases and sundry kinds of death.

a John 6.

And therefore, in the name and authority of the eternal God, and of His Son Jesus Christ, I excommunicate from this Table all blasphemers of God, all idolaters, all murderers, all adulterers, all that be in malice or envy; all disobedient persons to father or mother, Princes or Magistrates, Pastors or Preachers; all thieves and deceivers of their neighbours ; and, finally, all such as live a life directly fighting against the will of God :*b* charging them, as they will answer in the presence of Him who is the righteous Judge, that they presume not to profane this most holy Table. And yet this I pronounce not, to seclude any penitent person, how grievous soever his sins before have been, so that he feel in his heart unfeigned repentance for the same ;*c* but only such as continue in sin without repentance. Neither yet is this pronounced against such as aspire to a greater perfection than they can in this present life attain unto: for, albeit we feel in ourselves much frailty and wretchedness, as that we have not our faith so perfect and constant as we ought, being many times ready to distrust God's goodness through our corrupt nature; and also that we are not so thoroughly given to serve God, neither have so fervent a zeal to set forth His glory, as our duty requireth, feeling still such rebellion in ourselves, that we have need daily to fight against the lusts of our flesh ;*d* yet nevertheless, seeing that our Lord hath dealt thus mercifully with us, that He hath printed His Gospel in our hearts,*e* so that we are preserved from falling into desperation and misbelief; and seeing also that He hath endued us with a will and desire to renounce and with-

b Gal. 5.

c Mat. 3.

d Rom. 7. Gal. 5.

e Heb. 8. Jer. 31. Ezek. 36.

stand our own affections, with a longing for His righteousness and the keeping of His commandments,[f] we may be now right well assured, that those defaults and manifold imperfections in us shall be no hindrance at all against us, to cause Him not to accept and impute us as worthy to come to His spiritual Table: For the end of our coming thither is not to make protestation that we are upright or just in our lives;[g] but contrariwise, we come to seek our life and perfection in Jesus Christ, acknowledging in the mean time that we of ourselves be the children of wrath and damnation.[h]

Let us consider, then, that this Sacrament is a singular medicine for all poor sick creatures, a comfortable help to weak souls, and that our Lord requireth no other worthiness on our part, but that we unfeignedly acknowledge our naughtiness and imperfection. Then, to the end that we may be worthy partakers of His merits, and most comfortable benefits, which is the true eating of His flesh and drinking of His blood,[i] let us not suffer our minds to wander about the consideration of these earthly and corruptible things (which we see present to our eyes, and feel with our hands), to seek Christ bodily present in them, as if He were enclosed in the bread and wine, or as if these elements were turned and changed into the substance of His flesh and blood; for the only way to dispose our souls to receive nourishment, relief, and quickening of His substance, is to lift up our minds by faith above all things worldly and sensible, and thereby to enter into heaven, that we may find and receive Christ, where He dwelleth undoubtedly very God

f Rom. 7. Phil. 3.

g Luke 18.

h Eph. 2. Luke 5.

Transubstantiation, transelementation, transmutation, and transformation, as the Papists use them, are the doctrine of devils.
i John 6.

The true eating of Christ in the Sacrament.

and very Man. in the incomprehensible glory of
His Father,*k* to Whom be all praise, honour. and
glory, now and ever. Amen.

*The exhortation ended, the Minister cometh down
from the Pulpit, and sitteth at the Table, every man
and woman in like wise taking their place as occasion best serveth: Then he taketh bread, and giveth
thanks,*^l *either in these words following, or like in
effect:—*

k 1 Tim. 6.

l Mat. 26.
Mark 14.
Luke 22.
1 Cor. 11.

O FATHER of mercy, and God of all consolation, seeing all creatures do acknowledge and confess Thee as Governor and Lord,"' it becometh us. the workmanship of Thine own hands, at all times to reverence and magnify Thy godly Majesty, first, for that Thou hast created us to Thine own image and similitude," but chiefly because Thou hast delivered us from that everlasting death and damnation into the which Satan drew mankind, by the mean of sin,^o from the bondage whereof neither man nor angel was able to make us free,^p but Thou, O Lord, rich in mercy, and infinite in goodness, hast provided our redemption to stand in Thine only and well beloved Son,^q whom of very love Thou didst give to be made Man like unto us, in all things, sin except,^r that in His body He might receive the punishment of our transgression,^s by His death to make satisfaction to Thy justice,^t and by His resurrection to destroy him that was author of death,^u and so to bring again life to the world,^w from which all the whole offspring of Adam most justly was exiled.^x

O Lord, we acknowledge that no creature is

m Rev. 5.

n Gen. 1.

o Eph. 2.
Gal. 1.
Gen. 3.

p Acts 4.
Heb. 1.

q Rev. 5.

r John 3.
Heb. 2, 4.
s 1 Pet. 2.
Isa. 53.
t Mat. 3, 17.
Rom. 5.
u Heb. 2.
w John 6.

x Gen 3.
Rom. 5.

able to comprehend the length and breadth, the deepness and height of that Thy most excellent love,^y which moved Thee to show mercy where none was deserved,^z to promise and give life where death had gotten the victory,^a to receive us into Thy grace when we could do nothing but rebel against Thy justice.^b O Lord, the blind dulness of our corrupt nature will not suffer us sufficiently to weigh those Thy most ample benefits;^c yet, nevertheless, at the commandment of Jesus Christ our Lord, we present ourselves to this His Table, which He hath left to be used in remembrance of His death, until His coming again,^d to declare and witness before the world,^e that by Him alone we have received liberty and life,^f that by Him alone Thou dost acknowledge us Thy children and heirs,^g that by Him alone we have entrance to the throne of Thy grace,^h that by Him alone we are possessed in our spiritual Kingdom, to eat and drink at His Table,ⁱ with whom we have our conversation presently in heaven,^k and by whom our bodies shall be raised up again from the dust,^l and shall be placed with Him in that endless joy, which Thou, O Father of mercy, hast prepared for Thine Elect before the foundation of the world was laid.^m And these most inestimable benefits we acknowledge and confess to have received of Thy free mercy and grace, by Thine only beloved Son Jesus Christ,ⁿ for the which therefore, we Thy congregation, moved by Thy Holy Spirit,^o render Thee all thanks, praise, and glory, for ever and ever. Amen.

This done, the Minister breaketh the bread, and

THE LORD'S SUPPER.

delivereth it to the people, who distribute and divide the same amongst themselves, according to our Saviour Christ's commandment, and likewise giveth the cup: ᵖ *During the which time some place of the Scriptures is read, which doth lively set forth the death of Christ, to the intent that our eyes and senses may not only be occupied in these outward signs of bread and wine, which are called the visible word, but that our hearts and minds also may be fully fixed in the contemplation of the Lord's death, which is by this holy Sacrament represented. And after this action is done, he giveth thanks, saying,*

p Mat. 26.
Mark 14.
Luke 22.
1 Cor. 10, 11.

MOST merciful Father, we render to Thee all praise, thanks, and glory, for that it hath pleased Thee of Thy great mercies to grant unto us, miserable sinners, so excellent a gift and treasure, as to receive us into the fellowship and company of Thy dear Son Jesus Christ our Lord,ᵠ whom Thou deliveredst to death for us,ʳ and hast given Him unto us as a necessary food and nourishment unto everlasting life.ˢ And now we beseech [Thee] also, O heavenly Father, to grant us this request, that Thou never suffer us to become so unkind as to forget so worthy benefits, but rather imprint and fasten them sure in our hearts, that we may grow and increase daily more and more in true faith,ᵗ which continually is exercised in all manner of good works,ᵘ and so much the rather, O Lord, confirm us in these perilous days and rages of Satan,ʷ that we may constantly stand and continue in the confession of the same, to the advancement of Thy glory,ˣ who art God over all things, blessed for ever. So be it.

q 1 Cor. 10.
r Rom. 4.
s John 6.

t Luke 17.
u Gal. 5.

w 1 Tim. 4.
Eph. 5.
2 Peter 3.
x Mat. 5.
1 Pet. 2.

The action thus ended, the people sing the 103d *Psalm,* My soul give laud, &c., *or some other of thanksgiving, which ended, one of the blessings before mentioned* * *is recited, and so they rise from the Table and depart.*

* Page 90.

TO THE READER.

Why this Order is observed rather than any other.

IF so be that any would marvel why we follow rather this Order than any other, in the administration of this Sacrament, let him diligently consider that first of all we utterly renounce the error of the Papists; secondly, we restore unto the Sacrament his [its] own substance, and to Christ His proper place. And as for the words of the Lord's Supper, we rehearse them, not because they should change the substance of the bread or wine, or that the repetition thereof, with the intent of the sacrificer, should make the Sacrament, as the Papists falsely believe, but they are read and pronounced to teach us how to behave ourselves in that action, and that Christ might witness unto our faith, as it were with His own mouth, that He hath ordained these signs to our spiritual use and comfort; we do, first, therefore, examine ourselves, according to St Paul's rule, and prepare our minds, that we may be worthy partakers of so high mysteries; then, taking bread, we give thanks, break and distribute it as Christ our Saviour hath taught us; finally, the administration ended, we give thanks again according to His example, so that without His word and warrant there is nothing in this holy action attempted.

THE
FORM OF MARRIAGE.

After the banns or contract hath been published three several days in the Congregation (to the intent that if any person have interest or title to either of the parties, they may have sufficient time to make their challenge), the parties assemble at the beginning of the sermon, and the Minister at time convenient saith as followeth:—

The Exhortation.

DEARLY beloved brethren, we are here gathered together in the sight of God, and in the face of His Congregation, to knit and join these parties together in the honourable estate of Matrimony,[a] which was instituted and authorised by God Himself in Paradise, man being then in the estate of innocency:[b] For what time God made heaven and earth, and all that is in them, and had created and also fashioned man after His own similitude and likeness, unto whom He gave rule and lordship over all the beasts of the earth, fishes of the sea, and fowls of the air, He said, "It is not good that man live alone; let us make him an helper like unto himself;" and God brought a fast sleep upon him, and took one of his ribs, and shaped Heva thereof, giving us there-

[a] Heb. 13. Prov. 18.

[b] Gen. 2.

THE FORM OF

by to understand, that man and wife are one body, one flesh, and one blood;[c] signifying also unto us, the mystical union that is between Christ and His Church,[d] for the which cause man leaveth his father and mother, and taketh him to his wife, to keep company with her,[e] whom also we ought to love, even as our Saviour loveth His Church;[f] that is to say, His elect and faithful Congregation,[g] for the which He gave His life.[h]

And semblably [in like manner] also it is the wife's duty to study to please and obey her husband, serving him in all things that be godly and honest,[i] for she is in subjection, and under the governance of her husband, so long as they continue both alive.[k]

And this holy Marriage, being a thing most honourable, is of such virtue and force, that thereby the husband hath no more right or power over his own body, but the wife; and likewise the wife hath no more right or power over her own body, but the husband;[l] forasmuch as God hath so knit them together in this mutual society, to the procreation of children, that they should bring them up in the fear of the Lord, and to the increase of Christ's Kingdom.[m]

Wherefore, they that be thus coupled together by God cannot be severed, or put apart, unless it be for a season, with the consent of both parties, to the end to give themselves the more fervently to fasting and prayer, giving diligent heed, in the mean time, that their too long being apart be not a snare to bring them into the danger of Satan through incontinency:[n] And therefore, to avoid fornication, every man ought to have his own wife, and every

Margin notes:
c In Hebrew man is called *Isch*, and the woman *Ischa*, whereby is well expressed the natural affinity betwixt the man and his wife.
d Eph. 5.
e Gen. 2. Mat. 19. Mark 10. Eph. 5. 1 Pet. 3
f Eph. 5. Col. 3.
g John 17.
h Rom. 5. Heb. 9. 1 Pet. 3.
i Eph. 5. Col. 3. 1 Pet. 3. 1 Cor. 11. 1 Tim. 2.
k Rom. 7. 1 Cor. 7. Mat. 19.
l 1 Cor. 7.
m Eph. 6.
n 1 Cor. 7.

MARRIAGE.

woman her own husband,^o so that so many as cannot live chaste, are bound by the commandment of God to marry,^p that thereby the holy Temple of God, which is our bodies, may be kept pure and undefiled: For since our bodies are now become the very members of Jesus Christ, how horrible and detestable a thing is it, to make them the members of an harlot!^q Every one ought therefore to keep his vessel in all pureness and holiness,^r for whosoever polluteth and defileth the Temple of God, him will God destroy.^s

o 1 Cor. 7.
p 1 Cor. 7. Mat. 19.
q 1 Cor. 6. 2 Cor. 6. 1 Pet. 2.
r 1 Thes. 4. Rom. 6. Eph. 5.
s 1 Cor. 3.

Here the Minister speaketh to the parties that are there present to be married, in this wise:—

I REQUIRE and charge you, as you will answer at the day of judgment, when the secrets of all hearts shall be disclosed,^t that if either of you do know any impediment why you may not be lawfully joined together in Matrimony, that ye confess it: For be ye well assured, that so many as be coupled otherwise than God's Word doth allow, are not joined together by God, neither is their Matrimony lawful.

t 1 Cor. 4. Rom. 2. Mat. 7.

If no impediment be by them declared, then the Minister saith to the whole Congregation:—

I TAKE you to witness that be here present, beseeching you all to have good remembrance hereof; and, moreover, if there be any of you which knoweth that either of these Parties be contracted to any other, or knoweth any other lawful impediment, let them now make declaration thereof.

If no cause be alleged, the Minister proceedeth, saying [to the Man],

^u Col. 3.
1 Pet. 3.
Mat. 19.
Eph. 5.
Mal. 2..

FORASMUCH as no man speaketh against this thing, You N. shall protest here before God and His holy Congregation, that you have taken, and are now contented to have M. here present for your lawful Wife, promising to keep her, to love and intreat her in all things, according to the duty of a faithful Husband,^u forsaking all other during her life; and briefly, to live in an holy conversation with her, keeping faith and truth in all points, according as the Word of God and His holy Gospel doth command.

The Answer.

Even so I take her, before God, and in the presence of this His Congregation.

The Minister to the Spouse also saith,

^x Eph. 5.
Col. 3.
1 Tim. 2.
1 Pet. 3.

YOU M. shall protest here before the face of God, and in presence of this His Congregation, that ye have taken, and are now contented to have N. here present for your lawful Husband, promising to him subjection and obedience,^x forsaking all other during his life; and, finally, to live in an holy conversation with him, keeping faith and truth in all points, as God's Word doth prescribe.

The Answer.

Even so I take him, before God, and in the presence of this His Congregation.

MARRIAGE.

The Minister then sayeth [to the Parties married],

GIVE diligent ear then to the Gospel, that ye may understand how our Lord would have this holy contract kept and observed, and how sure and fast a knot it is, which may in no wise be loosed, according as we are taught in the nineteenth chapter of St Matthew's Gospel.

"The Pharisees came unto Christ to tempt Him, and to grope His mind, saying, Is it lawful for a man to put away his wife for every light cause? He answered, saying, Have ye not read, that He which created man at the beginning made them male and female, saying, For this thing shall man leave father and mother, and cleave unto his wife, and they twain shall be one flesh, so that they are no more two, but one flesh? Let no man therefore put asunder that which God hath coupled together."

IF ye believe assuredly these words, which our Lord and Saviour did speak (according as ye have heard them now rehearsed out of the holy Gospel), then may ye be certain, that God hath even so knit you together in this holy estate of Wedlock; wherefore, apply yourselves to live together in Godly love, in Christian peace, and good example, ever holding fast the band of charity without any breach, keeping faith and truth the one to the other, even as God's Word doth appoint.

Then the Minister commendeth them to God, in this or such like sort:—

The Lord sanctify and bless you, the Lord pour the riches of His grace upon you, that ye may please Him, and live together in holy love to your lives' end. So be it.

Then is sung the 128*th Psalm*, Blessed are they that fear the Lord, *&c., or some other appertaining to the same purpose.*

THE
ORDER OF BAPTISM.

First note, that forasmuch as it is not permitted by God's Word, that women should preach or minister the Sacraments, and it is evident that the Sacraments are not ordained of God to be used in private corners, as charms, or sorceries, but left to the Congregation, and necessarily annexed to God's Word as seals of the same:* Therefore, the infant that is to be baptised shall be brought to the Church on the day appointed to Common Prayer and Preaching, accompanied with the Father and Godfather, so that, after the Sermon, the child being presented to the Minister, he demandeth this question:—

DO ye here present this child to be baptised, earnestly desiring that he may be ingrafted in the mystical body of Jesus Christ?

The Answer.

Yea, we require the same.

The Minister proceedeth.

THEN let us consider, dearly beloved, how Almighty God hath not only made us His children by adoption, and received us into the

* The transgression of God's ordinance is called iniquity and idolatry, and is compared to witchcraft and sorcery, 1 Sam. 15. How dangerous also it is to enterprise anything rashly, or without the warrant of God's Word, the examples of Saul, 1 Sam. 13; of Uzzah, 2 Sam. 6; of Uzziah, 2 Chron. 26; and of Nadab and Abihu, Lev. 10, sufficiently do warn us.

fellowship of His Church,[a] but also hath promised that He will be our God, and the God of our children, unto the thousandth generation :[b] Which thing, as He confirmed to His people of the Old Testament by the Sacrament of Circumcision,[c] so hath He also renewed the same to us in His New Testament, by the Sacrament of Baptism ;[d] doing us thereby to wit, that our infants appertain to Him by covenant, and therefore ought not to be defrauded of those holy signs and badges whereby His children are known from Infidels and Pagans.[e]

Neither is it requisite that all those that receive this Sacrament have the use of understanding and faith, but chiefly that they be contained under the name of God's people, so that the remission of sins in the blood of Christ Jesus doth appertain unto them by God's promise,[f] which thing is most evident by St Paul, who pronounceth the children begotten and born (either of the parents being faithful) to be *clean* and *holy*.[g] Also our Saviour Christ admitteth children to His presence, embracing and blessing them.[h] Which testimonies of the Holy Ghost assure us, that infants be of the number of God's people, and that remission of sins doth also appertain to them in Christ. Therefore, without injury they cannot be debarred from the common sign of God's children. And yet is not this outward action of such necessity, that the lack thereof should be hurtful to their salvation,[i] if that, prevented by death, they may not conveniently be presented to the Church.[k] But we (having respect to that obedience which Christians owe to the voice and ordinance of Christ

[a] Rom. 8.
Gal. 4.
Eph. 1, 2.
[b] Gen. 17.
Ex. 20.
Deut. 9.
Isa. 56.
[c] Gen. 17.
Rom. 4.
[d] Col. 2.
Rom. 6.
Gal. 3.
Acts 2.

[e] Acts 10.

[f] Acts 2.

[g] 1 Cor. 7.

[h] Mat. 19.
Mark 10.
Luke 18.
Ps. 22.

[i] Rom. 4.
Gal. 3.
James 2.
Gen. 15.
[k] Gen. 17.
Lev. 12.

BAPTISM. 137

Jesus, who commanded to preach and baptise all without exception *l*) do judge them only unworthy of any fellowship with Him, who contemptuously refuse such ordinary means, as His wisdom hath appointed to the instruction of our dull senses.

Furthermore, it is evident that Baptism was ordained to be ministered in the element of water, to teach us, that like as water outwardly doth wash away the filth of the body, so inwardly doth the virtue of Christ's blood purge our souls from that corruption and deadly poison,*m* wherewith by nature we were infected,*n* whose venomous dregs, although they continue in this our flesh,*o* yet by the merits of His death are not imputed unto us,*p* because the justice of Jesus Christ is made ours by Baptism; *q* not that we think any such virtue or power to be included in the visible water, or outward action, for many have been baptised, and yet never inwardly purged;*r* but that our Saviour Christ, who commanded Baptism to be ministered, will, by the power of His Holy Spirit, effectually work in the hearts of His Elect, in time convenient, all that is meant and signified by the same.*s* And this the Scripture calleth our Regeneration, which standeth chiefly in these two points—in mortification, that is to say, a resisting of the rebellious lusts of the flesh, and in newness of life, whereby we continually strive to walk in that pureness and perfection, wherewith we are clad in Baptism.*t*

And although we, in the journey of this life, be encumbered with many enemies, who in the way assail us,*u* yet fight we not without fruit; for this continual battle, which we fight against sin,

l Mat. 28.
Mark 16.

m Mat. 3.
1 Pet. 3.
1 John 5.
1 Cor. 10.
n Eph. 2.
o Rom. 7.
p Rom. 4.
Gal. 3.
Ps. 32.
q Rom. 6.
Gal. 3.

r As Judas, Simon Magus, Hymeneus, Alexander, Philetus.

s Acts 2, 13.

t Eph. 2.
1 Cor. 12.
Rom. 6.
Col. 2.

u 1 Pet. 5.
Luke 22.
Job 1.

death, and hell, is a most infallible argument, that God the Father, mindful of His promise made unto us in Christ Jesus, doth not only give us motions and courage to resist them,[w] but also assurance to overcome, and obtain victory.[x]

Wherefore, dearly beloved, it is not only of necessity that we be once baptised, but also it much profiteth oft to be present at the ministration thereof, that we (being put in mind of the league and covenant made between God and us,[y] that He will be our God, and we His people, He our Father, and we His children[z]) may have occasion as well to try our lives past as our present conversation, and to prove ourselves, whether we stand fast in the faith of God's Elect, or, contrariwise, have strayed from Him, through incredulity and ungodly living,[a] whereof if our consciences do accuse us, yet by hearing the loving promises of our heavenly Father, who calleth all men to mercy, by repentance,[b] we may from henceforth walk more warily in our vocation. Moreover, ye that be fathers and mothers may take hereby most singular comfort to see your children thus received into the bosom of Christ's Congregation, whereby ye are daily admonished, that ye nourish and bring up the children of God's favour and mercy, over whom His fatherly providence watcheth continually.[c]

Which thing, as it ought greatly to rejoice you, knowing that nothing can come unto them without His good pleasure,[d] so ought it to make you diligent and careful to nurture and instruct them in the true knowledge and fear of God,[e] wherein if ye be negligent, ye do not only injury to your own

w Rom. 5.
James 1.
Eph. 6.
1 Pet. v.
x 1 Cor. 15.
Hos. 13.
Heb. 2.
John 16.

y Deut. 6, 11.
Josh. 1.

z Jer. 31.
Heb. 8.

a Eph. 4.
Heb. 13.
Col. 3.

b Ezek. 18.
Acts 11.
2 Pet. 3.
Deut. 4.

c Mat. 18.

d Mat. 10.
Luke 12.

e Deut. 4.
Eph. 6.

BAPTISM.

children, hiding from them the goodwill and pleasure of Almighty God their Father,*f* but also heap damnation upon yourselves, in suffering His children, bought with the blood of His dear Son, so traitorously, for lack of knowledge, to turn back from Him. Therefore it is your duty, with all diligence to provide that your children, in time convenient, be instructed in all doctrine necessary for a true Christian, chiefly that they be taught to rest upon the justice of Christ Jesus alone, and to abhor and flee all superstition, Papistry, and idolatry.

Finally, to the intent that we may be assured that you, the father and the surety, consent to the performance hereof, declare here before [God, and in] the face of His Congregation, the sum of that Faith wherein ye believe, and will instruct this child.*g*

Then the Father, or in his absence the Godfather, shall rehearse the Articles of his Faith, which done, the Minister expoundeth the same as after followeth.

[An Exposition of the Creed.]

THE Christian Faith, whereof now ye have briefly heard the sum, is commonly divided in [to] Twelve Articles; but that we may the better understand what is contained in the same, we shall divide it into four principal parts. The first shall concern God the Father; the second, Jesus Christ our Lord; the third shall express to us our faith in the Holy Ghost; and the fourth and last shall declare what is our faith concerning the Church, and of the graces of God freely given to the same.

What danger hangeth over those parents who neglect the bringing up of their children in godliness.
f 1 Sam. 2.
2 Kings ii.

The true use of the Catechism, to the execution whereof the Fathers and Godfathers bind themselves.
g Gen. 18.
Deut. 32.

THE ORDER OF

I believe in God the Father Almighty, maker of heaven and earth.

First, of God we confess three things; to wit, that He is our Father, Almighty, maker of heaven and earth. Our Father we call Him, and so by faith believe Him to be, not so much because He hath created us (for that we have common with the rest of creatures, who yet are not called to that honour to have God to them a favourable Father), but we call Him Father by reason of His free adoption, by the which He hath chosen us to life everlasting in Jesus Christ, and this His most singular mercy we prefer to all things, earthly and transitory; for without this there is to mankind no felicity, no comfort, nor final joy; and having this, we are assured that by the same love, by the which He once hath freely chosen us, He shall conduct the whole course of our life, that in the end we shall possess that immortal Kingdom that He hath prepared for His chosen children; for from this fountain of God's free mercy or adoption springeth our vocation, our justification, our continual sanctification, and, finally, our glorification,

h Rom. 8.

as witnesseth the Apostle.[h]

The same God our Father we confess Almighty, not only in respect of that He may do, but in consideration that by His power and godly wisdom are all creatures in heaven and earth, and under the earth, ruled, guided, and kept in that order that His eternal knowledge and will hath appointed them. And that is it which in the third part we do confess, that He is Creator of heaven and earth—that is to say, the heaven and the earth, and the contents thereof, are so in His hand, that there is nothing done without His knowledge, neither yet against His will; but that He ruleth

BAPTISM.

them so, that in the end His godly name shall be glorified in them. And so we confess and believe that neither the devils, nor yet the wicked of the world, have any power to molest or trouble the chosen children of God, but in so far as it pleaseth Him to use them as instruments, either to prove and try our faith and patience, or else to stir us to more fervent invocation of His name, and to continual meditation of that heavenly rest and joy that abideth us after these transitory troubles. And yet shall not this excuse the wicked, because they never look in their iniquity to please God, nor yet to obey His will.

In Jesus Christ we confess two distinct and perfect natures, to wit, the eternal Godhead and the perfect Manhood joined together, so that we confess and believe, that that eternal Word who was from the beginning, by whom all things were created, and yet are conserved and kept in their being, did, in the time appointed in the counsel of His heavenly Father, receive our nature of a Virgin, by operation of the Holy Ghost, so that in His conception we acknowledge and believe that there is nothing but purity and sanctification, yea, even in so much as He is become our brother: For it behoved Him, that should purge others from their sins, to be pure and clean from all spot of sin, even from His conception. *And in Jesus Christ His only Son our Lord.*

Conceived by the Holy Ghost.

And as we confess and believe Him conceived by the Holy Ghost, so do we confess and believe Him to be born of a Virgin, named Mary, of the tribe of Judah, and of the family of David, that the promise of God and the prophecy might be fulfilled, to wit, "That the seed of the woman shall *Born of the Virgin Mary.*

break down the serpent's head,"[i] and that "a Virgin should conceive and bear a child, whose name should be *Emmanuel*, that is to say, *God with us.*"[k]

The name *Jesus*, which signifieth a Saviour, was given unto Him by the Angel,[l] to assure us, that it is He alone that saveth His people from their sins. He is called *Christ*, that is to say, *Anointed*, by reason of the offices given unto Him by God His Father, to wit, that He alone is appointed King, Priest, and Prophet; King, in that, that all power is given to Him in heaven and on earth, so that there is none other but He in heaven, nor on earth, that hath just authority and power to make laws, to bind the consciences of men; neither yet is there any other that may defend our souls from the bondage of sin, nor yet our bodies from the tyranny of man. And this He doth by the power of His Word, by the which He draweth us out of the bondage and slavery of Satan, and maketh us to reign over sin, while that we live and serve our God in righteousness and holiness of our life. A Priest, and that perpetual and everlasting, we confess Him; because that by the sacrifice of His own body, which He once offered up upon the cross, He hath fully satisfied the justice of His Father in our behalf, so that whosoever seeketh any means, besides His death and passion, in heaven or on earth, to reconcile unto them God's favour, they do not only blaspheme, but also, so far as in them is, renounce the fruit and efficacy of that His only one sacrifice. We confess Him to be the only Prophet, who hath revealed unto us the whole will of His Father, in all things appertaining to our salvation. This our Lord Jesus we confess to be the only Son of God, because there is none such by nature but He alone. We confess Him also our Lord, not only by reason we are His creatures, but chiefly because He hath redeemed us by His precious blood, and so hath gotten just dominion over us, as over the people whom He hath delivered from bondage of sin, death, hell, and the devil, and hath made us kings and priests to God His Father.

We further confess and believe, that the same our Lord Jesus was accused before an earthly Judge, Pontius Pilate, under whom, albeit oft and divers times He was pronounced to be innocent, He suffered the death of the cross, hanged upon a tree betwixt two thieves: which death, as it was most cruel and vile before the eyes of men, so was it accursed by the mouth of God Himself, saying, "Cursed is every one that hangeth on a tree." And this kind of death sustained He in our person, because He was appointed of God His Father to be our pledge, and He that should bear the punishment of our transgressions. And so we acknowledge and believe that He hath taken away that curse and malediction that hanged on us, by reason of sin.

He verily died, rendering up His spirit into the hands of His Father, after that He had said, "Father, into Thine hands I commend my spirit." After His death, we confess His body was buried, and that He descended to the hell. But because He was the Author of life, yea, the very life itself, it was impossible that he should be retained under the dolours of death.

Suffered under Pontius Pilate.
Was crucified.

Died, and was buried, and descended into hell.

The third day He rose again from the dead.

And therefore the third day He rose again, victor and conqueror of death and hell, by the which His resurrection, He hath brought life again into the world, which He, by the power of His Holy Spirit, communicateth unto His lively members, so that now unto them corporal death is no death, but an entrance into that blessed life wherein our Head, Jesus Christ, is now entered: for after that He had sufficiently proved His resurrection to His disciples, and unto such as constantly did abide with Him to the death, He

He ascended into heaven, and sitteth on the right hand of God the Father Almighty.

visibly ascended to the heavens, and was taken from the eyes of men, and placed at the right hand of God the Father Almighty, where presently He remaineth in His glory, only Head, only Mediator, and only Advocate for all the members of His body, of which we have most especial comfort, first, for that, that by His ascension the heavens are opened unto us, and an entrance made unto us that boldly we may appear before the throne of our Father's mercy. And, secondarily, that we know that this honour and authority are given to Jesus Christ our Head, in our name, and for our profit and utility: for albeit that in body He now be in the heaven, yet by the power of His Spirit he is present here with us, as well to instruct us, as to comfort and maintain us in all our troubles and adversities, from the which He shall finally deliver His whole Church, and every true member of the same, in that day when He shall visibly appear again, Judge of the quick and the dead.

For this, finally, we confess of our Lord Jesus Christ, that as He was seen visibly to ascend, and

BAPTISM. 145

so left the world, as touching that body that suffered and rose again, so do we constantly believe that He shall come from the right hand of His Father, when all eyes shall see Him, yea, even those that have pierced Him; and then shall He gather as well those that then shall be found alive, as those that before have slept. Separation shall be made betwixt the lambs and the goats,*m* that is to say, betwixt the elect and the reprobate; the one shall hear this joyful voice, "Come, ye the blessed of my Father, possess the Kingdom that is prepared for you before the beginning of the world:" the other shall hear that fearful and irrevocable sentence, "Depart from Me, ye workers of iniquity, to the fire that never shall be quenched." And for this cause, this day in the Scriptures is called, "The day of refreshing,"*n* and "of the revelation of all secrets,"*o* because that then the just shall be delivered from all miseries, and shall be possessed in the fulness of their glory. Contrariwise, the reprobate shall receive judgment, and recompense of all their impiety, be it openly or secretly wrought.

As we constantly believe in God the Father, and in Jesus Christ, as before is said; so we do assuredly believe in the Holy Ghost, whom we confess God equal with the Father and the Son, by whose working and mighty operation our darkness is removed, our eyes spiritually are illuminated, our souls and consciences sprinkled with the blood of Jesus Christ, and we retained in the truth of God, even to our lives' end. And for these causes we understand, that this eternal Spirit, proceeding from the Father and the Son,

From thence He shall come to judge the quick and the dead.

m Mat. 25.

n Acts 3.
o Rom. ii.
1 Cor. iv.

I believe in the Holy Ghost.

hath in the Scriptures divers names; sometimes called water, by reason of His purgation, and giving strength to this our corrupt nature to bring forth good fruit, without whom, this our nature should utterly be barren, yea, it should utterly abound in all wickedness. Sometimes the same Spirit is called fire, by reason of the illumination and burning heat of fire that He kindleth in our hearts: The same Spirit also is called oil or unction, by reason that His working mollifieth the hardness of our hearts, and maketh us receive the print of that image of Jesus Christ, by whom only we are sanctified.

The Holy Catholic Church: the communion of saints.

We constantly believe that there is, was, and shall be, even till the coming of the Lord Jesus, a Church, which is holy and universal; to wit, the Communion of Saints. This Church is holy, because it receiveth free remission of sins, and that by faith only in the blood of Jesus Christ. Secondly, because it being regenerate, it receiveth the Spirit of sanctification and power, to walk in newness of life, and in good works, which God hath prepared for His chosen to walk in. Not that we think the justice of this Church, or of any member of the same, ever was, is, or yet shall be, so full and perfect that it needeth not to stoop under mercy; but that because the imperfections are pardoned, and the justice of Jesus Christ imputed unto such as by true faith cleave unto Him. Which Church we call universal, because it consisteth and standeth of all tongues and nations, yea, of all estates and conditions of men and women, whom of His mercy God calleth from darkness to light, and from the bondage and thral-

BAPTISM.

dom of sin, to His spiritual service and purity of life : unto whom He also communicateth His Holy Spirit, giving unto them one faith, one Head and Sovereign Lord, the Lord Jesus, one Baptism and right use of Sacraments, whose heart also He knitteth together in love and Christian concord.

To this Church, holy and universal, we acknowledge and believe three notable gifts to be granted ; to wit, remission of sins, which by true faith must be obtained in this life ; resurrection of the flesh, which all shall have, albeit not in equal condition, for the reprobate (as before is said) shall rise, but to fearful judgment and condemnation, and the just shall rise to be possessed in glory : and this resurrection shall not be an imagination, or that one body shall rise for another, but every man shall receive in his own body as he hath deserved, be it good or evil. The just shall receive the life everlasting, which is the free gift of God, given and purchased to His chosen, by Jesus Christ our only Head and Mediator : to Whom, with the Father and the Holy Ghost, be all honour, praise, and glory, now and ever. So be it.

The forgiveness of sins.
The resurrection of the body.

And life everlasting.

Then followeth this Prayer.

ALMIGHTY and everlasting God, who of Thine infinite mercy and goodness hast promised unto us that Thou wilt not only be our God, but also the God and Father of our children, we beseech Thee, that as Thou hast vouchsafed to call us to be partakers of this Thy great mercy, in the fellowship of faith,*p* so it may please Thee to sanctify with Thy Spirit,*q* and to receive into the

p Gal. 3.
Phil. 3.
q 1 Pet. 1.
2 Cor. v.
Rom 8.
Eph. 2, 3.

number of Thy children, this Infant, whom we shall baptise according to Thy Word,^r to the end that he, coming to perfect age, may confess Thee only, the true God, and whom Thou hast sent, Jesus Christ,^s and so serve Him, and be profitable unto His Church in the whole course of his life,^t that after his life be ended, he may be brought, as a lively member of His body, unto the full fruition of Thy joys in the heavens,^u where Thy Son, our Saviour Christ, reigneth world without end; in whose Name we pray, as He hath taught us, saying, *Our Father which art, &c.*

r Mat. 28.
Mark 16.
Acts 2.

s Rom. 10.
John 17.
t Rom. 12.
1 Cor. 12.
1 Thes. 5.

u 1 Cor. 2.
Rom. 6.
Tit. 3.

When they have prayed in this sort, the Minister requireth the Child's name, which known, he saith,

N., I baptise thee IN THE NAME OF THE FATHER, OF THE SON, AND OF THE HOLY GHOST.^w

w Mat. 28.

And as he speaketh these words, he taketh water in his hand, and layeth it upon the Child's forehead; which done, he giveth thanks, as followeth :—

FORASMUCH, most holy and merciful Father, as Thou dost not only beautify and bless us with common benefits, like unto the rest of mankind, but also heapest upon us most abundantly, rare and wonderful gifts;^x of duty we lift up our eyes and minds unto Thee, and give Thee most humble thanks for Thine infinite goodness, who hast not only numbered us amongst Thy Saints,^y but also of Thy free mercy dost call our children unto Thee, marking them with this Sacrament, as a singular token and badge of Thy love;

x Eph. 2.
1 Pet. 2.
Hos. 2.

y 1 Pet. 2.
Eph. 2.

BAPTISM. 149

wherefore, most loving Father, though we be not able to deserve this so great a benefit (yea, if Thou wouldest handle us according to our merits, we should suffer the punishment of eternal death and damnation),[z] yet, for Christ's sake, we beseech Thee that Thou wilt confirm this Thy favour more and more towards us, and take this Infant into Thy tuition and defence, whom we offer and present unto Thee, with common supplications, and never suffer him to fall into such unkindness whereby he should lose the force of Baptism,[a] but that he may perceive Thee continually to be his merciful Father, through Thy Holy Spirit working in his heart, by whose divine power he may so prevail against Satan, that in the end, obtaining the victory, he may be exalted into the liberty of Thy Kingdom. So be it.

[z] Rom. 3. Jer. 2. Isa. 40. Luke 17.

[a] 1 Cor. 5.

OF FASTING.

The Superintendents, Ministers, and Commissioners of Churches reformed, within the Realm of Scotland, meeting in the General Assembly at Edinburgh, the 25th day of December 1565 : To all that truly profess the Lord Jesus within the same Realm, or elsewhere, wish grace and mercy from God the Father, and from His only Son our Lord Jesus Christ, with the Holy Spirit.

THE present troubles being somewhat considered, but greater feared shortly to follow, it was thought expedient, dearly beloved in the Lord Jesus, that the whole faithful within this Realm should together, and at one time, prostrate themselves before their God, craving of Him pardon and mercy for the great abuse of His former benefits, and the assistance of His Holy Spirit, by whose mighty operation we may yet convert to our God, that we provoke Him not to take from us the light of His Gospel, which He of His mercy hath caused so clearly of late days to shine within this Realm.

But because that such public supplications require always fasting to be joined therewith, and public fasting craveth certain time, and certain exercises of godliness then to be used with greater straitness than at other times, the whole Assembly, after deliberation, hath appointed the second Sunday of May and the third, next following the date of the said Assembly, to that most necessary exercise (as time now standeth) of public fasting. And further, did require the same to be signified by all Ministers to their people, the Sunday immediately before the said second Sunday of May. But lest that the Papists shall think that now we begin to authorise and praise that which sometimes we have reproved and damned in them, or else that the ignorant, who know not the commodity of this most godly exercise, shall contemn the same, we have thought expedient somewhat to speak to the one and to the other.

And unto the Papists first we say, that as in purity of conscience we have refused their whole abominations, and amongst the rest, that their superstitious and Pharisaical manner of fasting: so, even unto this day, we do continue in the same purpose, boldly affirming that their fasting is no fasting that ever God approved, but that it is a deceiving of the people, and a mere mocking of God, which most evidently will appear, if in thé Scriptures we search what is the right end of fasting, what fasting pleaseth God, and which it is that His soul abhorreth.

Of fasting in the Scriptures we find two sorts, the one private. the other public. The private is that which man or woman doeth in secret, and before their God, for such causes as their own consciences bear record unto them, as David during the time that his son, which was begotten in adultery, was stricken with mortal sickness, fasted, wept, and lay upon the ground, because that in the sickness of the child he did consider God's displeasure against himself, for the removing whereof he fasted, mourned, and prayed, until such time as he saw God's will fulfilled, by the taking away of the child. Privately fasted Hannah, wife to Elkanah, even in the very solemn feasts, during the time of her barrenness. For she wept and ate nothing, but in the bitterness of her heart she prayed unto the Lord; neither ceased she from sorrow and mourning until such time as Eli the high priest concurred with her in prayers, by whose mouth, after that he had heard her pitiful complaint, she received comfort.

Of this fasting speaketh our Master Jesus Christ in these words: "When ye fast, be not sad * as the hypocrites, for they disfigure their faces, that they may seem unto men to fast; but thou, when thou fastest, anoint thine head and wash thy face, that thou seem not unto men to fast, but unto thy Father which seeth in secret, and will reward thee openly." Of the same, no doubt, speaketh the Apostle when he saith, "Defraud not one another, except it be with consent for a time, that ye may give yourselves to fasting and prayer." To this private fasting, which standeth chiefly in a temperate diet, and in pouring forth of our secret thoughts and necessities before God, can be prescribed no certain rule, certain time, nor certain ceremonies, but as the causes and occasions why that exercise is used are diverse (yea, so diverse, that seldom it is that many at once are moved with one cause), so are diet, time, together with all other circumstances required to such fasting, put in the liberty of them that use it. To this fasting we have been faithfully and earnestly exhorted by our preachers, as oft as the Scriptures which they intreated, offered unto them occasion. And we doubt not but the godly within this Realm have used the same as necessity craved, albeit with the Papists we blew no trumpets, to appoint thereto certain days.

The other kind of fasting is public, so called because that it is openly commanded,† sometimes of a Realm, sometimes of a multitude, sometimes of a city, and sometimes of a meaner company, yea, sometimes of particular persons, and yet publicly used, and that for the wealth of a multitude. The causes thereof are also diverse, for sometimes the fear of enemies, sometimes the angry face of God punishing, sometimes His threatening to destroy, sometimes iniquity found out that was not rightly before considered, and sometimes the earnest zeal that some bear for the preservation of God's people, for advancing of His glory, and performing of His work, according to His promise, move men

* *Sour* in early editions.

† *Avowed* in early copies.

ON FASTING.

to public fasting, confession of their sins, and solemn prayers for defence against their enemies, recovering of God's favour, removing of His plagues, preservation of His people, and setting forward of that work which He hath of His mercy promised to finish, as in the probations following evidently shall appear :—

When messengers came to Jehoshaphat, saying, There cometh a great multitude against thee from beyond the sea, out of Aram, that is Syria, &c., Jehoshaphat feared, and set himself to seek the Lord, and proclaimed a fast throughout all Judah. And Judah gathered themselves together, to ask counsel of the Lord : they came even out of all the cities of Judah to inquire of the Lord. And Jehoshaphat stood in the congregation of Judah and Jerusalem, in the house of the Lord, before the new court. And all Judah stood before the Lord with their young ones, their wives, and their children. And Jehoshaphat said, "O Lord God of our fathers, art not Thou God in heaven, and reignest not Thou in all kingdoms of the heathen? And in Thy hand is power and might, and none is able to withstand Thee. Hast not Thou our God cast out the inhabitants of this land before Thy people Israel, and hast given it to the seed of Abraham Thy friend for ever? &c. But now the Amorites and Moabites, and Mount Seir, are come to cast us out of Thy possession. O Lord our God, shalt Thou not judge them? In us there is no strength to stand against the great multitude that cometh against us, neither know we what to do; but unto Thee are our prayers bent," &c. Of this history we have the first cause of public fasting, and the solemnity thereof sufficiently proved. For the fear of enemies compelled Jehoshaphat to seek the Lord ; he, knowing himself burdened with the care of the people, exhorted them to do the same. They from all cities and quarters repaired unto Jerusalem, where, upon an appointed day, the king and the people, yea, wives and children, presented themselves before the Lord, in His holy Temple, opened their necessity, craved His help against that raging multitude, that always was enemy to God's people, and gave open confession of their own weakness, leaning only to the promise and protection of the Omnipotent. Which example we, and every people likewise assaulted, may and ought to follow in every point.

This only excepted, that we are not bound to meet at any one appointed place as they did at Jerusalem. For to no one certain and several place, is that promise made that then was made to the Temple of Jerusalem, which was, that whatsoever, men in their extremity should ask of God in it, God should grant it from His holy habitation in the heaven. Jesus the Messias then looked for, whose presence was sought in the mercy-seat, and betwixt the cherubim, is now entered within the veil, that is, in the heaven, and there abideth only Mediator for us, unto whom, from all the coasts of the earth, we may lift up our hands, direct our prayers, supplications, and complaints, and be assured that they shall be received, in whatsoever place we meet. And yet in time of such public exercises, we would wish that all men and women should repair to such places as their consciences may be best instructed, their faith most edified, repentance most lively stirred up in them, and they by God's Word may be most assured that their just petitions shall not be repelled. Which things cannot be done so lively in secret and private meditation, as they are in public assembly where Christ Jesus is truly preached. And this much shortly for the first cause.

Of the second, to wit, that the angry face of God punishing ought to drive us to public fasting, and to humiliation of our souls before our God, we have two notable examples, the one written in Joshua, who, hearing and understanding that Israel had turned the back before the Canaanites, and the Elders of Israel rent their clothes, fell upon their faces before the Ark of the Lord until the night, and cast dust upon their heads, in sign of their humiliation and dejection. The other is expressed in the book of Judges, where Israel being commanded by God to fight against Benjamin, because that they maintained wicked men that deserved death, lost the first day twenty thousand of their army, and the second day eighteen thousand. At the first loss they were lightly touched, and asked counsel if they should renew the battle, but at the second overthrow, the whole people repaired unto the house of the Lord, sat there, wept before the Lord, and fasted that day until night, for then began they to consider God's angry face against them.

In this last history, there appeareth just cause why the

ON FASTING.

people should have run to the only refuge of God, because that their first army of forty thousand men was utterly destroyed.

But what just occasion had Joshua so lamentably to complain, yea, so boldly, as it were, to accuse God, that He had deceived him in that, that against His promise He had suffered Israel to fall before their enemies? Was the loss of thirty men (no more fell that day in [by] the edge of the sword) so great a matter that he should despair of any better success, that he should accuse God that He had brought them over Jordan, and that he should fear that the whole army of the Lord should be environed about and consumed in the rage of their enemies? Yea, if Israel had only looked no further than to the loss of the forty thousand men, they had been but feeble soldiers, for they had sufficient strength remaining behind. For what were forty thousand in respect of all the tribes of Israel? Nay, nay, dear brethren, it was another thing than the present loss that terrified and feared their consciences, and made them so effeminately (so would flesh judge) to complain, weep, and howl before God, to wit, they saw His angry face against them, they saw His hand fortify their enemies, and to fight against them, whom both He had commanded to fight, and had promised to endue with victory. For every commandment of God to do anything against His enemies, hath included within it a secret promise of His godly assistance, which they found not in the beginning of their enterprises, and therefore they did consider the fierceness of His displeasure, and did tremble, before His angry face, whose mighty hand they found to fight against them; and that was the cause of their grievous complaints and fearful crying before their God. What was the cause that God dealt so strangely with the one and with the other? We may perchance somewhat speak, when that we shall intreat of the fruits of fasting, and of those things that may hold back from us the assistance of God, even when we prepare us to put His commandment in execution.

The third cause of public fasting, is God's threatenings pronounced, either against a multitude, or against a person in particular. Of the former, the example is Nineveh, unto the which Jonah cried, " Yet forty days, and Nineveh shall be destroyed;" which unpleasant tidings coming to the ears of the King, he proclaimed a fast, he humbled his own soul, yea, even in sackcloth, and, sitting in the dust, he straitly commanded reformation of manners in all estates, yea, and that signs of repentance, of terrors, and fear should appear not only in men and women, but also in the brute beasts, from which was all kind of nourishment commanded to be withdrawn, to witness that they feared as well God's judgment to fall upon the creatures that served them in their impiety, as upon themselves that had provoked God to that hot displeasure. Of the other, the example is most notable (most notable we say), because that it fell in a wicked man, to wit, in Ahab, who, by instigation of his wicked wife Jezebel, gave himself to do all iniquity. And yet when that he heard the fearful threatenings of God pronounced by the Prophet Elias against him, against his wife, and house, he rent his royal garments, put on sackcloth, slept therein, fasted, and went bare-footed. What ensued the one and the other, of these we shall hear hereafter.

The fourth cause of public fasting and mourning (for they two must ever be joined) is iniquity descried that was not before rightly considered: the testimony whereof we have in Ezra, after the reduction of the captivity, and that the Temple and the work of the Lord's house was stayed; it was shown unto Ezra that the people of Israel, the Priests, and the Levites were not separated from the people of the Nations, but that they did according to their abominations, for they married unto themselves, and unto their sons, the daughters of the Canaanites, the Perizzites, Hivites, Jebusites, Amorites, Moabites, and Egyptians, so that the holy seed was mixed with profane idolaters; which thing being understood and more deeply considered than it was before, then Ezra saw just cause why the work of the Lord prospered not in their hands.

This considered, we say, Ezra, taking upon him the sin and offence of the whole people, rent his clothes, and pulled forth the hairs of his head and beard, sat as a man desolate of all comfort till the evening sacrifice, and then rising, he bowed his knees, and stretched forth his hands before the Lord, and made a most simple and humble confession of all the enormities that were committed by the people, as well before the captivity as after their returning, and ceased not his lamentable complaint, until such time as a great multitude of men, women, and children, moved by his example, wept vehemently, and promised redress of that present disorder and impiety.

Of the last cause of public fasting, to wit, the zeal that certain persons bear for the preservation of God's people, for advancing of His glory, and performing of His work according to His promise, we have example in Mordecai, Daniel, and in the faithful assembled at Antioch. For when that Mordecai heard of that cruel sentence, which, by the procurement of Haman, was pronounced against his nation ; to wit, that upon a certain appointed day, the Jews in all the provinces of the King Artaxerxes should be destroyed, old and young, men and women, and that their substance should be distributed in prey,—this bloody sentence, we say, being heard, Mordecai rent his clothes, put on sackcloth and ashes, passed forth through the midst of the city, and cried with a great and bitter cry : and, coming to the King's gate, gave knowledge to Esther what cruelty was decreed against the nation of the Jews, willing her to make intercession to the King for the contrary, who, after certain excuses, said, " Go and gather all the Jews that are in Shushan, and fast for me ; eat not, nor drink not, three days and three nights, and I also, and my handmaids, shall likewise fast, although that I should perish." In this we may clearly see, that the zeal that Mordecai had to preserve the people of God, moved not only himself to public fasting, but also Esther the Queen, her maids, and the whole Jews that heard of the murder intended, and moved Esther also to hazard her life, in going unto the King without his commandment.

Of the other, to wit, that the earnest desire that God's servants have, that God will perform His promise, and maintain [the work] that He hath begun, example we have in Daniel, and in the Acts of the Apostles. For Daniel, understanding the number of the years forespoken by the Prophet Jeremiah, that Jerusalem should be waste, to have been ended in the first year of the reign of Darius, turned himself unto God, fasted, humbled himself in sackcloth and ashes, and with unfeigned confession of his own sins, and of the sins of the people, he vehemently prayed, that according to the promises sometimes made by Moses, after rehearsed by the Prophets Isaiah and Jeremiah, He would suddenly send them deliverance, and that He would not delay it for His own name's sake.

When the Gentiles began to be illuminated, and that Antioch had so boldly received the Gospel of Jesus Christ, that the Disciples in it first of all took upon them the name of Christians, the principal men of the same Church, trusting no doubt that the Kingdom of Jesus Christ should further be enlarged, and that the multitude of the Gentiles should be instructed in the right way of salvation, fasted and prayed, and while that they were so exercised, charge was given that Paul and Barnabas should be separated from the rest, to the work whereunto God had called them, &c.

Of these former histories and Scriptures, we may clearly see, for what causes public fasting and general supplications have been made in the Church of God, and ought to be made whensoever the like necessities appear or occasions are offered. Now let us shortly hear what comfort and fruit ensued the same. For the enemy, yea, the murderer, of all godly exercise is desperation; for with what courage can any man with continuance call upon God, if he shall desperately doubt whether God shall accept his prayer or not? How shall he humble himself before His throne? Or to what end shall he confess his offences, if he be not persuaded that there is mercy and goodwill in God to pardon his sins, to accept him in favour, and to grant unto him more than his own heart, in the midst of his dolour, can require or imagine?

True it is, that this venom of desperation is never thoroughly purged from our hearts, so long as we carry this mortal carcass. But yet the constant promises of our God, and the manifold documents of His mercy and help, shown unto men in their greatest extremity, ought to animate us to follow their example, and to hope for the same success that they have gotten above man's expectation. Jehoshaphat, after his humiliation and prayer, obtained the victory without the loss of any of his soldiers, for the Lord raised Ammon and Moab against the inhabitants of Mount Seir, who being utterly destroyed, every one of the enemies of God's people lifted up his sword against another, till that of that

ON FASTING.

godless multitude there was not one left alive. Joshua and the Israelites, after their dejection, were comforted again. Nineveh was preserved, albeit that Jonah had cried destruction; yea, Ahab, notwithstanding all his ungodliness, lost not the fruit of his humiliation, but was recompensed with delay of the uttermost of the plagues during his lifetime. The mourning of Ezra was turned into joy, when that he saw the people willing to obey God, and the work of the house of the Lord go forward. The bitter crying of Mordecai, and the painful fasting of Esther, were abundantly rewarded, when not only the people of God were preserved, but Haman, their mortal enemy, was hanged upon the same gallows that he had prepared for Mordecai. Daniel, after his fasting, confession, and prayer, got most notable revelations and assurance that his people should be delivered, yea, that in all extremities they should be preserved, till that the Messias promised unto them should come, and manifestly show Himself. And the godly of Antioch were not frustrate of their comfort, when they had heard how mightily God had wrought amongst the Gentiles by the ministry of Barnabas and Paul; so that we may boldly conclude, that as God hath never despised the petitions of such as with unfeigned hearts have sought His comfort in their necessities, so He will not send us away empty and void, if with true repentance we seek His face.

If any would ask, in what extremity we find ourselves now to be that heretofore we have not seen, and what are the occasions that should move us now to humble ourselves before our God by public fasting, more than we did in the beginning, when this Gospel was now last offered unto us, for then, by all appearance, we and it in our persons stood in greater danger than we do yet; we answer, that the causes are more than for grief of heart we can express. First, because that in the beginning we had not refused God's graces, but contrariwise with such fervency we received them, that we could bear with no kind of impiety; but for the suppressing of the same we neither had respect to friend, possession, land, or life, but we put all in hazard, that God's truth might be advanced, and idolatry might be suppressed. And therefore did our God, by the mouth of His Messengers, in all our adversities, assure us that our enemies should not prevail against us, but that they should be subdued under us, that our God should be glorified in our example and upright dealing. But now, since that carnal wisdom hath persuaded us to bear with manifest idolatry, and to suffer this Realm which God hath once purged, to be polluted again with that abomination, yea, alas! since that some of us, that God made sometimes instruments to suppress that impiety, have been the chief men to conduct and convey that Idol throughout all the quarters of this Realm, yea, to the houses of them that sometimes detested the Mass as the devil and his service; since that time, we say, we have found the face of our God angry against us, His threatenings have been sharp in the mouths of His Messengers, whom albeit for the time we despised and mocked, yet just experience convicteth us that we were wicked, and that they in threatening us did nothing but the duty of God's true Messengers.

And this is the second cause that moveth us to this public humiliation rather now than in the beginning, to wit, that then we followed God, and not carnal wisdom, and therefore made He few in number fearful to many; fools before the world, to confound the wise; and such as before never had experience in arms, God made so bold and so prosperous in all their enterprises, that the expertest soldiers feared the poor ploughmen; yea, our God fought for us by sea and by land, He moved the hearts of strangers to support us, and to spend their lives for our relief. But now, alas! we see no sign of His former favour: for wisdom or manhood, strength and friends, honour and blood joined with godliness, are fallen before our eyes, to let us understand what shall be our destruction, if in time we turn not to our God, before that His wrath be further kindled. But this is not the end. For men had before hope (or at least some opinion), that God would move the Queen's Majesty's heart to hear the blessed Gospel of Jesus Christ truly preached, and so, consequently, that she would abandon all idolatry and false religion. But now she hath given answer in plain words, That that religion in which she hath been nourished (and that is mere abomination) she will maintain and defend. And in declaration whereof, of late days there is erected a displayed banner against Jesus Christ. For corrupted hypocrites,

ON FASTING.

and such as have been known deceivers of the people, are now authorised to spew out their poison against Jesus Christ, His eternal truth, and true Messengers of the same. That idol the Mass is now again in divers places erected. And what hereof may ensue, yea, or what may we look shall be the end of such unhappy beginnings, we desire the godly deeply to consider.

But let it be granted, that we had not fallen back from our former fervency, that we saw not God's angry face threatening us with more fearful plagues to follow, that the best part of our Nobility were not exiled this Realm, neither yet that our Sovereign were enemy to our religion, that she bear no greater favour to flattering Friars and to corrupted Papists than she doth to our pure Preachers : supposing, we say, that we had none of these foresaid causes to move us (howbeit we have them all, and more, if that we list to remember them), yet is there one which, if it move us not to humiliation, we show ourselves more than insensible. For now is Satan so enraged against Jesus Christ, and so odious is the light of His Gospel unto that Roman Antichrist, that to suppress it in one province, realm, or nation, he thinketh it nothing, unless that in all Europe, the godly, and such as abhor the Papistical impiety, be therewith also utterly destroyed, and so razed from the face of the earth, that no memory of them shall after remain.

If any think that such cruelty cannot fall into the hearts of men, we send them to be resolved of those Fathers of the last Council of Trent, who in one of their sessions have thus concluded :—" All Lutherans, Calvinists, and such as are of the new religion, shall utterly be rooted out. The beginning shall be in France, by conducting of the Catholic King, Philip of Spain, and by some of the Nobility of France; which matter," they say, "put in execution, the whole power of both, together with the Pope's army and force of the Duke of Savoy, and Ferrara, shall assault Geneva, and shall not leave it till they have put it to the sack, saving in it no living creature."

And with the same mercy shall so many of France, as have tasted of the new religion, be served. From thence expedition shall be made against the Germans, to reduce them to the obedience of the Apostolic seat. And so shall they proceed to other realms and nations, never ceasing till that all be rooted out, that will not make homage to that Roman idol. How fearful a beginning this conclusion and determination had, France will remember more ages than one. For how many, above a hundred thousand men, women, babes, virgins, matrons, and aged fathers, suffered, some by sword, some by water, some by fire, and other torments, the very enemies themselves are compelled to acknowledge. And albeit that God of His mercy in part disappointed their cruel enterprises, yet let us not think that their will is changed, or their malice assuaged. No; let us be assured that they abide but opportunity to finish the work, that cruelly against God, against His truth, and the true professors of the same, they have begun. The whisperings whereof are not secret, neither yet the tokens obscure. For the traffic of that dragon, now with the Princes of the earth, his promises and flattering enticements, tend to none other end but to inflame them against Jesus Christ, and against the true professors of His Gospel. For who can think that the Pope, Cardinals, and horned Bishops, will offer the greatest portion of their rents for sustaining of a war, whereof no commodity should redound (as they suppose) to themselves? If any think that we accuse them without cause, let them hear their own words, for this they wrote near the end of the same decree :—

"And to the end that the holy Fathers on their part appear not to be negligent, or unwilling to give their aid and support unto so holy a war, or to spare their own rents and money, have added that the Cardinals shall content themselves of the yearly rent of 5 or 6 thousand ducats, and the richest Bishop of 2 or 3 thousand at the most ; and to give frankly the rest of their revenues to the maintaining of the war, which is made for the extirpation of the Lutherans and Calvinists sect, and for re-establishing of the Roman Church, till such time as the matter be conducted to a good and happy end." If these be not open declarations, in what danger all the faithful stand, if they can bring their cruelty to pass, let very idiots judge. But let us hear their conclusion. "France and Germany," say they, "being by these means so chastised, abased, and brought to the obedience of the holy Roman Church, the Fathers doubt not but time shall provide both counsel and commodity; that the rest of the realms about may be reduced to one flock, and one Apostolic governor and pastor," &c.

By this conclusion we think that the very blind may see what is purposed against the Saints of God in all realms and nations; to wit, destruction with cruelty, or else to make them worship that blasphemous beast, who, being an idol, usurpeth to himself the name of universal Pastor, and being known to be the Man of sin and perdition, will be holden for an Apostolic governor. But some shall say they are yet far from the end of their purpose, and therefore we need not be so fearful, nor so troubled. We answer, The danger may be nearer than we believe; yea, perchance a part of it hath been nearer to our necks than we have considered. But howsoever it be, seeing that God of His mercy hath brought forth to light their cruel and bloody counsel, in which we need not doubt, but still they continue, it becometh us not to be negligent or slothful. But we ought to follow the example of Hezekiah, the King of Judah, who, receiving not only the despiteful answer, but also the blasphemous and threatening letter of Sennacherib, first sent unto the Prophet Isaiah, and pitifully complained of the instant troubles, willing him to make intercession unto God for the remnant that were left. Unto whom, albeit that the Prophet answered comfortably, assuring the King that the enemy should not come so near as to shoot dart or arrow within Jerusalem, yet ceased not the godly King to present himself in the Temple of the Lord, and, as a man despairing of all worldly comfort, spread abroad the letters that proud Sennacherib had sent unto him, and made unto God his most fervent prayer, as in the 37th chapter of the Prophet Isaiah we may read. The enemy had turned back, and God had put a bridle in his nostrils. And so men might have thought, that the King needed not to have been so troubled. But the Spirit of God instructed the heart of His servant to seek help where it was only to be found, and from the hands of God, who only was able to put final end to that tyranny. The example, we say, of this approved servant of God we ought to follow now, when the like destruction is intended against us, yea, not against one realm only, but against all that profess the

Lord Jesus, as before we have heard. Albeit that God of His mercy hath stayed the fury of the Papists for a time, we ought not to think that their malice is changed, neither that such as truly profess the Lord Jesus can be in security, so long as that Babylonian whore hath power to enchant the Princes of the earth. Let us, therefore, understanding that she, being drunken with the blood of the Saints, can never repent of cruelty and murder, use against her the spiritual weapons, to wit, earnest invocation of God's Name, by the which we find the proud tyrants of the earth, in times past, to have been overthrown.

Above all these causes aforesaid, we have yet one that ought not to be omitted; to wit, the body of this Realm hath long enjoyed quietness, while that other nations about us have been severely plagued. What thousands died in the East countries, and in England, of the pestilence, anno 1564, their own confessions bear record; what cruelty hath been executed in France; what towns spoiled, and murder committed, somewhat before we have declared, and more we might, if we had not respect to brevity and time. And what trouble is presently, and long hath been, betwixt Denmark and Sweden, the posterity of that country will after understand.

And in all this time, now six years and more, hath God spared us, so that the public estate hath always remained quiet, except within these few months. Ought not the deep consideration of this move us now to stoop before our God? For have we been spared, because that our rebellion to God is less than is the rebellion of those nations that we have seen punished? If we think so, we are far deceived.

For in so great light of the Gospel, we think that greater disobedience was never shown unto God, nor greater ingratitude unto His Messengers, since the days of the Apostles, than of late years hath been (and yet is) within this Realm. Idolatry is obstinately maintained; whoredom and adultery are but pastimes of the flesh; slaughter and murder are esteemed small sin, if any man have a friend in court; crafty dealing with the simple, deceit, and oppression are counted good conquest (yea, alas! almost universally); partiality in judgment is but interpretation of laws; yea, delaying of justice, what matter is that? What reverence is had to

God's Messengers, and what respect unto the poor, that now so multiply within this Realm (that the like hath seldom been seen)? Though we will cease, the stones will cry, and condemn us; and yet what superfluity, what vanity, what feasting, riotous banqueting have been, and yet are used in court, country, and towns, although the tongues of men dare not speak, yet we think the purses of some do feel, and in their manner complain. If these be not sins that crave plagues from God, we humbly desire men to consider what are the sins that were laid to the charge of Sodom and Gomorrah by the Prophet Ezekiel.

Now, say we, God before our eyes hath punished others, and can He spare us, being more sinful than they were? Nay, He cannot. And therefore there rests nothing unto us but utter destruction, if we unfeignedly turn not unto our God, before that His wrath be further kindled against us. Judgment is begun in His own house, for if within Scotland amongst men of their estate there were to be found equity, justice, temperance, compassion upon the poor, and upright conscience, they did most clearly shine in them whom God before our eyes hath first dejected. Therefore (yet again) we say, that only repentance can save us from plagues more grievous than they have felt, or that we have seen of many years within this Realm.

But now we know that such as neither love God, nor truly fear His judgments—for many Atheists we have, and rank Papists within this Realm*—shall grudge and cry, What new ceremony is this that we now hear of? Wherefore shall we fast? And who hath power to command us so to do? A fig for their fasting; we will fill and stuff our bellies after the old fashion, &c. Let not the godly be offended at the taunts and reproaches of such godless people; but let us tremble before our God, and consider that such hath been the proud contempt of the wicked in all ages before us, as in the Prophets we may read. For Isaiah complaineth, saying, "When the Lord calleth to sackcloth and ashes, there is nothing heard but, Let us eat and drink, kill the fat beasts, and make banquets; let us bring wine in abundance, and more: if we must die, let us depart in joy;" for so they meant when they said, "Let us eat and drink, to-morrow we shall die." But let us consider what answer they receive:

* First edition has— *for more Atheists we have nor consummate Papists within this Realm.*

"As I live, saith the Lord, this your iniquity shall not be forgiven unto the death : I shall take from you the mirth of wine and oil, your young men shall fall by the sword, your aged men shall be led captives, your delicate dames shall trot upon their feet over the river (meaning Euphrates), their buttocks shall be naked, and their shame shall not be hid," &c. Jeremiah the Prophet preached and cried even to the King and to the Queen, and commanded them to walk in lowliness, to do justice, to repress impiety, and so he promised that they should sit still upon their throne in joy and quietness. But if they would not, he boldly pronounced that their carcasses should be cast to the heat of the sun, and to the frost, and cold of the night. Ezekiel, in his age, useth the same order, and in his own body showeth unto them signs of humiliation, and of the plagues that should apprehend them for their rebellion.

All their admonitions were despised, we confess; but thereto we should not look, but unto that which ensued such proud contempt.

If we would that our places should be so destroyed, that they should remain desolate, and be dens to dragons; if we would that our land should be laid waste, and be a prey to our enemies ; and if we would that the rest of the plagues threatened by the Prophets, and which have apprehended the disobedient before us, should come upon us in full perfection,—then we need neither to fast nor pray, repent nor turn to God. But if we desire either to find mercy in this life, or joy and comfort in the life to come, we must show ourselves unfeignedly sorry for the abominations that now universally reign ; we must be like Lot in Sodom, and Noah in that catholic defection from God which was in the first age ; and by their examples, and notable deliverance, ought we to be encouraged to show ourselves sorry for this present corruption, and to set ourselves against it to the uttermost of our powers, unless that we would have portion with the wicked.

Neither ought we to be discouraged because that the contemners, godless people, and mockers of all godliness, shall exceed us in number.

Their number, dear brethren, shall not hurt our innocency, if that we with unfeigned hearts turn unto our God ; for

ON FASTING.

the promise of His mercy is not bound unto the multitude, so that He will not hear but where the greatest part is godly. No, dear brethren, wheresoever two or three be gathered in His name, there is He in the midst of them : and again, whosoever calleth upon the name of the Lord, he shall be saved, yea, even when in God's displeasure the whole world shall be plagued. And therefore let us not follow the multitude in evil doing ; but let us decline from the ways of their vanity, and by unfeigned humiliation of ourselves, let us purchase favour before God's vengeance burst out like fire.

THE power that we have to proclaim this fasting is not of man, but of God, who by the mouth of His Prophet Ezekiel pronounceth this sentence : "If the watchman see the sword or any plague coming upon the land, if he blow not the trumpet, and plainly warn them to turn to God ; and if the sword come and take any away, the wicked shall perish in their iniquity ; but their blood shall be required from the hands of the watchman." Now so it is, that God of His mercy hath raised up amongst us more watchmen than one or two, of whose mouths we cannot deny but we have heard fearful threatenings of plagues to follow upon this proud contempt of all God's graces.

And therefore we, in the fear of our God, willing to avoid the uttermost of the plagues, have with one consent concluded this godly exercise to be used among us, in sign of our unfeigned humiliation ; which albeit the godless shall mock, yet are we assured that He who once pronounced this sentence, "The soul that shall not be afflicted that same day" (to wit, the day appointed to public humiliation), "shall perish from amongst his people ; yea, every soul that shall do any work that day, I shall destroy such a soul from the midst of his people." The ceremony and the certain appointed day we know to be abolished at the coming of Jesus Christ, together with the rest of the figural ceremonies ; but the effect thereof shall abide so long as there abideth any true Church upon the face of the earth, unto the which repentance and remission of sins are publicly preached. And therefore, albeit we have no corporal punishment to lay upon the contemners of that godly exercise, yet have we the spiritual sword, which once will strike sorer than any material sword can or may.

The judgments and justice of our God are immutable : He abideth the same and one God that drowned the world by water, that consumed Sodom and Gomorrah with fire from heaven, that plagued Pharaoh, destroyed Jerusalem, and hath executed His fierce judgments in all ages, yea, and even before our eyes. It is the same God (we say) that this day, by His faithful servants, calleth us to repentance, whose voice, if we contemn, we declare ourselves rebellious to our God, mockers of His threatenings, and such as sometimes in despite cried, "We will walk according to the lust of our own hearts, and let the counsel of the Holy One of Israel come as it list," &c. And if we do so, then woe, yea woe and double damnation unto us; for then even as assuredly as God liveth, so assuredly shall the plagues that our ears have often heard, be poured forth upon us, even in the eyes of this same perverse generation, with whom we contemn God, and before whom we are neither feared nor ashamed stubbornly to proceed from sin to contempt. Our hope is better of you, dear brethren, that have professed the Lord Jesus with us, within this Realm, albeit that this we speak to let you understand what rebellion hath been in flesh before us, and how it hath been punished, that we may learn to stoop before our God by unfeigned repentance; and then we shall be assured that, according to the promise made by the mouth of Joel, our God shall leave unto us a blessing, albeit that the vehement fire of His wrath shall consume the disobedient.

But now, lest that we should think that the observation of the ceremony is enough to please God, we must understand what things must be joined with fruitful fasting, and what things they are that may make our fasting odious to our God. And first we have to understand that fasting, by itself considered, is no such thing as the Papists heretofore have imagined, to wit, that it is a work meritorious, and a satisfaction for the sins before committed. No; all they that fast with that intent, renounce the merits of Christ's death and passion, in so much as they ascribe to fasting (which is but an exercise used by man) that which is only proper to Jesus Christ; which is, that He, by offering up Himself once for all, hath

ON FASTING.

made perfect for ever those that shall be sanctified. We must further understand, that as the Kingdom of God is neither meat nor drink, so is neither fasting, by itself simply considered, the cause why that Kingdom is granted to the chosen, neither yet eating (moderate, we mean) any cause why the reprobate are frustrate thereof. But unto fasting there must be somewhat joined, if that God shall look upon it at any time in His favour. The Prophet Joel is witness hereof, who in the person of God said unto such as He had severely threatened, "Turn unto me with your whole heart, in fasting and mourning:" In which words the Holy Ghost first requireth the conversion of the heart unto God, and thereto joineth fasting and mourning, as witnesses of the sorrow that we have for our former offences. and fear that we have of His severe judgments; the relief whereof, we publicly profess, we can obtain by no other means but by God's free mercy, from whom we have before declined. So that the very exercise of fasting and mourning, and prayer therewith annexed, so solemnly protested, that by our fasting we merit not; for he that still confesseth his offence, and in bitterness of heart crieth for mercy, doth not brag of his merits. If the Papists reply, Yet God looketh to the fasting and heareth the prayers of such as rightly humble themselves before Him,—we deny not; but thereto we add, that rightly did never man humble himself before God that trusted or gloried in the merits of his own works; for without faith it is impossible to please God, and faith dependeth upon the promise of God's free mercy through Jesus Christ, and not upon the merits of any works. The Pharisee in bragging was rejected, but the Publican in denying himself, and calling for mercy, was justified, not by his works, which he had not, but by grace and mercy, for the which he sobbed. Daniel fasted, confessed his sins, and the sins of the people, and thereto he added most earnest and fervent prayers. But doth he allege any of them as a cause why God should either be merciful to him or to the people? Nay, we find no such thing, but the plain contrary; for thus he concludeth : "Now therefore, our God, hear the prayer and supplication of Thy servant, and show Thy pleasing visage unto Thy Sanctuary that lieth waste, for the Lord's sake. O my God, give ear that Thou mayest hear, and open Thine eyes that Thou mayest see the waste places of the city which beareth Thy name ; for we allege not our righteousness in our prayers that we pour forth before Thee, but Thy most abounding mercy. Lord, hear ; Lord, be merciful ; Lord, take heed ; and help and delay not, for Thine own sake, my God." We may plainly see whereupon this excellent servant of God grounded himself to purchase God's favour, to wit, upon the Lord ; that is, upon the Saviour and Mediator promised, upon the most abundant mercy of God, and upon God Himself; for he understood what God had promised, as well by the mouth of Moses as by the Prophet Isaiah, saying, "Behold, yet I am, yea, even I am the Lord, and there is no God but I. I kill and I give life again. I give the wound, and I shall heal. For my own name's sake will I do it, saith the Eternal." Upon these and the like promises, we say, did all the Saints of God in all their extremities depend, and did look to receive comfort, without all respect to their own works : they damned the best of their own works, and called them nothing but filthiness before God. And therefore, yet as before, we boldly affirm, that the Papistical fasting was not only vain (for what fasting is it to abstain from flesh, and to fill the belly with fish, wine, spice, and other delicates?) but also it was odious unto God, and blasphemous to the death of Jesus Christ, for the causes fore-written. And thus much shortly for those things that must be joined with fruitful fasting.

Now we have to consider what things may make our fasting odious, besides this proud opinion of merit whereof we have spoken.

It is no doubt but that infidelity maketh all the works of the reprobate odious before God, yea, even when that they do the very works that God hath commanded, as we may read in Mat. 5, 6, and 7, Isa. 1 and 66, &c., and divers other places. But because that infidelity lurketh often in the heart, and cannot well be espied, but by the bitter and rotten fruits that spring thereof: the Spirit of God hath painted forth unto us in plain words, what vices may make us and all our works odious before our God, so that neither will He hear our prayers nor regard our fasting. Solomon saith, "He that stoppeth his ear from the cry of the poor, his prayer shall be abominable before God." And Isaiah in the person of God saith, "Albeit that ye shall stretch out your hands, and multiply your prayers, yet will I not hear you, for your hands are full of blood." But most plainly to our purpose speaketh the same Prophet, saying, "The house of Jacob daily seeketh me, and they would know my ways, as a nation that wrought justice, and that had not left the judgments of their God. They ask me judgments of justice (that is, they quarrel with me), and they desire that God shall draw near. Why have we fasted, say they, and Thou beholdest not? We have afflicted our souls, and Thou despisest it." The Prophet answereth in the person of God, and saith, "Behold, in the day of your fast ye will seek your will, and require all your debts; behold, ye fast to strife and debate, and to smite with the fist of wickedness: ye shall not fast as they do to-day, to make your voice be heard above;" that is, to oppress others, so that they are compelled to cry unto God. "Is it such a fast as I have chosen? That a man should afflict his soul for a day, and to bow down his head as a bulrush, and to lie down in sackcloth and ashes? Wilt thou call this a fasting, or an acceptable day unto the Lord? Is not this the fasting that I have chosen? to loose the bands of wickedness, to take away the heavy burdens, and to let the oppressed go free, and that ye break every yoke? Is it not to deal thy bread unto the hungry, and that thou bring the poor that wandereth unto thy house; when thou seest the naked, that thou cover him; and hide not thyself from thine own flesh? Then shall thy light break forth as the morning, and thy health shall grow speedily; thy righteousness shall go before thee, and the glory of the Lord shall embrace thee," &c. In these most notable sentences, and in such as follow in the same place, we have to mark what things may make our fasting to be rejected of God, what He craveth of such as fast fruitfully, and what promise He maketh to such as obey Him. This people externally professed God, they daily sought His face by repairing to the Temple, hearing of the Law, and exercising of the sacrifices; yet did God plague them in more sorts than one, as in the book of the Kings and Chronicles we may read. In their extremity they ran (as to them appeared) to the uttermost refuge; they fasted and unfeignedly humbled their bodies,—for that the Prophet meaneth when that he saith, that they fasted till their necks were weakened, and made faint as a bulrush, for very lack of corporal food. They laid off their gorgeous garments and put on sackcloth, &c. And yet were their troubles nothing relieved. And that was the cause why they quarrelled with God, and said, "Why have we fasted, and Thou hast not seen?" &c. And in very deed to the natural man it was strange; for God had promised that He would comfort His people whensoever they should humble themselves before Him, notwithstanding their former iniquity.

In the external ceremonies, or in the corporal exercises, there could no fault be espied. Why then doth not God hear them? complain they. God answereth that their outward profession was but hypocrisy, their fasting was but mocking of God, and their prayers could do nothing but provoke Him to further displeasure. Because that albeit they retained the name of God, and albeit that they appeared in His Temple, yet had they forsaken both His judgments, statutes, and holy ordinances. Albeit the body stooped, and was afflicted by fasting, yet remained the heart proud and rebellious against God; for they followed their own corrupted ways, they oppressed such as were subject unto them, their heavy yokes lay upon the necks of such as could not rid themselves from their bondage. Amongst them were strife, debate, whisperings of malice, yea open contention and manifest violence, which were all evident declarations of proud hearts and impenitent souls. And therefore God giveth unto them open defiance in the time when they think that they seek His face most earnestly. And hereto ought we this day, that profess the Lord Jesus, and have renounced abominations of Papistry within the Realm of Scotland, give diligent heed. For it is not the simple knowledge of the truth only, nor yet the external profession of the same, that is acceptable before God. Nay, nay, dear brethren, He requireth the fruits of repentance,—and they are, to decline from evil, and to do good, as we may read in many places of the Scripture. Think we it a thing agreeable with the nature of the Eternal God, that He shall receive us in favour, after that we have offended, and we will not for His sake remit the injuries that are done to us? Can we think to be at peace with Him, when that we stubbornly will continue in strife among ourselves? Shall He relieve our grief, bondage, or yoke, and we not relieve the burdens that unjustly we lay upon our brethren? Shall He bestow His undeserved mercy upon us, and we show no bowels of mercy to such as we see in misery before our eyes? Let us not be deceived; God cannot deny Himself. Murder, malice, hatred, cruelty, oppression, strife, theft, deceit, unjust dealing, covetousness, avariciousness, and unmercifulness unto the poor, besides pride, whoredom, adultery, wantonness, and the rest of the works of the flesh, are so odious before God, that while that any of them reigneth in the heart of man, he and his whole works are detestable before God. And, therefore, if we desire that God's fearful judgments shall be stayed, let us (that know the truth, and say that we profess the same) unfeignedly return unto our God. Let us not be inferiors to the King of Nineveh, who commanded every man to turn from his wicked ways, and from the iniquity that was in his hands. Let us consider what our God craveth of us, but especially let Earls, Lords, Barons, Burgesses, and Artificers consider by what means their substances are increased.

It is not enough to justify us before God, that civil laws cannot accuse us. Nay, brethren, the eyes of our God pierce deeper than the laws of men can stretch. The law of man cannot convince the Earl, the Lord, the Baron, or Gentleman, for the oppression of the poor labourers of the ground, for his defence is ready: I may do with mine own as best pleaseth me. The Merchant is just enough in his own conceit, if before men he cannot be convicted of theft and deceit. The Artificer or Craftsman thinketh himself free before God, albeit that he neither work sufficient stuff, nor yet sell it for reasonable price. The world is evil, saith he, and how can men live if they do not as others do? And thus doth every man lean upon the iniquity of another, and thinketh himself sufficiently excused when that he meeteth craft with craft, and repulseth back violence either with deceit or else with open injury. Let us be assured, dear brethren, that these be the sins which heretofore have provoked God, not only to plague but also to destroy and utterly overthrow strong realms and flourishing commonwealths.

Now, seeing that the justice and judgments of our God abide for ever, and that He hath solemnly pronounced that every realm, nation, or city that sinneth, as did Judah and Jerusalem, shall be likewise punished : let that fearful destruction that came upon them, in the which, after hunger and pestilence, the sword devoured without discretion the rich and poor, the noble and those that were of base degree, the young and old, the Priests and Prophets, yea, the matrons and virgins escaped not the day of that sharp visitation : let their punishment (we say) provoke us to repentance, and so no doubt we shall find favour in the sight of [our] God, albeit that He hath begun to show unto us evident signs of His displeasure, justly conceived against us. But (as God forbid) if we mock His Messengers, and despise His words, till that there be no remedy, as they did, then can we (whom God hath raised up to instruct and forewarn you) do nothing but take witness of heaven and earth, yea, and of your own conscience, that we have faithfully instructed you in the right way of God, as well concerning His true worshipping as in doing of your duties one to another ; and also that we have forewarned you of the plagues to come, first by our tongues, and now by our pen, for a perpetual memorial to the posterity that shall follow, who shall glorify God, either for your conversion, or else for your just condemnation, and severe punishments, if ye continue disobedient.

To prescribe to every man his duty in particular we cannot, because we know not wherein every man and every estate particularly offendeth ; but we must remit every estate, and every man in his vocation, to the examination of his own conscience, that according as God commandeth in His holy Law, and as Christ Jesus requireth, that such as shall possess the Kingdom with Him, shall do : which is, "Whatsoever," saith He, "that ye would men should do unto you, do ye the like unto them." By this rule, which the Author of all equity, justice, and policy hath established, if we appointed the Earls, Lords, Barons, and Gentlemen to try their own consciences, whether that they would be content that they should be intreated (if God had made them husbandmen and labourers of the ground) as they have intreated, and presently do intreat, such as sometimes had a moderate and reasonable life under their predecessors; whether (we say) that they would be content that their tenements and rents should be raised from rent to rent, from one farm to two, and so going upward, till that for poverty the ancient labourers are compelled to leave the ground in the hands of the lord,—if with this intreatment they would be content, we appeal to their own consciences. And if they think that they would not, then, in God's name, we require them to begin to reform themselves and to remember that it is not we, but that it is Christ Jesus, that so craveth of them. And unto the same rule we send Judges, Lawyers, Merchants, Artificers, and, finally, even the very labourers of the ground themselves, that every one in his own vocation may try how justly, uprightly, and mercifully he dealeth with his neighbour. And if he find his conscience accused by the former sentence of our Master, let him call for grace, that he may not only repent for the time past, but also amend in times to come, and so shall their fasting and prayers be acceptable unto God.

If men think that we require the thing that is impossible (for what were this else but to reform the face of the whole earth, which never was, nor yet shall be, till that the righteous King and Judge appear for the restoration of all things), we answer, that we speak not to the godless multitude, neither to such as are mockers of God's judgments, whose portion is in this life, and for whom the fire of hell (which now they mock) is assuredly prepared; but we speak to such as have professed the Lord Jesus with us, who have communicated with us in His blessed Sacraments, have renounced idolatry, and have avowed themselves to be new creatures in Jesus Christ in whom they are ingrafted as lively branches, apt to bring forth good fruit. Now, why it should be thought impossible that these men (of what vocation soever they be) should begin to express in their lives that which in word they have publicly professed, we see no good reason, unless that they would say that it is impossible that God shall now work in men of this age, as we read that He hath wrought in men before us (and that were blasphemy), seeing that the hand of our God is no more shortened towards us than it hath been towards those that have passed before us. At God's commandment Abraham left his father's house and native country ; Moses preferred the condition of the people of Israel, even in their greatest affliction, to the riches and glory of Pharaoh's court ; David, upon the unction of Samuel, did patiently abide the persecution of Saul many years ; Zaccheus, at a dinner with Christ Jesus, was not only content to restore whatsoever he had before defrauded, but also to give the half of all his substance to the relief of the poor ; and the faithful, in the days of the Apostles, sold their possessions, and ministered unto the needy. None of these excellent works crave we of the faithful in our age ; but only those without which the Spirit of sanctification cannot be known to be in man, to wit, that every man speak the truth to his brother, that none oppress nor defraud another in any business, that the bowels of mercy may appear amongst such as God hath called to His knowledge ; and, finally, that we altogether, that profess the Lord Jesus and do abhor idolatry, abhor also all kind of impiety, studying to abound in all good works, and to shine as lights in the midst of this wicked generation. Which if we do not, we declare no doubt that Christ Jesus dwelleth not within us, but that we are they that hear and know the will of our Lord, but do not the same. And unto what curse and malediction such persons are subject, the parable of the fig-tree which was threatened to be cut down if it brought not forth fruit,—the curse given to it, upon the which Christ Jesus, being hungry, found no fruit, and His last sentence against the reprobate, do sufficiently witness. Wherein we have to observe, that the reprobate are adjudged to the fire that never shall be quenched, not only because they committed iniquity, but also because they were not found fruitful in good works. Let every man therefore that will avoid plagues temporal and perpetual, unfeignedly study to accomplish in work that which in word and outward profession he doth avow ; and upon such, no doubt, shall the blessing of God rest when the manifest contemners and cloaked hypocrites shall be razed from the face of the earth, and shall be cast into utter darkness, where there shall be weeping and gnashing of teeth without end, which shall be the reward of their wicked works.

More things we would have written,—such as the notes upon the discomfiture of Joshua at Ai, and of the Israelites fighting against Benjamin, together with the foolish opinion of the Papists, who think themselves bound to fast forty days (which they call their Lent) because that Christ Jesus fasted forty days immediately after His baptism; but these we are compelled for this present to pretermit, by reason that the time appointed to this present exercise of fasting approacheth so nigh. If it shall please God of His mercy to continue the light of His Gospel amongst us, this argument will be enlarged and set forth with greater circumstances from time to time.

NOW to the Order, exercise, and abstinence that is to be kept in this public fasting: First, it is to be observed that the two days before expressed—to wit, the second and third Sunday of May instant—are not appointed for any religion of time, neither yet that those precise days shall be observed every year following, but because that shortly thereafter are the Estates of this Realm appointed to assemble in Parliament. Therefore the whole Assembly thought those days for the present necessity most meet, leaving in the liberty of the Church, what time they will appoint to that exercise in all times to come.

The Sundays are appointed not of superstition, neither yet to bring in any schism within the Church, but because that upon the Sunday the people (especially that dwell in country towns) may best attend upon prayer, and the rest of the exercises that ought to be joined with public fasting.

THE abstinence is commanded to be from Saturday at eight of the clock at night, till Sunday after the exercise at afternoon, that is, after five of the clock. And then only bread and drink to be used, and that with great sobriety, that the body craving necessary food, the soul may be provoked earnestly to crave of God that which it most needeth, that is, mercy for our former unthankfulness, and the assistance of His Holy Spirit in time to come.

Men that will observe this exercise may not any of the two days use any kind of games, but exercise themselves after the public assemblies, in private meditation with their God.

Gorgeous apparel should be abstained from during the whole time of our humiliation, which is from the one Sunday in the morning, till the next Sunday at night; albeit that the straitness of abstinence is to be kept but the two days only.

We do not bind the consciences of persons that be unable to bear the extremity of the abstinence, and yet do we exhort them to use their liberty (if any they take) in secret, lest that others either follow their evil example, or else judge them to be despisers of so necessary an exercise.

The time that shall be spent as well before noon as after, must be left to the wisdom of the discreet Ministers, who best can judge both what the auditors may bear and what themselves are able to sustain. But because this exercise is extraordinary, the time thereof would be somewhat longer than it is used to be in the accustomed assemblies. And yet we would not have it so tedious that it should be noisome to the people. And therefore we think that three hours and [or] less before noon, and two hours at afternoon, shall be sufficient for the whole public exercise. The

THE GENERAL FAST.

rest to be spent in private meditation by every family apart.

The Sunday before the second Sunday of May, as before is said, shall every Minister give advertisement to his flock, of such things as are to be done the next Sunday following, and of the causes of the same, with such exhortation as God shall put into their mouths, to make the people to embrace the just commandment of the Church with more glad minds.

In towns we think it expedient, that the exercise of the doctrine begin upon the Saturday at afternoon, immediately before the first Sunday of abstinence, that the people may be the better prepared religiously to use the observation of the next day. But in villages, we think good that the doctrine begin the Sunday before. The argument of the Sermon and exhortation to be taken from some proper place of the Prophets, as of Joel the first, where he saith, "Sanctify a fast, appoint the assembly," &c.; or of Jonah the third, where Jonah cried, "Yet forty days, and Nineveh shall be destroyed;" or of Jeremiah the seventh, where that he saith, "Hear the word of the Lord all Judah, and ye that enter in by these gates," &c.; or of the thirteenth of Luke, upon the declaration of them that show to our Master the cruelty of Pilate, and upon His answer; or upon any other proper place of Scripture that intreateth of repentance, of public humiliation, of the causes and of the fruits of the same.

This ended, as it were for preparation, the beginning shall be upon Sunday, from the Law of God, because that all that offendeth God's Majesty proceedeth from the transgression thereof; and therefore after a short prayer that it will please God to make His holy Word to fructify among us, this Confession following shall be made.

THE CONFESSION

That shall go before the Reading of the Law, and before every Exercise.

IT is of Thy mercy, O Lord, and not of our merits, that it hath pleased Thee to show Thyself unto the world, ever from the beginning and unto us now in this last and most corrupt age; yea, Lord, we further confess that neither Law nor Gospel can profit us to salvation, except that Thou of Thy mere grace work in us above all power that is in this our nature. For albeit Thou teach, we shall remain ignorant: albeit Thou threaten, we shall contemn: and albeit Thou promise mercy and grace, yet shall we despair and remain in infidelity, unless that Thou create in us new hearts, write thy Law in the same, and seal in us remission of our sins, and that sense and feeling of Thy Fatherly mercy, by the power of Thy Holy Spirit. To the old world Thou spakest by Noah; to Pharaoh and his people by Thy servant Moses; to all Israel by the fearful trumpet of Thy Law; to the city of Jerusalem by Thine own Wisdom, our Lord Jesus Christ; and to the multitude, as well of Jews as Gentiles, by the preaching of Thy holy Apostles. But who gave obedience? Who trembled, and constantly feared Thy hot displeasure? Who did rightly acknowledge the time of their visitation? And who did embrace and keep to the end Thy fatherly promises? Only they, O Lord, to whom Thy Spirit was the inward teacher, whose hearts Thou openedst, and from whom thou removedst rebellion and infidelity. The rest were externally called, but obeyed not: they heard as well mercy offered as threatenings pronounced, but neither with the one nor with the other were they effectually moved. We acknowledge, O Lord, that the same corruption lurketh in us that budded forth in them to their destruction and just condemnation. And therefore we most humbly beseech Thee, O Father of mercy, for Jesus Christ Thy Son's sake, that as Thou hast caused the light of Thy Word clearly to shine amongst us, and as Thou hast plainly instructed us, by the external ministry, in the right way of salvation, so it will please Thee inwardly to move our dull hearts, and by the power of Thy Holy Spirit, that Thou wilt write and seal in them that holy fear and reverence which Thou cravest of Thy chosen children, and that faithful obedience to Thy holy will, together with the feeling and sense, that our sins are fully purged and freely remitted by that only one Sacrifice, which only by itself is acceptable unto Thee, to wit, the obedience, death, and mediation of Thine only Son our Sovereign Lord, only Pastor, Mediator, and High Priest, our Lord Jesus Christ: To Whom, with Thee, and with the Holy Ghost, be all honour and glory, world without end. So be it.

This Confession ended, the Minister or Reader shall distinctly read the 27th and 28th chapters of

Deuteronomy; which ended, the Minister shall wish every man to descend secretly into himself, to examine his own conscience, wherein he findeth himself guilty before God. The Minister himself, with the people, shall prostrate themselves, and remain in private meditation a reasonable space, as the quarter of an hour or more.

Thereafter shall the Minister exhort the people to confess with him their sins and offences as followeth:—

JUST and righteous art Thou, O Lord God, Father everlasting; holy is Thy Law, and most just are Thy judgments, yea, even when Thou dost punish in greatest severity; we do confess as the truth is, that we have transgressed Thy whole Law, and have offended Thy godly Majesty in breaking and violating every precept of the same; and so most justly mayest Thou pour forth upon us all plagues that are threatened, and that we find poured forth upon the disobedient at any time from the beginning.

And so much the rather, O Lord, because that so long we have been called by Thy holy Word to unfeigned repentance and newness of life, and yet have we still remained in our former rebellion; and therefore, if Thou wilt enter into judgment with us, we can neither escape confusion in this life nor just condemnation in the life to come. But, Lord, Thy mercy is without measure, and the truth of Thy promise abideth for ever. Unworthy are we that Thou shouldest look upon us, but, Lord, Thou hast promised that Thou wilt show mercy to the most grievous offenders whensoever they repent. And, further, Thou, by the mouth of Thy dear Son our Lord Jesus Christ, hast promised that Thou wilt give Thy Holy Spirit to such as humbly call unto Thee. In boldness of the which promise, we most humbly beseech Thee, O Father of mercies, that it would please Thy godly Majesty to work in our stubborn hearts an unfeigned sorrow for our former offences, with some sense and feeling of Thy grace and mercy, together with an earnest desire of justice and righteousness, in which we are bound continually to walk. But because that neither we nor our prayers can stand before Thee, by reason of that imperfection which still remaineth in this our corrupt nature, we fly to the obedience and perfect justice of Jesus Christ, our only Mediator, in whom, and by whom, we call not only for remission of our sins, and for assistance of Thy Holy Spirit, but also for all things that Thy godly wisdom knoweth to be expedient for us, and for Thy Church universal, praying as He hath taught us, saying, *Our Father which art, &c.*

This ended, the Minister shall read the text whereupon he will ground his Sermon.

FIRST, he shall expound the dignity and equity of God's Law: Secondly, the plagues and punishments that ensue the contempt thereof, together with the blessings promised to the obedient observers of it: Thirdly, he shall teach Christ Jesus to be the end and perfection of the Law, who hath perfectly accomplished that which was impossible for the Law to do. And so shall he exhort every man to unfeigned repentance, to steadfast faith in Christ Jesus, and to show the fruits of the same.

The Sermon ended, the common prayer shall be used that is contained before in this book, beginning thus: "God almighty, and heavenly Father,"* &c. Which ended, the 51st Psalm shall be sung whole, and so with the blessing the assembly is to be demitted for that exercise.

The original copy has, In the Psalm Book the 45 page thereof.
* See p. 97.

At Afternoon.

AFTER invocation of God's Name publicly by the Minister, and secretly by every man and woman for a reasonable space, the Minister may take the argument of his Sermon from the beginning of the 119th Psalm, where the diligent reader shall observe the properties and conditions of such as in whose hearts God writeth His Law. Or if that be thought over hard, then may he take the text of John, " God is light, and in Him there is no darkness; if we say we have fellowship with Him," &c. The prayer is referred unto the Minister: The 6th Psalm shall be sung.

The blessing and exhortation, to call to mind wherefore that exercise is used, being ended, the public exercise shall be put to end for that day.

ALBEIT that in the country the people cannot well meet every day betwixt the two Sundays, yet in cities and towns we think they ought to assemble an hour before noon, and an hour and more at afternoon: the hour before noon, to be the hour accustomed to the common

THE GENERAL FAST.

prayers; the hour at afternoon to be at three of the clock, or after.

The Exercise of the Whole Week.

THE beginning ever to be with confession of our sins, and calling for God's graces. Then certain Psalms and certain Histories to be distinctly read, exhortation to be conceived thereupon, and prayers likewise, as God shall instruct and inspire the Minister or Reader.

Monday Forenoon.
Psalms ii., iii., x.
Hist. Judges ii.

Afternoon.
Psalms xii., xiii., xvii.
Hist. Judges vi.

Tuesday Forenoon.
Psalms xxv., xxviii.
Hist. Judges vii.

Afternoon.
Psalms xxxvi., xl.
Hist. Judges iv.

Wednesday Forenoon.
Psalms xiv., lv.
Hist. Judges xix.

Afternoon.
Psalms xliv., lvi.
Hist. Judges xx.

Thursday Forenoon.
Psalms xlix., lvii.
Hist. Esther iii., iv.

Afternoon.
Psalm xxxvii.
Hist. Esther v., vi., vii.

Friday Forenoon.
Psalms lix., lxi., lxiv.
Hist. 2 Chron. xx.

Afternoon.
Psalm lxix.
Hist. Isaiah xxxvi.

Saturday Forenoon.
Psalms lxviii., lxx.
Hist. Isaiah xxxvii.

Afternoon.
Psalms lxxiv., lxxvii.
Hist. Esdras ix., x.

Sunday, the last day of this public exercise for this

time, before noon shall be used in all things as the former Sunday, except that the 26th of Leviticus be read for the 28th of Deuteronomy, and for the Prayer shall be used that which is before in this book, beginning, "Eternal and everlasting," &c.*

<small>The original copy has, To be found in the Psalm Book the 165 page.
* See p. 85.</small>

Sunday Afternoon.

Psalm lxxviii.   Hist. Daniel ix.

The exhortation and prayers ended, for the conclusion shall be distinctly read the 80th Psalm, and so with exhortation to every man to consider to what end the whole exercise tendeth, with benediction, the assembly shall be demitted.

THE exhortation and prayers of every several exercise, we have remitted to be gathered by the discreet Ministers, for time pressed us so that we could not frame them in such order as was convenient, neither yet thought we it so expedient to pen prayers unto men, as to teach them with what heart and affection, and for what causes, we should pray in this great calamity, appearing shortly to overwhelm this whole Realm, unless God of His great mercy, above man's expectation, find the remedy, before whom it is that we have (and presently do) prostrate ourselves, for obtaining of those things, without which the light of His Evangel cannot long continue with us. And therefore yet once again, we exhort, and, by the power committed unto us by God, charge all that profess the Lord Jesus, and the sincerity of His Evangel, within this Realm, that even as they love the quietness of their commonwealth, the continu-

THE GENERAL FAST. 187

ance of Christ Jesus His holy Evangel within the same, and their own salvation, together with the salvation of their posterity, that unfeignedly they prostrate themselves before the throne of God's Majesty, and in bitterness of heart pray with us [as followeth]:—

Arise, O Lord, and let Thine enemies be confounded. Let them flee from Thy presence that hate Thy godly name. Let the groans of Thy afflicted enter in before Thee. And preserve Thou by Thy own power, such as be appointed to death. Let not Thine enemies thus triumph to the end; but let them understand that against Thee they fight. Preserve the Vine which Thy right hand hath planted. Oppose Thy power to the power of that Roman Antichrist, and let the glory of Thine anointed, Jesus Christ our Lord, shine before all nations. So be it.

Hasten, Lord, and tarry not.

CERTAIN CHAPTERS*

AND

PARTS OF THE SCRIPTURES

*What follows was not in Lekprevik's first edition 1566, but was added in his edition of 1574.

Used by the Ministers of Edinburgh and Holyrood House, in the time of God's visitation by the Pest: In the time when in the Court rang all Impiety, as Murder, Whoredom, and contempt of God's

THE ORDER OF

Word, but especially when the Queen was stricken by God's hand in Jedburgh: Also in the time of Famine and Dearth, and at other such times as God gave occasion, and according to the manner of the Scourge.

In time of Pest.

Numbers xxi. Ezekiel iii.
2 Samuel xxxiv. Psalm xci.
With other such places proper for the same.

In the time when Impiety aboundeth.

Ezekiel iii. Isaiah iii.
Zephaniah i. Jeremiah xxxiv.
Numbers xvi. Hosea iv.
Numbers xxv. Amos vi.
Joshua vii. Obadiah.
1 Samuel iv., vii. Micah 2.
1 Samuel xv. Zechariah v.
1 Kings xv. Ezra iv.
2 Chron. xxvi. Nehemiah ix.

In time of Famine.

Isaiah lviii. 1 Kings xvii., xviii.
Haggai i. 2 Kings iv.
Amos iv. 2 Kings vi., vii., viii.
Amos viii. Zechariah vii.

And other such like parts of the Scriptures, according as the correction was laid of God; for even as the Lord our God has divers and sundry wands wherewith He scourgeth the world, but mercifully correcteth His own children for their profit, so has He left divers examples in holy Scripture, how His chosen have used themselves under every sort of correction, by Him fatherly laid upon them, as in the Chapters before expressed was first noted, to stir men to prevent God's judgments, by true and unfeigned repentance before the plague came.

So these Chapters now noted were chosen by the Ministers of Edinburgh and Holyrood House, and others godly thereabout, at such time as God did visit them, as is above expressed: To testify also that the Church of God, nor the faithful and discreet Ministers, are not bound at every humiliation to stick scrupulously to the former, as no other may be chosen; but as God changeth His wands, so may our prayers with the examples of the saints so afflicted, be changed and ordered. Neither can the wicked justly accuse us in so doing of inconstancy; but rather ought the chosen to glorify God, that our public fasting and humiliation is not bound to man's commandment precisely, nor to old customs as the Papists use their ceremonies; but as God visiteth us, so in that manner seek we Him, as He teacheth us, and giveth us examples in His most holy Word, according to His Fatherly correction.

THREE CAUSES OF THIS PUBLIC FAST.

AS in these days we call unto God for mercy for our unthankfulness, being so oft and divers times delivered, and yet His benefits so suddenly forget; in that that we see sin so to abound in all estates, God's fearful threatenings not feared, but the pronouncers thereof mocked and disdained by the most part of the world.

Secondly, the great hunger, famine, and oppression of the poor, although the rich and wealthy, that keep their corn while the wild beasts eat it, feel not the famine, whose plague suddenly follows, if hastily they prevent not God's judgments by unfeigned repentance.

Thirdly and chiefly, we humble ourselves, and call upon our God for the comfort and deliverance of our afflicted brethren in France, Flanders, and other parts; for although the plague and cruel decree of Trent is begun at Shushan, or rather in filthy Sodom in Paris, that butcher-house of Satan, by those mansworn and cruel murderers, yet their mind is no less cruelly bent towards us. For if they had not pity to drink their own blood, and to see the same run in the streets with Manasses, much less will they be moved with compassion when they shall only hear cruelty used against strangers, except God drown Pharaoh, chase and slay Sennacherib, confound and beat down with shame Herod, which must be through the prayers of the Saints of God, humbled under His mighty hand.

Those and other manifold causes, as sin, unpunished in many places, the craftiness of the worldlings, with the apparent deceitfulness of false brethren, move us this day to stoop under His mighty hand; which we beseech Him, for His own Name's sake, we may do without hypocrisy; then not doubting but that the fruit and
profit thereof shall be found and seen,
as at divers times we have felt, to
His own glory, and comfort of
His Church: To Whom be
praise, glory, and hon-
our, for ever.
Amen.

THE CL.
PSALMES OF
David IN MEETER,
with diuers *Notes and Tunes*
augmented to them.
Alſo with the profe on the margen.
IAMES V.
If any be afflicted, let him pray: and if any would be
merie, let him sing Psalmes.

At Edinburgh,
Printed by Andro Hart, *and are to*
be ſold at his owne ſhoppe, a little beneath
.the Croſſe. *Anno* 1611.

THE
PSALMES
of DAVID.

Beatus vir qui non abiit.
PSALME I. T. Stern.

¶ *Whether it was Esdras or any other that gathered the Psalmes into a booke, it seemeth he did set this Psalme first, in maner of a preface, to exhort all godly men to studie and meditate the heauenly wisdome: for the effect hereof is, that they be blessed, which giue theselues wholy al their life to the holy Scripturs, and that the wicked contemners of God, though they seeme for a while fortunate, yet at length shall come to miserable destruction.*

HE man is blest

that hath not

bent to wicked

rede his eare: Nor led his life as sinners

B Lessed is the man that doeth not walk in the counsell of the wicked, nor stand in the way of sinners, nor sit in the seat of the scorneful.

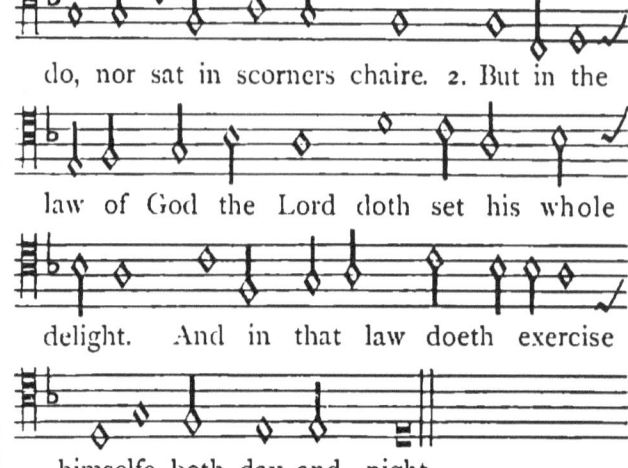

2 But his
delight is in
the lawe of
the Lord,
and in his
Law doth he
meditate day
and night.

do, nor sat in scorners chaire. 2. But in the
law of God the Lord doth set his whole
delight. And in that law doeth exercise
himselfe both day and night.

3 For he
shall be like
a tree plant-
ed by the
riuers of wa-
ters, that will
bring forth
her fruite in
due season:
whose leafe
shall not
fade: so
whatsoeuer
he shal doe,
shall prosper.
4 The wick-
ed are not so,
but as the
chaffe, which
the wind
drieuth away.
5 Therefore
the wicked
shall not
stand in the
iudgment,
nor sinners
in the assem-
blie of the
righteous.
6 For the
Lord know-
eth the way
of the right-
eous, and the
way of the
wicked shall
perish.

3 He shall be like the tree that grow'th
   fast by the riuer side:
Which bringeth forth most pleasant fruit
   in her due time and tide.
Whose leafe shall neuer fade nor fall,
   but flourish still and stand:
Euen so all things shall prosper well,
   that this man taketh in hand.
4 So shall not the vngodly men,
   they shall be nothing so:
But as the dust, which from the earth
   the windes driue to and fro.
5 Therefore shall not the wicked men,
   in iudgement stand vp-right:
Nor yet the sinners with the iust,
   shall come in place or sight.
6 For why? the way of godlie men
   vnto the Lord is knowen:
And eke the way of wicked men
   shall quite be ouerthrowen.

PSALMS.

Omnes gentes plaudite manibus.
PSALME XLVII. W. Ke.

¶ *The Prophet exhorteth all people to the worship of the true and euerliuing God, commending the mercie of God towards the posteritie of Jacob: and after prophecieth of the kingdome of Christ in this time of the Gospell.*

LET all folke with ioy clap hands and reioyce, And sing vnto God with most chearful voice. For high is the Lord and feared to be, The earth ouer all a great king is he: In daûting the folke, he hath so well wrought, That vnder our feete, whole Nations are brought.

All people clappe your hands: sing loud vnto God with a ioyful voice.

2 For the Lord is high and terrible, a great king ouer al the earth.

3 Hee that subdued the people vnder vs, and the nations vnder our feete.

PSALMS.

<small>4 He hath chosē our inheritance for vs, euen the glorie of Iaacob whom he loued. Selah.</small>

4 An heritage faire
   He chose, vs to moue,
   Which Iaakob enioyd,
   Whom he so did loue.

<small>5 God is gone vp with triumph, euen the Lord with the sound of the trumpet.</small>

5 Our God is gone vp,
   With triumph and fame,
   With sound of the trumpe,
   To witness the same.

<small>6 Sing praises to God, sing praises: sing praises vnto our King, sing praises.</small>

6 Sing prayses to God,
   Sing praises I say:
   To this our great King,
   Sing praises alway.

<small>7 For God is the king of all the earth: sing prayses euery one that hath vnderstanding.</small>

7 For of all the earth,
   Our God is the King,
   Such as vnderstand,
   Now praise to him sing.

<small>8 God reigneth ouer ye heathen: God sitteth vpō his holy throne.</small>

8 The heathen to rule,
   God also doth reigne,
   Who doth stil vpon,
   His high throne remaine,

<small>9 The princes of the people are gathered vnto the people of the God of Abrahā: for the shields of the world belong to God: he is greatlie to bee exalted.</small>

9 Strange Princes doe come,
   Vnto the Lords folde,
   Who are as his shields,
   His Church vp to hold.
   For shields of the world,
   Belong to the Lord,
   His Name to exalt,
   Let all men accord.

Iuxta flumina Babylonis sedimus.

PSALME CXXXVII. W. W.

¶ *The people of God in their banishment, seeing Gods true religion decay, liued in great anguish and sorow of heart, the which griefe the Chaldeans did so little pitie, that they rather increased the same dailie with tauntes, reproaches and blasphemie against God, wherefore the Israelites desire God, first to punish the Edomits who prouoked the Babylonians against them, and mooued by the spirit of God prophecie the destruction of Babylon, where they were handled so tyrannouslie.*

WHEN as we sate in Babylon,
 the riuers round about,
And in remembrance of Sion,
 The tears for griefe brast out.

2 We hangd our harpes and instruments,
 the willow trees vpon,
For in that place men for their vse,
 had planted manie one.

3 Then they to whom we prisoners were
 said to vs tauntingly,
Now let vs heare your Hebrew songs,
 and pleasant melodie.

4 Alace said we who can once frame,
 his sorowfull heart to sing,

BY the Riuers of Babell we sate, and there we wept, when we remembered Sion.

2 We hanged our harpes vpon the willowes in the mids thereof.

3 Then they that led vs captiues, required of vs songs and mirth, when we had hanged vp our harpes, saying: Sing vs one of ye songs of Sion.

4 How shall we sing, said

The praises of our louing God,
thus vnder a strange King?

5 But if that I Ierusalem,
   out of mine heart let slide,
Then let my fingers quite forget,
   the warbling Harpe to guide.

6 And let my tongue within my mouth,
   be tyed for euer fast,
If that I ioy before I see,
   thy full deliuerance past.

7 Therefore O Lord remember now,
   the cursed noyse and cry,
That Edoms sonnes against vs made,
   when they razde our Citie.
Remember Lord their cruel wordes,
   when as with one accord:
They cryde, on sacke and raze their wals,
   in despite of their Lord.

8 Euen so shalt thou O Babylon,
   at length to dust be brought:
And happie shall that man be calde,
   that our reuenge hath wrought.

9 Yea blessed shall that man be calde,
   that taketh thy children yong,
To dash their bones against hard stones.
   that lye the streets among.

CONCLUSIONS.

C.M.
GLORE to the FATHER, *to the* SONNE,
And to the Holy GHOST;
As it was in the Beginning,
Is now, and aye shall last

TO PSALM XXV.

O LORD, the strength and Rocke,
of all that trust in Thee;
Save and defend Thy chosen Flock,
from all calamitie.
Glore to the Father bee,
the Sonne, and Holy Ghost,
As it hath been continuallie,
is now, and aye shall last.

TO PSALM XLVII.

AND give him all glorie
In Psalmes most sweete:
And to his Sonne Christ,
And blest Paracleete.
Which from the beginning,
Did ever extend,
And so shall continue,
World without end.

TO PSALM LXX.

*T*O God bee glore interminable,
And his Sonne, verie God and Man:
And holy Ghost inseparable,
As was aye since the world began.

TO PSALM CXXII.

*C*OME let us forgather
To praise God the Father,
Ever ilk morning of the day.
Sing Psalmes in sweet sound,
Let our voyces redound
From earth unto heaven, and say;
To God our Creator,
And Christ our Salvator,
And the Paraclete most holie,
Our guide and Counsellour,
Be laude, glore, and honour,
For evermore, continuallie.

TO PSALM CXXXVI.

*G*LORE to the Father bee,
And to the Sonne most sweet:
The same glorie give wee
Unto the holy Sprite:
As was before
God create all,
Is now, and shall,
Last evermore.

THE X. COMMANDEMENTS
of Almightie God.

EXODVS XX.

ATTEND my people and giue eare
Of ferlie things I will thee tell,
See that my words in mind thou beare,
And to my precepts listen well.

1 I am thy Soueraine Lord and God,
 Which haue the brought frô careful thrall
 And eke reclaimde from Pharaos rod,
 Make thee no Gods on them to call :

2 Nor fashioned forme of any thing,
 In heauen, or earth to worship it,
 For I thy God by reuenging,
 With grieuous plagues this sin will smite.

3 Take not in vaine his holy Name,
 Abuse it not after thy will,
 For so thou mightst soone purchase blame
 And in his wrath he would thee spill.

4 The Lord frô work the seuenth day ceast
 And brought all things to perfite ende,
 So thou and thine that day take rest,
 That to Gods hestes ye may attend.

5 Vnto thy parents honour giue,
 As Gods commandements doe pretend,
 That thou long dayes and gude mayst liue
 In earth, where God a place doth lend.

6 Beware of murther and cruell hate,
7 All filthie fornication feare :

8 See thou steale not in anie rate,
9 False witnesse against no man beare.
10 Thy neighbours house wish not to haue,
His wife, or ought that he calles mine:
His field, his Oxe, his asse, his slaue,
Or any thing which is not thine.

¶ THE LORDS PRAYER.
D. Coxe.

OVR Father which in heauen art,
And makst vs all one brother-hood:
Wee call vpon thee with one heart,
Our heauenly Father and our God.
   Grant we pray not with lips alone,
   But with the hearts deepe sigh and grone.

Thy blessed Name be sanctified.
Thy holy word mought vs inflame,
In holy life for to abide,
To magnifie thy holy Name,
   From all errours defend and keepe,
   The little flocke of thy poore sheepe.

Thy kingdome come euen at this houre
And henceforth euerlastingly,
Thine holy Ghost into vs poure,
With all his giftes most plenteously.
   From Sathans rage and filthie band,
   Defend vs with thy mightie hand.

Thy will be done with diligence,
Like as in heauen in earth also:
In trouble grant vs patience,
Thee to obey in wealth and wo:

Let not flesh, blood, or any ill,
Preuaile against thy holy will.

Giue vs this day our daily bread,
And all other good giftes of thine,
Keep vs from warre, and from bloodshed,
Also from sicknesse, dearth and pine,
   That we may liue in quietnesse,
   Without all greedy carefulnesse.

Forgiue vs our offences all,
Relieue our carefull conscience,
As we forgiue both great and small,
Which vnto vs haue done offence,
   Prepare vs (Lord) for to serue thee,
   In perfite loue and vnitie.

(O Lord) into tentation,
Lead vs not when the fiend doth rage :
To withstand his inuasion,
Giue power and strength to euerie age :
   Arme and make strong thy feeble host,
   With faith and with the holy Ghost.

(O Lord) from euill deliuer vs,
The dayes and times are dangerous :
From euerlasting death saue vs,
And in our last neede comfort vs :
   A blessed end to vs bequeth,
   Into thy hands our soules receiue.

For thou, O Lord, art King of Kings.
And thou hast power ouer all :
Thy glorie shineth in all things,
In the wide world vniuersall :
   Amen, let it be done, O Lord,
   That we haue prayed with one accord.

VENI CREATOR.

COME holy Ghoste Eternall God,
   proceding from aboue :
Bothe from the Father and the Sonne,
   the God of peace and loue.
Visite our mindes and into vs
   thy heauenly grace inspire,
That in all treuth and godlynes
   we may haue true desire.

Thou art the very Comforter,
   in all woe and distresse :
The heauenly gift of God most high,
   which no toung can expresse.
The Fountaine and the liuely spring,
   of ioye Celestiall :
The fire so bright, the loue so cleare,
   and Vnction spirituall.

Thou in thy giftes art manifold,
   whereby Christes Kirk doth stand,
In faithfull heartes writing thy Law,
   the finger of Gods hand.
According to thy promise made
   thou gauest speache of grace :
That through thy helpe the prayse of God
   may stand in euery place.

O holy Ghost into our wittes,
   sende downe thy heauenly light :
Kindle our heartes with feruent loue,
   to serue God day and night.

Strength and stablish all our weakenes,
  so feeble and so fraile :
That neither flesh, the world, nor Deuill
  against vs doe preuaile.

Put backe our enemies farre from vs,
  and grant vs to obteine :
Peace in our hearts with God and man,
  without grudge or disdaine.
And grant (ô Lord) that thou being
  our leader and our guide :
We may eschew the snares of sinne,
  and from thee neuer slide.

To vs such plentie of thy grace,
  gude Lord, graunt, we thee pray :
That thou maist be our Comforter,
  at the last dreadfull day :
Of all strife and dissension,
  ô Lord dissolue the bands,
And make the knottes of peace and loue
  throughout all Christian lands.

Grant vs, ô Lord, through thee to know
  the Father of all might :
That of his deare beloued Sonne,
  we may attaine the sight.
And that with perfite faith also,
  we may acknowledge thee :
The Spirit of them both alway,
  one God in persons three.

Laude and prayse be to the Father,
  and to the Sonne equall,
And to the holy Spirite also,
  one God coeternall.

And pray we that the onely Sonne
vouchsafe his Spirite to send,
To all that do professe his Name,
vnto the worldes end.

THE SONG OF SIMEON

called, Nunc dimittis.

O LORD because my heartes desire
Hath wished long to see,
My onely Lord and Sauiour,
Thy Sonne before I die,
The ioye and health of all mankinde
Desired long before,
Who now is come into the worlde,
Of mercy bringing store.

Thou sufferest thy seruant now
In peace for to depart,
According to thy holy worde,
Which lighteneth my heart.
Because mine eyes, quhilk thou hast made
To giue my body light :
Haue now beheld thy sauing health,
Which is the Lord of might.

Whome thou mercifully hast set,
Of thine aboundant grace,
In open sight and visible,
Before all peoples face :
The Gentiles to illuminate,
And Sathan ouerquell :
And eke to be the glorie of
Thy people Israell.

THE XII. ARTICLES

of the Christian Faith.

ALL my beliefe and confidence,
    is in the Lord of might,
The Father who all things hath made,
    the day and eke the night.
The heauens and the firmament,
    and also many a starre,
The earth, and all that is therein,
    which passe mans reason farre.

And in lyke manner I beleeue,
    in Christ our Lord, his Sonne,
Coequall with the Deitie,
    and man in fleshe and bone.
Conceiued by the holy Ghost,
    his worde doeth me assure :
And of his mother Marie borne,
    yet she a Virgine pure.

Because mankinde to Sathan wes,
    for sinne in bonde and thrall :
He came and offred vp him selfe,
    to death, to saue vs all.
And suffering most grieuous paine,
    then Pilate being Iudge :
Wes crucified vpon the Crosse,
    and thereat did not grudge.

* And so he died in the fleshe,
    bot quickned in the Spirite :
His body then wes buried,
    as is our vse and rite :
His Spirite did after this descend,
    into the lower partes,
To them that long in darknes were,
    the trew light of their hartes.

And in the third day of his death,
    he rose to lyfe againe.
To th' end he might be glorified,
    out of all grief and paine.
Ascending to the heauens hie,
    to sit in glorie still.
On Gods right hand, his Father deare,
    according to his will

Vntill the day of iudgement come,
    when he shall come againe :
With Angels power ; yea, of that day,
    we all be vncertaine.
To iudge all people righteously,
    whome he hath dearely bought :
The liuing and the dead also,
    whom he hath made of nought.

---

* In place of the following eight lines, some editions have :—

    " He tholl'd the last assault of death
        which did life's torments ende :
    Thereafter was he buried,
        and did to hell descend."

And in the holy Spirite of God,
   my faith to satisfie :
The third persone in trinitie,
   beleue I stedfastlie.
The holy and Catholick Kirk,
   that Gods worde doth maintaine,
And holy Scripture doth allowe,
   which Sathan doth disdaine.

And also I do trust to haue,
   by Iesu Christ his death,
Release and pardon of my sinnes,
   and that onely by faith.
What time all fleshe shall ryse againe
   before the Lord of might:
And see him with their bodily eyes
   which now do giue them light.

And then shall Christ our Sauiour,
   the Shepe and Goates diuide :
And giue lyfe euerlastingly,
   to those whome he hath tride :
Which is the Realme Celestiall,
   in glorie for to rest,
With all the holy company,
   of Saintes and Angels blest.

Who serue the Lord Omnipotent,
   obediently each houre :
To whome be all Dominion,
   and praise for euermore.

THE SONG OF BLESSED

Marie, called Magnificat.

MY soule doth magnifie the Lord,
My Spirite eke euermore,
Reioyceth in the Lord my God,
Who is my Sauiour.
And why? because he did regarde,
And gaue respect vnto,
So base estate of his handmaid,
And let the Mightie go.

For now behold all Nations,
And Generations all:
From this time furth for euermore,
Shall me right blessed call.
Because he hath me magnified,
Who is the Lord of might:
Whose name be euer sanctified,
And praised day and night.

·For with his mercy and his grace,
All men he doth enflame:
Throughout all Generations,
To such as feare his Name.
He sheweth strength with his right arme,
And made the proude to start:
With all imaginations,
That they bare in their hart.

He hath put downe the mightie ones,
From their supernall seate :
And did exalt the meke in hart,
As he hath thought it mete.
    The hungrie he replenished,
With all things that were good :
And through his power he made the riche
Oft times to want their foode.

    And calling to rememberance,
His mercy euery deale :
Hath holpen vp assistantly,
His seruant Israell;
    According to his promise made,
To Abraham before,
And to his seede successivelie,
To stand for euermore.

THE
CATECHISME

or maner to teach Children
the Christian Religion.

Wherein the Minister demandeth the question,
and the Childe maketh answere : Made by the
excellent Doctor & Pastour in Christs Church,
IOHN CALVIN.

EPHES. 2.

*The doctrine of the Apostles and Prophets, is the
foundation of Christs Church.*

At Edinburgh, Printed by
Andro Hart. 1611.

OF THE ARTICLES
OF THE FAITH.

THE MINISTER.

WHAT is the principall and chiefe ende of mans life?

THE CHILDE.

To know God.

M. What mooueth thee to say so?

C. Because he hath created vs, and placed vs in this world, to set foorth his glorie in vs. And it is good reason that wee employ our whole life to his glorie, seeing he is the beginning and fountaine thereof.

M. What is then the chiefe felicitie of man?

C. Euen the selfe-same, I meane to know God, and to haue his glorie shewed foorth in vs.

M. Why doest thou call this, mans chiefe felicitie?

C. Because that without it, our condition or state were more miserable then the state of brute beastes.

M. Hereby then wee may euidentlie see that there can no such miserie come vnto man, as not to liue in the knowledge of God?

C. That is most certaine.

M. But what is the true and right knowledge of God?

Whereunto man was created and made.

The greatest felicitie that man can attain to.

The true knowledge of God.

THE ARTICLES

C. When a man so knoweth God, that hee giueth him due honour.

<small>The right maner to worshippe God, standeth in four points.</small>

M. Which is the way to honour God aright?

C. It is to put our whole trust and confidence in him: to studie to serue him, in obeying his will: to call vpon him in our necessities, seeking our saluation, and all good things at his hand, and finallie to acknowledge, both with heart and mouth, that he is the liuely fountaine of all goodnesse.

<small>II. *Sonday.*</small>

M. Well then, to the end that these things may be discussed in order, and declared more at large: Which is the first point?

C. To put our whole confidence in God.

<small>The first poynt of honoring God</small>

M. How may that be?

C. When wee haue an assured knowledge that he is almightie, and perfectlie good.

M. And is that sufficient?

C. No.

M. Shew the reason.

C. For there is no worthines in vs, why God should either shew his power to helpe vs, or vse his mercifull goodnesse to saue vs.

M. What is then further required?

C. That euerie one of vs be fully assured in his conscience, that he is beloued of God, and that he will be both his Father and Sauiour.

M. How shall we be assured hereof?

C. By his owne Word, wherein he vttereth vnto vs his mercie in Christ, and assureth vs of his loue towards vs.

<small>The foundation of our faith.</small>

M. Then the very ground to haue sure côfidence in God, is to know him in our Sauiour Christ.

C. Yea truely.

OF THE FAITH. 219

M. Then brieflie, what is the effect of this knowledge of God in Christ?

C. It is contained in the confession of the Faith vsed of all Christians, which is commonly called the Creede of the Apostles: both because it is a briefe gathering of the Articles of that Faith, which hath bene alwaies continued in Christs Church, and also because it was taken out of the pure doctrine of the Apostles.

M. Rehearse the same.

C. I beleeue in God the Father Almightie, maker of heauen and earth: And in Iesus Christ his onely Sonne our Lord: Who was conceiued by the holy Ghost, borne of the Virgine Marie: Suffered vnder Pontius Pilate, was crucified, dead, buried, and descended into Hell: Hee rose againe the third day from death: He ascended into heauen, and sitteth at the right hand of God the Father almightie: From thence he wil come to iudge the quicke and the dead.

I beleeue in the holie Ghost: The holie Church vniuersall: The communion of Saints: The forgiuenesse of sinnes: The rising againe of the bodies, and life euerlasting.

M. To the intent that this confession may be more plainly declared, into how many parts shall we diuide it?

C. Into foure principall parts.

The Creed of the Apostles.

III.
Sonday.
The Christian Faith standeth in four points.

※　※　※　※　※

NOTE.—In the foregoing specimens (fac-simile) of the Psalter and Catechism, we have followed the order in which they are given in the original edition, where, being printed in full, they occupy more than half the volume.

The Prayers that follow are chiefly for use in private houses, and were printed after the Catechism.

A FORM OF PRAYER

TO BE USED IN PRIVATE HOUSES EVERY MORNING AND EVENING.

MORNING PRAYER.

ALMIGHTY GOD, and most merciful Father, we do not *a* present ourselves here before Thy Majesty trusting in our own merits or worthiness, but in Thy manifold mercies, who hast promised to hear our prayers, and *b* grant our requests which we shall make to Thee in the name of Thy beloved Son, Jesus Christ our Lord, who hath also commanded us to assemble ourselves together in His name, with full assurance that He will not only be among us, but also be our Mediator and Advocate towards Thy Majesty, that we may *c* obtain all things which shall seem expedient to Thy blessed will for our necessities. Therefore we bebeseech Thee, most merciful Father, to turn Thy loving countenance towards us, and *d* impute not unto us our manifold sins and offences, whereby we justly deserve Thy wrath and sharp punishment; but rather receive us to Thy mercy, for thy well-beloved Son Jesus Christ's sake, accepting His death and passion as a just recompence for all our offences, *e* in whom only Thou art pleased, and through whom Thou canst not be offended with us.

And seeing that of Thy great mercies we have quietly passed this night, grant, O heavenly Father, that we may bestow this day wholly on Thy service, so that all our *f* thoughts, words, and deeds may redound to the glory of Thy name, and good example to all men; who, seeing our good works, may glorify Thee our heavenly Father. And forasmuch as of Thy mere favour and love Thou hast not only created us to Thine own *g* similitude and likeness, but

a Dan. 9.

b John 16.

c 1 Tim. 2.
1 John 3.

d Ps. 32.

e 1 John 2.

f Col. 3.

g Gen. 2.

also hast chosen us to be heirs with Thy dear Son Jesus Christ of that immortal kingdom which Thou preparedst for us before the beginning of the world, we beseech Thee to *h* increase our faith and knowledge, and to lighten our hearts with Thy Holy Spirit, that we may in the mean time live in godly conversation and integrity of life, knowing that *i* idolaters, adulterers, covetous men, contentious persons, drunkards, gluttons, and suchlike, shall not inherit the kingdom of God.

(.·.) And because Thou hast commanded us to pray one for another, we do not only make request, O Lord, for ourselves and them that Thou hast already called to the true understanding of Thy heavenly will, but for all people and *k* nations of the world, who, as they know by Thy wonderful works that Thou art God over all, so they may be instructed by Thy Holy Spirit, to believe in Thee, their only Saviour and Redeemer. But forasmuch as they cannot *l* believe except they hear, nor cannot hear but by preaching, and none can preach except they be sent, therefore, O Lord, raise up faithful distributors of Thy mysteries, who, setting apart all worldly respects, may, both in their life and doctrine, only seek Thy glory. Contrarily, confound *m* Satan, Antichrist, with all hirelings and Papists, whom Thou hast already cast off into a reprobate sense, that they may not by sects, schisms, heresies, and errors disquiet Thy little flock. And because, O Lord, we be fallen into the latter days, and *n* dangerous times, wherein ignorance hath gotten the upper hand, and Satan with his ministers seek by all means to quench the light of Thy Gospel; we beseech Thee to maintain Thy cause against those *o* ravening wolves, and strengthen all Thy servants whom they keep in prison and bondage. Let not Thy longsuffering be an occasion either to increase their tyranny or to discourage Thy children, neither yet let our sins and wickedness be an hindrance to Thy mercies; but with speed, O Lord, consider the great miseries and afflictions of Thy poor Church, which in sundry places, by the rage of enemies, is grievously tormented. And this we confess, O Lord, to come most justly for our sins, who (notwithstanding Thy manifold benefits, whereby Thou dost daily allure us to love Thee, and Thy sharp threatenings, whereby we have occasion to fear Thee, and

h Luke 17

i Gal. 5.

k Acts 10.
1 Tim. 2.

l Rom. 10.

m Rom. 16.

n 2 Tim. 3.

o Mat. 7.

speedily to repent) yet continue in our own wickedness, and feel not our hearts so touched with that displeasure of our sins as we ought to do. Therefore, O Lord, create in us new hearts, that with fervent minds we may bewail our manifold sins, and earnestly repent us for our former wickedness and ungodly behaviour towards Thee: and whereas we *p* cannot of ourselves purchase Thy pardon, yet we humbly beseech Thee for Jesus Christ's sake, to show Thy mercies upon us, and receive us again to Thy favour. Grant us, dear Father, these our requests, and all other things necessary for us and Thy whole Church, according to Thy promise in Jesus Christ our Lord: In whose name we beseech Thee, as He hath taught us saying, *Our Father, &c.*

p Rom. 5.
2 Cor. 3.
Luke 17.

A Prayer to be said before Meals.

ALL things depend upon Thy providence, O Lord, to receive at Thine hands due sustenance in time convenient. Thou givest to them, and they gather it; Thou openest Thine hand, and they are satisfied with all good things. *q*

q Ps. 104.

O heavenly Father, who art the fountain and full treasure of all goodness, we beseech Thee to show Thy mercies upon us Thy children, and sanctify these gifts *r* which we receive of Thy merciful liberality, granting us grace to use them *s* soberly and purely, according to Thy blessed will; so that hereby we may acknowledge Thee to be the Author and Giver of all good things, and, above all, that we may remember continually to seek *t* the spiritual food of Thy Word, wherewith our souls may be nourished everlastingly, through our Saviour Christ, who is the true *u* bread of life, which came down from heaven, of whom whosoever eateth shall live for ever, and reign with Him in glory, world without end. So be it.

r 1 Tim. 4.

s Tit. 2.

t John 6.

u John 6.

A Thanksgiving after Meals.

LET all nations magnify the Lord; let all people rejoice in praising and extolling His great mercies. For His fatherly kindness is plentifully showed forth upon us, and the truth of His promise endureth for ever. *w*

We render *x* thanks unto Thee, O Lord, for the manifold benefits which we continually receive at Thy bountiful hand;

w Ps. 117.

x Col. 3.

<small>y Rom. 8.
Tit. 3.

z 2 Tim. 1.

a 1 John 2.

b 1 Tim. 6.
1 Cor. 1.
Rom 8.</small>

not only for that it hath pleased Thee to feed us in this present life, giving unto us all things necessary for the same, but especially because thou hast of Thy free mercies *y*fashioned us anew into an assured hope of a far better life, the which Thou hast *z* declared unto us by Thy holy Gospel. Therefore we humbly beseech Thee, O heavenly Father, that Thou wilt not suffer our affections to be *a* so entangled or rooted in these earthly and corruptible things, but that we may always have our minds directed to Thee on high, continually *b* watching for the coming of our Lord and Saviour Christ, what time He shall appear for our full redemption : To Whom, with Thee and the Holy Ghost, be all honour and glory for ever and ever. So be it.

Another Thanksgiving before Meat.

<small>c 1 Tim. 4.
Acts 10.</small>

ETERNAL and everlasting God, Father of our Lord Jesus Christ, who of Thy most singular love which Thou bearest to mankind hast appointed to his sustenance not only the fruits of the earth, but also the fowls of the air, and beasts of the earth, and fishes of the sea; and hast commanded Thy benefits to be received as from Thine hands with *c* thanksgiving, assuring Thy children by the mouth of Thine Apostle that to the clean all things are clean, as the creatures which be sanctified by the word and by prayer; grant unto us so moderately to use these Thy gifts present, that, our bodies being refreshed, our souls may be more able to proceed in all good works, to the praise of Thy holy name, through Jesus Christ our Lord. So be it. *Our Father, &c.*

Another.

<small>d Ps. 145.</small>

THE eyes of all things do look up and trust in Thee, O Lord : Thou givest them meat in due season : Thou openest Thine hand, and fillest with Thy blessings every living creature. *d* Good Lord, bless us and the gifts which we receive of Thy large liberality, through Jesus Christ our Lord. So be it. *Our Father, &c.*

Another Thanksgiving after Meat.

GLORY, praise, and honour be unto Thee, most merciful and omnipotent Father, who of Thine infinite goodness hast created man to Thine own image and similitude, who also hast fed and daily feedest of Thy most bountiful hand all living creatures. Grant unto us that as Thou hast nourished these our mortal bodies with corporal food, so Thou wouldest replenish our souls with the perfect knowledge of the lively word of Thy beloved Son Jesus, to whom be praise, glory, and honour for ever. So be it.

God save the Church universal : God comfort them that be comfortless : Lord, increase our faith. O Lord, for Christ Thy Son's sake be merciful to the commonwealths where Thy Gospel is truly preached, and harbour granted to the afflicted members of Christ's body ; and illuminate, according to Thy good pleasure, all nations with the brightness of Thy word. So be it.

Another.

THE God of all glory and peace, who hath created, redeemed, and presently fed us, be blessed for ever. So be it.

The God of all power, who hath called from death that great Pastor of the sheep, our Lord Jesus, comfort and defend the flock which He hath redeemed by the blood of the eternal Testament; increase the number of true preachers ; repress the rage of obstinate tyrants ; mitigate and lighten the hearts of the ignorant ; relieve the pains of such as be afflicted, but especially of those that suffer for the testimony of His truth ; and finally confound Satan by the power of our Lord Jesus Christ. So be it.

EVENING PRAYER.

O LORD GOD, Father everlasting and full of pity, we acknowledge and confess that we are *e* not worthy to lift up our eyes to heaven; much less to present ourselves before Thy Majesty with confidence that Thou wilt hear our prayers and grant our requests, if we consider our own deservings. For our consciences do accuse us, and our sins

e Luke 18.

	witness against us, and we know that Thou art an upright judge, who dost not justify the sinners and wicked men,
f Exod. 20.	but *f* punishest the faults of all such as transgress Thy commandments. Yet, most merciful Father, since it hath pleased
g Ps. 50.	Thee to *g* command us to call on Thee in all our troubles and adversities, promising even then to help us, when we feel ourselves, as it were, swallowed up of death and
h Ps. 18.	*h* desperation; we utterly renounce all worldly confidence, and flee to Thy sovereign bounty, as our only stay and refuge,
i Ps. 79.	beseeching Thee not to call to *i* remembrance our manifold sins and wickedness, whereby we continually provoke Thy wrath and indignation against us: neither our negligence and unkindness, who have neither worthily esteemed, nor in our lives sufficiently expressed the sweet comfort of Thy Gospel revealed unto us: but rather to accept the obedience and death of Thy Son Jesus Christ,
k Heb. 10.	who by offering up His body in *k* sacrifice once for all, hath made a sufficient recompence for all our sins. Have
l Ps. 39.	mercy therefore upon us, O Lord, and forgive us our *l* offences. Teach us by Thy Holy Spirit, that we may rightly weigh them, and earnestly repent for the same; and so
m Ps. 58.	much the rather, O Lord, because that the *m* reprobate, and such as Thou hast forsaken, cannot praise Thee nor call
n Ps. 5.	upon Thy name; but the *n* repenting heart, the sorrowful
o Ps. 107.	mind, the conscience oppressed, *o* hungering and thirsting for Thy grace, shall ever set forth Thy praise and glory.
p Ps. 22.	And albeit we be but *p* worms and dust, yet Thou art our
q 2 Cor. 6.	Creator, and we are the work of Thine hands; yea, *q* Thou art our Father, and we Thy children—Thou art our Shepherd, and we Thy flock—Thou art our Redeemer, and we
r Jer. 10. Ps. 6.	Thy people whom Thou hast bought—Thou art our God,
s Ezek. 18.	and we Thine inheritance. *r* Correct us not therefore in
(.˙.) This mark directeth us to the part of the Morning Prayer that is for increase of the Gospel. Which also may be said here as time serveth.	Thine anger, O Lord, neither according to our deserts punish us, but mercifully chastise us with a fatherly affection, that all the world may know that at what *s* time soever a sinner doth repent him of his sin from the bottom of his heart, Thou wilt put away his wickedness out of Thy remembrance, as Thou hast promised by Thy holy Prophet.
	(.˙.) Finally, forasmuch as it hath pleased Thee to make the night for man to rest in, as Thou hast ordained him the

day to travail, grant, O dear Father, that we may so take our bodily rest, that our souls may continually *t* watch for the time that our Lord Jesus Christ shall appear for our deliverance out of this mortal life ; and in the mean season that we, not *u* overcome by any fantasies, dreams, or other tentations, may fully set our minds upon Thee, love Thee, fear Thee, and rest in Thee; furthermore, that our sleep be not excessive or overmuch after the insatiable desires of our flesh, *w* but only sufficient to content our weak nature, that we may be the better disposed to live in all godly conversation, to the glory of Thy holy name and profit of our brethren. So be it.

t Luke 12.

u Mat. 16.

w Luke 21.

A COMPLAINT OF THE TYRANNY USED AGAINST THE SAINTS OF GOD,

Containing a Confession of our Sins, and a Prayer for the Deliverance and Preservation of the Church, and Confusion of the Enemies.

ETERNAL and everlasting God, Father of our Lord Jesus Christ, who hast commanded us to pray and promised to hear us, even when we do call from the pit of desperation ; the miseries of these our most wicked days compel us to pour forth before Thee the complaints of our wretched hearts oppressed with sorrow. Our eyes do behold, and our ears do hear the calamities and oppressions which no tongue can express, neither yet, alas, do our dull hearts rightly consider the same. For the heathen are entered into Thine inheritance—they have polluted Thy sanctuary, profaned and abolished Thy blessed Institutions, most cruelly murdered, and daily do murder, Thy dear children. Thou hast exalted the arm and force of our enemies, Thou hast exposed us to a prey, to ignominy, and shame before such as persecute Thy truth. Their ways do prosper, they glory in mischief, and speak proudly against the honour of Thy name. Thou goest not forth as Captain before our hosts. The edge of our sword, which sometimes was most sharp, is now blunt, and doth return without victory in battle.

It appeareth to our enemies, O Lord, that Thou hast

broken that league which of Thy mercy and goodness
Thou hast made with Thy Church. For the liberty which
they have to kill Thy children like sheep, and to shed
their blood, no man resisting, doth so blind and puff
them with pride that they ashame not to affirm, that Thou
regardest not our intreating. Thy long suffering and
patience maketh them bold, from cruelty to proceed to the
blasphemy of Thy name. And in the mean season, alas, we
do not consider the heaviness of our sins which long have
deserved at Thy hands, not only these temporal plagues,
but also the torments prepared for the disobedient. For
we, knowing Thy blessed will, have not applied our diligence to obey the same, but have followed, for the most
part, the vain conversation of the blind world ; and, therefore, in very justice hast Thou visited our unthankfulness.
But, O Lord, if Thou shalt observe and keep in mind for
ever the iniquities of Thy children, then shall no flesh
abide nor be saved in Thy presence. And therefore we,
convicted in our own conscience, that most justly we suffer,
as punished by Thy hand, do nevertheless call for mercy,
according to Thy promise. And first we desire to be corrected with the rod of Thy children, by the which we may
be brought to a perfect hatred of sin and of ourselves ; and,
therefore, that it would please Thee, for Christ Jesus Thy
Son's sake, to show to us and Thy whole Church universally persecuted, the same favour and grace that sometimes
Thou didst when the chief members of the same for anguish
and fear were compelled to cry: Why have the nations
raged ? why have the people made uproars ? and why have
princes and kings conjured against Thine anointed Christ
Jesus? Then didst Thou wonderfully assist and preserve
Thy small and dispersed flock—then didst Thou burst the
bars and gates of iron—then didst Thou shake the foun-
dations of strong prisons—then didst Thou plague the cruel
persecutors, and then gavest Thou some tranquillity and
rest, after those raging storms and cruel afflictions.

O Lord, Thou remainest one for ever—we have offended
and are unworthy of any deliverance, but worthy art Thou
to be a true and constant God ; and worthy is Thy dear
Son Christ Jesus, that Thou shouldest glorify His name and
revenge the blasphemy spoken against the truth of His

Gospel, which is by our adversaries damned as a doctrine deceivable and false: yea, the blood of Thy Son is trodden under feet, in that the blood of His members is shed for witnessing of Thy truth; and, therefore, O Lord, behold not the unworthiness of us that call for the redress of these enormities, neither let our imperfections stop Thy mercies from us, but behold the face of Thine anointed Christ Jesus, and let the equity of our cause prevail in Thy presence. Let the blood of Thy saints which is shed, be openly revenged in the eyes of Thy Church, that mortal 'men may know the vanity of their counsels, and that Thy children may have a taste of Thine eternal goodness. And, seeing that from that Man of sin, that Roman Antichrist, the chief adversary to Thy dear Son, doth all iniquity spring and mischief proceed,—let it please Thy fatherly mercy more and more to reveal his deceit and tyranny to the world. Open the eyes of princes and magistrates, that clearly they may see how shamefully they have been and are abused by his deceivable ways, how by him they are compelled most cruelly to shed the blood of Thy saints, and by violence refuse Thy New and Eternal Testament; that they, in deep consideration of these grievous offences, may unfeignedly lament their horrible defection from Christ Jesus Thy Son, from henceforth studying to promote His glory in the dominions committed to their charges, that so yet once again the glory of Thy Gospel may appear to the world. And seeing also that the chief strength of that odious beast consisteth in the dissension of princes, let it please Thee, O Father, who hast claimed to Thyself to be called the God of peace, to unite and knit in perfect love the hearts of all those that look for the life everlasting. Let no craft of Satan move them to war one against another, neither yet to maintain by their force and strength that kingdom of darkness; but rather that godly they may conspire (illuminated by Thy Word) to root out from among them all superstition with the maintainers of the same. These Thy graces, O Lord, we unfeignedly desire to be poured forth upon all realms and nations; but principally, according to that duty which Thou requirest of us, we most earnestly require that the hearts of the inhabitants of England and Scotland, whom the malice and craft of

Satan and his supporters, of many years have dissevered, may continue in that godly unity which now of late it hath pleased Thee to give them, being knit together in the unity of Thy Word. Open their eyes, that clearly they may behold the bondage and misery which is purposed against them both; and give unto them wisdom to avoid the same in such sort, that in their godly concord Thy name may be glorified, and Thy dispersed flock comforted and relieved.

The commonwealths, O Lord, where Thy Gospel is truly preached, and harbour granted to the afflicted members of Christ's body, we commend to Thy protection and mercy. Be Thou unto them a defence and buckler, be Thou a watchman to their walls, and a perpetual safeguard to their cities, that the crafty assaults of their enemies, [being] repulsed by Thy power, Thy Gospel may have free passage from one nation to another; and let all preachers and ministers of the same have the gifts of Thy Holy Spirit in such abundance as Thy godly wisdom shall know to be expedient for the perfect instruction of that flock which Thou hast redeemed with the precious blood of Thine only and well-beloved Son Jesus Christ. Purge their hearts from all kind of superstition, from ambition and vainglory, by which Satan continually laboureth to stir up ungodly contention, and let them so consent in the unity of Thy truth, that neither the estimation which they have of men, nor the vain opinions which they have conceived by their writings, prevail in them against the clear understanding of Thy blessed Word.

And now last, O Lord, we most humbly beseech Thee, according to that prayer of Thy dear Son our Lord Jesus, so to sanctify and confirm us in Thine eternal verity, that neither the love of life temporal, nor yet the fear of torments and corporal death, cause us to deny the same when the confession of our faith shall be required of us; but so assist us with the power of Thy Spirit, that not only boldly we may confess Thee, O Father of mercies, to be the true God alone, and [Him] whom Thou hast sent, our Lord Jesus, to be the only Saviour of the world; but also, that constantly we may withstand all doctrine repugnant to Thy eternal truth, revealed to us in Thy most blessed Word. Remove from our hearts the blind love of ourselves, and so rule Thou all the actions of our life, that in us Thy godly name may be glorified, Thy Church edified, and Satan finally confounded by the power and means of our Lord Jesus Christ: to Whom, with Thee and the Holy Spirit, be all praise and glory before Thy congregation now and ever. So be it.

Arise, O Lord, and let Thine enemies be ashamed, let them flee from Thy presence that hate Thy godly name, let the groans of Thy prisoners enter in before Thee, and preserve by Thy power such as be appointed to death. Let not Thine enemies thus triumph to the end, but let them understand that against Thee they fight. Preserve and defend the vine which Thy right hand hath planted, and let all nations see the glory of Thine Anointed.

Hasten, Lord, and tarry not.

A GODLY PRAYER
To be said at all times.

HONOUR and praise be given to Thee, O Lord God Almighty, most dear Father of heaven, for all Thy mercies and loving-kindness showed unto us, in that it hath pleased Thy gracious goodness freely and of Thine own accord, to elect and choose us to salvation before the beginning of the world; and even like continual thanks be given to Thee for creating us after Thine own image—for redeeming us with the precious blood of Thy dear Son when we were utterly lost—for sanctifying us with Thy Holy Spirit in the revelation and knowledge of Thy holy Word—for helping and succouring us in all our needs and necessities—for saving us from all dangers of body and soul—for comforting us so fatherly in all our tribulations and persecutions—for sparing us so long, and giving us so large a time of repentance. These benefits, O most merciful Father, like as we acknowledge to have received them of Thine only goodness; even so we beseech Thee, for Thy dear Son Jesus Christ's sake, to grant us always Thy Holy Spirit, whereby we may continually grow in thankfulness towards Thee, to be led into all truth, and comforted in all our adversities. O Lord, strengthen our faith, kindle it more in ferventness and love towards Thee and our neighbours for Thy sake. Suffer us not, most dear Father, to receive Thy word any more in vain, but grant us always the assistance of Thy grace and Holy Spirit, that in heart, word, and deed we may sanctify and do worship to Thy name.

Help to amplify and increase Thy kingdom, that whatsoever Thou sendest, we may be heartily well content with Thy good pleasure and will. Let us not lack the thing, O Father, without the which we cannot serve Thee; but bless Thou so all the works of our hands that we may have sufficient, and not be chargeable but rather helpful unto others. Be merciful, O Lord, to our offences; and, seeing our debt is great, which Thou hast forgiven us in Jesus Christ, make us to love Thee and our neighbours so much the more. Be Thou our Father, our Captain, and Defender in all temptations; hold Thou us by Thy merciful hand, that we may be delivered from all inconveniences, and end our lives in the sanctifying and honouring of Thy holy name, through Jesus Christ our Lord and only Saviour. So be it.

Let Thy mighty hand and outstretched arm, O Lord, be still our defence—Thy mercy and loving-kindness in Jesus Christ, Thy dear Son, our salvation—Thy true and holy Word our instruction—Thy grace and Holy Spirit our comfort and consolation, unto the end and in the end. So be it.

O Lord, increase our faith.

A PRAYER TO BE SAID OF THE CHILD BEFORE HE STUDY HIS LESSON.

Out of the 119th Psalm.

" Wherein shall the Child address his way? in guiding himself according to Thy Word. Open mine eyes, and I shall know the marvels of Thy Law. Give me understanding, and I shall keep Thy Law; yea, I shall keep it with my whole heart."

LORD, who art the fountain of all wisdom and knowledge, seeing it hath pleased Thee to give me the means to be taught in my youth, for to learn to guide me godlily and honestly all the course of my life; may it also please Thee to lighten my understanding (the which of itself is blind), that it may comprehend and receive that doctrine and learning which shall be taught me ; may it please Thee to strengthen my memory to keep it well ; may it please Thee also to dispose my heart willingly to receive it with such desire as appertaineth, so that, by my ingratitude, the occasion which Thou givest me be not lost. That I may thus do, may it please Thee to pour upon me Thy Holy Spirit ; the Spirit, I say, of all understanding, truth, judgment, wisdom, and learning, the which may make me able so to profit, that the pains that shall be taken in teaching me be not in vain. And to what study soever I apply myself, make me, O Lord, to address it unto the right end : that is, to know Thee in our Lord Jesus Christ, that I may have full trust of salvation in Thy grace, and to serve Thee uprightly according to Thy pleasure, so that whatsoever I learn, it may be unto me as an instrument to help me thereunto.

And seeing Thou dost promise to give wisdom to the little and humble ones, and to confound the proud in the vanity of their wits, and likewise to make Thyself known to them that be of an upright heart, and also to blind the ungodly and wicked ; I beseech Thee to fashion me unto true humility, so that I may be taught first to be obedient unto Thee, and next unto my superiors that Thou hast appointed over me ; further that it may please Thee to dispose my heart unfeignedly to seek Thee, and to forsake all evil and filthy lusts of the flesh : and that in this sort I may prepare myself to serve Thee only, in that estate which it shall please Thee to appoint for me when I shall come to age.

"The Lord revealeth His secrets unto them that fear Him, and maketh them to know His alliance."—Ps. 25.

A PRAYER TO BE SAID BEFORE A MAN BEGIN HIS WORK.

O LORD GOD, most merciful Father and Saviour, seeing it hath pleased Thee to command us to travail, that we may relieve our need ; we beseech Thee of Thy grace so to bless our labour, that Thy blessing may extend unto us, without the which we are not able to continue, and that this great favour may be a witness unto us of Thy bountifulness and assistance, so that thereby we may know the fatherly care that Thou hast over us. Moreover, O Lord, we beseech Thee that Thou wouldest strengthen us with Thy Holy Spirit, that we may faithfully travail in our state and vocation without fraud or deceit: and that we may endeavour ourselves to follow Thy holy ordinance, rather than to seek to satisfy our greedy affections, or desire to gain. And if it please Thee, O Lord, to prosper our labour, give us a mind also to help them that have need, according to that ability that Thou of Thy mercy shalt give us; and knowing that all good things come of Thee, grant that we may humble ourselves to our neighbours, and not by any means lift ourselves above them who have not received so liberal a portion, as of Thy mercy Thou hast given unto us. And if it please Thee to try and exercise us by greater poverty and need than our flesh would desire; that Thou wouldest yet, O Lord, grant us grace to know that Thou wilt nourish us continually through Thy bountiful liberality, that we be not so tempted that we fall into distrust; but that we may patiently wait till Thou fill us, not only with corporal graces and benefits, but chiefly with Thy heavenly and spiritual treasures, to the intent that we may always have more ample occasion to give Thee thanks, and so wholly to rest upon Thy mercies. Hear us, O Lord of mercy, through Jesus Christ Thy Son our Lord. Amen.

A PRAYER NECESSARY FOR ALL MEN.

O MERCIFUL GOD, I a wretched sinner acknowledge myself bound to keep Thy holy commandments, but yet unable to perform them, and to be accepted for just, without the righteousness of Jesus Christ Thy only Son, who hath perfectly fulfilled Thy law, to justify all men that believe and trust in Him; therefore grant me the grace, I beseech Thee, to be occupied in doing of good works, which Thou commandest in Holy Scripture, all the days of my life, to Thy glory, and yet to trust only in Thy mercy, and in Christ's merits, to be purged from my sins, and not in my good works, be they never so many. Give me grace to love Thy Word fervently, to search the Scriptures diligently, to read them humbly, to understand them truly, to live after them effectually. Order myself* so, O Lord, that

* my life.

it may be always acceptable unto Thee. Give me grace not to rejoice in anything that displeaseth Thee, but evermore to delight in those things that please Thee, be they never so contrary to my desires. Teach me so to pray, that my petitions may be graciously heard of Thee. Keep me upright amongst diversities of opinions and judgments in the world, that I never swerve from Thy truth taught in Holy Scripture. In prosperity, O Lord, save me, that I wax not proud; in adversity help me, that I never despair nor blaspheme Thy holy name, but taking it patiently, to give Thee thanks, and trust to be delivered after Thy pleasure. When I happen to fall into sin through frailty, I beseech Thee to work true repentance in my heart, that I may be sorry without desperation, trust in Thy mercy without presumption, that I may amend my life and become truly religious without hypocrisy, lowly in heart without fainting, faithful and trusty without deceit, merry without lightness, sad without mistrust, sober without slothfulness, content with my own without covetousness, to tell my neighbour his faults without dissimulation, to instruct my household in Thy laws truly, to obey our King and all Governors under him unfeignedly, to receive all laws and common ordinances (which disagree not from Thy holy Word) obediently, to pay every man that which I owe unto him truly, to backbite no man, nor slander my neighbour secretly, and to abhor all vice, loving all goodness earnestly: O Lord, grant me thus to do, for the glory of Thy name.

F I N I S.

NOTES.

I.—LIST OF EDITIONS.

WITHOUT attempting a complete list, we shall mention the principal editions of the 'Book of Geneva' and of the 'Book of Common Order,' stating also, in most cases, where copies exist.

THE BOOK OF GENEVA.

Date.	Printer.	Place.	Copies.
1556	Crespin	Geneva	Advocates' Library. Library at Britwell House. Reprinted in Knox's Works, vol. iv. p. 149.
1561	Durand	Geneva, 16mo	Library, St Paul's, London.
1562	Lekprevik	Edinburgh	Advocates' Library.*

THE BOOK OF COMMON ORDER.

Date.	Printer.	Place.	Copies.
1564	Lekprevik	Edinburgh	C. C. College, Oxford.
1565	Lekprevik	Edinburgh	Library at Britwell House. St John's College, Cambridge. Advocates' Library.†
1566	Henry le Mareschal	16mo	Library, Peterborough Cathedral.
1575	Bassandyne	Edinburgh	Bodleian Library, Oxford. Mr David Laing, Edinburgh.
1578 (about)‡		Edinburgh	Soc. of Antiquaries of Scotland.

* This Scottish reprint contains some Prayers not in the Geneva editions.
† The same as that of 1564, excepting the date on title-page.
‡ A copy wanting the title-page. Printed in black-letter, apparently at Edinburgh, by John Ross.

NOTES.

Date.	Printer.	Place.	Copies.
1587	Vautrollier	London	British Mus. Mr D. Laing. Lambeth.
1594	Schilders	Middleburgh	Glas. Univ. Trin. Col., Dub.
1594	Charteris	Edinburgh	Mr D. Laing.
1596	Charteris	Edinburgh	Mr D. Laing.
1599	Schilders	Middleburgh, 16mo	Library of St Mary's Cath. Chapel, Edinburgh.
1601	Canin	Dort	Lea Wilson's Catalogue.
1602	Schilders	Middleburgh	Brit. Museum. Lambeth. Baliol College, Oxford.
1611	Hart	Edinburgh	Adv. Lib. Signet Lib. Univ. of Aber. Bodl. Lib. Mr D. Laing. Rev. J. M. Laing, Blairdaff, Aberdeenshire.*
1611	Hart	Edinburgh, 16mo	Mr D. Laing.
1615	Hart †	Edinburgh	Advocates' Lib. Brit. Mus. Public Lib., Cambridge.
1622	Hart	Edinburgh	Mr D. Laing.
1625	Raban	Aberdeen	Wm. Euing, Esq., Glasgow.
1629	Raban	Aberdeen, 16mo	Mr D. Laing.
1630	Hart's Heirs	Edinburgh, 16mo	Lea Wilson's Catalogue.
1633	Raban	Aberdeen	Glas. Univ. Aber. Univ. Brit. Mus. Bodl. Lib.
1634	Hart's Heirs	Edinburgh	British Museum.
1635	Hart's Heirs	Edinburgh	Univ. Edin. Glas. Univ. Aber. Univ. Adv. Lib. Signet Lib. Bodleian Lib., Ox.; and in many private collections.
1635 ‡	Raban	Aberdeen, 16mo	Mr Hill Burton.
1640	Bryson §	Edinburgh, 16mo	Mr D. Laing.
1643	Bryson	Edinburgh, 16mo	Mr D. Laing. Mr H. Burton.
1644	Tyler	Edinburgh, 16mo	Mr Gibson Craig.

* To whom we have to express our obligation for the use of his copy.

† For the use of a beautiful copy of this edition we have been indebted to the Rev. Dr Bisset, Bourtie, Aberdeenshire. On a book-plate it has the arms and name of the Hon. Archibald Campbell, Esq. (sic), with date 1708; and later, in 1768, the name of Gavin Mitchel, an eminent clergyman in his day.

‡ Supposed.   § This edition is Hart's of 1634, with a new title.

Besides pocket and other editions, such as those mentioned, the 'Book of Common Order' was frequently printed for binding up with Bibles. In more recent times it has been reprinted in Dunlop's Collection of Confessions; in the 'Phœnix,' vol. ii., London, 1708; as a separate volume, edited by Dr Cumming of London, in 1840; and (as mentioned above) in Laing's edition of Knox's Works, vols. iv. and vi. In 1864 the entire Psalter was reprinted from Hart's edition of 1635. The editor, the Rev. Neil Livingston, has added notes and dissertations, and though these refer more to the Psalter than to the Prayers, which he has not reprinted, we have been much indebted to them for information, and for suggesting sources of information.

Some other old editions, besides those we have mentioned, are referred to by Mr Livingston, and by Dr Lee in his 'Memorial for the Bible Society,' but we have omitted them, as being obscure, or because no copies are known to exist.

For assistance in drawing up the list we have given, or rather for furnishing us with a great part of it, we have to express our great obligations to Mr David Laing of the W.S. Library, Edinburgh, who has a very large private collection, and who, it may be safely said, knows more of the subject than any other person.

In the different editions there is a great variety of readings, many of them arising from the attempt to modernise expressions, and even the construction of sentences, in accordance with the change that passed over the language of Scotland during the period. This applies more to the Scottish portions of the book than to the Genevan, which was at first written in good English. Where there has been difficulty, we have generally followed the reading given in Dunlop's Confessions. Hart's edition of 1611 is one of the most complete as regards the prose documents, containing nothing, however, which was not in use before 1601.

The 'Book of Geneva' was entitled, 'The Form of Prayers and Ministration of the Sacraments, &c., used in the English Congregation at Geneva; and approved by the famous and Godly-learned Man, M. John Calvin:' the Scottish edition of 1564, 'The Form of Prayers and Ministration of the Sacraments, &c., used in the English Church at Geneva, approved and received by the Church of Scotland, whereunto besides that was in the former books are also added sundry other Prayers, with the whole Psalms of David in English Metre:' Hart of 1615, 'The Psalms, &c. Hereunto is added the whole Church Discipline, with many godly Prayers, &c.:' Raban of 1633, 'The Psalms, &c. With the whole Form of Discipline and

Prayers, according to the Church of Scotland.' The Book of Geneva is referred to in the First Book of Discipline as the Book of our Common Order, but this name does not appear to have been much used till modern times. The book seems to have been commonly referred to as the Psalm Book, the Prayers, the Common Prayers, and, after 1645, as the Old Liturgy.

II.—STATEMENT ILLUSTRATING THE PEDIGREE OF THE BOOK OF COMMON ORDER.

1525. It was in the German-Swiss Cantons that the earliest Reformed Liturgies appeared. Not to refer to some intermediate forms, such as Leo Juda's, little removed from those of the Church of Rome, a church-book was published at Zurich in or about 1525, containing verbatim the prayer so well known afterwards as 'Calvin's Confession.' — Ebrard's 'Ref. Kirkenbuch.'

1533. The first of the French-Reformed group of Liturgies was published at Neuchâtel in this year. Farel was there in 1532, and is believed to have been the author. The Marriage Service of Calvin's Liturgy, so called, appears in it almost verbatim. Our acquaintance with this draft of 1533 is through a reprint published at Strasburg in 1859, by Professor Baum.

1536 to 1538. Farel and Calvin Ministers at Geneva.

1538 to 1541. Calvin Minister of a congregation of French refugees at Strasburg.

1541. Calvin returned to Geneva and published his Liturgy, which had been compiled and brought gradually into use during the previous few years of his ministry.—Ebrard's 'Ref. Kirk.,' Intro., p. xxvi.; Dyer's 'Life of Cal.,' p. 140. The author of 'Eutaxia' mentions 1543 as the date of its first publication, though composed several years earlier. — 'Eutaxia' (New York, 1855), p. 28. (Having named this work, we must add that to it we have been greatly indebted in this and other kindred studies. More than any other publication in English it has had to do with the revived study of the Reformed Liturgies in late years.)

1545. Calvin republished his Liturgy in Latin; also a French edition

NOTES.

for the use of his old congregation at Strasburg, with some additions to the Genevan form.

1549. King Edward's first book was published.

1551. Pollanus, who had succeeded Calvin as Minister at Strasburg, and who, with his congregation, had taken refuge in England in 1549, published in London a Latin translation of the Strasburg Liturgy dedicated to King Edward VI. About the same time Alasco framed a Liturgy for the use of the Netherland congregation in London. This was founded on the Liturgy of Pollanus, and was published in Latin and in Dutch at Frankfort in 1555.—' Opera,' republished at Amsterdam in 1866. Alasco's Liturgy gives the Calvinistic forms, with additions and dissertations, resembling in its plan another work which had great influence in England— 'Hermann's Scheme of Doctrine and Worship for the Electorate of Cologne,' first published in 1543. There is a Latin copy of this rare book (Hermann's) in the Advocates' Library.

1552. King Edward's second book was published.

1554. Pollanus and his congregation having left England for Frankfort during Mary's reign, were joined there by the English exiles; and a second edition of his Liturgy was published. There is a copy of this Frankfort edition in the University Library, Glasgow. The Confession of Faith at the end is signed by the representatives of both the French and English congregations. As said above, this Liturgy is a translation of the form Calvin drew up for Strasburg. In addition to the Genevan prayers it provides sentences of absolution: at marriage the 128th Psalm is to be sung on entering the church; directions are given for private communion; and at funerals the pastor is to go before, and give an exhortation and prayer at the grave. A somewhat frequent rubric is, "The Minister to use this form unless he can do better of his own accord." The Liturgy is reprinted in Daniel's 'Codex Liturgicus,' but our notes are from the Glasgow copy.

1554. The 'Book of Geneva,' as it was afterwards called, was drawn up at Frankfort, and in

1556 was published at Geneva.

1562. Lekprevik's reprint was issued in Edinburgh.

1564. The first edition of the 'Book of Common Order' was published.

III.—CONTENTS OF THE BOOK OF COMMON ORDER.

1. *The Calendar.*—The 'Book of Geneva' began with a long address "to our brethren in England," ascribed to Whittingham, but this was never reprinted in Scotland. The edition of 1564-5 begins with a calendar, and this was continued in all the editions we have seen, though it is fuller in some than in others. In one account of the Glasgow Assembly it is said that exception was taken to the festivals and saints' days, but they were retained in the editions published till 1643. This was "for the use of their fairs" more than anything else. We have given a specimen leaf.

2. *The Fairs.*—Given in all editions.

3. *The Confession of the Christian Faith.*—From the 'Book of Geneva.' Till 1676, or even later, this Confession was frequently published in England, and bound up with the 'Book of Common Prayer.'—Pref. xx. 'Lit. Services,' Qu. Eliz. Par. Soc.

4. *Of the Ministers and their Election; of the Elders and Deacons.*—From the 'Book of Geneva,' one sentence in the note at the end, referring to "our dispersion and exile," being omitted in the Scottish edition of 1562, and in all editions of the 'Book of Common Order.'

5. *The Weekly Assembly of the Ministers, Elders, and Deacons.*—From the 'Book of Geneva.' This was the meeting of the Consistory.

6. *An Order for Interpretation of the Scriptures, and answering of doubts.*—From the 'Book of Geneva,' where to the heading as here given is added in the table of contents, *observed every Monday*. In the Church of Geneva itself at this time, the expository exercise took place on Thursday, when each minister in his turn explained a portion of Scripture and was criticised. "The Thursday Service, called *Congregation*," is still kept up in Geneva.—'Eutaxia,' p. 29, 30. These exercises or prophesyings were sanctioned in Scotland by the 'First Book of Discipline,' and were also introduced into many dioceses in England with the approval of the bishops. In Scotland, the *Exercise* in course of time became the *Presbytery*, which in prelatical times became the *Exercise* again. After 1638 meetings of Presbytery always began with the *Exercise.*—Henderson's 'Government and Order.'

7. *The Form and Order of the Election of the Superintendent.*—This was drawn up by Knox in 1560, and is generally printed with the 'Book of Common Order.' Considerable portions of this form are taken from Alasco's Ordination Service; but resemblance is only traceable in some parts of it. Knox, who had, no doubt, become familiar

with Alasco's Liturgy as used in London before Edward's death, would know it still better as published at Frankfort in 1555.

8. *An Order of Ecclesiastical Discipline.* — Retained from the 'Book of Geneva.'

9. *The Order of Excommunication and of Public Repentance.*—This was drawn up by Knox at the desire of the Assembly before 1567, was revised by a Committee of Assembly in 1568, and was printed by Lekprevik in 1569. The date 1571 in the title as given in Hart occurs in several editions of the 'Book of Common Order.' An edition of that year is mentioned, but no copy of it is known to exist. An Act of Assembly of date December 25, 1565, is in all the copies mentioned erroneously as of date December 26, 1568.

The Order is extracted almost verbatim from the longer treatise of Alasco on the same subject.—Works, ii. 179-222.

10. *The Visitation of the Sick, with a Prayer for the Sick.*—The Visitation is retained from the 'Book of Geneva,' the compilers of which had taken it from Calvin's Genevan Liturgy, where it occurs in substance. The prayer to be said was added in the 'Book of Common Order;' the style is peculiarly cumbrous and involved, and efforts to amend this have caused many variations in the different editions.

11. *The Manner of Burial.*—Retained from the 'Book of Geneva.' The words, however, "if he" (the Minister) "be present and required," were added in Scotland. They do not appear in the 'Book of Geneva,' nor in the Edinburgh reprint of 1562, nor till the first edition of the 'Book of Common Order' in 1564. This change is instructive, as showing that the Church wished to leave the question of a funeral service open, and that the Scottish rubrics were well considered.

12. *The Order of Public Worship.*—The first rubric is retained from the 'Book of Geneva,' except that "useth this confession" is substituted for "useth one of these two confessions." In the 'Book of Geneva' the first prayer was "A Confession of our Sins, framed to our time out of the 9th chapter of Daniel," but this never appears in the 'Book of Common Order.'

(1.) *The Confession of our Sins.*—This is the second confession of the 'Book of Geneva.' It is a translation of the common confession of the Reformed Liturgies, made probably from Calvin's Latin version of 1545. *Not for the worthiness thereof,* and what follows, is added. This prayer, minus the addition, has a place in all the Reformed Liturgies, and was published in England in 1566 in Bull's Collection of Prayers, 'Christian Prayers and Meditations,' Parker Soc., p. 46. It is sometimes called Beza's Confession, because he used it at Poissy :

more frequently it is called Calvin's. Ebrard, however, attributes it to Œcolampadius, and says that it appeared in the Zurich Liturgy of 1525. Others refer it to the Missal, and in all likelihood it was a pre-Reformation prayer.

(2.) *Another Confession and Prayer, commonly used in the Church of Edinburgh, on the day of Common Prayer.*—This appears first in the Edinburgh edition of 1562, as an addition to the reprint of the 'Book of Geneva.'—(See Laing's Knox, vol. vi. p. 371.) It was considerably altered, and printed again in its present shape in the edition of 1564. From the allusions in it, it was evidently composed in Scotland, and very likely by Knox himself.

(3.) *A Confession of Sin to be used before Sermon.*—This appears first in the 'Book of Common Order,' in the edition of 1575. It is a compilation from other Confessions.

(4.) *A Confession used in the time of extreme trouble.*—This is a Scottish prayer, appears in the edition of 1564, and may have been composed by Knox.

The rubric that follows these Confessions is from the 'Book of Geneva.' Calvin's Genevan Liturgy has also a similar rubric, leaving the Prayer before Sermon free.

After the Sermon,

(5.) *A Prayer for the Whole Estate of Christ's Church.*—This is retained from the 'Book of Geneva;' except that petitions for the King and Commonwealth take the place of a prayer for the city of Geneva, and a sentence relating to "our miserable country of England" is omitted. The petitions for all conditions of men are very much taken from Calvin's Genevan Liturgy. The preface to the Creed, the Creed itself, and the rubric that follows, are as in the 'Book of Geneva.'

The two benedictions are also retained from it. The "you," however, is in the 'Book of Common Order' changed into "us." In Calvin's Genevan and in most of the Reformed Liturgies, only the blessing from Numbers is given. "You" or "thee" are always used; and some have as a preface, "Receive the blessing of the Lord." "Go in peace, and remember the poor," was usually added.

The note or rubric that follows is also from the 'Book of Geneva;' the part of it referring to plagues also appears in Calvin's Liturgy.

13. *Other Public Prayers.*

(1.) *Another Manner of Prayer after the Sermon.*—This is not in the 'Book of Geneva,' but appears in the Edinburgh edition of 1562, and in all complete copies of the 'Book of Common Order;' also in Bull's 'Christian Prayers and Meditations,' p. 129. It is a translation of the Prayer after Sermon in Calvin's Genevan Liturgy. The long rendering of the Lord's Prayer is omitted in the later Genevan and French Liturgies, though it is still retained by the Walloon Churches. The 'Book of Common Order' calls the Genevan Church the *French Church of Geneva*, to distinguish it from that of the English exiles.

(2.) *Another Prayer.*—This also is from Calvin's Genevan Liturgy, designed for use when God threateneth His judgments. It appears in the Edinburgh edition of 1562. It was composed by Calvin for a special fast in 1541, and in the Dutch Liturgy was adopted as the regular morning prayer, where it remains a striking memorial to the Netherlanders of the sufferings and heroic struggles of their ancestors. Grindal borrowed it for use in the Church of England in 1563, on occasion of a fast for plague, and it served as a model in later times.— Eutaxia, p. 151, 211 ; Lit. Ser. Queen Eliz., Par. Soc., p. 483.

(3.) *A Prayer used in the Churches of Scotland in the time of Persecution by the Frenchmen, but principally when the Lord's Table was to be ministered.*—This appears in the edition of 1564, but part of it had been in use when both the kings of France were alive—therefore before 1559, when Henry the Second died. It was probably composed by Knox.

The Prayer referring to the Lord's Supper is a free translation from Calvin's Genevan Liturgy.

(4.) *A Thanksgiving unto God after our Deliverance from the Tyranny of the Frenchmen.*—This appears in the edition of 1564. There was a service of thanksgiving for this deliverance, held in St Giles's on the 19th of July 1560. Knox officiated, and the prayer used is given in his Works, Wod. Soc., vol. ii. 85. As given in the Liturgy, it is much altered.

(5.) *A Prayer used in the Assemblies of the Church, as well Particular as General.*—This appears in the edition of 1564, and is a Scots compilation apparently.

(6.) *A Prayer to be used when God threateneth His Judgment.*—This is not in the edition of 1564, but appears in that of 1575. It is a Scots prayer, and perhaps by Knox.

(7.) *A Prayer in time of Affliction.*—This is not in the edition of 1564, though from the references to "this noisome and destroying plague," it was probably composed in 1563 (Lit. Ser., Queen Eliz., p. 488), and perhaps by Knox. Like some of the other Scots prayers, it uses strong terms against sacrilege.

(8.) *A Prayer for the King.*—This is taken from the Primer or Book of Private Prayer of King Edward the Sixth—published in 1553. The Scots were familiar with it from 1557, but it does not appear in the edition of the 'Common Order' of 1564. We find it, however, in that of 1575. The relations of the nation to the occupants of the throne at these dates perhaps account for this.

Besides these public prayers, there is in the Edinburgh edition of 1562 *a godly prayer*,—see Laing's Knox, vi. 370. It is an expansion of Calvin's Prayer for Illumination, generally used by him and his colleagues before sermon.—Eutaxia, p. 35.

It was not afterwards printed in the 'Book of Common Order,' perhaps to insure the use of a "conceived" prayer in this part of the service.

Charteris's edition of 1596 has four prayers not found in other copies, but two of them at least are private prayers.—Laing, vi. 380.

14. *The Manner of the Lord's Supper.*—As in Calvin's Genevan Liturgy, the Communion service began immediately after the recitation of the Creed used at the close of the ordinary prayer after sermon. The Scottish form is retained from the 'Book of Geneva,' with the exception of a few clauses. The first rubric is the same in both, and the exhortation is the same till "sundry kinds of death." This part of the exhortation is from King Edward's Liturgy. The 'Book of Geneva' goes on with the "debarring" clauses from King Edward's Book, but, instead of these, the 'Book of Common Order' gives the "debarration" of Calvin's Genevan Liturgy. At "Albeit we feel in ourselves," the 'Book of Common Order' returns to the 'Book of Geneva,' and follows it to the end of the exhortation, this portion having been taken from Calvin's Genevan Liturgy. The last sentences of this, as in all the Reformed services, are an expansion of Sursum Corda, to which words the Reformers were wont to appeal, as a proof that the ancients did not hold the doctrine of a local presence.

The rubric that follows the exhortation is from the 'Book of Geneva,' and also the Eucharistic Prayer. There was no prayer in this place in Calvin's Liturgy, his Ante-Communion Prayer, which is also copied into the 'Book of Common Order,' being used at the close of the ordinary prayer after sermon, and before the recital of the Creed. In Scotland it was intended that both should be used.

The rubric following the Eucharistic Prayer is from the 'Book of Geneva.' There was a rubric nearly similar in Calvin's Genevan Liturgy. Instead of "some place of the Scripture is read," it however had "some psalms are sung, or some passage of Scripture read," and this was practically adopted in Scotland. In these rubrics the Lord's Supper is called the *Action*—hence the Scottish phrase, *action sermon*.

The thanksgiving that follows is from the 'Book of Geneva,' which had retained it *verbatim* from Calvin's Service.

The rubric that follows is from the 'Book of Geneva.' The Song of Simeon has since been used universally in this place by the Reformed Churches, but it is not mentioned in the earliest editions of Calvin's Liturgy, and it was perhaps not translated into English when the 'Book of Geneva' was framed.

The Note to the Reader is from the 'Book of Geneva.' There is a note of similar import in Calvin's Genevan Liturgy, except that it does not, like the former, disclaim the idea that the words of institution make the Sacrament.

15. *The Form of Marriage.*—This is retained from the 'Book of Geneva,' which had borrowed it (with the exception of a sentence or two from King Edward's Book) from Calvin's Genevan Liturgy, and Calvin's form again had been taken almost *verbatim* from Farel's Neûchatel Liturgy of 1533. This form and Calvin's had a prayer at the close of the service, which was omitted by the 'Book of Geneva.' Here, too, as elsewhere, the 'Book of Geneva' omits the preface universal in the Continental services of "Our help is in the name of the Lord," &c. This is given as a preface to Cowper's Sermons, but there are few traces of its use in Scotland, though it was no doubt common. In Scotland, in accordance with the rubric, marriage was at first performed after the Reader's service, and before sermon. Thus in 1600 the Glasgow session decrees that those who "go away after marriage or baptism, and stay not sermon, shall be counted totally absent."

16. *The Order of Baptism.*—This is retained from the 'Book of Geneva,' except the exposition of the Creed, which appears first in the 1564 edition of the 'Common Order.' In the rubric before the first prayer, the Genevan Book has, "The minister . . . saith in this manner, or such like, kneeling," where the Scots Book of 1564 has, "Then followeth this prayer." This prayer closely follows that given in Calvin's Genevan Liturgy, omitting, however, a petition for the remission of the original sin of the child.

17. *The Order of the Fast.*—This was drawn up in 1565 by Knox and Craig, in obedience to an order of the Assembly. Knox speaks as if he had written it himself.—Works, vol. ii. p. 517. It was printed by Lekprevik in 1566, and again in 1574, with the addition of a few pages, beginning at "Certain chapters," &c. It was printed in all the complete editions of the 'Book of Common Order,' but the text varies very much.

18. *The* 150 *Psalms of David.*—Of these we have merely given a

few specimens, *fac-simile.* Some of the psalms, translated by Wedderburn, vicar of Dundee, were used at first by the Protestants of Scotland. After this, along with King Edward's Book, it is believed that the 44 psalms translated by Sternhold and Hopkins were introduced into Scotland, and used in public worship.

The 'Book of Geneva,' first published in 1556, contained 51 psalms —viz., the 44 of Sternhold and Hopkins, somewhat modified, and 7 by Whittingham. In 1561 the 'Genevan Psalter' was enlarged to 87 psalms, 36 additional being added to the old 51, and these would be introduced into Scotland with all copies of the Book. In 1562 the translation of the whole psalms was completed in England for the use of the Church. In addition to the 44 of Sternhold and Hopkins, 20 of those which had been added by the exiles were retained.

In 1564 the 'Scottish Psalter' was completed. It retained the Genevan collection of 87, selected 42 from the additions in the English Psalter of 1562, and completed the number with 21 new renderings by Pont and J. C., supposed to be John Craig.

The Psalters of the Churches of Scotland and England had thus 109 translations of the psalms in common—viz., 40 by Sternhold, 37 by Hopkins, 10 by Kethe, 11 by Whittingham, 8 by Norton, 2 by M., and 1 by Pulleyn.

The other 41 were different, and of those in the Scots Book, 15 were by Kethe, 4 by Whittingham, 1 by Pulleyn, 6 by Pont, and 15 by J. C.

The same desire for uniformity, which gave us our present version of the Bible, caused King James to endeavour to introduce a common Prayer-Book and Psalter into both kingdoms. With the aid of Sir William Alexander, Earl of Stirling, he drew up a poetical version of the Psalms, which was printed in 1631 by order of King Charles. The Scots knew that it was a stepping-stone to a new Liturgy, and reasons against its reception were drawn up, it has been supposed, by Calderwood. In 1634 King Charles gave orders to the Scottish Privy Council that no other version was to be printed or imported; and in 1636 he brought out a new edition, a good deal changed from that of 1631. This was bound up with Laud's Service-Book of 1637, and was intended for immediate use, but both shared a similar fate.

The old Psalter continued in use till 1650, and for many years later among the Scottish congregations in Holland. The present or Westminster version was carefully revised in Scotland; and the Commission of Assembly, in 1650, ordered its introduction, and forbade the use of the old, in church or family, after the 1st May of that year.

It may be added that the present second version of the 100th Psalm, and the second version of the 124th, are, with a few verbal changes, from the old Psalter. The former was composed by Kethe, the latter by Whittingham. Others, such as the L. M. version of the 145th, closely resemble those in the old book.

The old Psalms have usually the Latin headings, and in many editions the long ones are divided into parts, as in the French Psalters.

The prose version is given in the margin of the edition of 1599, and in most of the subsequent editions. This is always taken from the Genevan Bible, except in the edition of Raban, 1633, which gives King James's version.

19. *Conclusions or Doxologies.*—These, of which we have given specimens, were renderings of Gloria Patri, 32 in number, to suit the great variety of metres in the Psalter, so that one might be sung at the close of each psalm or part of a psalm. One of these conclusions is given in the edition of 1575, the full set in that of 1595. Some of the later editions have part of them, some the whole, some none; but the use of Gloria Patri in some or in all the metres was universal in 1638. Baillie speaks of it as the "constant practice of our Church." Somewhat similar versions of Gloria Patri are still printed at the end of the Psalms, in the English Book of Common Prayer.

The edition of 1595 has a short collect after each Psalm founded upon it. These prayers seem to have been sometimes printed separately. They are given in full in Livingstone's edition of the Psalter.

20. *Hymns.*—The Continental Psalters had a few hymns appended to the Psalms. Thus the Dutch of 1640 had the Decalogue, the Song of Zacharias, of Mary, of Simeon, of Elizabeth, the Lord's Prayer, Creed, Te Deum, &c. Marot's French Psalter of 1543 had the Song of Simeon, Decalogue, Belief, the Lord's Prayer, and Ave Marie. Similar versions were added to the Psalms in the 'Book of Geneva' and in the English Psalter. They had appeared also in Scotland at an earlier period with Wedderburn's Psalms. (See Dr Mitchell's 'Wedderburns and their Work.') The Scottish Psalter, as printed in 1564, gave only the Psalms; but Bassandyne's edition of 1575 has five spiritual songs; that of 1587, and many others, have ten; while some of the later editions have fourteen, as follows:—

(1.) *The Ten Commandments.*—Retained from the 'Book of Geneva.' It is assigned to Whittingham.

(2.) *A Prayer after the Commandments.*—Taken from the English Psalter of 1560.

NOTES.

(3.) *The Lord's Prayer.*—From the English Psalter of 1560. Assigned to Cox, Bishop of Ely. It is, however, a translation of Luther's hymn on the same subject.—Mitchell's Wedderburns, p. 18 and 53.

(4.) *Veni Creator.*— From King Edward's Liturgy, the same version of this old hymn being given in the ordination services of his first book, 1549.—Liturgies of Edward VI., p. 172, Par. Soc.

(5.) *Song of Simeon.*—From the English Psalter of 1560.

(6.) *The Creed.*—From the English Psalter of 1560.

(7.) *The Humble Sute of a Sinner.*—From the English Psalter of 1562.

(8.) (1*st*) *Lamentation of a Sinner.*—From the English Psalter of 1562.

(9.) *The Complaint of a Sinner.*—From the English Psalter of 1562.

(10.) *The Magnificat.*—From the English Psalter of 1560.

(11.) (2*d*) *The Lamentation.*—From the English Psalter of 1562.

(12.) *The Song of Moses.*—This is peculiar to Scotland, and was composed by James Melville.

(13.) *A Thanksgiving after the Lord's Supper.*—From the English Psalter of 1562.

(14.) *What greater Wealth.*—Peculiar to Scotland.

There were versions of some of these hymns in most European languages soon after the Reformation, and Latin versions before. We have printed six from Hart of 1615, &c., and but for want of space would have given others. Most of them are to be found in those copies of the English Prayer-Book that have Sternhold and Hopkins's version of the Psalms. See also the Hymns printed with the English New Version.

All the hymns in the old Psalter appear to be even yet of "public authority" in the Church. When the new Psalter was under consideration, the Assembly in 1647 authorised Zachary Boyd to revise the hymns for incorporation with it. This was not done, but the hymns were not superseded with the psalms.

The music is always given with the psalms till 1650. Many of the tunes are from the French Psalter of Marot. For a century church music had been most carefully cultivated in Scotland, but it began to decline immediately after this time, as the new leaven of English sectarianism began to work.

For most of the above particulars relating to the Psalter we are indebted to Mr Laing's notes in the Appendix to Baillie's Letters, vol. iii. 525, and to Livingstone's reprint.

21. *The Catechism of Calvin.*—This Catechism, of which we have given a few pages *fac-simile*, appeared first in French in 1536, and in Latin in 1538. It was afterwards much altered, and was printed again in its complete form in French in 1541, and in Latin in 1545. Farel and Viret are said to have assisted in the compilation of it (Dyer's Calvin, p. 82), but Calvin speaks as if he were the sole author. It was translated by the English refugees, and bound up with the 'Book of Geneva.' It was approved by the 'First Book of Discipline,' was usually bound with the 'Book of Common Order,' and was the ordinary Church Catechism of Scotland till the time of the Westminster Assembly. It was also the Church Catechism of the French, French-Swiss, and Walloon Churches; and in 1578 it was ordered by statute to be used in the University of Oxford.—(Eutaxia, p. 196.) It is divided into portions for each Sunday in the year, or rather for 55 Sundays. Calvin's little catechism for the examination of children before admission to the Lord's supper was bound up with the larger one. The phrase "single and double carritches" occurs long before 1645, and refers to these two catechisms. Craig published two catechisms, the shorter of which took the place of Calvin's little catechism in 1592. The other great catechism of the Reformed, the Heidelberg, was also printed by public authority for the use of the Church of Scotland, and is sometimes bound up with the 'Book of Common Order.'

It was first published in 1563; was chiefly composed by Ursinus, a pupil of Melanchthon, and is sometimes called Ursine's catechism, sometimes the Palatine. It became the Church Catechism of the Dutch, German, and German-Swiss Reformed, was approved by the Synod of Dort, and is perhaps the best of all the Reformed symbols. It was in 159- that it received public authority in Scotland; but the Act of Assembly on the subject does not appear to be extant. In Hart's 1615 edition of the 'Book of Common Order' the title-page bears that it is "appointed to be printed for the use of the Kirk of Edinburgh." There were two translations in use. The one in Hart of 1615 differs from that in Dunlop's Confessions. In the Liturgy of the Dutch Church in America a translation is given which differs from both. Like Calvin's Catechism, it is divided into portions, fifty-two in number, for the Lord's days of a year.

The Catechisms of the Scottish Reformation have recently been carefully edited by the Rev. Dr Bonar, Edinburgh.

22. *Prayers for Private Houses.*

(1.) *Morning Prayer.*—Retained from the 'Book of Geneva,' one or two sentences towards the close, in which the exiles referred to their country, being changed in the Scottish editions. There was a morning prayer after the catechism in Calvin's Genevan Liturgy, but this has not much in common with it.

(2.) *Prayers to be said before and after Meals.*—Part of these are from the 'Book of Geneva.' The Blessing and first Thanksgiving appear in Calvin's Genevan Liturgy. Some of them are taken partly from graces as old as the time of St Chrysostom and St Athanasius.—Priv. Pray., Qu. Eliz., p. 400, 401.

(3.) *Evening Prayer.*—Retained from the 'Book of Geneva,' and taken partly from the Evening Prayer in Calvin's Liturgy. This was the last prayer in which Knox joined, it having been read at family worship in his room an hour before his death.—(Laing's Knox, vol. vi. 660; M'Crie's Life, p. 276.) Spottiswoode says—this prayer "being ordinarily read in the house;" but this, though probable enough, is not stated in the contemporary account. It may be added that Knox read through the Psalms every month (Cal. His., iii. 232), besides some chapters of the Old and New Testaments daily. The Morning and Evening Prayer and all the Graces, as in Hart, are printed in the 'Liturgical Services of the Reign of Elizabeth' from an English edition of 1566. The Evening Prayer and the Graces appear also in Bull's 'Christian Prayers' of the same date.—Parker Soc.

23. *Other Prayers.*—After the Evening Prayer Hart gives "a Prayer made at the first Assembly of the English Church at Geneva, when the Confession of the Faith, and whole orders were there read and approved." As it was never used in Scotland, and is omitted in many editions of the 'Book of Common Order,' we have not printed it, but have given at the end a more common one, which is not in Hart, instead.

(1.) *A Complaint of the Tyranny used against the Saints of God, &c.*—This is in the edition of the 'Book of Common Order' of 1564, and most of the subsequent editions. It is a Scottish compilation. The last paragraph is the same as a prayer, at the end of the Order of the Fast.

(2.) *A Godly Prayer.*—*Honour and Praise, &c.*—This prayer is in the 1564 edition, and generally afterwards. It is given in 'Bull's Christian Prayers,' p. 147, with the heading, "A thanksgiving to God for His great benefits, and prayer for grace to confirm and increase the same." The portion after the thanksgiving is an expansion of the Lord's Prayer. It is evidently an old prayer.

(3.) *A Prayer to be said of the Child before he study his Lesson, out of the* 119*th Psalm.*—This is taken from Calvin's 'Genevan Liturgy.' Part of it is given in the Liturgies of King Edward VI., Park. Soc., p. 539, under date 1553. The whole of it is given in Latin in the Orarium of 1560.—Private Prayers of the reign of Queen Eliz., p. 207. It was in all likelihood in use long before the Reformation.

(4.) *A Prayer to be said before a Man begin his Work.*—Appears in the edition of 1564. Probably an old prayer.

(5.) *A Prayer necessary for all Men.*—Though not in Hart, we have added this, as it is usually printed with the 'Book of Common Order.' It has an interesting history, being founded on a Latin prayer of Thomas Aquinas, which was translated into English by Queen Mary when she was only eleven years of age. Mary's translation appeared first in the Primer of 1545, again in the Primer of 1553, and in Queen Elizabeth's Primer of 1559. A Latin version is given in the Orarium of 1560. See Liturgies of King Ed., p. 466; Private Prayers of the reign of Queen Eliz., p. 107 and 201.

The version given in the Book of Common Order,' which differs considerably from that of Queen Mary, was taken from Godly Prayers printed in England in 1552, with the change of a word, *self* for *life*, apparently a misprint. — Liturgical Services, Qu. Eliz., Par. Soc., p. 246 and 250.

There are some prayers usually printed after the Heidelberg Catechism, which are chiefly different versions of some of those printed after Calvin's. The Morning Prayer for Families is a translation of a similar prayer in Calvin's Liturgy; the Prayer for Scholars, a different translation from that in Hart. The Grace and the Thanksgiving and the Evening Prayer are translations from Calvin's Liturgy. The last is supposed to have been founded on the hymn, "Salvator mundi, Domine."—Private Prayers, Queen Eliz., p. 131 and 445.

It thus appears that nearly the whole of Knox's Liturgy is from earlier Reformed Services; and though we have scarcely touched upon the wider field, there can be no doubt that these services themselves are, if we except Protestant expressions of doctrine and opinion, mainly from Catholic originals, and may be traced through the whole of Christianity.

G. W. S.

A DIRECTORY

FOR

THE PUBLIC WORSHIP

OF

GOD

INTRODUCTION

TO

THE DIRECTORY.

THE era of the Westminster Assembly was marked by a closer relation between the Scottish Church and English Puritanism than was ever possible before or since. The Scottish ideal of a Church, popular without being democratic, national without being a department of State, catholic without dependence on foreign Churches for its life, repelled the Puritan as well as the Erastian and the Anglican. He never clung, as the Scots did, to a belief in the federal character of the Christian Church. If a Nonconformist, he recognised no wider circle of fellowship than the little company with whom he worshipped. If he conformed to the Church of England, religious unity was associated in his mind with the decrees of courts rather than of councils. A common danger had now brought Puritan and Scotsman into close alliance, and in the first excitement of success they had united in an enterprise not unlike that which they had baffled, and set themselves to bring the three nations to a uniformity in worship, Church government, and creed. But they soon found that something more was needed to make them one than agreement in theology and in dislike to the ecclesiastical arrangements of the Tudors. The Scots, Huguenot rather than Puritan in their affinities, stood on the traditions of their own and the Reformed Churches of the Continent. The Parliamentarians wavered between a limited Episcopacy, such as Usher would have allowed, and Independency in various stages of development. The Scots Commissioners wrote from London to their own Assembly: "The prejudices against Presbyteriall government are many and great; the two extremes of Prelacie and Independencie, which latter is the generall claime of all sects and sectaries, have prevailed most in this Kirk, and no other thing known by the multitude but the one or the other."* And Baillie in his private letters wrote: "In the time of this anarchie the divisions of people weeklie does much encrease: the Independent partie growes; but the Anabaptists more, and the Antinomians most. . . . As yet a Presbytrie to this people is conceaved to be a strange monster. . . . . The humour of this people is very various, and inclinable to singularities, to differ from all the world, and one from another, and shortly from themselves. No people had so much need of a Presbytrie." † During the sitting of the Assembly, an alliance between the more moderate Puritans and the Scots restrained the Independents, and after much debate and compromise a constitution, formally Presbyterian, was adopted. But from the first it wanted the vigour of a native growth. Parliament would concede to it no divine right. The growing power of the Independents crippled its action. After its disestablishment at the Restoration, it gradually disappeared; and at the present day, the most genuine representatives of the Puritans, so far as they have not been comprehended in the National Church, are to be found in the ranks of Congregationalism. The Presbyterianism of Westminster would have been more likely to

* Acts of Assembly, p. 102. Edit. 1843.
† Letters, ii. 117, 177.

endure, if, instead of being fashioned on foreign models, it had been allowed to adapt itself to the circumstances and temperament of the nation. It is certain that in a later age much of what is most fervid in English religion has found an embodiment for itself in a system essentially Presbyterian. In not a few of its features—in its spirit of independent loyalty, in its combination of liturgical with free prayer, and in its subordination of congregational power to a graduated administration and firm central executive—the system of Wesley, though of a different school of theology, bears no small resemblance to what the Church of Scotland became after her Reformation was complete.

The traces of the Westminster alliance have in Scotland been more lasting. Ever since the union of the crowns, both her sympathies and antipathies had, more than in earlier times, been limited by the narrow confines of the island. The deep sense of wrong produced by the intrusion of an English Episcopate had called into existence a party having more in common with English nonconformity than their fathers had. Soon after the great Assembly of 1638, they had begun to act in organised opposition to those of their brethren who were content with the older Scottish Protestantism. Though the degree of divergence was much less, these two parties stood in the same relative position to each other as the two great sections of the Westminster Divines. Both sides had representatives among the Commissioners sent up to the Assembly. The advanced Puritans, even when opposed by the Scots, who usually acted in perfect concert, felt more sympathy with Gillespie and Rutherford than with Henderson and Baillie. There was as yet a wide interval between the Independent and the Protester (as he was afterwards called), but it was sensibly diminished during the sitting of the Assembly. The good understanding which was maintained between them during Cromwell's iron domination in Scotland, showed how far the process of assimilation had advanced. Much of the leaven then introduced is working still, as any one may observe who analyses the principles involved in most of our Church controversies, and not a few of our peculiarities of worship.

Though the idea of a United British Church was not realised by the Assembly, the fruits of their labours remain in the canons of theology, discipline, and worship which were to have been its standards, and the metrical Psalter prepared for its service of praise. These, now almost forgotten in England, have come to be considered the distinctive badges of Scottish religion. At first, it seems incredible that a people, so tenacious of their independence, should have so readily accepted, and so reverently preserved, the decrees of a foreign Convocation, acting under the commission of a foreign legislature. But when we consider the influence which Scottish opinion had in the Assembly, we may rather wonder that England so readily adopted them. The proposal for such a council had first come from the Assembly in Edinburgh. When the six Commissioners "from the Kirk and kingdom of Scotland" took their seats in the Jerusalem Chamber, they refused to have their suffrages lost among those of a hundred and fifty Englishmen. They would sit, they said, as a body of assessors, with voices, but no votes, treating in the name of Scotland for uniformity with England; and their claim, after some demur, was allowed.* At every stage of the Assembly's proceedings, their influence over its decisions was greater than either their numbers or their undoubted talents could account for. Men who had hitherto been living in enforced conformity,

* Baillie, ii. 110.

THE DIRECTORY.

or unorganised nonconformity, may have conceded something to their experience in Church legislation. But we cannot forget the great names on the other side, or the sensitiveness to Scottish dictation which then prevailed in England. The chief reason for the extreme deference paid to them was the importance of the northern alliance, at a time when the great issues of the civil war were trembling in the balance. On one occasion Baillie says dryly, " Mr Henderson's hopes are not great of their conformitie to us, before our armie be in England." But whatever we assume to be the causes, the results were such as to justify his words before the Scottish Assemby in 1645 : " That in place of Episcopacie, a Scotts Presbytrie should be concluded in ane English Assemblie, and ordained in ane English Parliament, as it is already ordained in the House of Commons; that the practice of the Church of Scotland, sett down in a most wholesome, pious, and prudent Directorie, should come in the place of a Liturgie in all the three dominions ; such stories, lately told, would have been counted fancies, dreams, meer impossibilities : yet this day we tell them as truths, and deeds done."*

All that is known of English opinion up to the meeting of the Assembly shows that Baillie might well be almost incredulous of their success in superseding the Liturgy by the Directory. For it is plain that at first nothing more than a revision of the Prayer-Book had been contemplated. A declaration of the English Parliament, April 9, 1642, says "that they intend a due and necessary reformation of the government and liturgy of the Church, and to take away nothing in the one or the other but what shall be evil, and justly offensive, or at least unnecessary and burdensome." The Act summoning the Assembly bears

* Ibid., p. 256.

that "many things as yet remain in the discipline, liturgy, and government of the Church, which necessarily require a more perfect reformation." Nor was the intention of Parliament overborne by the popular voice. No doubt there had always been among a section of the Puritans a preference for an unliturgical worship. Neal has preserved a Directory which was found among Cartwright's papers after his death, "anciently contended for, and as far as the times would suffer, practised by the first nonconformists in the days of Queen Elizabeth."* The order of service is, a psalm, "the minister noting the end of their singing," an exhortation to devotion, a prayer, ending with the Lord's Prayer, a sermon, a prayer for blessing on the Word, the Church, and all mankind, followed by the Lord's Prayer, a psalm, and blessing. But preference for such a service was seldom made a matter of conscience. In the end of the sixteenth century, a modification of the Reformed Liturgy common to France, Switzerland, and Scotland, was extensively used among the Puritans.† Their scruples were aroused by the ceremonies, vestments, and inflexibility of the Common Prayer rather than by its forms. Both in 1643, and at the Restoration,‡ a large body of them would have been satisfied with certain alterations of it. Undoubtedly the Scots were pleased to see it abolished. It was connected in their minds with the long-continued endeavour to force on the Northern Church the peculiarities of the Southern. But even amid the intense excitement of 1638, there had been no declaration against Liturgies as such, but only against one of the various Liturgies used in Reformed

* Neal's Puritans, 2d ed., ii. 816.
† See Middleburg Prayer-Book in Hall's Reliq. Liturg.
‡ See Debate at the Savoy Conference, where about one-half of the Presbyterian Commissioners were Westminster Divines.

THE DIRECTORY.   263

Christendom. Certainly no voice was raised against the simpler and more elastic forms of their own Common Order. Henderson himself, in his interesting tract 'The Government and Order of the Church of Scotland, 1641' speaks of it as an order to which they conformed, though not tied to the words. But those were days in which opinions and parties were rapidly matured. By the time that the Assembly met, the opinion that all forms of prayer are a restraining of the Spirit, had been widely adopted. We shall see that on this point the views of the Divines themselves underwent no little change during the few months that it was under their consideration; and when they rose, both kingdoms, one formally and for a time, the other silently and for ever, had abandoned their distinctive forms of ritual. Still the Scottish Liturgy as then used was the mould on which the new manual was fashioned. To see this it is only necessary to set side by side the order of service for the Lord's Day required by each :—

COMMON ORDER.		DIRECTORY.
Prayer,		Prayer,
Scripture from both Testaments,	Reader's Service,	Scripture from both Testaments,
Psalm,		Psalm,
Prayer,		Prayer,
Psalm, Prayer, } in morning only,*		
Sermon,		Sermon,
Prayer,		Prayer,
Lord's Prayer,		Lord's Prayer,
Creed,		
Psalm,		Psalm,
Benediction.		Benediction.

When we come to inquire into the details of the

* Henderson's Government and Order.

Assembly's work, the most distinct information is found in the Journal of Dr John Lightfoot (Works, vol. xiii. ed. 1825). Baillie's letters to his friends in Scotland, though less regular, and less copious in their details, abound in vivid sketches of parties and debates. Gillespie's Notes, published a few years ago, are chiefly memoranda of the discussions on Church government; but the few that refer to the Directory are interesting and important. Another source of information is the MS. Record preserved at Queen's Square, Bloomsbury, in the library founded by Dr Williams. The editor has to express his thanks to the Trustees and Librarian for the ready permission and help which they gave him when he applied for access to these volumes. The debates on the Directory are recorded under fifty-four sessions in the end of the second volume, and twenty-one at the beginning of the third. They are believed to be the notes of Byfield, the scribe (whose name is on the blank leaf), jotted down while the discussions went on, and, in all probability, afterwards extended in a register now lost. Words and sentences are constantly left unfinished, and whole speeches are represented by blanks of half a page following the name of the speaker. To decipher these records is a work of very great difficulty; but after as careful an examination as was possible of every session, they have been found to add little of importance to Lightfoot's more careful summary.

The Assembly was divided into three committees, in which its business was matured for open discussion. As no records of their sittings are known to exist, the incidental notices of Baillie tell us almost all that we know of the history of the Directory in this first stage. In October 1643, three months after the opening of the Assembly, the subject was assigned to one of these com-

THE DIRECTORY.

mittees;* and in December the preparation of the rough draft of a Directory was left to a small sub-committee, consisting of Marshall, Palmer, Goodwin, Young, Herle, and the Scots Commissioners, with Marshall as chairman.† As Young (the "T. Y." of Smectymnuus) was a Scotsman by birth,‡ and Goodwin the only decided Independent of the number, the general cast of the Directory was more likely to be Scottish than English. Moreover, the most important sections of it, those on Prayer, Preaching, and the Administration of the Sacraments, were left ultimately to Henderson and his friends.§ In spring, the draft was in the hands of the grand committee, and on the 24th of May was submitted to the Assembly. It occupied them almost exclusively till the middle of August, was resumed in October, and was completed in the end of December, receiving the sanction of Parliament immediately after. In February it was accepted by the Scottish Assembly and Parliament. Nothing can better illustrate the difference between the English and Scottish theories of the relations between the civil and ecclesiastical estates than the language in which it was confirmed by the two Legislatures. The English "have consulted with the reverend, pious, and learned divines called together to that purpose, and do judge it necessary that . . . the Directory for the Public Worship of God, hereinafter mentioned, be established and observed in all the churches within the kingdom." The Scottish "do heartily and cheerfully agree to the said Directory, according to the Act of the General Assembly approving the same; which Act, together with the Directory itself, the Estates of Parliament do, without a contrary voice, ratify and approve in all the heads and articles thereof, and do interpone and add the

---

* Neal, ii. 106.   † Baillie, ii. 117.
‡ Baillie, i. 366, ii. 148.   § Ibid., p. 131, 140, 148.

authority of Parliament to the said Act of the General Assembly."

The Directory was less comprehensive in its range than many other works of the same kind have been. Even as it stands, it contains sections which were added almost at the last moment. Certain offices, such as those for Confirmation or the Private Administration of the Sacraments, were excluded on principle. Regulations for Discipline and Ordination, as well as a Catechism, were provided for by the Assembly elsewhere. The Assembly of Scotland, before they accepted it, thought it necessary to supplement it by several declaratory enactments. The Act establishing it defined the sense in which they received the passage concerning communicating at a table, and made a reservation in favour of their existing laws, so far as these were not altered by the Directory.* At the same time they passed another Act which, as virtually an Appendix to the Directory, is here inserted at length :—

Sess. 14, February 7, 1645.—*The opinion of the Committee for keeping the greater uniformity in this Kirk, in the practice and observations of the Directory in some points of public worship.*

1. It is the humble opinion of the Committee for regulating that exercise of reading and expounding the Scriptures read upon the Lord's Day, mentioned in the Directory, that the Minister and people repair to the kirk half an hour before that time at which ordinarily the Minister now entereth to the public worship ; and that that exercise of reading and expounding, together with the ordinary exercise of preaching, be perfected and ended at the time which formerly closed the exercise of public worship.

II. In the administration of Baptism, it will be convenient that that Sacrament be administered in face of the Congregation, that what is spoken and done may be heard and seen of all, and that it be administered after the sermon, before the blessing.

III. In the administration of the Lord's Supper, it is the judgment of the Committee :—

---

* See page 284 of this volume.

1. That congregations be still tried and examined before the Communion, according to the bygone practice of this Kirk.

2. That there be no reading in the time of communicating, but the Minister making a short exhortation at every table ; that thereafter there be silence during the time of the communicants' receiving, except only when the Minister expresses some few short sentences, suitable to the present condition of the communicants in the receiving, that they may be incited and quickened in their meditations in the action.

3. That distribution of the elements among the communicants be universally used ; and for that effect, that the bread be so prepared that the communicants may divide it amongst themselves, after the Minister hath broken and delivered it to the nearest.

4. That while the tables are dissolving and filling, there be always singing of some portion of a Psalm, according to the custom.

5. That the communicants, both before their going to and after their coming from the table, shall only join themselves to the present public exercise then in hand.

6. That when the Communion is to be celebrate in a parish, one Minister may be employed for assisting the Minister of the parish, or at the most two.

7. That there be a sermon of preparation delivered in the ordinary place of public worship upon the day immediately preceding.

8. That before the serving of the tables there be only one sermon delivered to those who are to communicate, and that in the kirk where the service is to be performed. And that in the same kirk there be one sermon of thanksgiving after the Communion is ended.

9. When the parishioners are so numerous that their parish kirk cannot contain them, so that there is a necessity to keep out such of the parish as cannot conveniently have place, that in that case the brother who assists the Minister of the parish may be ready, if need be, to give a word of exhortation in some convenient place appointed for that purpose, to those of the parish who that day are not to communicate ; which must not be begun until the sermon delivered in the kirk be concluded.

10. That of those who are present in the kirk when the Communion is celebrate none be permitted to go forth whill [until] the whole tables be served and the blessing pronounced, unless it be for more commodious order, and in other cases of necessity.

11. That the Minister who cometh to assist have a special care to provide his own parish, lest, otherwise, while he is about to minister comfort to others, his own flock be left destitute of preaching.

12. That none coming from another parish shall be admitted to the Communion without a testimonial from their own Minister: and no Minister shall refuse a testimonial to any of his parish who communicates ordinarily at their own parish kirk, and are without scandal in their life for the time. And this is no ways to prejudge any honest person who occasionally is in the place where the Communion is celebrate; or such as by death or absence of their own Minister, could not have a testimonial.

IV. It is also the judgment of the Committee, that the Ministers' bowing in the pulpit, though a lawful custom in this Kirk, be hereafter laid aside, for satisfaction of the desires of the reverend Divines in the Synod of England, and for uniformity with that Kirk, so much endeared to us.

> The Assembly, having considered seriously the judgment of the Committee above written, doth approve the same in all the articles thereof, and ordains them to be observed in all time hereafter.

The next enactment concerning the Directory is a recommendation in an Interim Act of 1652 :—

That every Minister do so dispose of the time appointed for the reading of Scripture, as both the order of the Directory and Act of Uniformity, in the point of lecture, may be observed; that two chapters being read, one of the Old Testament and the other of the New, after reading of the first, some few observations of the chief doctrines being held forth and propounded briefly and plainly to the people, time may be left to read the second chapter, and to give some brief observations on it also, as the time allowed will suffer.

Since the Restoration, the Directory has never been acknowledged by civil authority. The Parliamentary recognition of it in 1645 was annulled by the Act Rescissory. When the old order of things was restored at the Revolution, no notice was taken of it in the new compact between Church and State. The story, as told by Sage,[*] is that it had been intended to ratify the Catechisms and Directory, but that, after the reading of the Confession, the Parliament became impatient, and voted that to be

[*] Account of the Late Establishment, &c., p. 43.

THE DIRECTORY. 269

sufficient; so that it is the only one of the Westminster standards embodied in the Revolution Settlement. The Church, however, though not rigidly conforming to the Directory, has never treated it as an obsolete statute. The following Statutes contain all that has been enacted regarding it since the Revolution :—

1694. Sess. 9. Act anent Lecturing.—The General Assembly of this National Church, considering how necessary and edifying it is that the people be well acquainted with the Holy Scriptures, doth therefore commend to the several Presbyteries that they endeavour that the ministers within their respective bounds shall, in their exercise of lecturing, read and open up to the people some large and considerable portion of the Word of God : and this to the effect the old custom introduced and established by the Directory may by degrees be recovered.

1705. Sess. 12. Recommendation concerning the observation of the Directory for Worship.—The General Assembly hereby seriously recommends to all ministers and others within this National Church the due observation of the Directory for the Public Worship of God, approven by the General Assembly held in the year 1645, sess. 10.

1736. Sess. 8. Act concerning Preaching.—The General Assembly . . . do hereby recommend to all ministers and preachers seriously to consider and observe the Directory of this Church, concerning the preaching of the Word, which is approven by the General Assembly 1645, and in particular, &c.

1856. Sess. ult. Recommendation and Declaratory Act on Public Worship.—The General Assembly had laid before them an overture on Public Worship, the tenor whereof follows :—" Whereas it has always been the desire of the Church of Scotland, that in every part of its bounds the people should, as far as practicable, enjoy in an equal degree the benefits of public instruction and the administration of Divine ordinances, it is overtured to this General Assembly, that a Recommendation or Declaratory Act shall be issued for the purpose of reminding all who labour in word and doctrine that every congregation, at each diet of public worship, should have access to the advantage of hearing a portion of the Old and New Testament read,—and that there should always be included in the service of every Lord's Day, not only a sermon, but a lecture on a passage of the Holy Scriptures."

The General Assembly approve of the overture, and enjoin all the ministers of this Church to observe the recommendations contained in it respecting the reading of the Holy Scriptures of the Old and New Testament at each diet of public worship : And further, on the subject of the overture, the Assembly earnestly call the attention of all the Presbyteries and ministers of this Church to the regulations on this and other particulars connected with public worship and spiritual instruction contained in the Directory for the Public Worship of God, trusting that the principles maintained in that Directory will be duly observed.

From the day of its publication, the Directory has had more of official recognition than of hearty conformity accorded to it. In England, it was assailed by that large party who believed the Liturgy of Elizabeth to be the purest existing type of Christian worship. Their views are set forth with much vigour by Dr Henry Hammond, in his 'View of the New Directory.' While, as was to be expected, he unsparingly attacks the Preface, the Directory itself is blamed rather for its omissions than its enactments. It excited also the bitter enmity of the sectaries who held that "a Directory or Order to help in the way of worship is a breach of the second commandment,"* and who, even in the sub-committee, had an advocate in Goodwin.† In Scotland, there seems to have been on the one side of the Church a disposition to maintain the old national customs of worship, notwithstanding the Directory; on the other, to find a warrant for further changes in the partial licence which it gave. "I hear that the Lord's Prayer was generally used in the kirks of Edinburgh till the year 1649, and read forms of prayer till the 1647. In the 1648, instead of these, every afternoon, the ministers went in by turns and prayed, and caused read two chapters of the Bible, and a little after they turned it to a lecture, that was used for

* Edwards's Gangræna, p. 31. † Baillie, ii. 123.

THE DIRECTORY.

some years after."* We need not doubt Dr Monro's facts, because his language is that of a hot partisan, when he says, "After the year 1638, until Cromwell's army invaded our nation, they never left off the using of those Catholic and Christian forms [the Lord's Prayer, Doxology, and Creed]. But such of the Remonstrators as were deeply in the interests of the usurper, then left off the use of such forms, drawing as near as was possible to the spiritual heights and pretended purity of the Independents in the army."† The dislike which the Protesters had to the use of the Lord's Prayer is well known. We may suppose, from the position which they occupied in relation to the Assembly of 1652, that the Act of that year, enforcing the reading of both Testaments, was directed against them; and they have always been considered the originators of the new customs at the Communion which date from that period.‡

At the Restoration, the change in the existing form of worship was not great. The Directory was not acknowledged. But the nation would not endure an attempt to impose a fixed Liturgy. It was to be expected that the nearest approach to a liturgical service would be found in Aberdeenshire. But it did not go beyond "a sett form of prayer, especially with the Lord's Prayer," followed by Scripture, the Creed (the people all standing), and the Ten Commandments; all read by the reader, where there was one; and in towns the Common Order was to be read at daily service.§ But over the rest of Scotland, there seems to have been merely a revival of the old Scottish service, with the Common Order as a directory rather

---

* Wodrow's Analecta, i. p. 274. See also Correspondence, iii. 494.
† Apology for the Clergy, 1693, p. 18.
‡ Principal Lee's History, ii. 312; and Burnet's History.
§ Synod Records, p. 263.

than a liturgy. A few exceptions, such as there will always be where a law of uniformity is not absolutely inflexible, have been noticed and remembered from their very rarity. The observances which the school of 1640 had denounced resumed their former places in the service, with the exception of bowing in the pulpit.* It was natural that two parties, differing so widely as to the source and form of Church government, should adopt distinctive differences in their worship; and the curious result was that for half a century the use of the Lord's Prayer, Doxology, and Creed, which had once distinguished the old Scottish Presbyterians from those of English sympathies, was the badge of ritual distinction between Presbyterian and Episcopalian. † Nothing can be more unlike the reality than the picture which many call up before their imaginations, of surpliced priests reading the Anglican service in the old parish churches of Scotland, or dispensing the Eucharist to communicants kneeling at chancel rails. Attention has repeatedly been drawn to the fact that even Sir Walter Scott, as we gather from his tales, particularly from 'Old Mortality,' supposed the English worship to have been universally adopted during this period. When we remember how many people of superficial education have formed, and are forming, from those most charming of fictions, strong opinions on the gravest problems of Scottish history, it is of importance to remark this ignorance of what was the established worship of his country till within a lifetime of his own birth.

Two Englishmen have described the Scottish service, as they found it celebrated at the very moments of transi-

* Full and Final Answer Examined, 1703, p. 17.
† See Fife Synod Records, p. 184; and the Revolution Pamphlets, *passim*.

tion in 1661 and 1689. Ray, the naturalist,* says, "The minister there, in the public worship, doth not shift places out of the desk into the pulpit, as in England, but at his first coming in ascends the pulpit. They commonly begin their worship with a Psalm before the minister comes in, who, after the Psalm is finished, prayeth, and then reads and expounds in some places, in some not; then another Psalm is sung, and after that their minister prays again and preacheth as in England." This was just before the restoration of Episcopacy. The state of things before the restoration of Presbytery is thus described by Morer, in the 'Short Account of Scotland,' first published in 1702, in which he gave his recollections of what the country was, when he was serving there as chaplain to an English regiment in 1689: "First, the precentor, about half an hour before the preacher comes, reads two or three chapters to the congregation, of what part of Scripture he pleases, or as the minister gives him directions. As soon as the preacher gets into the pulpit, the precentor leaves reading and sets a psalm, singing with the people, till the minister by some sign orders him to give over. The Psalm ended, the preacher begins confessing sins and begging pardon, exalting the holiness and majesty of God, and setting before Him our vileness and propensity to transgress His commandments. Then he goes to sermon, delivered always by heart, and, therefore, sometimes spoiled with battologies,† little impertinencies, and incoherence in their discourses. The sermon finished, he returns to prayer, thanks God for that opportunity to deliver His Word; prays for all mankind, for all Christians, for that particular nation, for the Sovereign and Royal Family (without naming any), for subordinate

* Itinerary, p. 208.
† The "vain repetitions" of St Matt. vi. 7.

magistrates, for sick people (especially such whose names the precentor hands up to him), then concludes with the Lord's Prayer, to sanctify what was said before. After this, another Psalm is sung, named by the minister, and frequently suited to the subject of his sermon; which done, he gives the benediction, and dismisses the congregation for that time." He says that the Presbyterians do it after the same manner, except that they do not use the Lord's Prayer and Doxology.* Of the Episcopalians he says, "I know of no book of canons they have, except the Perth Articles, *and the Directory above mentioned, which they also seem to have an eye to*,"† though he says afterwards, speaking of the Service-Book of 1637, "I know withal, that not only the Episcopal clergy, but, generally speaking, the nobility and gentry, think very well of it, wish it established by law, and could be content to be made a province to England that the English service might take place in that country."‡

It was to be expected that at the revival of Presbyterian government in 1690 all purely ecclesiastical arrangements would be largely influenced by the principles of the Protesters. At the Restoration, the strength of that party had lain among the younger clergy, and as none but those who had been admitted after 1649 were required to accept a fresh collation to their benefices, with its testing accompaniment, the oath of canonical obedience to a bishop, the outed ministers were mostly of this school. Observances, which they had disliked in their brethren the Resolutioners, had not become less objectionable when adopted by the curates. The service at the moorland meeting would of necessity differ somewhat from that which the minister had used in the church from which he had been driven, and the change would be more in the direction of freedom than of

* P. 60, 61. † Ibid., p. 52. ‡ P. 59.

regulated order. Those who accepted the irritating restrictions of an indulged incumbency were prompted both by feeling and by public opinion to recede as far as possible from the customs of their Episcopal neighbours. Kirkton tells us that when they were forbidden to lecture, some of them who, in accordance with their own Directory, read two passages of Scripture instead, were blamed by their people " for learning of the Erastian magistrate to worship God."* The Presbyterian clergy of the Revolution consisted of a few old Protesters, retaining the opinions of their youth, intensified by persecution, and a younger race of men who had been trained under the same influences, and licensed at home or in Holland. We need not wonder, therefore, that the mode of worship which was now gradually consolidated into an unwritten law wanted many of the most distinctive features of that which Knox, and Calderwood, and Henderson had defended. Episcopacy when established by Charles II. had been forced to forego, or at least defer, its design of introducing an English ritual, and to content itself with the national worship, which was being changed by those who ought to have preserved it. The result was that in some parts of the country, paradoxical as it may seem, Presbyterian customs were saved from extinction by the Episcopal incumbents who conformed at the Revolution. But, on the whole, the worship of the eighteenth century rested on associations more recent than the days of the Westminster Assembly. The attempt made by the Assembly of 1705 to secure conformity to the Directory was probably induced by the fact that the paper war between Episcopalian and Presbyterians had just then been raging in its greatest fury, and the constant taunts directed at their neglect of their own standard had reminded them of the propriety of more exact conformity to it. But

* Hist., p. 292.

though public opinion refused to be guided in this direction, either then or for long after, it created and maintained an unacknowledged standard of its own. It is remarkable that, with so little reference to any written authority, the worship of Scotland, not only in the National Church but in all indigenous communions, should have undergone so little change. Some way on in the eighteenth century, the difference with Episcopacy as to government was further widened by a difference in worship. But, with this limited exception, the Scottish service, conformist and nonconformist, has been singularly uniform. Of late years, however, the Church of Scotland, feeling the influence of a movement which has reached every corner of the Christian world, has begun to inquire into the origin, the authority, and the results of the customs in which she had hitherto acquiesced. These inquiries have been stimulated by the Act of Assembly which in 1856 called attention to the Directory's claims on our obedience. It has thus become a question of some importance, how far it is binding on the present generation of the Scottish clergy.

We have seen that it pretends to no civil authority. Its ecclesiastical sanction in 1645 was distinct and emphatic, but not more so than that of the Covenant, by which few Scotsmen, and no Scottish Churchmen, of the present day, feel themselves bound. But the claims of the Directory have from time to time been revived by the various Acts of Assembly quoted above. No doubt their language is only that of recommendation. To those who measure the moral obligation of a law by the probability of its being enforced, they may appear without authority. But all who are accustomed to acquiesce loyally in the Assembly's injunctions, and those especially who feel the want of a common standard by which they may try any disturbing question as to the details of public worship, will surely pay all due deference to what is at least the latest utterance of the Church of Scotland on such subjects. We need not, of course, offer more rigid obedience than the Directory asks for itself, and its demands are not excessive. Its name and spirit both show that it intended to allow a large measure of liberty to individual discretion. The letter which accompanied it when sent down to Scotland said, "We have not advised any imposition which might make it unlawful to vary from it in anything." It must be admitted that its language is not free from a defect common to the decrees of all councils with more deliberative than executive power—a proneness to dispose of disputed questions by using ambiguous language, or compromising opposing customs. We shall have to notice cases in which the Divines are known from other sources to have intended the text to bear meanings which the letter of it would never have suggested.

The injunctions of the Directory apply to *things which are to be spoken* and *things which are to be done.* The concluding words of the Preface, a passage made much more vague by the Assembly than it was in the original draft, explain how the materials for Prayer and Exhortation are to be used. It is left to each minister's sense of duty to see that the right of expansion, contraction, re-arrangement, or change, shall not become in his hands a hindrance to uniformity " in those things that contain the substance of the service and worship of God." When we examine the *agenda*, we find that the injunctions are issued with varying degrees of authority. They are evidently meant to be peremptory "when they hold forth such things as are of divine institution," or where variations in practice would make any approach to uniformity impossible. In other cases they are no more than recommendations. In others again they are mere permissions. In most cases, the language used is sufficiently precise to show the force of each injunction. The obligation to a practice is not the same when it is called *necessary*, *requisite*, *expedient*, *convenient*, or *sufficient;* or when in one place the minister *is to* or *shall*, in another *may*, do such and such things.

But the right of modifying the Directory, where its language is permissive, being conceded, this privilege ought to be exercised, not empirically, but with a wise regard to our own traditions and historical identity. Some changes in the arrangements of our worship are unavoidable; for it is vain to fancy that change can be stayed at the point to which ceaseless change has brought us. But it seems likely that the inevitable innovations of our age will partake largely of the character of restoration. Perhaps the following rules may commend themselves to those who are anxious to regulate their improvements by the Directory, in the hope that our future may retain the likeness of our past.

Where existing custom is in accordance with the Directory, change ought to be avoided.

Where custom has varied from it, the changes will be found to be of two kinds. There were points as to which our forefathers never accepted the recommendations of the Directory, but adhered to their own older customs, sometimes under the express sanction of permissive clauses; as when they used the Prayer of General Intercession after the sermon instead of before. If our fathers adhered to those customs on the ground of prescription, while the league with England lasted, there is still less reason for abandoning them now, when the lapse of two more centuries has made them more venerable, and the national compact has long been fallen from on the other side.

The other class of variations are those of more recent origin, such as the disuse of the Lord's Prayer, or the celebration of Marriage and Baptism in private. It will be found that as a rule these later changes may be given up without injury to the character of our service. One obvious exception is in the case of the section which forbids religious service at funerals, even in the house where the dead lie. This change was one so obviously necessary that no one would wish to see it reversed.

If, in any case, existing custom seems undesirable, and a return to the practice of the Directory impracticable, the Common Order has the next claim upon our attention. If a legitimate basis for any alteration cannot be found in one or other of our former standards of worship, it may safely be pronounced inconsistent with the constitution and spirit of our Church.

In the two other kingdoms for which the Directory was intended, it is now acknowledged only by Churches of Scottish descent. In America the Presbyterian Church uses a Directory, which, though not that of Westminster, has been based upon it, and retains to a great extent its enactments, and even its language. It wants the greater part of the materials for Prayer and Exhortation, and has several chapters on subjects not treated of in the older form. The Westminster sections are represented by the chapters on the Lord's Day, on the Assembling of the Congregation, Reading of Scripture, Singing of Psalms, Prayer, Preaching, the Sacraments, Marriage, Visitation of the Sick, Burial of the Dead, Fasting, and Thanksgiving. On the whole, these subjects do not occupy more than half the space given to them in the original Directory.

In the following reprint the text is that of the first Scottish edition, issued by Evan Tyler in 1645. Different readings in other editions, and such variations in the original draft as do not call for notice in the Appendix, are added as footnotes. T. L.

A

DIRECTORY

FOR

The Publike WORSHIP

OF

GOD

Throughout the three KINGDOMS

OF

SCOTLAND, ENGLAND,
and *IRELAND.*

WITH

An Act of the Generall Assembly of the Kirk of Scotland, *for establishing and observing this present Directory.*

EDINBURGH:
Printed by *Evan Tyler*, Printer to the Kings most Excellent Majestie. 1645.

CONTENTS.

	PAGE
THE Act of the General Assembly,	284
The Preface,	287
Of the Assembling of the Congregation,	291
Of Public Reading of the Holy Scriptures,	292
Of Public Prayer before the Sermon,	293
Of the Preaching of the Word,	299
Of Prayer after the Sermon,	303
Of the Sacrament of Baptism,	304
Of the Sacrament of the Lord's Supper,	308
Of the Sanctification of the Lord's Day,	311
Of the Solemnisation of Marriage,	312
Of the Visitation of the Sick,	315
Of Burial of the Dead,	318
Of Public Solemn Fasting,	319
Of the Observation of Days of Public Thanksgiving,	321
Of Singing of Psalms,	322
An Appendix touching Days and Places for Public Worship,	323

ASSEMBLY AT EDINBURGH, February 3, 1645.
Sess. 10.

ACT *of the* GENERAL ASSEMBLY *of the* KIRK *of* SCOTLAND, *for the establishing and putting in Execution of the* DIRECTORY *for the Public Worship of God.*

WHEREAS an happy unity and uniformity in religion amongst the Kirks of Christ in these three Kingdoms, united under one Sovereign, hath been long and earnestly wished for by the godly and well-affected amongst us, was propounded as a main article of the large Treaty, without which band and bulwark no safe, well-grounded, and lasting peace could be expected; and afterward, with greater strength and maturity, revived in the Solemn League and Covenant of the three Kingdoms, whereby they stand straitly obliged to endeavour the nearest uniformity in one form of Church government, Directory of Worship, Confession of Faith, and Form of Catechising; which hath also before, and since our entering into that Covenant, been the matter of many supplications and remonstrances, and sending Commissioners to the King's Majesty, of declarations to the Honourable Houses of the Parliament of England, and of letters to the Reverend Assembly of Divines, and others of the ministry of the Kirk of England; being also the end of our sending Commissioners, as was desired, from this Kirk, with commission to treat of uniformity in the four particulars afore-mentioned, with such Committees as should be appointed by both Houses of Parliament of England, and by the Assembly of Divines sitting at Westminster; and beside all this, it being, in point of conscience, the chief motive and end of our adventuring upon manifold and great hazards, for quenching the devouring flame of the present unnatural and bloody war in England, though to the weakening of this Kingdom within itself, and the advantage of the enemy which hath invaded it; accounting nothing too dear to us, so that this our joy be fulfilled. And now this great work

ACT OF ASSEMBLY.

being so far advanced, that a Directory for the Public Worship of God in all the three Kingdoms being agreed upon by the Honourable Houses of the Parliament of England, after consultation with the Divines of both kingdoms there assembled, and sent to us for our approbation, that, being also agreed upon by this Kirk and Kingdom of Scotland, it may be in the name of both Kingdoms presented to the King, for his Royal consent and ratification; the General Assembly, having most seriously considered, revised, and examined the Directory afore-mentioned, after several public readings of it, after much deliberation, both publicly and in private committees, after full liberty given to all to object against it, and earnest invitations of all who have any scruples about it, to make known the same, that they might be satisfied; Doth unanimously, and without a contrary voice, agree to and approve the following Directory, in all the heads thereof, together with the Preface set before it; and doth require, decern, and ordain, That, according to the plain tenor and meaning thereof, and the intent of the Preface, it be carefully and uniformly observed and practised by all the ministers and others within this Kingdom whom it doth concern; which practice shall be begun, upon intimation given to the several Presbyteries from the Commissioners of this General Assembly, who shall also take special care for timeous printing of this Directory, that a printed copy of it be provided and kept for the use of every kirk in this Kingdom; also that each Presbytery have a printed copy thereof for their use, and take special notice of the observation or neglect thereof in every congregation within their bounds, and make known the same to the Provincial or General Assembly, as there shall be cause. Provided always, That the clause in the Directory of the Administration of the Lord's Supper, which mentioneth the Communicants sitting about the Table, or at it, be not interpreted as if, in the judgment of this Kirk, it were indifferent, and free for any of the Communicants not to come to, and receive at the Table; or as if we did approve the distributing of the Elements by the Minister to each Communicant, and not by the Communicants among themselves. It is also provided, That this shall be no prejudice to the order and practice of this Kirk, in such particulars as are appointed by the Books of Discipline and Acts of General Assemblies, and are not otherwise ordered and appointed in the Directory.

Finally, the Assembly doth, with much joy and thankfulness, acknowledge the rich blessing and invaluable mercy of God, in bringing the so much wished for uniformity in religion to such a happy period, that these Kingdoms, once at so great a distance in the Form of Worship, are now, by the blessing of God, brought to a nearer uniformity than any other Reformed Kirks; which is unto us the return of our prayers, and a lightening of our eyes, and reviving of our hearts, in the midst of our many sorrows and sufferings; a taking away, in a great measure, the reproach of the people of God, to the stopping of the mouths of malignant and disaffected persons; and an opening unto us a door of hope, that God hath yet thoughts of peace towards us, and not of evil, to give us an expected end; in the expectation and confidence whereof we do rejoice; beseeching the Lord to preserve these Kingdoms from heresies, schisms, offences, profaneness, and whatsoever is contrary to sound doctrine and the power of godliness; and to continue with us, and the generations following, these His pure and purged Ordinances, together with an increase of the power and life thereof, to the glory of His great Name, the enlargement of the kingdom of His Son, the corroboration of peace and love between the Kingdoms, the unity and comfort of all His people, and our edifying one another in love.

PREFACE.

IN the beginning of the blessed Reformation, our wise and pious ancestors took care to set forth an Order for redress of many things, which they then, by the Word, discovered to be vain, erroneous, superstitious, and idolatrous, in the Public Worship of God. This occasioned many godly and learned men to rejoice much in the Book of Common Prayer, at that time set forth; because the Mass, and the rest of the Latin service being removed, the Public Worship was celebrated in our own tongue: many of the common people also received benefit by hearing the Scriptures read in their own language, which formerly were unto them as a book that is sealed.

Howbeit, long and sad experience hath made it manifest, that the Liturgy used in the Church of England (notwithstanding all the pains and religious intentions of the compilers of it) hath proved an offence, not only to many of the godly at home, but also to the Reformed Churches abroad. For, not to speak of urging the reading of all the prayers, which very greatly increased the burden of it, the many unprofitable and burdensome ceremonies contained in it have occasioned much mischief, as well by disquieting the consciences of many godly ministers and people, who could not yield unto them, as by depriving them of the ordinances of God, which they might not enjoy without conforming or subscribing to those ceremonies. Sundry good Christians have been, by means thereof, kept from the Lord's Table; and divers able and faithful ministers debarred from the exercise of their ministry (to the endangering of many thousand souls, in a time of such scarcity of faithful pastors), and spoiled of their livelihood, to the undoing of them and their families. Prelates, and their faction, have laboured to raise the estimation of it to such a height, as if there were no other worship, or way of worship of God amongst us, but only the Service-book; to the great hindrance of the preaching of the Word, and (in some places, especially of late) to the justling of it out as unnecessary, or (at best) as far inferior to the reading of Common Prayer; which was made no better than an idol by many ignorant and superstitious people, who, pleasing themselves in their presence at that Service, and their lip-labour in bearing a part in it, have thereby hardened themselves in their ignorance and carelessness of saving knowledge and true piety.

In the mean time, Papists boasted that the book was a compliance with them in a great part of their service; and so were not a little confirmed in their superstition and idolatry, expecting rather our return to them, than endeavouring the reformation of themselves: in which expectation they were of late very much encouraged, when, upon the pretended warrantableness of imposing of the former ceremonies, new ones were daily obtruded upon the Church.

Add hereunto (which was not foreseen, but since hath come to pass), that the Liturgy hath been a great means, as on the one hand to make and increase an idle and unedifying ministry, which contented itself with set forms made to their hands by others, without putting forth themselves to exercise the gift of prayer, with which our Lord Jesus Christ pleaseth to furnish all His servants whom He calls to that office : so, on the other side, it hath been (and ever would be, if continued) a matter of endless strife and contention in the Church, and a snare both to many godly and faithful ministers, who have been persecuted and silenced upon that occasion, and to others of hopeful parts, many of which have been, and more still would be diverted from all thoughts of the ministry to other studies; especially in these latter times, wherein God vouchsafeth to His people more and better means for the discovery of error and superstition, and for attaining of knowledge in the mysteries of godliness, and gifts in Preaching and Prayer.

Upon these, and many the like weighty considerations in reference to the whole book in general, and because of divers particulars contained in it; not from any love to novelty, or intention to disparage our first Reformers (of whom we are persuaded, that, were they now alive, they would join with us in this work, and whom we acknowledge as excellent instruments, raised by God, to begin the purging and building of His house, and desire they may be had of us and posterity in everlasting remembrance, with thankfulness and honour), but that we may in some measure answer the gracious providence of God, which at this time calleth upon us for further reformation, and may satisfy our own consciences, and answer the expectation of other Reformed Churches, and the desires of many of the godly among ourselves, and withal give some public testimony of our endeavours for uniformity in Divine Worship, which we have promised in our Solemn League and Covenant; We have, after earnest and frequent calling upon the name of God, and after much consultation, not with flesh and blood, but with His holy

Word, resolved to lay aside the former Liturgy, with the many rites and ceremonies formerly used in the worship of God; and have agreed upon this following Directory for all the parts of Public Worship, at ordinary and extraordinary times.

Wherein our care hath been to hold forth such things as are of Divine institution in every Ordinance; and other things we have endeavoured to set forth according to the rules of Christian prudence, agreeable to the general rules of the Word of God;* our meaning therein being only, that the general heads, the sense and scope of the Prayers, and other parts of Public Worship, being known to all, there may be a consent of all the Churches in those things that contain the substance of the Service and Worship of God, and the Ministers may be hereby directed, in their administrations, to keep like soundness in Doctrine and Prayer, and may, if need be, have some help and furniture; and yet so as they become not hereby slothful and negligent in stirring up the gifts of Christ in them; but that each one, by meditation, by taking heed to himself, and the flock of God committed to him, and by wise observing the ways of Divine Providence, may be careful to furnish his heart and tongue with further or other materials of Prayer and Exhortation, as shall be needful upon all occasions.

* In the original draft this clause was wanting.—M.S. Records.

A DIRECTORY

FOR

Public Prayer, Reading the Holy Scriptures, Singing of Psalms, Preaching of the Word, Administration of the Sacraments, and other parts of the Public Worship of God, Ordinary and Extraordinary.

Of the Assembling of the Congregation, and their Behaviour in the Public Worship of God.

WHEN the Congregation is to meet for public worship, the people (having before prepared their hearts thereunto) ought all to come and join therein; not absenting themselves from the Public Ordinances through negligence, or upon pretence of private meetings.

Let all enter the assembly, not irreverently, but in a grave and seemly manner, taking* their seats or places without adoration, or bowing themselves towards one place or other.

The Congregation being assembled, the Minister, after solemn calling on them to the worshipping of the great name of God, is to begin with Prayer,—

In all reverence and humility acknowledging the incom-

---

* In original draft, "Let all enter the assembly reverently, taking."—MS. Records.

prehensible greatness and majesty of the Lord (in whose presence they do then in a special manner appear), and their own vileness and unworthiness to approach so near Him, with their utter inability of themselves to so great a work; And humbly beseeching Him for pardon, assistance, and acceptance, in the whole Service then to be performed; and for a blessing on that particular portion of His Word then to be read: And all in the Name and Meditation of the Lord Jesus Christ.

The Public Worship being begun, the people are wholly to attend upon it, forbearing to read any thing, except what the Minister is then reading or citing; and abstaining much more from all private whisperings, conferences, salutations, or doing reverence to any person present, or coming in; as also from all gazing, sleeping, and other undecent behaviour, which may disturb the Minister or people, or hinder themselves or others in the service of God.

If any, through necessity, be hindered from being present at the beginning, they ought not, when they come into the Congregation, to betake themselves to their private devotions, but reverently to compose themselves to join with the assembly in that Ordinance of God which is then in hand.

Of Public Reading of the Holy Scriptures.

READING of the Word in the Congregation, being part of the Public Worship of God (wherein we acknowledge our dependence upon Him, and subjection to Him), and one means sanctified by Him for the edifying of His people, is to be performed by the Pastors and Teachers.

Howbeit, such as intend the ministry, may occasionally both read the Word, and exercise their gift in preaching in the Congregation, if allowed by the Presbytery thereunto.

All the Canonical Books of the Old and New Testament (but none of those which are commonly called *Apocrypha*) shall be publicly read in the vulgar tongue, out of the best allowed translation, distinctly, that all may hear and understand.

How large a portion shall be read at once, is left to the wisdom of the Minister; but it is convenient, that ordinarily one Chapter of each Testament be read at every meeting; and sometimes more, where the chapters be short, or the coherence of matter requireth it.

It is requisite that all the Canonical Books be read over in order, that the people may be better acquainted with the whole body of the Scriptures; and ordinarily, where the reading in either Testament endeth on one Lord's Day, it is to begin the next.

We commend also the more frequent reading of such Scriptures as he that readeth shall think best for edification of his hearers, as the Book of Psalms, and suchlike.

When the Minister who readeth shall judge it necessary to expound any part of what is read, let it not be done until the whole Chapter or Psalm be ended; and regard is always to be had unto the time, that neither Preaching or other Ordinance be straitened, or rendered tedious. Which rule is to be observed in all other public performances.

Besides Public Reading of the Holy Scriptures, every person that can read is to be exhorted to read the Scriptures privately (and all others that cannot read, if not disabled by age or otherwise, are likewise to be exhorted to learn to read), and to have a Bible.

Of Public Prayer before the Sermon.

AFTER Reading of the Word (and Singing of the Psalm), the Minister who is to preach is to endeavour to get his own and his hearers' hearts to be rightly affected with their sins, that they may all mourn in sense thereof before the Lord, and hunger and thirst after the grace of God in Jesus Christ, by proceeding to a more full Confession of sin, with shame and holy confusion of face, and to call upon the Lord to this effect:—

To acknowledge our great sinfulness, First, by reason of original sin, which (beside the guilt that makes us liable to everlasting damnation) is the seed of all other sins, hath depraved and poisoned all the faculties and powers of soul and body, doth defile our best actions, and (were it not restrained, or our hearts renewed by grace) would break forth into innumerable transgressions, and greatest rebellions against the Lord, that ever were committed by the vilest of the sons of men; and next, by reason of actual sins, our own sins, the sins of magistrates, of ministers, and of the whole nation, unto which we are many ways accessory: which sins of ours receive many fearful aggravations, we having broken all the commandments of the holy, just, and good law of God, doing that which is forbidden, and leaving undone what is enjoined; and that not only out of ignorance and infirmity, but also more presumptuously, against the light of our minds, checks of our consciences, and motions of His own Holy Spirit to the contrary, so that we have no cloak for our sins; Yea, not only despising the riches of God's goodness, forbearance, and long-suffering, but standing out against many invitations and offers of grace in the Gospel; not endeavouring, as we ought, to receive Christ into our hearts by faith, or to walk worthy of Him in our lives.

To bewail our blindness of mind, hardness of heart, unbelief, impenitency, security, lukewarmness, barrenness; our not endeavouring after mortification and newness of life, nor after the exercise of godliness in the power thereof; and that the best of us have not so steadfastly walked with God, kept our garments so unspotted, nor been so zealous of His glory, and the good of others, as we ought: And to mourn over such other sins as the congregation is particularly guilty of, notwithstanding the manifold and great mercies of our God, the love of Christ, the light of the Gospel, and Reformation of religion, our own purposes, promises, vows, solemn covenant, and other special obligations, to the contrary.

To acknowledge and confess, that, as we are convinced of our guilt, so, out of a deep sense thereof, we judge ourselves unworthy of the smallest benefits, most worthy of God's fiercest wrath, and of all the curses of the law, and heaviest judgments inflicted upon the most rebellious sinners; and that He might most justly take His kingdom and Gospel from us, plague us with all sorts of spiritual and temporal judgments in this life, and after cast us into utter darkness, in the lake that burneth with fire and brimstone, where is weeping and gnashing of teeth for evermore.

Notwithstanding all which, to draw near to the throne of grace, encouraging ourselves with hope of a gracious answer of our prayers, in the riches and all-sufficiency of that only one oblation, the satisfaction and intercession of the Lord Jesus Christ, at the right hand of His Father and our Father; and in confidence of the exceeding great and precious promises of mercy and grace in the new covenant, through the same Mediator thereof, to deprecate the heavy wrath and curse of God, which we are not able to avoid or bear; and humbly and earnestly to supplicate for mercy, in the free and full remission of all our sins, and that only for the bitter sufferings and precious merits of that our only Saviour Jesus Christ.

That the Lord would vouchsafe to shed abroad His love in our hearts by the Holy Ghost; seal unto us, by the same Spirit of adoption, the full assurance of our pardon and reconciliation; comfort all that mourn in Zion, speak peace to the wounded and troubled spirit, and bind up the broken-hearted: And as for secure and presumptuous sinners, that He would open their eyes, convince their consciences, and turn them from darkness unto light, and from the power of Satan unto God, that they also may receive forgiveness of sin, and an inheritance among them that are sanctified by faith in Christ Jesus.

With remission of sins through the blood of Christ, to pray for sanctification by His Spirit; the mortification of sin dwelling in, and many times tyrannising over us; the quickening of our dead spirits with the life of God in Christ; grace to fit and enable us for all duties of conversation and callings towards God and men; strength against temptations; the sanctified use of blessings and crosses; and perseverance in faith and obedience unto the end.

To pray for the propagation of the Gospel and Kingdom of Christ to all nations; for the conversion of the Jews, the fulness of the Gentiles, the fall of Antichrist, and the hastening of the second coming of our Lord; for the deliverance of the distressed Churches abroad from the tyranny of the Antichristian faction, and from the cruel oppressions and blasphemies of the Turk; for the blessing of God upon the Reformed Churches, especially upon the Churches and Kingdoms of Scotland, England, and Ireland, now more strictly and religiously united in the Solemn National League and Covenant; and for our plantations in the remote parts of the world: more particularly for that Church and Kingdom whereof we are members, that therein God would establish peace and truth, the purity of all His Ordinances, and the power of godliness; prevent and remove heresy, schism, profaneness, superstition, security, and unfruitfulness under the means of grace; heal all our rents and divisions, and preserve us from breach of our Solemn Covenant.

To pray for all in authority, especially for the King's Majesty; that God would make him rich in blessings, both in his Person and Government; establish his Throne in religion and righteousness, save him from evil counsel, and make him a blessed and glorious instrument for the conservation and propagation of the Gospel, for the encouragement and protection of them that do well, the terror of all that do evil, and the great good of the whole Church, and of all his Kingdoms; for the conversion of the Queen, the religious education of the Prince, and the rest of the Royal Seed; for the comforting of the afflicted

Queen of Bohemia, sister to our Sovereign; and for the restitution* and establishment of the illustrious Prince Charles, Elector Palatine of the Rhine, to all his dominions and dignities; for a blessing upon the High Court of Parliament (when sitting in any of these Kingdoms respectively), the Nobility, the subordinate Judges and Magistrates, the Gentry, and all the Commonality; for all Pastors and Teachers, that God would fill them with His Spirit, make them exemplarily holy, sober, just, peaceable, and gracious in their lives; sound, faithful, and powerful in their ministry; and follow all their labours with abundance of success and blessing; and give unto all His people pastors according to His own heart; for the Universities, and all Schools and Religious Seminaries of Church and Commonwealth, that they may flourish more and more in learning and piety; for the particular City or Congregation, that God would pour out a blessing upon the ministry of the Word, Sacraments, and Discipline, upon the Civil Government, and all the several families and persons therein; for mercy to the afflicted under any inward or outward distress; for seasonable weather, and fruitful seasons, as the time may require; for averting the judgments that we either feel or fear, or are liable. unto, as famine, pestilence, the sword, and suchlike.

And, with confidence of His mercy to His whole Church, and the acceptance of our persons, through the merits and mediation of our great High Priest, the Lord Jesus, to profess that it is the desire of our souls to have fellowship with God in the reverend and conscionable use of His holy Ordinances; and, to that purpose, to pray earnestly for His grace and effectual assistance to the sanctification of His holy Sabbath, the Lord's Day, in all

---

* " Restauration."—Ed. 1689.

the duties thereof, public and private, both to ourselves, and to all other Congregations of His people, according to the riches and excellency of the Gospel, this day celebrated and enjoyed.

And because we have been unprofitable hearers in times past, and now cannot of ourselves receive, as we should, the deep things of God, the mysteries of Jesus Christ, which require a spiritual discerning; to pray that the Lord, who teacheth to profit, would graciously please to pour out the Spirit of grace, together with the outward means thereof, causing us to attain such a measure of the excellency of the knowledge of Christ Jesus our Lord, and, in Him, of the things which belong to our peace, that we may account all things but as dross in comparison of Him; and that we, tasting the first-fruits of the glory that is to be revealed, may long for a more full and perfect communion with Him, that where He is we may be also, and enjoy the fulness of those joys and pleasures which are at His right hand for evermore.

More particularly, that God would in special manner furnish His Servant (now called to dispense the bread of life unto His household) with wisdom, fidelity, zeal, and utterance, that he may divide the Word of God aright, to every one his portion, in evidence and demonstration of the Spirit and power; and that the Lord would circumcise the ears and hearts of the hearers, to hear, love, and receive with meekness the ingrafted Word, which is able to save their souls; make them as good ground to receive in the good seed of the Word, and strengthen them against the temptations of Satan, the cares of the world, the hardness of their own hearts, and whatsoever else may hinder their profitable and saving hearing; that so Christ may be so formed in them, and live in them, that all their thoughts may be brought into captivity to the obedience of Christ, and their hearts established in every good word and work for ever.

We judge this to be a convenient order in the ordinary Public Prayers; yet so, as the Minister may defer (as in prudence he shall think meet) some part of these Petitions till after his Sermon, or offer up to God some of the Thanksgivings hereafter appointed, in his Prayer before his Sermon.

Of the Preaching of the Word.

PREACHING of the Word, being the power of God unto salvation, and one of the greatest and most excellent works belonging to the ministry of the Gospel, should be so performed that the workman need not be ashamed, but may save himself and those that hear him.

It is presupposed (according to the Rules for Ordination) that the Minister of Christ is in some good measure gifted for so weighty a service, by his skill in the original languages, and in such arts and sciences as are handmaids unto divinity; by his knowledge in the whole body of theology, but most of all in the Holy Scriptures, having his senses and heart exercised in them above the common sort of believers; and by the illumination of God's Spirit, and other gifts of edification, which (together with reading and studying of the Word) he ought still to seek by prayer and an humble heart, resolving to admit and receive any truth not yet attained, whenever God shall make it known unto him. All which he is to make use of, and improve, in his private preparations, before he deliver in public what he hath provided.

Ordinarily, the subject of his Sermon is to be some text of Scripture holding forth some principle or head of religion, or suitable to some special occasion emergent; or he may go on in some Chapter, Psalm, or Book of the Holy Scripture, as he shall see fit.

Let the introduction to his text be brief and perspicuous, drawn from the text itself, or context, or some parallel place, or general sentence of Scripture.

If the text be long (as in histories or parables it sometimes must be), let him give a brief sum of it; if short, a paraphrase thereof if need be: in both, looking diligently to the scope of the text, and pointing at the chief heads and grounds of doctrine which he is to raise from it.

In analysing and dividing his text, he is to regard more the order of matter than of words; and neither to burden the memory of the hearers in the beginning with too many members of division, nor to trouble their minds with obscure terms of art.

In raising Doctrines from the text, his care ought to be, *First*, That the matter be the truth of God. *Secondly*, That it be a truth contained in or grounded on that text, that the hearers may discern how God teacheth it from thence. *Thirdly*, That he chiefly insist upon those doctrines which are principally intended,* and make most for the edification of the hearers.

The Doctrine is to be expressed in plain terms; or, if anything in it need explication,† it is to be opened, and the consequence also from the text cleared. The parallel places of Scripture, confirming the doctrine, are rather to be plain and pertinent than many, and (if need be) somewhat insisted upon, and applied to the purpose in hand.

The Arguments or Reasons are to be solid, and, as much as may be, convincing.‡ The illustrations, of what kind soever,§ ought to be full of light, and such as may convey the truth into the hearer's heart with spiritual delight.

If any doubt, obvious from Scripture, reason, or prejudice of the hearers seem to arise, it is very requisite to remove it, by reconciling the seeming differences, answering the reasons, and discovering and taking away the causes of prejudice and mistake. Otherwise it is not fit to detain the hearers with propounding or answering vain or wicked cavils, which, as they are endless, so the propounding and answering of them doth more hinder than promote edification.

He is not to rest in general Doctrine, although never so much cleared and confirmed, but to bring it home to special use by application to his hearers: which albeit it prove a work of great difficulty to himself, requiring much prudence, zeal, and meditation, and to the natural and corrupt man will be very unpleasant; yet he is to endeavour to perform it in such a manner that his auditors may feel the Word of God to be quick and powerful, and a discerner of the thoughts and intents of the heart; and that, if any unbeliever or ignorant person be present, he may have the secrets of his heart made manifest, and give glory to God.

* Here originally the paragraph ended.—Lightfoot.
† In original draft, "be obscure."—MS. Records.
‡ In original draft, "the reasons are not to be subtle or conjectural, but convincing."—Lightfoot.
§ In original draft, "whether from comparisons, contraries, &c."—Lightfoot. "Contraries and similes."—MS. Records.

In the use of Instruction or Information in the knowledge of some truth, which is a consequence from his Doctrine, he may (when convenient) confirm it by a few firm arguments from the text in hand, and other places of Scripture, or from the nature of that commonplace in divinity, whereof that truth is a branch.

In confutation of false doctrines, he is neither to raise an old heresy from the grave, nor to mention a blasphemous opinion unnecessarily: but, if the people be in danger of an error, he is to confute it soundly, and endeavour to satisfy their judgments and consciences against all objections.

In exhorting to duties, he is, as he seeth cause, to teach also the means that help to the performance of them.

In dehortation, reprehension, and public admonition (which require special wisdom), let him, as there shall be cause, not only discover the nature and greatness of the sin, with the misery attending it, but also show the danger his hearers are in to be overtaken and surprised by it, together with the remedies and best way to avoid it.

In applying comfort, whether general against all tentations, or particular against some special troubles or terrors, he is carefully to answer such objections as a troubled heart and afflicted spirit may suggest to the contrary.

It is also sometimes requisite to give some notes of trial (which is very profitable, especially when performed by able and experienced ministers with circumspection and prudence, and the signs clearly grounded on the Holy Scripture), whereby the hearers may be able to examine themselves whether they have attained those graces, and performed those duties to which he exhorteth, or be guilty of the sin reprehended, and in danger of the judgments threatened, or are such to whom the consolations propounded do belong; that accordingly they may be quickened and excited to duty, humbled for their wants and sins, affected with their danger, and strengthened with comfort, as their condition, upon examination, shall require.

And, as he needeth not always to prosecute every Doctrine which lies in his text, so is he wisely to make choice of such Uses, as, by his residence and conversing with his flock, he findeth most needful and seasonable; and, amongst these, such as may most draw their souls to Christ, the fountain of light, holiness, and comfort.

This method is not prescribed as necessary for every man, or upon every text; but only recommended, as being found by experience to be very much blessed of God, and very helpful for the people's understandings and memories.

But the Servant of Christ, whatever his method be, is to perform his whole ministry :—

1. Painfully, not doing the work of the Lord negligently.

2. Plainly, that the meanest may understand; delivering the truth not in the enticing words of man's wisdom, but in demonstration of the Spirit and of power, lest the Cross of Christ should be made of none effect; abstaining also from an unprofitable use of unknown tongues,* strange phrases, and cadences of sounds and words; sparingly citing sentences of ecclesiastical or other human writers, ancient or modern, be they never so elegant.

3. Faithfully, looking at the honour of Christ, the conversion, edification, and salvation of the people, not at his own gain or glory; keeping nothing back which may promote those holy ends, giving to every one his own portion, and bearing indifferent respect unto all, without neglecting the meanest, or sparing the greatest in their sins.

4. Wisely, framing all his doctrines, exhortations, and especially his reproofs, in such a manner as may be most likely to prevail; showing all due respect to each man's person and place, and not mixing his own passion or bitterness.

5. Gravely, as becometh the Word of God; shunning all such gesture, voice, and expressions, as may occasion the corruptions of men to despise him and his ministry.

6. With loving affection, that the people may see all coming from his godly zeal, and hearty desire to do them good. And,

7. As taught of God, and persuaded in his own heart, that all that he teacheth is the truth of Christ; and walking before his flock as an example to them in it; earnestly, both in private and public, recommending his labours to the blessing of God, and watchfully looking to himself and the flock whereof the Lord hath made him overseer: So shall the Doctrine of truth be preserved uncorrupt, many souls converted and built up, and himself receive manifold comforts of his labours even in this life, and afterward the crown of glory laid up for him in the world to come.

Where there are more Ministers in a Congregation than one, and they of different gifts, each may more especially apply himself to Doctrine or Exhortation, according to the gift wherein he most excelleth, and as they shall agree between themselves.

* " From speaking of Latin, Greek, and Hebrew."—Lightfoot.

Of Prayer after the Sermon.

THE Sermon being ended, the Minister is

To give thanks for the great love of God, in sending His Son Jesus Christ unto us; for the communication of His Holy Spirit; for the light and liberty of the glorious Gospel, and the rich and heavenly blessings revealed therein; as, namely, election, vocation, adoption, justification, sanctification, and hope of glory; for the admirable goodness of God in freeing the land from Antichristian darkness and tyranny,* and for all other national deliverances; for the Reformation of religion; for the Covenant; and for many temporal blessings.

To pray for the continuance of the Gospel, and all Ordinances thereof, in their purity, power, and liberty: to turn the chief and most useful heads of the Sermon into some few petitions; and to pray that it may abide in the heart and bring forth fruit.

To pray for preparation for death and judgment, and a watching for the coming of our Lord Jesus Christ: to entreat of God the forgiveness of the iniquities of our holy things, and the acceptation of our spiritual sacrifice, through the merit and mediation of our great High Priest† and Saviour the Lord Jesus Christ.

And because the Prayer which Christ taught His disciples is not only a pattern of prayer, but itself a most comprehensive prayer, we recommend it also to be used in the Prayers of the Church.

And whereas, at the Administration of the Sacraments, the holding Public Fasts and days of Thanksgiving, and other special occasions, which may afford matter of special petitions and thanksgivings, it is requisite to express somewhat in our Public Prayers (as at this time it is our duty to pray for a blessing upon the Assembly of Divines, the

---

* This clause was wanting in the original draft.—Lightfoot.
† In original draft, "for the merits of our High Priest."—Lightfoot.

armies by sea and land, for the defence of the King. Parliament, and Kingdom), every Minister is herein to apply himself in his Prayer, before or after his Sermon, to those occasions : but, for the manner, he is left to his liberty, as God shall direct and enable him in piety and wisdom·to discharge his duty.

The Prayer ended, let a Psalm be sung, if with conveniency it may be done. After which (unless some other Ordinance of Christ, that concerneth the Congregation at that time, be to follow) let the Minister dismiss the Congregation with a solemn blessing.

THE ADMINISTRATION OF THE SACRAMENTS:

And first, of Baptism.

BAPTISM, as it is not unnecessarily to be delayed, so it is not to be administered in any case by any private person, but by a Minister of Christ, called to be the steward of the mysteries of God.

Nor is it to be administered in private places, or privately, but in the place of Public Worship, and in the face of the Congregation, where the people may most conveniently see and hear ; and not in the places where fonts, in the time of Popery, were unfitly and superstitiously placed.

The Child to be Baptised, after notice given to the Minister the day before, is to be presented by the Father, or (in case of his necessary absence) by some Christian friend in his place, professing his earnest desire that the Child may be Baptised.

Before Baptism the Minister is to use some words of instruction, touching the institution, nature, use, and ends of this Sacrament, showing,—

That it is instituted by our Lord Jesus Christ: That it is a Seal of the Covenant of Grace, of our ingrafting into Christ, and of our union with Him, of remission of sins, regeneration, adoption, and life eternal : That the water, in Baptism, representeth and signifieth both the blood of Christ, which taketh away all guilt of sin, original and actual; and the sanctifying virtue of the Spirit of Christ against the dominion of sin, and the corruption of our sin-

BAPTISM.

ful nature: That Baptising, or sprinkling and washing with water, signifieth the cleansing from sin by the blood and for the merit of Christ, together with the mortification of sin, and rising from sin to newness of life, by virtue of the death and resurrection of Christ: That the promise is made to believers and their seed; and that the seed and posterity of the faithful, born within the Church, have, by their birth, interest in the covenant, and right to the Seal of it, and to the outward privileges of the Church, under the Gospel, no less than the children of Abraham in the time of the Old Testament; the Covenant of Grace, for substance, being the same; and the grace of God, and the consolation of believers, more plentiful than before: That the Son of God admitted little children into His presence, embracing and blessing them, saying, *For of such is the kingdom of God:* That children, by Baptism, are solemnly received into the bosom of the Visible Church, distinguished from the world and them that are without, and united with believers; and that all who are Baptised in the name of Christ, do renounce, and by their Baptism are bound to fight against, the devil, the world, and the flesh: That they are Christians, and federally holy before Baptism, and therefore are they Baptised: That the inward grace and virtue of Baptism is not tied to that very moment of time wherein it is administered, and that the fruit and power thereof reacheth to the whole course of our life; and that outward Baptism is not so necessary, that, through the want thereof, the infant is in danger of damnation, or the parents guilty, if they do not contemn or neglect the Ordinance of Christ, when and where it may be had.

In these or the like instructions, the Minister is to use his own liberty and godly wisdom, as the ignorance or errors in the doctrine of Baptism and the edification of the people shall require.

He is also to admonish all that are present,

To look back to their Baptism; to repent of their sins against their Covenant with God; to stir up their faith; to improve and make right use of their Baptism, and of the Covenant sealed thereby betwixt God and their souls.

He is to exhort the Parent,—

To consider the great mercy of God to him and his Child; to bring up the Child in the knowledge of the grounds of the Christian religion, and in the nurture and admonition of the Lord; And to let him know the danger of God's wrath to himself and Child if he be negligent: Requiring his solemn promise for the performance of his duty.

This being done, Prayer is also to be joined with the Word of Institution, for sanctifying the Water to this spiritual use; and the Minister is to pray to this or the like effect:—

That the Lord, who hath not left us as strangers without the covenant of promise, but called us to the privileges of His ordinances, would graciously vouchsafe to sanctify and bless His own Ordinance of Baptism at this time: That He would join the inward Baptism of His Spirit with the outward Baptism of Water; make this Baptism to the Infant a Seal of Adoption, Remission of sin, Regeneration, and Eternal Life, and all other promises of the Covenant of grace; That the Child may be planted into the likeness of the Death and Resurrection of Christ; And that, the body of sin being destroyed in him, he may serve God in newness of life all his days.

Then the Minister is to demand the name of the Child; which being told him, he is to say (calling the Child by his name),

I BAPTISE THEE IN THE NAME OF THE FATHER, OF THE SON, AND OF THE HOLY GHOST.

As he pronounceth these words, he is to Baptise the Child with

Water: which, for the manner of doing of it, is not only lawful but sufficient, and most expedient to be, by pouring or sprinkling of the water on the face of the Child, without adding any other ceremony.

This done, he is to give thanks and pray, to this or the like purpose:—

Acknowledging with all thankfulness, that the Lord is true and faithful in keeping covenant and mercy: That He is good and gracious, not only in that He numbereth us among His saints, but is pleased also to bestow upon our children this singular token and badge of His love in Christ: That, in His truth and special providence, He daily bringeth some into the bosom of His Church, to be partakers of His inestimable benefits, purchased by the blood of His dear Son, for the continuance and increase of His Church.

And praying, That the Lord would still continue, and daily confirm more and more this His unspeakable favour: That He would receive the Infant now Baptised, and solemnly entered into the household of faith, into His Fatherly tuition and defence, and remember him with the favour that He showeth to His people; that, if he shall be taken out of this life in his infancy, the Lord, who is rich in mercy, would be pleased to receive him up into glory; and if he live, and attain the years of discretion, that the Lord would so teach him by His Word and Spirit, and make his Baptism effectual to him, and so uphold him by His divine power and grace, that by faith he may prevail against the devil, the world, and the flesh, till in the end he obtain a full and final victory, and so be kept by the power of God through faith unto salvation, through Jesus Christ our Lord.

Of the Celebration of the Communion, or Sacrament of the Lord's Supper.

THE Communion, or Supper of the Lord, is frequently to be celebrated; but how often, may be considered and determined by the Ministers, and other Church-governors of each Congregation, as they shall find most convenient for the comfort and edification of the people committed to their charge. And, when it shall be administered, we judge it convenient to be done after the Morning Sermon.

The ignorant and the scandalous are not fit to receive the Sacrament of the Lord's Supper.

Where this Sacrament cannot with conveniency be frequently administered, it is requisite that public warning be given the Sabbath Day before the administration thereof: and that either then, or on some day of that week, something concerning that Ordinance, and the due preparation thereunto, and participation thereof, be taught; that, by the diligent use of all means sanctified of God to that end, both in public and private, all may come better prepared to that heavenly Feast.

When the day is come for administration, the Minister, having ended his Sermon and Prayer, shall make a short Exhortation,—

Expressing the inestimable benefit we have by this Sacrament, together with the ends and use thereof: setting forth the great necessity of having our comforts and strength renewed thereby in this our pilgrimage and warfare: how necessary it is that we come unto it with knowledge, faith, repentance, love, and with hungering and thirsting souls after Christ and His benefits: how great the danger to eat and drink unworthily.

Next, he is, in the name of Christ, on the one part, to warn all such as are ignorant, scandalous, profane, or that live in any sin or offence against their knowledge or conscience, that they presume not to come to that Holy Table; showing them that he that eateth and drinketh unworthily eateth and drinketh judgment unto himself:

THE LORD'S SUPPER.

And, on the other part, he is in especial manner to invite and encourage all that labour under the sense of the burden of their sins, and fear of wrath, and desire to reach out unto a greater progress in grace than yet they can attain unto, to come to the Lord's Table; assuring them, in the same name, of ease, refreshing, and strength to their weak and wearied souls.

After this exhortation, warning, and invitation, the Table being before decently covered, and so conveniently placed, that the Communicants may orderly sit about it, or at it, the Minister is to begin the Action with sanctifying and blessing the Elements of Bread and Wine set before him (the Bread in comely and convenient vessels, so prepared, that, being broken by him, and given, it may be distributed amongst the Communicants; the Wine also in large cups), having first, in a few words, showed that those Elements, otherwise common, are now set apart and sanctified to this holy use by the Word of Institution and Prayer.

Let the Words of Institution be read out of the Evangelists, or out of the first Epistle of the Apostle Paul to the Corinthians, chap. xi. 23: *I have received of the Lord*, &c., to the 27th verse, which the Minister may, when he seeth requisite, explain and apply.

Let the Prayer, Thanksgiving, or Blessing of the Bread and Wine, be to this effect:—

With humble and hearty acknowledgment of the greatness of our misery, from which neither man nor angel was able to deliver us, and of our great unworthiness of the least of all God's mercies; to give thanks to God for all His benefits, and especially for that great benefit of our redemption, the love of God the Father, the sufferings and merits of the Lord Jesus Christ the Son of God, by which we are delivered; and for all means of grace, the Word and Sacraments; and for this Sacrament in particular, by which Christ and all His benefits are applied and sealed up unto us, which, notwithstanding the denial of them unto others, are in great mercy continued unto us, after so much and long abuse of them all.

To profess that there is no other name under heaven by which we can be saved, but the name of Jesus Christ, by Whom alone we receive liberty and life, have access to the Throne of grace, are admitted to eat and drink at His own Table, and are sealed up by His Spirit to an assurance of happiness and everlasting life.

Earnestly to pray to God, the Father of all mercies, and God of all consolation, to vouchsafe His gracious presence, and the effectual working of His Spirit in us; and so to sanctify these Elements both of Bread and Wine, and to bless His own Ordinance, that we may receive by faith the Body and Blood of Jesus Christ, crucified for us, and so to feed upon Him, that He may be one with us, and we one with Him; that He may live in us, and we in Him, and to Him who hath loved us, and given Himself for us.

All which he is to endeavour to perform with suitable affections, answerable to such an holy Action, and to stir up the like in the people.

The Elements being now sanctified by the Word and Prayer, the Minister, being at the Table,* is to take the Bread in his hand, and say, in these expressions (or other the like, used by Christ or His Apostle upon this occasion):—

According to the holy institution, command, and example of our blessed Saviour Jesus Christ, I take this Bread, and, having given thanks, break it and give it unto you.

There the Minister, who is also himself to communicate, is to break the Bread and give it to the Communicants.

TAKE YE, EAT YE; THIS IS THE BODY OF CHRIST WHICH IS BROKEN FOR YOU: DO THIS IN REMEMBRANCE OF HIM.

In like manner the Minister is to take the Cup, and say, in these expressions (or other the like, used by Christ or the Apostle upon the same occasion):—

* In original draft, "still keeping his place at the Table."—MS. Records.

According to the institution, command, and example of our Lord Jesus Christ, I take this Cup, and give it unto you.

Here he giveth it to the Communicants.

THIS CUP IS THE NEW TESTAMENT IN THE BLOOD OF CHRIST, WHICH IS SHED FOR THE REMISSION OF THE SINS OF MANY: DRINK YE ALL OF IT.

After all have communicated, the Minister may, in a few words, put them in mind

Of the grace of God in Jesus Christ held forth in this Sacrament; and exhort them to walk worthy of it.

The Minister is to give solemn Thanks to God,

For His rich mercy, and invaluable goodness, vouchsafed to them in that Sacrament; and to entreat for pardon for the defects of the whole service, and for the gracious assistance of His good Spirit, whereby they may be enabled to walk in the strength of that grace, as becometh those who have received so great pledges of salvation.

The Collection for the Poor is so to be ordered that no part of the public worship be thereby hindered.

Of the Sanctification of the Lord's Day.

THE Lord's Day ought to be so remembered beforehand, as that all worldly business of our ordinary callings may be so ordered, and so timely and seasonably laid aside, as they may not be impediments to the due sanctifying of the day when it comes.

The whole day is to be celebrated as holy to the Lord, both in public and private, as being the Christian Sabbath. To which end it is requisite that there be a holy cessation, or resting all the day, from all unnecessary labours; and an abstaining, not only from all sports and pastimes, but also from all worldly words and thoughts.

That the diet on that day be so ordered, as that neither servants be unnecessarily detained from the public worship of God, nor any other persons hindered from the sanctifying that day.

That there be private preparations of every person and family, by prayer for themselves, and for God's assistance of the Minister, and for a blessing upon his ministry; and by such other holy exercises as may further dispose them to a more comfortable communion with God in His public Ordinances.

That all the people meet so timely for Public Worship, that the whole Congregation may be present at the beginning, and with one heart solemnly join together in all parts of the Public Worship, and not depart till after the Blessing.

That what time is vacant, between or after the solemn meetings of the Congregation in public, be spent in reading, meditation, repetition of sermons; especially by calling their families to an account of what they have heard, and catechising of them, holy conferences, prayer for a blessing upon the public Ordinances, singing of Psalms, visiting the sick, relieving the poor, and suchlike duties of piety, charity, and mercy, accounting the Sabbath a delight.

The Solemnisation of Marriage.

ALTHOUGH Marriage be no Sacrament, nor peculiar to the Church of God, but common to mankind, and of public interest in every commonwealth; yet, because such as marry* are to marry in the Lord, and have special need of instruction, direction, and exhortation from the Word of God at their entering into such a new condition, and of the blessing of God upon them therein, we judge it expedient that Marriage be solemnised by a lawful Minister of the Word, that he may accordingly counsel them, and pray for a blessing upon them.

Marriage is to be betwixt one man and one woman only; and they, such as are not within the degrees of consanguinity or affinity prohibited by the Word of God; and the parties are to be of years of discretion, fit to make their own choice, or, upon good grounds, to give their mutual consent.

Before the solemnising of Marriage between any persons, their purpose of Marriage shall be published by the Minister three several Sabbath Days, in the Congregation, at the place or places of their

---

* In original draft, "because it was instituted by God in innocency, and those that marry," &c.—Lightfoot.

most usual and constant abode, respectively. And of this publication the Minister who is to join them in Marriage shall have sufficient testimony before he proceed to solemnise the Marriage.

Before that publication of such their purpose (if the parties be under age), the consent of the parents, or others under whose power they are (in case the parents be dead), is to be made known to the Church officers of that Congregation to be recorded.

The like is to be observed in the proceedings of all others, although of age, whose parents are living, for their first Marriage. And, in after Marriages of either of those parties, they shall be exhorted not to contract Marriage without first acquainting their parents with it (if with conveniency it may be done), endeavouring to obtain their consent.

Parents ought not to force their children to marry without their free consent, nor deny their own consent without just cause.

After the purpose or contract of Marriage hath been thus published, the Marriage is not to be long* deferred. Therefore the Minister, having had convenient warning, and nothing being objected to hinder it, is publicly to solemnise it in the place appointed by authority for Public Worship, before a competent number of credible witnesses, at some convenient hour of the day, at any time of the year except on a day of public humiliation. And we advise that it be not on the Lord's Day.

And because all relations are sanctified by the Word and Prayer, the Minister is to pray for a blessing upon them, to this effect :—

Acknowledging our sins, whereby we have made ourselves less than the least of all the mercies of God, and provoked Him to embitter all our comforts ; earnestly, in the name of Christ, to entreat the Lord (whose presence and favour is the happiness of every condition, and sweetens every relation) to be their portion, and to own and accept them in Christ, who are now to be joined in the honourable estate of Marriage, the covenant of their God : and that, as He hath brought them together by His providence, He would sanctify them by His Spirit, giving them a new frame of heart fit for their new estate ; enrich-

* The word "long" omitted in the English edition of 1644.—Hall's Reliquiæ Liturgicæ.

ing them with all graces whereby they may perform the duties, enjoy the comforts, undergo the cares, and resist the temptations which accompany that condition, as becometh Christians.

The Prayer being ended, it is convenient that the Minister do briefly declare unto them, out of the Scripture,

The institution, use, and ends of Marriage, with the conjugal duties, which, in all faithfulness, they are to perform each to other; exhorting them to study the holy Word of God, that they may learn to live by faith, and to be content in the midst of all marriage cares and troubles, sanctifying God's Name in a thankful, sober, and holy use of all conjugal comforts; praying much with and for one another; watching over and provoking each other to love and good works; and to live together as the heirs of the grace of life.

After solemn charging of the persons to be married, before the great God who searcheth all hearts, and to whom they must give a strict account at the last day, that if either of them know any cause, by precontract or otherwise, why they may not lawfully proceed to marriage, that they now discover it; the Minister (if no impediment be acknowledged) shall cause first the Man to take the Woman by the right hand, saying these words:—

I N. do take thee N. to be my married Wife, and do, in the presence of God, and before this Congregation, promise and covenant to be a loving and faithful Husband unto thee, until God shall separate us by death.

Then the Woman shall take the Man by his right hand, and say these words:—

I N. do take thee N. to be my married Husband, and I do, in the presence of God, and before this Congregation, promise and covenant to be a loving, faithful, and obedient Wife unto thee, until God shall separate us by death.

Then, without any further ceremony, the Minister shall, in the face of the Congregation, pronounce them to be Husband and Wife, according to God's Ordinance; and so conclude the Action with Prayer to this effect:—

That the Lord would be pleased to accompany His own Ordinance with His blessing, beseeching Him to enrich the persons now married, as with other pledges of His love, so particularly with the comforts and fruits of marriage, to the praise of His abundant mercy, in and through Christ Jesus.

A Register is to be carefully kept, wherein the names of the parties so married, with the time of their marriage, are forthwith to be fairly recorded in a book provided for that purpose, for the perusal of all whom it may concern.

Concerning Visitation of the Sick.

IT is the duty of the Minister not only to teach the people committed to his charge in public, but privately; and particularly to admonish, exhort, reprove, and comfort them, upon all seasonable occasions, so far as his time, strength, and personal safety will permit.

He is to admonish them, in time of health, to prepare for death; and for that purpose they are often to confer with their Minister about the estate of their souls; and, in times of sickness, to desire his advice and help, timely and seasonably, before their strength and understanding fail them.

Times of sickness and affliction are special opportunities put into his hand by God to minister a word in season to weary souls: because then the consciences of men are or should be more awakened to bethink themselves of their spiritual estates for eternity; and Satan also takes advantage then to load them more with sore and heavy temptations: therefore the Minister, being sent for, and repairing to the sick, is to apply himself, with all tenderness and love, to administer some spiritual good to his soul, to this effect:—

He may, from the consideration of the present sickness, instruct him out of Scripture, that diseases come not by chance, or by distempers of body only, but by the wise and orderly guidance of the good hand of God to every particular person smitten by them. And that, whether it be laid upon him out of displeasure for sin, for his correction and amendment, or for trial and exercise of his graces, or for other special and excellent ends, all his sufferings shall turn to his profit;

and work together for his good, if he sincerely labour to make a sanctified use of God's visitation, neither despising His chastening, nor waxing weary of His correction.

If he suspect him of ignorance, he shall examine him in the principles of religion, especially touching repentance and faith; and, as he seeth cause, instruct him in the nature, use, excellency, and necessity of those graces; as also touching the covenant of grace; and Christ the Son of God, the Mediator of it; and concerning remission of sins by faith in Him.

He shall exhort the sick person to examine himself, to search and try his former ways, and his estate towards God.

And if the sick person shall declare any scruple, doubt, or temptation that are upon him, instructions and resolutions shall be given to satisfy and settle him.

If it appear that he hath not a due sense of his sins, endeavours ought to be used to convince him of his sins, of the guilt and desert of them; of the filth and pollution which the soul contracts by them; and of the curse of the law and wrath of God due to them; that he may be truly affected with and humbled for them: and withal to make known the danger of deferring repentance, and of neglecting salvation at any time offered; to awaken his conscience and rouse him up out of a stupid and secure condition, to apprehend the justice and wrath of God, before whom none can stand but he that, being lost in himself, layeth hold upon Christ by faith.

If he have endeavoured to walk in the ways of holiness, and to serve God in uprightness, although not without many failings and infirmities; or, if his spirit be broken with the sense of sin, or cast down through want of the sense of God's favour, then it will be fit to raise him up by setting before him the freeness and fulness of God's grace, the sufficiency of righteousness in Christ, the gracious offers in the Gospel, that all who repent and believe with all their heart in God's mercy through Christ, renouncing their own righteousness, shall have life and salvation in Him. It may be also useful to show him that death hath in it no spiritual evil to be feared by those that are in Christ, because sin, the sting of death, is taken away by Christ, who hath delivered all that are His from the bondage of the fear of death, triumphed over the grave, given us victory, is Himself entered into glory to prepare a place for His people: so that neither life nor death shall be able to separate them from God's love in Christ, in whom such are sure, though now they must be laid in the dust, to obtain a joyful and glorious resurrection to eternal life.

OF THE SICK. 317

Advice also may be given, as to beware of an ill-grounded persuasion on mercy, or on the goodness of his condition for heaven, so to disclaim all merit in himself, and to cast himself wholly upon God for mercy, in the sole merits and mediation of Jesus Christ, who hath engaged Himself never to cast off them who in truth and sincerity come unto Him. Care also must be taken that the sick person be not cast down into despair by such a severe representation of the wrath of God due to him for his sins, as is not mollified by a sensible propounding of Christ, and His merit for a door of hope to every penitent believer.

When the sick person is best composed, may be least disturbed, and other necessary offices about him least hindered, the Minister, if desired, shall pray with him and for him to this effect :—

Confessing and bewailing of sin original and actual; the miserable condition of all by nature, as being children of wrath, and under the curse; acknowledging that all diseases, sicknesses, death, and hell itself, are the proper issues and effects thereof; imploring God's mercy for the sick person through the blood of Christ; beseeching that God would open his eyes, discover unto him his sins, cause him to see himself lost in himself, make known to him the cause why God smiteth him, reveal Jesus Christ to his soul for righteousness and life, give unto him His Holy Spirit, to create and strengthen faith to lay hold upon Christ, to work in him comfortable evidences of His love, to arm him against temptations, to take off his heart from the world, to sanctify his present visitation, to furnish him with patience and strength to bear it, and to give him perseverance in faith to the end.

That, if God shall please to add to his days, He would vouchsafe to bless and sanctify all means of his recovery, to remove the disease, renew his strength, and enable him to walk worthy of God, by a faithful remembrance and diligent observing of such vows and promises of holiness and obedience, as men are apt to make in times of sickness, that he may glorify God in the remaining part of his life.

And, if God have determined to finish his days by the present visitation, he may find such evidence of the pardon of all his sins, of his interest in Christ, and eternal life by Christ, as may cause his inward man to be renewed, while his outward man decayeth; that he may behold death without fear, cast himself wholly upon Christ without doubting, desire to be dissolved and to be with Christ, and so receive the end of his faith, the salvation of his soul, through the only merits and intercession of the Lord Jesus Christ, our alone Saviour and all-sufficient Redeemer.

The Minister shall admonish him also (as there shall be cause) to set his house in order, thereby to prevent inconveniences; to take care for the payment of his debts, and to make restitution or satisfaction where he hath done any wrong; to be reconciled to those with whom he hath been at variance, and fully to forgive all men their trespasses against him, as he expects forgiveness at the hand of God.

Lastly, The Minister may improve the present occasion to exhort those about the sick person to consider their own mortality, to return to the Lord and make peace with Him; in health to prepare for sickness, death, and judgment; and all the days of their appointed time so to wait until their change come, that when Christ, who is our life, shall appear, they may appear with Him in glory.

Concerning Burial of the Dead.

WHEN any person departeth this life, let the dead body, upon the day of burial, be decently attended from the house to the place appointed for public burial, and there immediately interred without any ceremony.

And because the custom of kneeling down and praying by or towards the dead corpse, and other such* usages, in the place where it lies before it be carried to Burial, are superstitious; and for that praying, reading, and singing, both in going to and at the grave, have been grossly abused, are no way beneficial to the dead, and have proved many ways hurtful to the living; therefore let all such things be laid aside.

* In original draft, "other usages."—Lightfoot.

PUBLIC FASTING.

Howbeit, we judge it very convenient that the Christian friends which accompany the dead body to the place appointed for public Burial, do apply themselves to meditations and conferences suitable to the occasion; and that the Minister, as upon other occasions, so at this time, if he be present, may put them in remembrance of their duty.

That this shall not extend to deny any civil respects or differences at the Burial, suitable to the rank and condition of the party deceased while he was living.

Concerning Public Solemn Fasting.

WHEN some great and notable judgments are either inflicted upon a people, or apparently imminent, or by some extraordinary provocations notoriously deserved; as also when some special blessing is to be sought and obtained, Public Solemn Fasting (which is to continue the whole day) is a duty that God expecteth from that nation or people.

A religious Fast requires total abstinence, not only from all food (unless bodily weakness do manifestly disable from holding out till the Fast be ended, in which case somewhat may be taken, yet very sparingly, to support nature when ready to faint), but also from all worldly labour, discourses, and thoughts, and from all bodily delights (although at other times lawful), rich apparel, ornaments, and suchlike, during the Fast; and much more from whatever is in the nature or use scandalous and offensive, as gaudish attire, lascivious habits and gestures, and other vanities of either sex ; which we recommend to all Ministers, in their places, diligently and zealously to reprove, as at other times, so especially at a Fast, without respect of persons, as there shall be occasion.

Before the public meeting each family and person apart are privately to use all religious care to prepare their hearts to such a solemn work, and to be early at the Congregation.

So large a portion of the day as conveniently may be is to be spent in Public Reading and Preaching of the Word, with Singing of Psalms fit to quicken affections suitable to such a duty: but especially in Prayer, to this or the like effect :—

Giving glory to the great Majesty of God, the Creator, Preserver, and supreme Ruler of all the world, the better to affect us thereby with a holy reverence and awe of Him; acknowledging His manifold, great, and tender mercies, especially to the Church and Nation, the more effectually to soften and abase our hearts before Him; humbly confessing of sins of all sorts, with their several aggravations; justifying God's righteous judgments as being far less than our sins do deserve; yet humbly and earnestly imploring His mercy and grace for ourselves, the Church and Nation, for our King, and all in authority, and for all others for whom we are bound to pray (according as the present exigent requireth), with more special importunity and enlargement than at other times; applying by faith the promises and goodness of God for pardon, help, and deliverance from the evils felt, feared, or deserved; and for obtaining the blessings which we need and expect; together with a giving up of ourselves wholly and for ever unto the Lord.

In all these the Ministers, who are the mouths of the people unto God, ought so to speak from their hearts, upon serious and thorough premeditation of them, that both themselves and their people may be much affected, and even melted thereby, especially with sorrow for their sins; that it may be indeed a day of deep humiliation and afflicting of the soul.

Special choice is to be made of such Scriptures to be read, and of such texts for Preaching, as may best work the hearts of the hearers to the special business of the day, and most dispose them to humiliation and repentance: insisting most on those particulars which each Minister's observation and experience tells him are most conducing to the edification and reformation of that Congregation to which he preacheth.

Before the close of the public duties the Minister is, in his own and the people's name, to engage his and their hearts to be the Lord's, with professed purpose and resolution to reform whatever is amiss among them, and more particularly such sins as they have been more remarkably guilty of; and to draw nearer unto God, and to walk more closely and faithfully with Him in new obedience than ever before.

He is also to admonish the people, with all importunity, that the work of that day doth not end with the public duties of it, but that they are so to improve the remainder of the day, and of their whole life, in reinforcing upon themselves and their families in private all those godly affections and resolutions which they professed in public, as that they may be settled in their hearts for ever, and themselves may more sensibly find that God hath smelt a sweet savour in Christ from their performances, and is pacified towards them by answers of grace, in pardoning of sin, in removing of judgments, in averting or preventing of plagues, and in conferring of blessings suitable to the conditions and prayers of His people by Jesus Christ.

Besides solemn and general Fasts enjoined by authority, we judge that, at other times, Congregations may keep days of Fasting, as Divine Providence shall administer unto them special occasions; and also that families may do the same, so it be not on days wherein the Congregation to which they do belong is to meet for Fasting, or other public duties of Worship.

Concerning the Observation of Days of Public Thanksgiving.

WHEN any such day is to be kept, let notice be given of it, and of the occasion thereof, some convenient time before, that the people may the better prepare themselves thereunto.

The day being come, and the Congregation (after private preparations) being assembled, the Minister is to begin with a word of Exhortation, to stir up the people to the duty for which they are met, and with a short Prayer for God's assistance and blessing (as at other conventions for Public Worship), according to the particular occasion of their meeting.

Let him then make some pithy narration of the deliverance obtained, or mercy received, or of whatever hath occasioned that assembling of the Congregation, that all may better understand it, or be minded of it, and more affected with it.

And, because Singing of Psalms is of all other the most proper Ordinance for expressing of joy and thanksgiving, let some pertinent Psalm or Psalms be sung for that purpose, before or after the Reading of some portion of the Word suitable to the present business.

Then let the Minister who is to preach proceed to further Exhortation and Prayer before his Sermon, with special reference to the present work: after which, let him preach upon some text of Scripture pertinent to the occasion.

The Sermon ended, let him not only pray, as at other times after preaching is directed, with remembrance of the necessities of the Church, King, and State (if before the Sermon they were omitted), but enlarge himself in due and solemn Thanksgiving for former mercies and deliverances; but more especially for that which at the present calls them together to give thanks: with humble petition for the continuance and renewing of God's wonted mercies, as need shall be, and for sanctifying grace to make a right use thereof. And so, having sung another Psalm suitable to the mercy, let him dismiss the Congregation with a Blessing, that they may have some convenient time for their repast and refreshing.

But the Minister (before their dismission) is solemnly to admonish them to beware of all excess and riot, tending to gluttony or drunkenness, and much more of these sins themselves, in their eating and refreshing; and to take care that their mirth and rejoicing be not carnal, but spiritual, which may make God's praise to be glorious, and themselves humble and sober; and that both their feeding and rejoicing may render them more cheerful, and enlarged further to celebrate His praises in the midst of the Congregation when they return unto it in the remaining part of that day.

When the Congregation shall be again assembled, the like course in praying, reading, preaching, singing of Psalms, and offering up of more praise and thanksgiving, that is before directed for the Morning, is to be renewed and continued so far as the time will give leave.

At one or both of the public meetings that day a Collection is to be made for the Poor (and in the like manner upon the day of Public Humiliation), that their loins may bless us and rejoice the more with us. And the people are to be exhorted at the end of the latter meeting to spend the residue of that day in holy duties, and testifications of Christian love and charity one towards another, and of rejoicing more and more in the Lord, as becometh those who make the joy of the Lord their strength.

Of Singing of Psalms.

IT is the duty of Christians to praise God publicly, by Singing of Psalms together in the Congregation, and also privately in the family.

In Singing of Psalms the voice is to be tunably and gravely ordered, but the chief care must be to sing with understanding, and with grace in the heart, making melody unto the Lord.

That the whole Congregation may join herein, every one that can read is to have a Psalm-Book; and all others not disabled by age or otherwise are to be exhorted to learn to read. But for the present, where many in the Congregation cannot read, it is convenient that the Minister, or some other fit person appointed by him and the other Ruling Officers, do read the Psalm line by line before the singing thereof.

An Appendix touching Days and Places for Public Worship.

THERE is no day commanded in Scripture to be kept holy under the Gospel but the Lord's Day, which is the Christian Sabbath.

Festival days, vulgarly called *Holy-days*, having no warrant in the Word of God, are not to be continued.

Nevertheless, it is lawful and necessary, upon special emergent occasions, to separate a day or days for public fasting or thanksgiving, as the several eminent and extraordinary dispensations of God's providence shall administer cause and opportunity to His people.

As no place is capable of any holiness, under pretence of whatsoever dedication or consecration, so neither is it subject to such pollution by any superstition formerly used, and now laid aside, as may render it unlawful or inconvenient for Christians to meet together therein for the Public Worship of God. And therefore we hold it requisite that the places of public assembling for worship among us should be continued and employed to that use.

END OF THE DIRECTORY.

APPENDIX TO THE DIRECTORY.

NOTES.

The Preface.

THE Preface was the work of a separate sub-committee, composed of Nye, Bridges, Burges, Goodwin, Vines, Reynolds, Marshall, Dr Temple, and the Scots Commissioners. It was not drawn up till the larger and most important part of the Directory had been completed. After it was brought in on the 28th of October, the Independents proposed to dispense with a preface altogether, which was vigorously resisted, especially by the Scots. The discussion of it occupied six sessions. Some of the debates are noticed in the MS. Record, but it is seldom possible to connect them with the text as it now stands. The most important was on the last paragraph. Five months before, when Mr Marshall was bringing in the first draft of the Directory, he had said, "This doth not only set down the heads of things, but * as that with the altering of here a word and there a word, a man may mould it into a prayer."† And when the Preface was tabled, it contained these words :—"Our meaning in the Directory is not that the ministers should not turn the material of it into an ordinary form of prayer and exhortation."‡ When a debate rose on this passage, Dr Gonge objected that "it was said in the beginning that this was soe compiled that we might turne it into a prayer. Too much invention will hinder devotion." Gillespie said that "that man who stirres up his own gifts doth better the best use of set formes. Good to hold out what is the best."§ Unfortunately Lightfoot was absent from this interesting debate. He was present next day, when he spoke of it "as dangerous to hint anything against a form of prayer."

* Illegible in the MS. Record.—T. L.   † MS. Record, May 26.
‡ Lightfoot, p. 304, 322.   § MS. Record, Nov. 6.

Henderson proposed to end the Preface thus :—"So to furnish his heart, &c., that he may be able to pray, &c., as if he had no help or furniture from this Directory;" which was accepted, but without the last clause. On the whole, the changes seem to have been made to satisfy the Independents. The Assembly were at last unanimous in accepting the passage as it now stands ; "those who were for set forms of prayer resolving to confine themselves to the very words of the Directory, while others made use of them only as heads for their enlargement."* Dr. Hammond speaks of a book entitled 'A Supply of Prayer for the Ships that want Ministers to pray for them, agreeable to the Directory established by Parliament—published by authority.' He describes it as "word for word formed out of it—the Directory turned into a prayer." †

There is printed among Gillespie's Notes a paper which has the appearance of having been a rejected amendment on the Preface. It is to be found among Wodrow's MSS. in the Advocates' Library, and had been copied by him from the original in Gillespie's hand. In the manuscript it stands exactly as follows :—

"*On the backside—*

"Gloria Patri.
Saying the Creed.
Standing up at the reading of the Gospel.
Preaching on Christmas.
Funeral sermons.
Churching of women, &c.
The saying of the three Creeds, after reading of Scripture.
The people's responsals.

"*And on the foreside—*

"Concerning other customs or rites in the worship of God, formerly received in any of the Kingdoms, which, though not condemned in this Directory, have been, or apparently will be, occasions of divisions and offences, as it is far from our intention that those or the like unnecessary burdens should be laid upon any, or any compelled thereto, so we judge it most expedient that the practice and use of them be not continued, as well for the nearer uniformity betwixt the Churches of both Kingdoms, as for their greater peace and harmony within themselves, and their edifying one another in love. Wherein we would be so understood as not having the least thought to discredit or blame our worthy Reformers or others who have since practised them. Only

* Neal, ii. 107. † View of the New Directory, p. 79.

we hold forth what we have learned from the rules of Christ and His Apostles, that even those of the learned and godly who satisfy their own judgments concerning the lawfulness of those customs, shall henceforth do well to abstain for the law of love, and for the bond of peace."

The first part of this document is evidently an endorsement descriptive of the second. What makes it probable that the second was intended to be part of the Preface is, that Christmas sermons are included among the things not condemned. We shall see that when the Preface was passed, the Appendix concerning holy days—which undoubtedly condemns the observance of Christmas—had not yet been drawn up nor thought of.

On the 20th of November the Preface received its last review. The Independents objected to the passages concerning the Covenant and the rules of Christian prudence; when "we were in great fear," says Baillie, "all should be cast in the howes." But the addition of some words removed their scruples. "Sure I am," Gillespie says, "the Directory had never passed the Assembly of Divines if it had not been for the qualifications in the Preface." *

Of the Assembling of the Congregation, and their Behaviour in the Public Worship of God.

The passage in the first paragraph concerning private meetings was a late addition. It was first proposed by Wilkinson, as part of the section on preaching. But it was afterwards inserted here, and the words forbidding salutations, gazing, etc., were added at the same time.†

It has been often supposed that the second paragraph forbids the offering of silent prayer on entering the church. Gillespie in his Notes says that the last paragraph of the section was added at the request of the English, because many ignorant people, coming in after service had begun, would not join in the minister's prayer till they had said over the Lord's Prayer. But that prohibition would have been unnecessary if the practice of private devotion had been absolutely forbidden before. What is protested against is not *oratio*, but *adoratio*—not prayer, but prayer accompanied by gestures, which seem to recognise a more real presence of the Divine Being in one part of the building than in another. What makes this certain is that Baillie, speaking of the minister's kneeling in the pulpit for secret prayer at the beginning of service, says that there "was nothing of it in the

* Baillie, ii. 506. † Gillespie's Notes, p. 102.

Directory." This *bowing in the pulpit*, with the Metrical Doxology and Lord's Prayer, were the *three nocent ceremonies* so much disliked by the new school in Scotland. A proof that it was not forbidden in the Directory is the prohibition of it in the Supplementary Act of Assembly as a thing repugnant to English feeling, "though a lawful custom in this Kirk." A law avowedly based on this ground alone may be considered as in abeyance, now that England is no longer a party to the contract. Up to this time private prayer on entering church had been usual in Scottish congregations. But after this the people followed the example of their ministers, and laid it aside.*

There is here no reference to the psalm which has long been the prelude to Scottish worship. This is often spoken of as one of our departures from the Directory. Granting that it is so, there is nothing inconsistent with the spirit of the book in the use of a psalm before the prescribed service begins. In Scotland, both before and after the Westminster Assembly, the opening psalm was not given out by the minister, and was often sung before he entered the church. The singing of psalms at the beginning of worship was a common custom in the Reformed Churches, and even though it had been forbidden by the Directory, it was likely to be continued in Scotland. However, a better explanation seems to be that our first psalm is that which the Directory mentions at the beginning of the section on Prayer before Sermon. Up to the time of the Westminster Assembly, there had been two distinct services in the Scottish worship :—the Reader's, consisting of the Common Prayers, Scriptures, and Psalm ; and the Minister's, consisting of a Sermon with Prayer before and after it, a Psalm, and the Benediction. The Reader was now to be displaced, and his duty assigned to the Preacher. Among Baillie's unprinted MSS. is "a paper to my colleagues" at the Assembly, in which he objects to the proposed suppression of the office that "we put downe that exercise of publique prayers in all our townes, we cast out all our readers as unlawfull officers, we lay a very heavy burden on the most of our ministers, besides twice preaching, catechising, baptising, marying, and holding a session, all which are very ordinar in most of our congregations, we will have him to pray, sing, read both before and after noon." To provide for this change, the supplementary Act of 1645 required the Minister's service to be lengthened by half-an-hour. But practically his duty remained the same as before. He took up the new service at the point where he had been accustomed to succeed his Reader. The preface, the short prayer, the two lessons, he omitted. The

* Sage's Presbytery Examined, p. 360.

Directory service, thus mutilated, is exactly the Scottish worship, as many can still remember it—the Psalm, the long Prayer, the Sermon, concluding Prayer, Psalm, and Benediction. Henderson's Tract shows that in 1641 it was usual at the morning service to have a second prayer and psalm before the sermon. These, combined with the new custom of lecturing before preaching, complete the full morning service of later times, as it is still to be heard in St Giles's Church, when the Assembly is sitting, and in the majority of the rural parishes, in which afternoon service has been suppressed. But the Reader's service gradually disappeared. The Common Prayers were disused almost at once. The reading of the Scripture, *ab inferiore cathedra*, continued till this century, though it was never general. The Psalm alone remained, but it was given out by the Minister instead of the Reader. Proclamation of banns is the only ecclesiastical function of this ancient official performed by his modern representative.

Both here and in the section on Thanksgiving, the Directory requires *prefacing*, or calling on the people to worship God. In the sub-committee, there was much difference of opinion regarding it, though it was sanctioned by the customs of both kingdoms, by the form begining, *Dearly beloved brethren*, in the Common Prayer, by Cartwright's Directory, and by the rubric in the Common Order. The preface has long disappeared from the Scottish service. An exposition of the psalm seems to have been at an early period substituted for it. In 1675 this practice had been for some time in use in the Scots Church at Rotterdam.* It is still observed in some of the older Dissenting congregations in Scotland.

There is a significant silence as to the posture to be used in prayer. In all the Reformed Churches, this was at first regulated more by custom than by statute, and even in the same congregation uniformity was not always the rule. In the Church of England there was for a time no attempt to enforce kneeling. The Prayer-Book of 1549 says, "As touching kneeling, crossing, holding up of hands, knocking upon the breast, and other gestures, they may be used or left, as every man's devotion serveth, without blame." Henderson told the Westminster Divines that in Scotland, communicants either sat or knelt at the Consecration Prayer. His own practice may be gathered from a volume of his sermons lately published, where in several of the prefaces he calls the congregation to pray, by saying, "Let us now fall down," &c.; and once, at the end of a sermon, he says, "I would have all of you to bend your knees," &c. In the Synod of Aberdeen, in

* Steven's History, p. 104.

1662, the Bishop required the people to "pray either standing or kneeling, as the most reverend gesture in prayer." The pamphlets after the Revolution frequently refer to the subject. The defenders of the Kirk say, "It's certain Presbyterians either stand or kneel in time of prayer, and allow of no other gesture to be so decent."* "He knows perfectly well that the forbearance of these postures is not required of the Church as a term of communion. . . . I am very sure Presbyterians do stand, that is to say, many of them; it cannot be said of all, at all times, nor can it be said of all the Prelatists in the nation."† On the other side it is said, "The Presbyterians in Scotland for the most part sit all of them in time of public prayer."‡ "I observed six sitting for one standing, and not one kneeling at prayer."§ "Many parts in the nation sitting at prayers, leaning on their elbows."|| "Though the minister perform prayer in a standing or leaning position, yet all the congregation, few or none excepted, sit all the while. . . . When you [the ministers] are hearers only, you sit as close as any of them."¶ Some of them speak as if to stand was not a practice only, but a principle among Episcopalians: one, speaking of the invitation to conform, says, "Who knows but by virtue of this uniformity we must forbear . . . to stand at prayer"** "The far greater part, if not all of them, that frequent your [the Episcopal] meetings do stand in time of public prayers, and that constantly, and think themselves bound so to do."†† Most readers would be more ready to take the following for a coarse caricature of Episcopalian worship by a Presbyterian, than of Presbyterian worship by an Episcopalian. "Should a foreigner come into your assemblies when you are at public prayers, he would hardly think the people at all concerned in them, when he sees them in so careless and sleepy like a posture; some leaning on their elbows, others leaning on the back or shoulders of another; others lying with their arms folded close upon their faces, as if they were asleep.' ‡‡ The natural explanation of these contradictions is, that various attitudes were used in prayer, sometimes standing, sometimes kneeling, and very frequently that of sitting, then and still practised in the Swiss and other Reformed Churches; and that some-

* Toleration's Fence Removed, 1703, p. 17.
† Full and Final Answer Examined, 1703, p. 18, 41.
‡ Apology for the Clergy, 1692, p. 57.
§ Short Character of Presbyterian Spirit, 1703, p. 9.
|| Calder on Set Forms, 1706, p. 50.
¶ Dialogue between a Presbyterian Minister, &c., 1704, p. 48, 132.
** Plain Dealing, 1703, p. 7.
†† Dialogue, p. 133.   ‡‡ Ibid. p. 131.

times a slight variation of this irreverent posture passed for kneeling. In time standing became universal in the Scottish Church, more from a sense of the decency of uniformity, than from submission to any decree of their own or the Westminster Assembly.

These pamphlets frequently refer to another point of difference on which the Directory is silent—that of uncovering the head in church. The Scottish usage seems to have been the same as that which is still preserved in some Continental churches, to wear the hat in time of preaching, and uncover at prayer—an unseemly practice, but one which at least proves that they did not hold the opinion so often imputed to them, that the sermon is more worthy of respect than the prayers. It would seem that, after the Reformation, this fashion prevailed in England. Cartwright, describing the Anglican worship as it was in Elizabeth's time, says, "When Jesus is named, then off goeth the cap, and down goeth the knees."* In Scotland, at the Revolution, an Episcopal writer could say no more for his party, than that "some persons more reverent think fit to be uncovered." † The custom was changing in the beginning of the eighteenth century. "Many uncover their heads in time of sermon, and for my part, I very much approve of it, and so do all I have spoken with upon that head," says a Presbyterian writer. ‡ But even in the last generation the hat was sometimes to be seen worn during sermon in country churches.

The Record mentions that when Mr Marshall gave in the draft of the Directory, he said, "All the prayers for the Lord's Day are drawn up into one body without any dividing of them, that if they do appear to be fit, the rest may be done suddenly, if returned." The division was afterwards made in Committee, and, as Gillespie, in his Notes, seems to hint, without the knowledge of the Scots. There must have been some difficulty in reconciling the practice of the two nations. Baillie says that the Puritans were accustomed to have only one prayer before sermon, while the Scots had two. The Independents, on the authority of 1 Tim. ii. 1, began their single prayer with "a large solemn prayer for the king and the Church," and were anxious to have this adopted. § The moderate Puritans objected to the English Liturgy that it had no preparatory prayer for "assistance or acceptance," such as Baxter afterwards introduced into the Savoy Prayer-Book. In Scotland, the first and longer prayer of the minister was,

* Whitgift's Works, iii. 384.   † Burton's History, ii. 31.
‡ Full and Final Answer Examined, p. 18.
§ Baillie, Dissuasive, p. 118. Letters, ii. 123.

as Henderson informs us, "for remission of sin, sanctification, and all things needful, joining also confession of sins and thanksgiving, with special relation to the hearers;" the second for a blessing upon the preaching of the Word, while the Prayer of General Intercession followed the sermon.

Baillie, in his 'Paper to my Colleagues,' calls the one long prayer "a new fancy of the Independents, grounded on no solid reason, and contrair to all the practice of the Church, old or late, who divided always ther prayers in mor small parts, and did not have any one of a disproportionable length."

We may assume that the words "forbearing to use," &c., were intended to prevent the private reading in service-time of either of the disused Liturgies. Nothing is said as to the use of Amen, which is, perhaps, what is referred to as "the people's responsals," in Gillespie's manuscript. A Scottish pamphlet of 1690 says that even under the Episcopal system "*Amen* gives great offence, though neither the clerk nor people use it, only the minister sometimes shuts up his prayer with it." *

Of Public Reading of the Holy Scriptures.

In the Assembly's discussions on Church Government in November 1643, the question whether the reading of the Word is a pastoral function had been debated for several days. Some who held the affirmative did so on the ground that it ought always to be read with exposition. When this section of the Directory, drawn up by Thomas Young, † was presented in June, the discussion was revived, and continued for three days on the question of the right of expectants to read in public. The limitation of the right to them did not altogether abolish the Scottish Readers, as it was intended to do. Not only under the Restoration, but under the Commonwealth, and after the Revolution, down to a recent period, Scripture was often read from the desk, before the minister began his duty. In 1792 a small endowment was founded by a minister of Dunbar for the schoolmaster of Forglen, on condition that he should read in church between the second and third bells.‡ Within the present century, there was a Reader in Aberdeen Cathedral, who read portions of the Psalter and lessons from both Testaments before morning service. § To this hour the

\- Burton's History, ii. 31. † Gillespie's Notes, p. 101.
‡ Scott's Fasti, i. 369.
§ History of Scots Affairs, Spalding Club, i. p. xxv.

desk is known in many districts of Scotland by no other name than the lettern. In Holland and Switzerland the office has been kept up ever since the Reformation.

The original draft of the earlier paragraphs, so far as Lightfoot has preserved it, ran thus :—" It belongs to the pastor's and teacher's office publicly to read the Word ; yet such as intend the ministry may occasionally both read the Scripture and exercise their gifts in preaching in the congregation, if allowed thereunto by the Presbytery. . . . How great a portion of the Scripture is to be read at every meeting may be determined by the discretion of the minister ; but we judge it convenient that ordinarily one chapter of either Testament be read at each meeting, and sometimes more than one when the shortness of the chapter or order of the matter requireth it." The words "either Testament" do not mean that only one passage of the Word was to be read. At that time the common meaning of *either*, used as an adjective, was *both of two*, not *one of two* as with us. A single lesson would have been directly opposed to the Scottish custom, which, as Henderson's Tract shows, was to read from both Testaments.

The passage recommending more frequent reading of select parts of Scripture does not mean that these may be substituted at discretion for one or other of the ordinary lessons. The intention of the Committee at their latest review of the section, undoubtedly was to enjoin the reading of a third portion, as the prose Psalter is read in the Church of England. Gillespie says that there was then added a direction "to read a portion of the Psalms before the Chapters." And soon afterwards there was in the Assembly itself "a debate about the reading of the Psalms every day," and "a debate about the length." We have seen that the words were thus understood and obeyed by the Reader in Aberdeen after 1800.

The next paragraph is of considerable importance, as on it rests the authority for the forenoon lecture, which held so prominent a place in the later Scottish worship. Hitherto, the reading of Scripture without comment had always formed a part of divine service in Scotland, while in England the Puritans (especially the more extreme section of them) had disliked it.* It is therefore remarkable, that when the Assembly were discussing the question, Nye and Goodwin, the Independent leaders, advocated, and many of the Presbyterians opposed, reading without exposition. Gillespie in committee objected to the clause which forbids exposition till the reading is ended. Both sides were perhaps influenced less by their former practice than by

* Zurich Letters, i. 281. Dissuasive, 30, 118. Gangræna, p. 16.

their desire to exclude or allow lay ministrations. The permissive language of the paragraph was the result. It is a mistake to suppose that the Scottish lecture is an English custom, adopted after the Westminster Assembly. Baillie evidently sees no novelty in an exposition, but only in an exposition followed by a sermon—a combination which does date from that period.* The English lecture was something different. It was a discourse delivered on a week-day or a Sunday afternoon, by a Puritan minister, in the orders of the Church of England, but prevented by the scruples of his party from reading the service, and therefore unbeneficed and dependent on his hearers for support. In Scotland the expository sermon had been long in use, though it was not till after this that the English name of *lecture* was applied to it. What is most remarkable is, that, by some tacit understanding, the cautious permission of the Directory was, from the first, received and obeyed in Scotland as a strict command. That very year, the Scots Church at Rotterdam, after a dispute with their minister on the question, referred it to their countrymen at the Westminster Assembly. Their decision was, that "the exposition of a chapter at once is not only lawful, but since the Reformation has been alwyse practised in some of the Kirkes of Scotland, and now is appointed by the Synod of London to be a parte of the uniformitie of divine service in all the Kirkes of the three Kingdomes."† The supplementary Act of 1645 assumes that reading and expounding are equally enjoined by the Directory. This not very obvious interpretation of it was obeyed with such zeal that reading was not only supplemented by exposition, but displaced by it. The Act of 1652 implies that already the due proportion of Scripture was being diminished. In 1661, Ray found the minister reading and expounding in some places, in some not. The Act of 1694 speaks of lecturing as *introduced and established* by the Directory. The subject is often discussed in the pamphlets after the Revolution, but the Scottish clergy so excuse as to accuse themselves. It is plain that the Word of God has been banished from the afternoon service altogether, and that the Westminster minimum of a chapter from each Testament at both services is represented by nothing but a shorter discourse with a longer text preceding the morning sermon. Unfortunately the lecture, like the Lord's Prayer, had become a party distinction. In 1692, an Episcopal incumbent, applying to the Assembly for leave to conform, says that his former brethren had blamed him for opening some portion of Scripture before sermon. At the same period we read of Church courts libelling ministers for

* Letters, ii. 122.   † Steven's History, p. 9.

neglecting the lecture which the Directory allowed,* though we never hear of discipline reaching those who omitted the reading which it required. The first sign of the Church's return to her earlier practice was the passing of an Act in 1812, which, while enjoining the continuance of lecturing, commends the course taken by the Synod of Aberdeen in reviving the regular reading of Scripture from one or both Testaments. It must be admitted that in its own way the lecture has done much to further the end for which the reading of Scripture was appointed. Now that the written Word is being restored to its proper place and proportion in God's worship, we need not lay aside a mode of teaching which the experience of two centuries has shown to be full of interest and profit, from the breadth and simplicity of treatment which it admits. Its reputation, like that of our free prayer, has often been injured by loose and unpremeditated effusions. But the Scottish service will have lost one of its best and most characteristic features if it does not frequently contain, either in the place indicated by the Directory, or in the room of the sermon, a carefully-prepared expository discourse on one of the Scriptures for the day.

Gillespie's paper includes, among things not forbidden in the Directory, the repeating in this place of the three Creeds, meaning probably any one of the three. It is certain that the Westminster Divines did not reject the Creeds. At one of their earlier sittings, when they were revising the Thirty-nine Articles, before a separate Confession was thought of, it was proposed to re-translate the Creeds, and to explain the harsher clauses of the Athanasian, but no motion to disown them is recorded by Lightfoot. On the contrary, they sent up to Parliament the following modification of the eighth article :— " The Creeds that go under the name of the Nice Creed, Athanasian Creed, and that which is commonly called the Apostles' Creed, are thoroughly to be received and believed, for that the matter of them may be proved by most certain warrants of Holy Scripture."

Of Public Prayer before the Sermon.

The sections on Prayer gave rise to very little discussion. The whole subject was disposed of on the 28th of May, with short debates on the 11th of June and 11th of November. In a debate on the pastoral office, Mr Young had proposed that the pastor should be bound to pray when he preached, " because of the tie for prayer in

* Continued Relation, p. 60.

the pulpit that the bishop laid upon us," in allusion apparently to the controversy on bidding of prayers, arising out of the 55th canon of the Church of England. The words, "the minister who is to preach," may have been introduced to carry out this proposal; or they may have been meant to discourage the Independent custom of dividing the different parts of the service among different persons in the congregation: "one to pray, and another to preach, a third to prophesie, and a fourth to dismiss with a blessing."* It was afterwards made a charge against the Protesters also, that they admitted elders and private persons to pray publicly when ministers were present.† The Puritans were accustomed to object to the General Confession in the English Liturgy, that it did not acknowledge the doctrine of Original Sin, though the words "there is no health in us" seem to contain a statement of it sufficiently distinct in a form of words not meant to be dogmatic. A recognition of it was inserted at the beginning of this prayer. The original words were different from the present, for Gataker signified his dissent from the expression, "the sin of Adam derived to us from our first parents."

When the division was made, the prayer of General Intercession was appointed to be before the sermon, and that of Thanksgiving after it. But as the Scottish custom had been to offer the prayer of Intercession after preaching, the last paragraph was added to allow this as an alternative arrangement.

Of the Preaching of the Word.

This section was discussed on the 3d of June and the four following days. Whitaker proposed to have no Directory for preaching, but he was defeated after a long argument, in which Rutherford took a leading part against him. The paragraph about the requisites of a minister seems to have been objected to as a whole; and when this point was decided, it was moved that it should begin with the vague words, "it is convenient." The Rules of Ordination spoken of are those in the Form of Church Government agreed to by the Assembly, and usually printed among its Standards.

When the next paragraph came to be considered, there was, says the Record, "debate about that, *text or argument*, because it gives liberty to preach without a text," which was a practice among the Independents ‡ Accordingly *argument* has been omitted. The As-

* Dissuasive, p. 117.   † Answer to Protesters, p. 28.
‡ Dissuasive, p. 118.

sembly at first directed "that sermons be made either upon some text of Scripture, or else upon a whole Psalm or chapter." But the last words were afterwards struck out, probably after the passage which allows lecturing was introduced. The custom sanctioned in the end of this paragraph, of preaching continuously on some one book of Scripture, was then almost universal in Scotland, both in the congregation and at the Exercise. This liberty, however, might be regulated by Presbyterial authority. There is a curious case noticed in the printed Records of the Presbytery of Cupar for 1650, in which an old minister was censured for having his ordinary text in "impertinent places of Scripture"—namely, the book of Job for lecture, and the last chapters of the Revelation for sermon.

There were many debates on the wording of the next paragraphs, some of them on points sufficiently minute. Thus Lightfoot records with satisfaction that he was successful in opposing the words "several parts of the text," so as to meet the possible case of a sermon preached on the word *Amen*. It will show how completely the language of the draft was sometimes altered by discussion, if we set down in their original shape the paragraphs which follow the words "In exhorting." "In exhorting to Christian duty, he is to teach, if he see cause, means to be used in attaining to it, &c., and these to press by places of Scripture, &c.; and because some may think they have attained it already, he may give, if need be, some signs for trial. In dehortation, reprehension, and public admonition, which requires special wisdom, he is not only to discover the nature and greatness of the sin and misery that attends it, but also to show the danger the hearers be in to be surprised by it, and means to escape the danger of it. In making his use for comfort, &c., it is requisite that he give some clear notes that such comforts belong to afflicted consciences. As he needs not always to handle every doctrine that ariseth out of the text, so is he to make choice of such uses as by his residence he findeth to be most necessary and seasonable."

The whole of the directions for the construction of a sermon are founded on that mode of preaching by Doctrine, Reason, and Use, which Bishop Burnet says was brought in by the Scottish preachers after 1638. It did not long continue. Baillie, a few years after this, complains that Binning and Leighton had introduced "a new guyse of preaching, contemning the ordinary way of expoting and dividing a text, of raising doctrines and uses." It was not sanctioned at Westminster without some opposition. To satisfy the objectors, the paragraph was inserted which begins, "This method is not prescribed as necessary."

The longest debate was on the propriety of quoting the dead languages in the pulpit. In the Record, we find Calamy, on the one side, arguing, "A minister told me he was converted by a Latin sentence—*Mallem esse porcus Herodis quam filius.*"* On the other, Rutherford characteristically says, "The pot may be used in the lithing, but not brought in with the porridge." After two days' debate, they agreed upon the cautiously guarded words, "abstaining from an unprofitable use of unknown tongues." The last paragraph corresponds so exactly with the section on the office of Doctor in the Form of Church Government, as to show that it referred to the distinction, then thought so important, between pastors and teachers. The length and number of sermons were matters with which the Assembly did not interfere. The first subject was discussed, and dropped. The second was frequently legislated on in the Scottish Assembly. In 1648 an Act was passed requiring two sermons to be preached every Lord's Day. Kirkton says that before the Restoration every minister preached three times a-week, and lectured and catechised once. Two sermons seem to have been the rule under the second Episcopacy.† The regulations of 1705 anent the visitation of Kirks require a lecture and sermon at morning service, the preaching of catechetic doctrine in the afternoon, and a sermon on some day of the week. The law seems to have been generally obeyed. "There are nine hundred parishes in Scotland," says Calder, "and consequently eighteen hundred worships every Lord's Day.‡ The latest notice of the service for catechetical doctrine is in an Act of 1720, earnestly enjoining its observance. The question of reading of sermons is another on which the Westminster Assembly gave no opinion. At that time, the practice, though not unknown in England, was a novelty in Scotland. Baillie says that Nye, when he preached in Edinburgh in 1643, "did not please because he read much out of his paper-book." In 1731, a discussion was raised in the General Assembly, because a sermon was read before His Majesty's Commissioner. § The last Act on the general subject of preaching is the long one of 1736, called forth by the theological controversies of the previous years.

* Macrobius, Saturn, ii. 4. † Fife Synod Records, p. 186. Morer, p. 61.
‡ Miscellany, 1713, p. 8. § Wodrow Corresp., ii. 498, iii. 489.

Of Prayer after the Sermon.

The only matter connected with the last prayer, which gave rise to any difference of opinion, was the use of the Lord's Prayer, about which there was a debate, as was to be expected from the opinions of some of the Independents.* On the 11th of June, however, it was ordered "with little debate." It is not to be supposed that the Assembly forbade its use anywhere but at the end of the last prayer. The direction would originally stand at the end of the *body of prayer*, given in by the Committee, and when this was divided into three portions, it remained attached to the last. The Scottish usage in this matter has not been uniform. In the Common Order the Lord's Prayer is at the end of the service. Henderson's Sermons imply that it was used at the end of the prayer before sermon. After the Restoration, it was repeated after the last prayer.† It is now most frequently used before the sermon.

In Scotland, up to this period, the Psalm had always ended with what was known as the Conclusion, Doxology, or *Gloria Patri*. The laying of it aside was one of the Western *novations*, which had been disturbing the Church since the Glasgow Assembly. Baillie says of the English, "Independents and all sang it, as far as I know, where it was printed at the end of two or three Psalms." The objection to its being sung at the end of every Psalm was very early heard in England.‡ At the present day, the Liturgy of the American Episcopalians requires it to be used only at the end of the whole portion of Psalms. In Scotland, it fell into disuse after the Westminster Assembly. Baillie says distinctly that there was nothing of it in the Directory. In Gillespie's manuscript it stands first in the list of the things not condemned. An attempt was made in the Assembly of 1645 to lay it aside by a formal Act, as was done with bowing in the pulpit. But Calderwood, evidently against Gillespie's mind,§ defended it as a primitive usage, and "it was thought good to let desuetude abolish it." A story was still current after the Revolution, that when the motion was made, the old historian burst out with, "Let that alone, for I hope to sing it in glory."|| At the Restoration, the Doxology was again heard. Ray, in 1661, says that in Dunbar "they sung

---

* Dissuasive, p. 119.
† Morer, Mene Tekel, p. 9.   Wodrow's Corr., iii. 493.   Pardovan.
‡ Zurich Letters, i. 283. § Notes, p. 120.
|| Dialogue, p. 39.

their Gloria Patri at the end of the Psalm after sermon, as had been ordered by the Parliament, in these words :—

> " Glore to the Father and the Sonne,
> And to the Holy Gheast,
> As it was in the beginning,
> Is now, and aye doth last. "

In 1662 the Bishop of Aberdeen in Synod recommended " that at the singing of the Doxologie, the people shall stand up and not sit," showing that the usage was to sit at the singing of the Psalm.* The charge of paying more honour to a human than to an inspired composition by this change of posture is met by an Episcopal writer of the next age with the answer, that the Doxology is not only an act of praise, but a profession of belief in the Holy Trinity, and as such ought to be repeated standing. At the same time, he does not deny that his party mostly sat at Psalms, though he regrets it.† In that age, they sang the Doxology before the blessing, and then only.‡ It had come to be considered a form belonging exclusively to Episcopacy. So well was this understood, that the incumbent of Burntisland was, immediately after the Revolution, libelled, among other things, for " keeping at his old forms of singing the Doxologie, &c."§ The Church of Scotland has long ceased to object to this ancient ascription of praise to the Trinity. For more than a century it has stood at the end of one of her authorised Hymns, and is often sung, in accordance with her older practice, between the last psalm and the benediction.

The only discussion connected with the Benediction was on the question whether, when the Communion was to be administered, it ought to be pronounced both after the ordinary service, and after the Sacrament. After two debates it was left an open question. The words of benediction are not prescribed. The blessing of the people in the name of God was considered a function belonging exclusively to the ministerial office.‖ It has been the custom in the Scottish Church for ministers alone to use the words *be with you*. Licentiates are supposed not to bless, but to pray, using the form, *be with us ;* and their repeating it with uplifted hands, as ministers do, is probably a modern nnovation. Pardovan lays down an exception to the above rule in the case of the blessing of the General Assembly by their Moderator, when he, too, says *be with us*, obviously as an acknowledgment that he is only *primus inter pares.*

* Synod Records, p. 267. † Dialogue, p. 47.
‡ Mene Tekel, p. 10. § Contin. of Hist. Rel. 1691, p. 68.
‖ Form of Church Government.

The Administration of the Sacrament of Baptism.

This section was considered by the Assembly at intervals between July and November, and occupied in all twelve sessions. The caution against delay was at one time more definite, and required that the Sacrament should be administered on the second Lord's Day at furthest. From a fear that this caution might be misunderstood, and open the door to lay baptism in cases of emergency, the words were added which limit the right of baptising to ministers.[*] Henderson would have had the passage worded, " by the minister of Christ." This was not approved, because it confined it too strictly to one person. Mr Seaman, on the other hand, proposed to leave out " in any case," so as to allow lay baptism in times of persecution, but he had no support.

The debate on private baptism extended into a second day. Both Rutherford and Gillespie took a prominent part in it. Baillie says—" We have carried, with much greater ease than we expected, the publickness of baptism. The abuse was great over all this land. In the greatest parosch in London scarce one child in a year was brought to the church for baptisme." After this was carried, an unsuccessful attempt was made to insert in the Directory reasons for public baptism. At a later session, it was proposed to enact that it should' be administered only in that congregation to which the child belonged. This was first amended by a permission to take it to any nearer church, and finally passed in the present general form. Public baptism was enjoined as *convenient* in the supplementary Act of 1645, and with much more stringency by the first Assembly after the Revolution. It was a frequent subject of dispute with the Episcopalians during the next generation. In 1718 Wodrow in his Correspondence bitterly laments the growth of private baptism in the Church, though he says it was less common in the west than in the east. The same difference between the two sides of Scotland is to be observed at the present day.

It was proposed to make it imperative that all fonts should be removed, and baptism administered at the place where the minister stands in his ministry. This last, which was the Scottish custom, was pressed by Gillespie and his friends.[†] To meet in part their wishes, Baptism at the church door was forbidden. The demolition of fonts was opposed and dropped. The clause requiring notice to be given

---

[*] Gillespie's Notes, p. 89.   [†] Notes, p. 89.

was added at the last moment on Lightfoot's suggestion. The Directory does not fix the part of the service at which Baptism shall be administered. This deficiency was supplied by the supplementary Act of the Scottish Assembly. Henderson's Tract shows the usage of 1641 to have been exactly the same as at present. Children were baptised as soon as the afternoon sermon was over, the prayer of Thanksgiving and Intercession following the Sacrament.

The presenting of the child by the father was a Scottish custom, incorporated in the Directory. "We have carried," says Baillie, "the parent's presenting of his child, and not their midwives, as was their universal custom." The Record also mentions that there was some "debate about taking the child into the father's arms." Each nation kept to its own fashion notwithstanding. Morer describes the father as holding the child in his arms during the ceremony, exactly as at present. The custom of the English Nonconformists is illustrated by an amusing passage in Calamy's own 'Life,' when he is describing his visit to Scotland in Queen Anne's time. He had been asked to preach in Liberton Church, and was told that four men had children to be baptised. "When sermon was over they presented themselves before me in a row, in the face of a numerous congregation, with their children in their arms. Before I proceeded to baptise them I briefly hinted at the nature and end of baptism, and then, putting up a prayer, leaned forward to receive the first of the four children from the father. To my great surprise he, instead of freely delivering it, drew back, and a number of the people smiled. I thereupon applied myself to the other fathers in their order, but they were as unwilling to part with them as the first. . . . Being come out of the church, I inquired into the reason of the shyness of these honest men, and found that it is not the practice in Scotland for ministers to take children into their arms when they baptise them; and that the honest men were in fear that I might sign their children with the cross."*

Godparents in the Anglican sense are forbidden by the words which lay the duty of sponsorship on the father in the first instance, and admit a substitute only in the case of his necessary absence. This is in accordance with the doctrine of the Westminster Standards, that a child's title to Baptism is its federal holiness in right of descent from those who are by profession under the covenant of grace. The Act of Assembly 1712, sess. 5, directs when and in what order another sponsor than the immediate parent may be admitted :—First, a kins-

* Vol. ii. p. 180.

man ; failing him, a Christian friend ; and in the case of unknown children, the office-bearers of the church.

The Record mentions, among other debates on the Baptismal responses, one "about I or We." This may refer to some proposal to allow secondary godparents, not displacing the parent, but standing along with him, and taking ever afterwards a Christian interest in his child. This relationship had some historical warrant in the Scottish Church. The Common Order, following Continental precedents, sanctioned it. Customs springing from it can be traced in later times. In Wodrow's 'Collections on the Life of Weems,' it is said that in 1646 the session of Glasgow ordered "that those who baptise on Sabbath have no more *gossips* nor six." In the last century the names of two *witnesses* were always added to each entry in the baptismal register. This could hardly be to preserve evidence of the public administration of a Sacrament, especially as the names are not usually signatures. This very name of *witness* was often given to the godparents of the Dutch, Swiss, and other Reformed Churches. We may suppose that those who bore the same name in Scotland were the representatives of the gossips of former times.

The Record shows that objections were made to prescribing the matter of the long Exhortation, and the short paragraph which follows must have been added to satisfy these scruples. Still the fact of such objections having been made, and the care with which the terms of the Exhortation were weighed, show that it was meant to be received as a form. At the beginning and end we recognise language afterwards adopted in the Confession and Larger Catechism. Another passage recalls the words of the English office, "Manfully to fight under His banner against sin, the world, and the devil." There was a debate "about the order of remission of sins and regeneration," possibly on the same grounds which led the Puritans at the Savoy Conference to propose that in the Liturgy the words " may receive remission of his sins by spiritual regeneration" should be changed into " may be regenerated and receive the remission of sins." The Record mentions a long debate, which seems to have turned on the question, whether the primary reference of the water in Baptism is to the blood of Christ, or to the influences of the Holy Spirit. Gillespie and Rutherford strongly supported the first view. Both significations were embodied in the text. The words *solemnly*, *visible*, and *federally* were inserted in one of the sentences, after as many debates. Such minute verbal criticism seems to show that the Exhortation was intended not only for a model but for a form.

The short address to the parent is a part of the service very different
from what was at first proposed. The Scots, after the Eastern fashion,
caused the parent to repeat the Apostles' Creed. The Puritans disliked
this custom,* and some of the Independents disliked the Creed itself.†
There were various debates before it was decided in what form the vows
should be taken. It was questioned first whether there ought to be a
profession of faith at all. The Independents opposed it. The Scots
insisted on it as a custom common to all Reformed Churches, Rutherford even saying, "We intend to put a *jus divinum* upon it." When
this point was carried, the next issue was whether the profession should
be made by question and answer, or by a "select speech" by the
minister. After this came debates as to what the questions should be,
whether there should be one or more, and about the use of the
Apostles' Creed. The questions which the Committee had proposed
were the four following :—"Do you believe all the articles of faith
contained in Scripture? That all men and this child are born in sin?
That the blood and Spirit washeth away sin? Will you have therefore
this child baptised?" Afterwards, these were reduced to two:
"Whether the parent or vice-parent desires the child to be baptised,
and whether he believes in God the Father, Son, and Holy Ghost."
At last it was "recommended that he make a profession of his faith,
by answering to these or the like questions : Dost thou believe in God
the Father, Son, and Holy Ghost ? Dost thou hold thyself obliged to
observe all that Christ hath commanded you ? And will you endeavour
so to do ? Dost thou desire this child to be baptised into the faith and
profession of Jesus Christ?" An unsuccessful attempt was made to
throw out the queries at the final revision of the section on the 12th of
November. No account is given of their subsequent disappearance,
or of the substitution of the present very imperfect form. Perhaps it
is to be explained by a passage in Clarendon, who says, on the authority of Lord Pembroke, that the Commons, after a debate, refused to
have the Creed and Decalogue in the Directory. The words, "or the
like questions," certainly permitted the use of the Creed in place of the
first query, which is indeed only a summary of it ; and Gillespie's manuscript includes, among the things not forbidden, another saying of the
Creed in addition to the use of the three Creeds after the Scripture.
Whether or not the passage in Clarendon explains the change made on
this part of the Directory, after it had passed the Assembly, it must
be remembered that the Apostles' Creed is one of the Westminster
Standards. It is much to be regretted that what profess to be autho-

* Baillie, ii. 258. † Dissuasive, p. 30.

rised editions of the Shorter Catechism so often omit both the Creed and the note defining its authority, though these are as much parts of the text as any question or answer in the book. The use of the Creed in Baptism was revived at the Restoration, and becoming, for the first time, associated in the popular mind with Episcopacy, had a prejudice excited against it, which is not yet altogether extinct.

It appears from Henderson's Tract that the prayer was in his time said at the commencement of the baptismal service. The Directory places it immediately before the Administration, thus restoring it to the place which it had in the Common Order. Readers are apt to overlook the fact that the rubric not only enjoins a prayer for the Divine blessing upon the sacramental element and rite, but requires that, as in the other Sacrament, the words of Institution (Matt. xxviii. 19) shall first be repeated, or incorporated in the prayer, as is done in the English office. Morer found two prayers used in Baptism—one, for present blessing, between the exhortation and vows; another, before the action, for future help. From the Record, it appears that the controversy on the efficacy of Baptism was raised by the words, "join the inward baptism with the outward baptism." There was another debate on words now deleted, "into the Communion of the Saints."

The mode of administration was discussed at great length. All admitted the validity of sprinkling. But the original draft declared that it was agreeable to the institution of Christ, which was objected to by some. By a majority of one, it was resolved to say merely, "The minister shall take water, and sprinkle or pour it," &c. This did not close the controversy, and it was the third day before they agreed on the present words, expressing a preference for pouring or sprinkling, but not excluding dipping. The words "without adding any other ceremony," refer to signing with the cross, which, in the eyes both of the Puritans and the Scots, was one of the most objectionable requirements in the English Liturgy. Coleman proposed to fix the number of sprinklings, but he met with no support. Probably he had in his mind the threefold sprinkling of the Dutch Reformed, founded on the trine immersion of the primitive Church. The Book of the Discipline of the Dutch Churches in England, published in 1645, makes it optional to sprinkle once or thrice.

Dr Hammond objects very much to the want of a service for the Churching of Women. It is certain, however, that one was, by the Assembly's directions, drawn up and discussed. It was finally laid aside, but Gillespie's paper shows that it was not understood to be absolutely forbidden. It has never been known in Scotland as a distinct service, but the post-baptismal prayer usually contains a thanksgiving in behalf of the mother.

Of the Celebration of the Communion.

This section caused longer and warmer discussion than any other part of the Directory. Out of seventy-five sittings, eighteen were given to it alone. The keenest contests were between the Scots and the Independents, each of whom believed their distinctive principles to be involved in their mode of celebrating the Sacrament. When the question of the frequency of Communion was before the Committee, it was proposed to require at least four celebrations a-year. This was opposed by Gillespie, as an attempt to regulate what Scripture had not decided. The dispute was renewed in the Assembly, on a motion " to set down a uniformitie of the time ;" but the final decision was in very general terms. In Scotland the tendency has always been towards a less frequent celebration of the ordinance than the statutes of the Church enjoined. There were three Communions annually in Edinburgh for at least four years after the Reformation.* Wodrow's ' Life of Weems' shows that in Glasgow, from 1583 to 1645, the Communion was an annual one except in six years, when it was administered twice. But between 1645 and the Restoration there were only six celebrations. During the latter period St Andrews and Edinburgh were for six years in succession without the Communion, though it was being regularly administered twice a-year in the parish of Canongate.† Under Episcopacy the same irregular state of things continued. In Glasgow there were but two Communions between the Restoration and the Revolution. The pamphlets of the next age contain mutual recriminations on the subject.‡ The Assembly enjoined more frequent Communion, but they laid down no definite rule, except a recommendation that in contiguous parishes the days of celebration should be as much as possible distributed over the year. Then, and long afterwards, the popular feeling was that the Communion, like the Passover, ought to be an annual feast. There is every reason to believe that this opinion was an inheritance transmitted from Romish times. In 1215, the fourth Council of Lateran passed

---

* Lee's History, i. 390.
† Lee's History, i. 398, 401. Nicoll's Diary.
‡ Full and Final Answer, p. 28. Calder's Miscellany, p. 47. Anderson's Answer, p. 4.

the celebrated canon which requires all persons come to years of discretion to confess and communicate at least once a-year, and that at Easter; and when the Reformation came this extreme case had been adopted as a rule by the majority of the people. Under the new order of things the feast of Easter was suppressed; but the annual Communion, the Holy Week, the preparatory Fast, the examination of the whole congregation by the minister, were all continued, or were revived at a later period without any thought of the source whence the suggestion came. Notwithstanding the undoubted usage of the early Church, the recommendations of quarterly Communion in the Book of Discipline, of monthly in the Common Order, of frequent celebration in the Directory, strengthened by many Acts of Assembly, and the appeals of such men as Willison and Dr Erskine—to say nothing of the *dictum* of Calvin, " consuetudo quæ semel quotannis communicare jubet, certissimum est diaboli inventum"—annual Communions kept their place in the great majority of Scottish parishes till a few years ago.

There were in the Assembly two debates, evidently raised by the Independents—one " about that—the ministers before the officers," the other " whether the officers shall be expressed, and whether not the people." There seems to have been in the Church of Scotland, long afterwards, a party who questioned the right of the kirk-session to fix the time.* Their right, subject to the Presbytery's control, was confirmed by the Assembly of 1833, though they condemned the conduct of the session whose acts were under review, in appointing so many Communions as to prevent uniformity within the bounds of the same city. The provision in the Directory for having the Sacrament at morning service was probably aimed at certain newly-gathered churches, which were reported to the Committee as having it every Sunday afternoon.†

The subject disposed of in the second paragraph had been the cause of much discord when the Assembly were discussing church government. The Committee now gave in the words as they stand, with the choice of two passages to precede them. The first is taken nearly *verbatim* from Henderson's 'Government and Order,' and was, we may suppose, the Presbyterian alternative:—" None to be admitted but such as, being baptised, are found, upon careful examination by the minister before the officers, to have a competent measure of knowledge of the grounds of religion, and ability to examine themselves, and who profess their willingness, and promise to submit themselves

* Wodrow's Corr., ii. 540. † Gillespie's Notes, p. 102.

to all the ordinances of Christ." The other was, "Who give just
grounds, in the judgment of charity, to conceive that there is faith and
regeneration wrought in them," a modification by Henderson and
Marshall of what had been proposed in Committee by the Independent Goodwin, "that they be such as profess a work of faith and
regeneration."* The paragraph was perhaps reduced to its present
dimensions when it came before the House of Commons, who were
very jealous of any legislation on this point except their own, as they
showed next year when preparing their Ordinance for suspension from
the Lord's Supper. Hitherto in Scotland the whole congregation had
been examined as to their fitness before each Communion. The
supplementary Act of 1645 provided for the continuance of this
practice, but it has long been abandoned. The Act 1706, xi. though
applying specially to the examination of catechumens for their first
Communion, maintains the theory of a congregational examination.
The Act 1727, viii. enjoins the observance of the Act 1645, particularly
in regard to this point.

The next paragraph requires one week-day service, except where
the Sacrament is so frequently administered as to make notice and
preparatory worship unnecessary. Such services were not unknown
in England. One of the charges brought in Parliament against Wren,
Bishop of Norwich, was that he forbade the preaching of preparation
sermons two or three days before the Communion. The Act of Assembly 1645, makes imperative the Saturday service, which had long
been a Scottish usage.† Up to this time there seems to have been no
general observance of sacramental fasts, though a national fast and the
Communion were sometimes observed in the same week.‡ Wodrow
does not seem to have found in the Glasgow Session Record any instance of a Communion fast before 1655,§ except an injunction to
keep a fast on the Communion Sundays of 1596. Tradition has
connected the origin of the Monday service with Livingstone's
sermon after the celebrated Shotts Communion in 1630. There
were, of course, the same week-day services as in any other week
of the year, usually on Tuesday and Thursday. But the days of
fasting and of thanksgiving did not become general till they were em-
braced in the new Communion customs brought in by the Protesters.
These are described in a tract of 1657, a copy of which is preserved in
the Advocates' Library. It is entitled 'A True Representation, Rise,

* Gillespie, p. 102.
† Government and Order. Lee's History, i. 393, 396.
‡ Lee's History, i. 391, 399. § Weems's Life.

Progress, and State of the Divisions of the Church of Scotland.' At page 35 it says, "Our dissenting brethren have taken up a new and irregular way. To omit their way of admitting persons who come from other congregations, they do not now usually celebrate that ordinance, but they have a great many ministers gathered unto it, six or seven, and sometimes double or more, whose congregations most part are left destitute of preaching that day; great confluences from all the country, and many congregations about are gathered at them; and on every day of their meeting (which are Saturday, the Lord's Day, and Monday), many of these ministers do preach successively one after another; so that three or four, and sometimes more, do preach at their preparation, and as many on the Monday following. And on the Lord's Day, sometimes three or four preach before they go to the Action; beside those who preach to the multitude of people that cannot be contained in the church." It seems that even then the fast-day was not a recognised part of the observances. There is, in the same volume, a Latin tract of that year, entitled *Uldericus Veridicus*, which says :—"Cum ad rem ipsam ventum est, maxima pars eorum, ad quos beneficium pertinet, tanquam semi-Muscovitæ excluduntur; suis autem cujuscumque demum parochiæ, tanquam veris Dei filiis, cibus ille cœlestis distribuitur; tot illic habentur conciones, quot in nulla unquam antea Ecclesia tam brevi tempore." The new days seem to have kept their place under the second Episcopacy;* and after the Revolution the whole system was perpetuated. The Acts of Assembly 1701 and 1724 tried, but in vain, to enforce the provisions of 1645, which forbade the shutting of neighbouring churches on the Communion day. Wodrow, speaking in 1709 of "those fair-days of the Gospel," mentions cases as exceptional in which there was only one sermon on Saturday and Monday, and where there was either no open-air preaching, or it did not begin till the Action sermon was over. These customs continued with little change throughout the century. In 1751 and 1762 attempts by the Synods of Sutherland and Argyll to dispense with some of the preaching days were disapproved of by the Assembly. In the Campbelton decision in the latter year, it seems to be implied that the authority for the Saturday service was higher than for the Monday. In an Independent tract ('Series of Interesting Questions,' &c., Edinburgh, 1800) the following services are said to be more or less generally in use :—A fast-day a month before the Communion, two or three services on the fast-day, evening service on Friday, two or three on Saturday, one on the evening of the Com-

* Lee's History, i. 402.

munion, and two on Monday—a large extension certainly of the Saturday preparation and Sunday thanksgiving services of the Act 1645. During the last half-century all change has been in the direction of more frequent Communion with fewer attendant services.

Whatever may have been the origin of other peculiarities of the Protesters, their sacramental usages cannot be attributed to English influence. Their new terms of communion bound them to debar from the Table of the Lord all parishioners who were not of their party, a course so full of difficulty that the Sacrament was postponed year after year. When it was administered, the rarity of the event attracted all the Protesters for many miles round. Much fervid feeling was awakened on these occasions, and the nation by degrees became familiar with the system of assembling the whole ministry and population of a district for prolonged evangelistic services at any church where the Communion was being administered. After the Revolution, the open-air preaching became dearer from recollections of field-meetings in the days of persecution. Their union with the Sacrament gave these services a deeper solemnity than might otherwise have attended them, but this was too dearly purchased by the rarity of the Communion.

The Assembly were occupied for two days with the questions, whether there should be a benediction at the close of the ordinary service, and whether non-communicants might be present at the Sacrament? Henderson pleaded for their admission, which was and is the Scottish practice. Both questions were at last passed over in silence. There was a debate on the reading of the Decalogue at some point in the Communion Service. Probably it was in the first instance recommended, as the House of Commons found some occasion for forbidding its use in the Directory. The Record speaks of a debate about the time of reading, which may refer either to the Decalogue or to the Words of Institution. According to the Common Order and 'Altare Damascenum,' these last were to be read from the pulpit. But when Henderson's Tract was published, they were not read till the minister, after debarring the unworthy, had gone to the Table. In Pardovan's time, an exhortation was delivered from the pulpit, and, after a Psalm, the minister went to the Table to "fence and open it," as the phrase was. Then followed the Words of Institution and Consecration Prayer.

The language of exclusion in the Exhortation is much less strict than in the Common Order. It was probably softened by the English, as Lightfoot says that it raised a sad dispute in the Assembly. Even as it stands, it retains more of the Scottish principle of fencing the Lord's Table from intruders than the corresponding exhortation of the Savoy Liturgy.

The most obstinate contest was concerning the words, "sit at or about it." The customs of England and Scotland were here altogether at variance. In England, from the time of the Reformation, the Elements had been consecrated at a small table, so placed in the church that all might see and hear. From this they were taken by the minister, and given to the people, kneeling for the most part in their pews. Laud's new fashion of setting the Table at the eastern wall, and obliging all to communicate at the rails, had hardly been introduced when the civil war began. The Scottish Table, on the other hand, was intended for the communicants as well as for the Elements. It was made as long as the size of the church would allow, and the communicants sat along its sides. The Scots believed that only in this way could the true significance of the Sacrament be preserved. They would not kneel when they received the Elements, from a fear that the attitude might in time revive the doctrine of a material presence. Of the three other modes used in the Reformed Churches—standing, passing, and sitting—they preferred the last, because it best reminded them that they were Christ's guests, bidden to His Supper. They objected to an altar-table, because it was suggestive of sacrifice; and yet they would not dispense with a table, because they believed the Sacrament to be not only a commemoration but a feast, wherein, in the words of the Confession, "the faithful, in the right use of the Lord's table, do so eat the body and drink the blood of the Lord Jesus, that He remaineth in them, and they in Him. As it was seldom possible to receive all the communicants in a congregation at one table, they admitted them either at different services, or in successive companies, at the same service. Out of these conflicting practices questions rose regarding the posture and the place of communicating. On the first, the Scots had already had many contests, but with the Anglicans, not with the Puritans. The difference at Westminster did not go beyond this, that while the Scots would have made sitting imperative, the Englishmen were disposed to leave it indifferent. Many of them had no objections to kneeling. Many, who objected to it, would have preferred standing, which was afterwards allowed in the Savoy Liturgy.* However, says Baillie, "they were content of sitting, though not as a ryte institute," and accepted the Scottish usage, thus described in the Assembly by Henderson: "The minister comes, reads the words of institution, and

* See also Calamy's Life of Baxter, p. 297.

prays standing; and the people either sit or kneel at prayer-time indifferently, but are sure to sit in the act of receiving."

But the question of place was not so easily settled. "To come out of their pewes to a table," Baillie says, "they deny the necessity of it: we affirme it necessare, and will stand to it." All were willing to agree to a table, and even that as many as it would admit should receive at it. But the Independents insisted that all should communicate at once, and the other Puritans stood aloof from the contest. The question seems to have been this—where there could not be both communion at a table and simultaneous communion, which was to be retained? The controversy began in the Committee, where Gillespie used much the same arguments as are to be found in his Miscellany Questions.* It continued with much heat in the Assembly, particularly in one day's discussion, the violence of which is noticed both by Baillie and Lightfoot. Henderson said, "We sent from the Church of Scotland are all of one mind on this point. We can hardly part from it—nay, I may add, we may not possibly part from it."

Compromises were tried in vain, and the matter had to be referred to Scotland for advice. At last in November the words passed in their present alternative form "*at* or *about* a table." But this ambiguous deliverance did not satisfy the Scots; and an explanatory clause was inserted in the Act authorising the Directory. The result was that each nation adhered to its own custom. The Scots received *at* a table, and the Puritans *about* it, in the nearest pews. Even under the Restoration sitting at a table continued to be the ordinary custom in Scotland.† Dr Somerville of Jedburgh found the practice of receiving in pews observed in Dr Price's meeting-house in London, and speaks of it as if it were to him a novelty. The merits of this controversy, which put the whole scheme of uniformity in peril, are now almost forgotten. The custom of the Westminster Independents is rapidly effacing the last traces of the Scottish usage, once so strenuously defended. Towards the end of the last century the separate table for consecration began to be introduced, not without murmurs. Then pews which could be converted into tables came into use, and filled the broad open space in the middle of the church, where the long table had been on the Communion-day. Even these new tables were in some cases not provided. The Assembly 1825 found, in reference to some churches in Glasgow, where the people received in their pews, "that it is the law, and has been the immemorial practice of the Church of Scotland, to dispense

* Notes, p. 101. † Morer.

the Sacrament of the Lord's Supper to the people seated at or round a Communion table or tables." The change went on notwithstanding, and now it is quite common to have the elements carried from pew to pew, where there is nothing but a narrow strip of linen on the book-shelf to represent the table spread for the spiritual nourishment of the Lord's guests, in which our fathers saw so much of the symbolism of the Sacrament.

Undoubtedly the use of a table to receive both the Elements and the communicants had much to recommend it. No other mode of celebration so well recalls the circumstances of the Last Supper, and it must have been an aid to faith to have the Sacrament associated in the mind with a part of the Church not used for any other act of worship. On the other hand, there was a difficulty in the necessity of having the administration many times repeated. This was met in two ways— either by having several services, or by admitting the communicants in successive companies at the same service. Of the first mode there were several varieties. One of Principal Lee's transcripts, in an interesting appendix to the first volume of his History, seems to say that in Edinburgh, in 1560, Knox administered the Communion daily for a whole week. For a century after that time it was very common to continue the celebration from Sunday to Sunday, till all had communicated. Sometimes there was sermon and Communion in the early morning, and the same repeated at a new service later in the day. These arrangements were often further simplified by having many tables ranged side by side in the spacious unpewed churches raised for a more gorgeous worship. But all these modes have long given place to the other practice of having many administrations in one extended service. When the parish was not large there was only a single table erected, serving both for consecration and for Communion. If it had been used for these purposes alone, with nothing spoken to each company of communicants, but the words of administration and a few versicles or sentences as the Bread and Cup passed from hand to hand, our old usages might have been preserved. But the modern fashion of delivering two long exhortations at every administration made this impossible. When the table came to be used as a pew, the use of the pew as a table naturally followed.

We learn from Lightfoot that there was something in this place about the minister's coming to the table. The Record also mentions a debate about "the minister's still keeping his place at the table," after the Consecration, where the words are now simply "being at the table." As some of the extreme Independents preferred to consecrate in the pulpit,* it is likely that the objections which caused the one passage to be struck out and the other to be altered, so as to allow the ministers remaining longer in the pulpit, came from that side of the Assembly. The following were the original words of the Directory in this place :—"The other officers attending that service, the minister is to begin the action with sanctification of the elements of bread and wine set before him, the bread in platters." The clause about the officers of the church was admitted in June, but was erased at some later stage.

The alterations made on this paragraph have left its meaning somewhat indistinct as to the order in which the Words of Institution and Consecration Prayer are to stand. The words "he is to begin the action with sanctifying and blessing the elements," do not mean that the Prayer goes before the Scripture, for the last words of the paragraph show that both the Word and Prayer are included in the word *sanctify*. This point was strongly insisted on by Gillespie in his 'English Popish Ceremonies,' in protest against the doctrine that the words *This is my body*, &c., are the Consecration. The whole paragraph is a summary of what is thereafter set forth at more length. *First* must mean *before* the distribution, spoken of in the previous clause, for the "few words" are to be spoken *after* the consecration. The intimate connection between the Word and Prayer make it fitting that both should be repeated at the table, according to the original command and present permission of the Directory, as well as the custom of Scotland described by Henderson. The words *sanctifying and blessing* were fixed on after a long discussion, in which the terms *sanctification*, *consecrating*, and *setting apart* were in succession proposed. The Prayer itself is in three parts—first, the Eucharistic Thanksgiving, then the profession of Belief, and last the Prayer of Invocation. The Independents strove hard to obtain some sanction for what Baillie calls "their two short graces," or double consecration of the elements, such as was afterwards allowed in the Savoy Liturgy. The Record shows that Gillespie opposed at great length their arguments, which rested on the words of the first two Evangelists. It may have been to allow them the option of reading the Words of Institution from these Gospels, that the Directory does not insist on the use of St Paul's version. This last has always been that read in Scotland, from the days of the Common Order and the First Book of Discipline, which appeals to "Christ's action, and to the perfect practice, as we reade in St Paul."

* Dissuasive, p. 121.

THE DIRECTORY.

The only warrant in the Directory for our Table Addresses is the place which allows a few words to be spoken after consecration. Both Gillespie and Baillie refer to Table exhortations as a Scottish custom, but it must have been one of recent growth. Neither the Common Order, the 'Altare Damascenum,' nor Henderson's Discipline and Order mention them, though there are short addresses of this kind published among his Sermons. The Act of 1645, in plainer terms than the Directory uses, requires one short exhortation at each table before the elements are given. The second address is of much later origin; Sage, after the Revolution, when descanting on the many services of the Scottish Communion, would have been too glad to add it to the number, but he does not speak of it.* Pardovan too is silent regarding it.

The Words of Administration were at first absolutely prescribed. The Record mentions a debate "about the words in the giving of the sacrament, whether the forme stand, or say in such like wordes." The amendment has been limited to the parallel passages of Scripture. In Scotland this point has never been definitely fixed. The Common Order prescribes no form. But that such words were used is plain from the First Book of Discipline, which says "that commandment ought to be given that the bread should be taken and eaten, and that all should likewise drink of the cup of wine, with declaration what both the one and the other is; we suppose no godly man will doubt." The 'Altare Damascenum' says that the words then used were, "Our Lord, on that night on which He was betrayed, took bread, and gave thanks, as we have now done, and brake it, as I also now break, and gave it, saying, This is My body," &c. Gillespie, in his 'English-Popish Ceremonies' (1637), gives the same form, with this variation, "as we also give thanks to God, who gave His Son to die for us . . . as we also give thanks to God, who gave His Son to shed His blood for us." Henderson gives as the form used in 1641, part of what the Directory prescribes, beginning with *Take ye*, and *This cup*. The Savoy form is almost the same. Of all these forms, the oldest, that of Calderwood, most exactly represents the present Scottish custom.

The Scots considered the breaking of the bread, not *before* or *at*, but *after* consecration, an important part of the Sacramental Action.† To this no opposition was made in the Assembly. Indeed the Savoy Liturgy shows that the moderate Puritans were disposed to go further, and, following an ancient use, to make it a distinct part of the service with appropriate words. Another form which the Scots thought equally

* Presbytery Examined, p. 366.   † English-Popish Ceremonies, p. 351.

important was the distribution of the elements from hand to hand among the communicants. After some discussion on minor points, "the great query was, whether, if one communicant take up one piece of bread, and break off a piece for himself, whether he must lay the rest in the dish again, or give it to his next fellow." This was one of those points on which Baillie says, "We were forced to take to general expressions, which by a benigne exposition, would infer our church practices." The Scottish Assembly made the sense in which they accepted the passage very distinct both in the Act authorising the Directory, and the Act supplementary. In Aberdeenshire the bread is sometimes cut into portions for each communicant, except so much as is required for the sacramental breaking by the minister. But, generally speaking, Scotland has preserved her ancient usage. In Dumfries, and some other places in the south, a custom has long continued of using for the communion, not common wheaten bread, but the cake well known in Scotland as *shortbread*. The Record says that there was some debate about the minister giving the Sacrament to himself, and, perhaps in consequence of this difference of opinion, the language used is not clear. Henderson's Tract says that the minister was always the first to partake. When more than one minister is present, it has been the custom for the first to receive the elements from another at a later table. But where this cannot be, Pardovan says, that the minister is to be the first to communicate. It was a practice among the Independents, corresponding to their double consecration, not to give the cup to any till every communicant had received the bread. This point was discussed for two days, and it has been left undecided. Gillespie and Rutherford both spoke against the proposal, and the first has written against it in his 'Miscellany Questions.' Henderson, however, says that in 1641, at any one table, the minister neither partook of the cup, nor gave it, till all the communicants had taken and eaten. We find from Baillie's 'Paper to his Colleagues' that there was in this part of the Directory a clause "discharging all privat prayer befor and after the participation," which he calls "the ordinare practise of the most, if not all, pastors and people I am acquaint with," and "which, to the most part of our Church, are taken for lawfull and laudable customs." He pleads against the clause that it rests on "the general maxime that all privat worshipe in the time and place of publique worshipe is to be discharged. This directly does decide the controversie of our Church in favors of that side who challenges the minister's and people's privat prayers in their entry to the publique as unlawfull worship." His protest seems to have been successful. The Directory also recommended that while the people were receiving, the minister should stir up their affections by short sentences spoken at intervals. The Scots argued strongly for this provision against some of the Independents. It was struck out, but restored in the Scottish Act of 1645. Sage, in his description of the Scottish Communion, calls these sentences a shorter discourse. The same Act condemned a custom which was as old as the Reformation—the reading of one of the histories of the Passion during the administration. Calderwood had written against it both in 'Pastor and Prelate,' and in the 'Altare Damascenum,' on the ground that the voices of the reader and the minister were often heard at the same moment. There was also at first in the Directory a regulation that some psalm, as the 22d or 103d, should be sung as they left the table. Here, as in other cases, Henderson's hand in the draft is discovered by the resemblance to a place in his Tract, where he says, "they gently depart, the whole congregation singing such psalms as 22 or 103." This clause, like everything else which implies a succession of tables, was removed, but it was inserted in the supplementary Act.

It was also appointed that "the minister, after sacrament, shall go into the pulpit, and give an admonition." But the change of places was much objected to, and a week afterwards all mention of going to the pulpit was dropped, and the present short permissive enactment was substituted. Henderson describes the minister as going to the pulpit, and after a short speech tending to thanksgiving, giving thanks and praying as on other Sabbaths. This custom of adding the ordinary Prayer of General Intercession to the sacramental Prayer of final Thanksgiving is still continued, and supplies a deficiency in the Directory for Communion, which nowhere requires prayer to be made in behalf of the whole Church of Christ.

The last paragraph refers to the Anglican Offertory. An offering for the poor has been a usual accompaniment of the service in Scotland. There are said to be places in the north where it is even now collected at the table. Collections in the middle of divine service on ordinary Sundays were not unknown in 1648, when they were forbidden by Act of Assembly. Since then they have been made either in the church before the benediction, or at the door before service.

The Directory says nothing of a second service on the evening of the Communion day. But the supplementary Act requires a sermon of thanksgiving. This, and that on Saturday, are the only additional services which have the statutory authority of the Church.

With this section the first and most important part of the Directory ends: when it was finished, the Preface was added, and the whole sent up to Parliament. The later sections were taken up at intervals during the next two months.

Of the Sanctification of the Lord's Day.

The second Committee had been ordered in August to prepare "a Directory for the Sabbath day." It was brought in and discussed for three days in November. After a long debate it was agreed that the title should be "For the sanctifying of the Lord's Day, the Christian Sabbath," but the three last words were afterwards struck out, on the ground that they were in the body of the section. The same point had been discussed in the previous January, on a motion that the words "Lord's Day" in a letter to foreign Churches, should be changed into "Sabbath." A number of debates are mentioned by Lightfoot, as, whether the subject ought to have a place in the Directory, or in the Catechism and Confession; how to avoid offence of Judaism on the one hand and profaneness on the other; how to bring in family duties, and whether discipline ought to be exercised on the Lord's Day. This was left to be decided in the Directory on Censures, where it is virtually allowed. The expression "is to be remembered before it come" was objected to and altered. First a prohibition of worldly words, and then of worldly thoughts, was added. The words "that there be no feasting on the Sabbath" were extended into the present third paragraph. To meet the case of those who lived at a distance from church, words in the fourth paragraph which required private reading of Scripture, and the following at the beginning of the sixth, "between the times of public worship, after a little time for refreshing, the time to be spent," were changed. Finally a motion was negatived, which proposed to insert "brief and discreet" before "repetition of sermons."

Of the Solemnisation of Marriage.

This section was brought up in November, and passed after six days' debate. There was much opposition to the first paragraph. Goodwin and his friends held marriage to be a civil contract, in which the minister acts only as the magistrate's delegate. The debates in the Record are not very intelligible, but the Scots seem to take much higher ground than this. Henderson in his Tract had said that marriage ought to be before the congregation with instruction, "blessing by the minister, and with the prayers of the Church." He now says, "I doubt it is not a mere civil contract. It is the commandment of God. A civil contract may be dissolved with consent of parties." Gillespie, who in his 'English-Popish Ceremonies' claims Scriptural authority for the "matrimonial benediction," says here, "I would be sorry any child of mine should be married but by a minister." Rutherford makes a distinction between marriage, of which the essence is consent, and solemnisation, to which belongs the vow; but he says, "They that are married without any vow or oath of God are not lawfull marriages." The second clause of the section is an addition of Gillespie's. The original text of the next passage stood thus: "Because it was instituted by God in innocency, and those that marry," &c. It was objected that this gave no warrant for a ministerial blessing, "as the first man and first woman were joyned together by God himself," and the clause was struck out. Lightfoot and Rutherford both defended it. To satisfy Goodwin, the word "bless" was changed into "pray for a blessing." There is a memorandum in the Record "that something be prepared for the Assembly concerning the degrees of contiguity and affinity prohibited." The subject was afterwards treated of in the 24th chapter of the Confession. The Committee was also instructed, on Henderson's motion, to "consider of something concerning contracts or espousals to be added to the Directory." Perhaps it was intended to have, as in primitive times, and as Cartwright's Directory enjoins, two services—one of Espousals, and one of Nuptials. Lightfoot and others spoke against requiring any contract before marriage. This is, however, implied in proclamation, or what the Common Order calls "publishing of banns, or *contract*." In Scotland it was long the custom to require the consignation of a sum of money by two sureties, as a guarantee that the persons proclaimed should marry within forty days. Proclamation has been enjoined by Acts of Assembly in 1690, 1698, and 1782. The notice has usually been read, not by the minister, but by the session-clerk, or his deputy the precentor. By an Act of 1784, session-clerks are not allowed to proclaim till a written intimation has been given to the minister, and his permission obtained.

There was a "long and large debate what remedy children should have if their parents be unreasonable, and what parents, if children match without their consent;" but these delicate questions were left to the wisdom of Parliament. It was with some difficulty that private marriages were prohibited. Baillie says, "After two dayes' tough debate, and great appearance of irreconcilable difference, thanks to God, we have gotten the Independents satisfied, and ane unanimous consent of all the Assemblie, that marriage shall be celebrate only by the minister, and that in the church, after our fashion." Here, as in the case of communicating in pews, time has won for the Independents the battle which they lost. Marriage in church has fallen so much into disuse in Scotland, that where it is revived many people suppose it to be an English innovation, which is a more correct description of the private ceremony. Dr Somerville, in his Autobiography, says that marriages in church were still the rule among the humbler classes in the middle of the last century; and there are districts in which it has never been altogether discontinued. The change may have been in part the cause of those loose notions as to the ceremony of marriage with which our countrymen are often taunted. A service of two or three minutes, hurried over in the manse kitchen, could not strongly impress upon ignorant spectators the sacred character of the marriage-vow.

The Record shows that it was at first ordered that marriages should be solemnised between eight o'clock and twelve. This was objected to, and among others by Gillespie, who said that as it stood it would make a great debate, because the Papists gave as a reason that mass was before twelve. Mr Ley proposed to limit the time to daylight. The words allowing marriages at any season of the year are a protest against the opinion that they ought not to be in Lent. Marriage on the Lord's Day is forbidden. At the Reformation it had been recommended in both countries, though other days were allowed by the broad principle that it should be both in the place and time of divine service, as is still required in the 62d Canon of the Church of England. Afterwards week-days were preferred. Sunday marriages were forbidden in Glasgow in 1641, and in Edinburgh also in 1643, not as sinful in themselves, but because needless work was caused in preparing a feast. Baillie's Paper to his colleagues includes marrying among the ordinary duties of Scottish ministers on the Lord's Day. Morer says that they were celebrated indifferently on any day of the week. In some places Sunday marriages were kept up within the memory of persons now living. On the whole, however, the wise advice of the Directory has been followed.

The passages "out of the Scripture" are not specified. It is known that any allusion to that in Eph. v. regarding the mystical union of Christ and His Church, which is embodied in the opening exhortations of the Common Prayer and Common Order, would have been distasteful to the Puritans, who feared that it might be used to support the notion that marriage is a sacrament.*

The vows are to be spoken by the parties themselves. In this, as in many other things, Scotland has adhered to her older way. The vows generally imposed at the present day are those of the Directory. But they are repeated by the minister as in the Common Order, and accepted by a word or sign of assent. The words "without any further ceremony," refer to the use of the ring, to which the Scots were always opposed, on account of its Pagan origin and Romish use. Their scruples may seem to us as superfluous as the ceremony appeared to them. But this at least has to be said for them, that if they had taken a lower view of marriage, they would not have objected to the ring. "Hunc ritum non damnaremus," says Calderwood, "si fœdera nuptialia civili modo celebrarentur." Morer says that he found the vows followed not by a prayer, but by a short harangue, which was in conformity with the Common Order.

Concerning Visitation of the Sick.

It was not at first intended to have a section on this subject, but in the debate on Burial a wish was expressed that the Committee should prepare one. It was given in on the 11th of December, and at first met with almost no opposition. On the 16th the subject was resumed in a more critical spirit. Along with various debates, which we cannot now refer to their places in the text, the Record mentions that it was discusssd whether the words "out of displeasure for sin" and "being lost in himself," should stand, and that Mr Tuckney moved to add something about the Sacrament. Nothing is said of public prayers for the sick, which might have been expected in a Directory for public worship.

Concerning Burial of the Dead.

This section was given in by Dr Temple on the 3d of December, and occupied the Assembly six days. Some would have thrown it out altogether. Many of the Puritans had long held that, in Cartwright's words, "the care of burying the dead does not belong more to the ministerial office than to the rest of the Church." They were supported by Rutherford, who said that he saw no more occasion for an act of worship at a man's leaving the world than at his entering it.

* Neal, i. 282. Savoy Exceptions.

Whitaker's answer was, that presently after birth he was brought to baptism. The discussions turned on the questions what should be done before, at, and after the interment? On the first there was no difference of opinion. It is distinctly enacted that neither in the house, nor on the way to the grave, should any religious office be performed. The praying beside the corpse was forbidden at Lightfoot's suggestion. Wheatley says that in his time, long after this, it was still the custom in England to sing psalms all the way from the house to the churchyard gate. At first sight, it seems as if service at the grave had also been prohibited. But Lightfoot says that a proposal that something might be said at the very interment was passed over in silence, "and so the minister left something to his liberty." He continues—" Dr Temple moved again, Whether a minister, at putting the body in the ground, may not say, *We commit the body to the ground*, &c. And it was conceived by the Assembly that he might, and the words, *without any ceremony more*, do not tie him up from this." This, though not an obvious, is a possible rendering of the passage. A ceremony, in the common use of the word, and in the Directory itself, means not a form of words but a symbolical action, such as the signing of the cross in baptism, the use of the ring in marriage, or, as here, the sprinkling of earth, when the words of committal are spoken. These words are not a prayer, could not well be sung, and need not be read, and so the letter of the statute may be obeyed. But without Lightfoot's hint no ordinary reader would so interpret it. The greatest contest was on the question whether there might be a funeral sermon after the interment. On this the Scots and English Divines were directly opposed to each other. Baillie says—"Our difference about funerall sermons seems irreconcileable : as it has been here and everywhere preached, it is nothing but ane abuse of preaching, to serve the humours of rich people only for a reward ; our Church expresslie has discharged them on many good reasons : it's here a good part of the minister's livelyhood ; therefore they will not quit it." We find Lightfoot twice accounting for his absence from the Assembly by saying that he had to preach sermons at funerals. In Scotland, the Common Order had allowed them. But the First Book of Discipline had anticipated that they would unduly occupy the time of ministers, "or else they shall have respect of persons, preaching at the burialls of the rich and honourable, but keeping silence when the poore and despised departeth." Scottish feeling had become much opposed to them, so much so that their Commissioners would not attend Pym's funeral on account of the sermon. The Record shows that in the draft the words were—"Nevertheless this doth not inhibit any minister, at that time being present, to give some seasonable word of exhortation." Lightfoot says that the mind of the Assembly was that the present words give liberty for funeral sermons, his own contribution to the ambiguity of the passage being the substitution of "*their*" for "*that* duty." Extreme as Rutherford's opinions probably were, it would have been better to follow his counsel and omit the whole subject, than to expend so much ingenuity in constructing sentences with the permission which the Englishmen desired underlying the prohibition insisted on by the Scots. This old controversy was revived for a moment in Scotland at the death of the Princess Charlotte, when Dr Andrew Thomson refused to preach on the day of her funeral. An interesting paper in defence of him is to be found among Dr M'Crie's works.

In Scotland this section has always been read in its more obvious sense, and till this century was rigidly obeyed. Ray says that the people went to the grave with the bell before them, "where there is nothing said, but only the corpse laid in." Morer says that the crier went round with his bell, announcing the death thus : " Faithful brethren and sisters, I let you to wot that there is a faithful brother [or sister] departed, as it hath pleased Almighty God. He was called ———, and lived in ———." In the same way the invitation to the funeral was given. There was no minister present ; herbs and flowers were scattered on the mortcloth, and women followed in the rear. These customs are referred to in an order issued in 1652 by the session of Glasgow, mentioned in 'Weems's Life'—"The Dead Bellman is ordeaned to omit the word *faithfull*, and to eshew the repetition of the name of God." Dr Somerville's description mentions the dead-bell, and the attendance of women, with the addition that these did not pass the churchyard gate. The hospitality offered to those who met in the house of the dead, which in old times often exceeded the bounds of decency, has in later days been made the occasion of introducing a kind of burial service. The custom has now become general of asking a minister to *say grace* and *return thanks*, and sometimes Scripture is read. But, unquestionably, the observance of praying where the corpse lies, except in so far as it is shielded by this fiction, is more at variance with the Directory than words of committal at the grave or service in the church after the interment would be.

It was at one time intended to specify the superstitious usages of both kingdoms ; but they were found to be too numerous, and were therefore excluded in general terms. Among the things which the

Puritans disapproved was the wearing of mourning garments.* In Scotland great efforts were made to suppress lykwakes, or watchings by the dead, but they kept their place for more than a hundred years after this. The Synod of Fife, in 1641, forbade "the carrying the dead about the kirk, and burying unchristened children apart." The customs observed in 1712 at the burial of unchristened children are enumerated in the 4th part of Anderson's 'Dialogue.' Few were called to accompany the corpse. There was no tolling of the bell at the burial, nor intimation of the death; and they were buried near the wall of the church or the churchyard, that none might pass over their graves. Recently it was the rule to bury suicides and the unbaptised on the north side of the church; and even to this day in most rural churchyards which have not become crowded with the dead, the northern part lies unused, from an unconscious adherence to the medieval superstition, which left that side of the church to the powers of evil.

Concerning Public Solemn Fasting.

This section was given in on the 13th of December, and is described by Lightfoot as "exceeding long and full on controvertible matters." Three days were given to it. The first day they considered the length of time during which abstinence was to last—a natural day, as the Record, or a day of twenty-four hours, as Lightfoot calls it. Next day there was a debate about fasting and eating, in reference, probably, to the first parenthesis of the second paragraph. On the third there was a debate " on the liberty of divers families to meet together in private to fast." Several things are to be noted in this section. Among the occasions which call for the appointment of fasting days, the celebration of the Lord's Supper is not mentioned. Special Scriptures were to be chosen, and not those which fell to be read in ordinary course. In Scotland, the practice, as set down by Henderson and in the Common Order, was to read the Law at such times. The singing of penitential Psalms and the public Prayers have a more prominent place than in an ordinary service. We find Wodrow, in his 'Correspondence,' speaking of customs among the Irish Presbyterians, which were evidently in more strict accordance with the Directory than what he was accustomed to see in Scotland : " their altering our ordinary practice on fast-days, and haranguing instead of preaching upon a portion of Scripture, and spending the rest of time in prayer." There is perhaps some connection between this appointment of the

* Whitgift, i. 368, 378.

Directory and the old custom by which, on the morning of a Sacramental Fast-day, the minister of the parish offered a long prayer without preaching, leaving the sermon to another—a division of duty hardly ever seen on any other occasion. The passage is also worthy of notice in which unpremeditated prayer is discouraged. Another feature, characteristic of the age, is the solemn engagement to be the Lord's, entered into by the minister for himself and his people. There was a debate concerning the authority by which fasts ought to be appointed. In Scotland there was a controversy on this subject in the next century. Wodrow, speaking of it, says that he finds the right of the civil magistrate to fix them questioned by no authority except Rutherford and James Guthrie. We have no expression of Rutherford's views on the subject among any of the recorded proceedings of the Assembly.

Concerning the Observation of Days of Public Thanksgiving.

This section passed sooner than the others in this part of the Directory. It was brought in in August, when it was proposed to lay it aside, that Marriage, Burial, and the Churching of Women might be considered. But as it had been introduced, it was then finished in four sessions. It at first began, "Convenient warning is to be given of the day to be set apart;" but this was altered, for the not very obvious reason, that the words might mean that the right of setting apart such days belonged to the congregation. Rutherford and others maintained that the Church had no right to set apart from common uses more of the day than was to be spent in public worship. The mention of private preparation was opposed, as going beyond the limits of a Directory for public worship. Some objected that the order of service was too strictly imposed. It was made a question, whether the narration, which is peculiar to this service, should be ordered to be given "first," or "in the forenoon." And lastly, there was a debate about the magistrates "giving due information of the occasion." But this was omitted.

Of Singing of Psalms.

There seems to have been no intention of taking up this subject till the Directory for ordinary worship and administration of the Sacraments was receiving a final revision in November. It was then for the first time entered on the list of contents, after repeated motions made by Lightfoot. There must have been many who would have preferred to see it left an open question. Baillie says that in London the Puritans had two Psalms before sermon. But there was a party among them to whom "the singing of Psalms in meeter, not being formal Scripture, but a paraphrase, is unlawfull;"* and a more extreme section, in their abhorrence of set forms, had singing prophets, "making one man alone to sing, in the midst of the silent congregation, the hymns which he out of his own gift had composed." † But apart from such fantastic opinions, the prevalent feeling of that time was, that singing was what the First Book of Discipline had called it, "a profitable, but not necessary act of worship." The section was brought in on the 19th of December, and met with no opposition, except from Henderson, who disapproved of the reading of Psalms line by line, introduced in anticipation of a new version of the Psalms. It was less necessary in Scotland, where, after the fashion of some foreign churches, the Psalm was always repeated by the minister or reader before it was sung. This was given up, and the alternate reading and singing here enjoined were adopted—each line being read in monotone, on the note in which the first syllable was to be sung. In time this artificial form of praise became so dear to the people of Scotland, that they forgot that it was a modern and provisional arrangement. The Assembly of 1746 recommended that it should be discontinued in private worship. At a later period much angry feeling was excited when the natural system of continuous singing in the congregation was restored. The *giving out of the line* is now heard only where a Psalm is being sung in the intervals between the Communion table services.

The intention of the Assembly was that a new version should supersede that of Sternhold and Hopkins in both kingdoms. It was already understood, both by Parliament and Assembly, that the one most likely to be adopted was that of Francis Rous, a member of the House of Commons. It was not formally sanctioned in England till 1646, by which time it had undergone considerable alteration; and after further changes by various hands, it was finally accepted in Scotland in 1650. This is our present version, or, as it was then called, Paraphrase, and sometimes Metaphrase, of the Psalms of David. The Scottish Assembly intended the other songs of the Old and New Testament to be paraphrased in the same way. They were making provision for this at the same time that Rous's version was being revised for the last time; but their intentions were frustrated by the

* Dissuasive, p. 29. † Ibid., p. 81. Gangræna, i. 27; ii. 11.

religious anarchy which followed the battle of Dunbar. Soon after the Revolution the subject was revived. In the Assembly of 1696 it was remitted to the Commission to have the Scripture Songs revised. It was again taken up among the many plans for consolidating the system of the Church which occupied the Assembly immediately before the Union with England. But nothing permanent was done till the publication of the present Paraphrases in 1745, and their revision in 1782.

The Directory prescribes nothing here as to the number of Psalms to be sung. We may assume, therefore, that the two, which are so incidentally spoken of under the directions for ordinary service, fix the minimum, and not the measure of praise.

An Appendix touching Days and Places for Public Worship.

Apparently we owe this Appendix to the accidental circumstance that on the 19th of November the Assembly, through a derangement of their plans, found themselves without any work to do. First they ordered " that in the Directory for the Sabbath day something be expressed against wakes and feasts, commonly called by the name of rush-bearing, as profane and superstitious, whitsunales and garlands." Then they spoke of declaring against holy days as such, and yet keeping up some days for relief of servants. Having thus opened up the whole subject, they agreed to " consider of something concerning holy days and holy places," and the result was that this Appendix was brought up on the 10th of December. There was some debate about the mention of the Sabbath in it. The views of the Divines on holy days had somewhat changed during the year. On the 22d of December 1643 they adjourned till the 28th, refusing to give any opinion as to the propriety of having service on Christmas Day. The London clergy met, and, with a few exceptions, agreed to have it, resolving generally to cry down the superstition of the day. But in 1644 the Assembly applied to the Houses for an order for the observance of the next *fast* day, " because the people will be ready to neglect it, being Christmas Day."

This was a matter on which the Scots held decided opinions. Their historical position in reference to it is stated in the Act of Assembly 1638, sess. 17. The Assembly 1645 so far confirmed this Appendix by an Act of great stringency against the observance of Yule Day. Between the Restoration and the Revolution, the holy days were little regarded.* The regular observance of them by Scottish Episcopalians was of a later date. Among the people at large the feeling against them was very strong. No act of Queen's Anne's government was more unpopular than the repeal of a law which forbade a *Yule vacance*, or Christmas recess, in the Court of Session.

The last paragraph originally began thus :—"All holiness of place ceasing under the Gospel, no one place is now holier than another." This was objected to, and in the debate which followed Gillespie and Rutherford spoke, the latter in favour of the passage as it stood. At last it was altered so as to admit that places of worship have a relative holiness, but not derived from any ceremonial consecration. The extreme opinion referred to in the end of the section, that a church, once polluted by superstition, is unfitted for God's worship, was not uncommon at that period.† Hooker had thought it necessary to argue against it at some length. It is to be observed that, out of deference to the Independents, the word *Church* is neither here nor in any part of the Directory applied to the House of God.

* Toleration's Fence Removed, p. 17.   Full and Final Ans. Exam., p. 17.   Morer.
† Gangræna, 26.   Dissuasive, 27.

T. L.

THE END.

EDINBURGH: PRINTED BY WILLIAM BLACKWOOD AND SONS.

BOOKS

PUBLISHED BY

WILLIAM BLACKWOOD & SONS,

EDINBURGH AND LONDON.

Knox's Liturgy & the Westminster Directory.

THE

BOOK OF COMMON ORDER

COMMONLY KNOWN AS JOHN KNOX'S LITURGY,

AND THE

DIRECTORY FOR PUBLIC WORSHIP

OF THE

CHURCH OF SCOTLAND,

WITH HISTORICAL INTRODUCTIONS AND ILLUSTRATIVE NOTES

BY THE

REV. GEORGE W. SPROTT, B.A.

AND THE

REV. THOMAS LEISHMAN, M.A.

Handsomely printed, in imitation of the large Editions of Andro Hart, on toned paper, bound in cloth, red edges, price 7s. 6d.

"Besides the reprints, carefully edited, this work gives the history of Knox's Liturgy, its sources and relation to the Reformed Liturgies of the Continent and the English Book of Common Prayer; also full details as to the discussions at Westminster on the Directory, and the sense in which it was understood; and, by extracts from MSS., pamphlets, records of Church Courts, &c., illustrates the worship of the Church of Scotland from the Reformation till the present time."

Principal Campbell.

THE THEORY OF THE RULING ELDERSHIP;

Or, The Position of the Lay Ruler in the Reformed Churches Examined. By P. C. CAMPBELL, D.D., Principal of the University of Aberdeen. Price 3s.

"Principal Campbell deserves the best thanks of the whole community for setting forth this subject so opportunely, and in a work so lucid in arrangement, so accurate in statement, so irresistible in reasoning, and so perspicuous and pleasing in style. We most heartily recommend his production to the most anxious attention of the Churches and the public generally."—*Glasgow Herald.*

Professor Caird.

I.
SERMONS.

By the Rev. JOHN CAIRD, D.D., Professor of Divinity in the University of Glasgow. Twelfth Thousand. Foolscap octavo, 5s.

"They are noble sermons; and we are not sure but that, with the cultivated reader, they will gain rather than lose by being read, not heard. There is a thoughtfulness and depth about them which can hardly be appreciated unless when they are studied at leisure; and there are so many sentences so felicitously expressed that we should grudge being hurried away from them by a rapid speaker, without being allowed to enjoy them a second time."—*Fraser's Magazine.*

II.
RELIGION IN COMMON LIFE:

A Sermon Preached in Crathie Church, October 14, 1855, before Her Majesty the Queen and Prince Albert. Published by Her Majesty's Command. Bound in cloth, 8d. Cheap Edition, 3d.

Professor Charteris.

LIFE OF THE LATE REV. JAMES ROBERTSON,

D.D., F.R.S.E.,

Professor of Divinity and Ecclesiastical History in the University of Edinburgh. By the Rev. A. H. CHARTERIS, D.D. With a Portrait. Octavo, price 10s. 6d.

"The Memoir of Professor Robertson now published shows a depth in his spiritual life, a simplicity and energy in his faith, a genuine warmth of heart, love of evangelical truth, and high-toned self-consecration, that was but imperfectly indicated in his public life, and could scarcely have been guessed at by those who only knew him as the Assembly debater."—*Witness.*

Professor Crawford.

I.
THE FATHERHOOD OF GOD,

Considered in its General and Special Aspects, and particularly in relation to the Atonement; with a Review of Recent Speculations on the Subject, and a Reply to the Strictures of Dr Candlish. By THOMAS J. CRAWFORD, D.D., Professor of Divinity in the University of Edinburgh. Third Edition. In demy octavo, price 9s.

NOTICES OF THE FIRST EDITION.

"It is with sincere pleasure that I declare my concurrence in the whole substance of these two Lectures (on the Atonement). Dr Crawford has rendered a signal and seasonable service to the cause of truth, by the clear, cautious, and able exposition which he has given of the great catholic doctrine of the Atonement, and by his thorough vindication of it against Socinian and Neo-Socinian objections, founded on its alleged inconsistency with right notions of the character and government of God."—*Dr Candlish's Reply to Professor Crawford*, p. 19.

"We are acquainted with no abler and simpler exposure of the fallacies of the Broad Church School on the doctrine of the Atonement, than is to be found in the third and fourth lectures of Professor Crawford on 'The Fatherhood of God,' though we do not agree with some of his minor points."—*Wright's Divine Fatherhood*, p. 155.

"We have great satisfaction in recommending to the particular attention of students in theology a book so candid and so orthodox, so judicious and so seasonable.—*London Quarterly Review*.

"We regard this as one of the ablest of the theological treatises which have recently appeared. . . . In relation to the Atonement especially, his reasonings are well-timed and valuable. Indeed we do not know of any work in which the views of Maurice, Campbell, Robertson, and others, on that important doctrine, are so admirably refuted. . . . We earnestly commend this able volume to the attention of our readers, and do not hesitate to place it side by side with such recognised standards in systematic theology as the works of Hill, Dick, and Cunningham."—*United Presbyterian Magazine*.

II.
ADDRESS DELIVERED AT THE CLOSE OF THE GENERAL ASSEMBLY OF THE CHURCH OF SCOTLAND, 3d June 1867.

By the MODERATOR, T. J. CRAWFORD, D.D., Professor of Divinity in the University of Edinburgh. Second Edition, to which is appended a Notice of the Strictures of Bishop Wordsworth. Price 6d.

III.
PRESBYTERIANISM DEFENDED AGAINST THE EXCLUSIVE CLAIMS OF PRELACY,

As urged by Romanists and Tractarians. 2d edition. Also, PRESBYTERY or PRELACY, which is the more conformable to the pattern of the Apostolic Churches? By the Rev. T. J. CRAWFORD, D.D. 2d edition, 2s.

BOOKS PUBLISHED BY

The Church Service Society
EUCHOLOGION ; OR, BOOK OF PRAYERS:
Being Forms of Worship issued by the Church Service Society. Price 6s. 6d.

"We anticipate great good from the publication of such a work as this. It can hardly fail to encourage and carry forward that effort to improve the worship of our Churches which not a few feel to be the most urgent demand of the day. In conclusion, we commend this work to the laity as well as the clergy. If the latter ought to be the pioneers and guides in all Church reform, the former may be assured that what they are their ministers will in great measure be."—*Aberdeen Journal*.

"Their volume is, therefore, a magazine of prayers rather than a manual of devotion, consisting of specimens or examples of prayers—original but mainly selected, as full, as suggestive of solemn, earnest devotion as words can be, and these very skilfully arranged, so as to fit in with the simple order of the existing service. Wellnigh every similar work of any value seems to have been consulted, and as every selected sentence is referred to its source, the result is a work of very considerable interest."—*Dublin Evening Mail*.

Professor Flint
CHRIST'S KINGDOM UPON EARTH.
A SERIES OF DISCOURSES. By the Rev. ROBERT FLINT, Professor of Moral Philosophy in the University of St Andrews. Crown octavo, 7s. 6d.

Principal Lee
LECTURES ON THE HISTORY OF THE CHURCH OF SCOTLAND,
From the Reformation to the Revolution Settlement. By the Very Rev. JOHN LEE, D.D., LL.D., Principal of the University of Edinburgh. Edited by the Rev. WILLAM LEE. Two vols. octavo, 21s.

INAUGURAL ADDRESSES IN THE UNIVERSITY OF EDINBURGH.
To which is prefixed a Memoir of the Author, by Lord NEAVES. Foolscap octavo, 2s. 6d.

PASTORAL ADDRESSES OF THE GENERAL ASSEMBLY.
Foolscap, octavo, 2s. 6d.

UNION, ESPECIALLY BETWEEN THE ESTABLISHED AND FREE CHURCHES, VIEWED IN CONNECTION WITH THE LAW OF PATRONAGE.
By THOMAS MYLES, Minister of Aberlemno. Price 6d.

WILLIAM BLACKWOOD AND SONS. 5

Publications of the General Assembly's Committees

FAMILY PRAYERS.

Prepared by a Special Committee, and authorised by the General Assembly of the Church of Scotland. To which is prefixed, a Pastoral Letter from the General Assembly on Family Worship. A New Edition, price 2s., bound in cloth. Also an Edition in large type, price 4s. 6d.

PRAYERS FOR SOCIAL AND FAMILY WORSHIP.

For the use of Soldiers, Sailors, Colonists, Sojourners in India, and other Persons, at home and abroad, who are deprived of the ordinary services of a Christian Ministry; also, Prayers and Thanksgivings on particular occasions. Third Edition, crown octavo, 4s. Cheap Edition, 1s. 6d. Another Edition, on toned paper, 2s. 6d.

HYMNS FOR PUBLIC WORSHIP.

Selected by the Committee of the General Assembly of the Church of Scotland on Psalmody. In various sizes of type—price, respectively, 4d., 6d., and 1s., bound in cloth; also, an Edition for Schools, at 1½d.

INDEX TO THE ACTS AND PROCEEDINGS OF THE GENERAL ASSEMBLY OF THE CHURCH OF SCOTLAND,

From the Revolution to the present time. By the Rev. JOHN WILSON, Dunning. 5s.

THE LAW OF CREEDS IN SCOTLAND:

A Treatise on the Legal Relation of Churches in Scotland, Established and not Established, to their Doctrinal Confessions. By ALEXANDER TAYLOR INNES, M.A. In octavo, price 15s.

"I cannot quote this work without expressing my strong admiration of its learning, ability, and (with a very few exceptions) impartial statement of the whole question discussed in this address."—*Dean Stanley's Address "On the Connection of Church and State."*

"Stirs questions of the widest range of consequences in our own part of the island, as well as across the Tweed."—*The Guardian.*

"We commend Mr Innes's unanswerable reasonings, which have indeed an application far beyond the special points to which they are addressed."—*Nonconformist.*

THE INCREASE OF FAITH.

A New Edition, enlarged. Price 4s.

"Evidently the work of a man of wide culture as well as piety."—*Contemporary Review.*

"We strongly recommend the volume."—*Journal of Sacred Literature.*

"A thoughtful and earnest work on an important subject."—*Methodist Magazine.*

"Full of sound sense and practical purpose, and brings a wide range of practical experience and not very common illustration to bear on the subject."—*Literary Churchman.*

BOOKS PUBLISHED BY

Reb. Dr M'Crie

A New and Uniform Edition of his works. Edited by Professor M'CRIE. Four Volumes, crown octavo, 24s. Sold separately,—viz. :

LIFE OF JOHN KNOX.
Containing Illustrations of the History of the Reformation in Scotland. Crown octavo, 6s.

LIFE OF ANDREW MELVILLE.
Containing Illustrations of the Ecclesiastical and Literary History of Scotland in the Sixteenth and Seventeenth Centuries. Crown octavo, 6s.

HISTORY OF THE PROGRESS AND SUPPRESSION OF THE REFORMATION IN ITALY IN THE SIXTEENTH CENTURY.
Crown octavo, 4s.

HISTORY OF THE PROGRESS AND SUPPRESSION OF THE REFORMATION IN SPAIN IN THE SIXTEENTH CENTURY.
Crown octavo, 3s. 6d.

SERMONS, AND REVIEW OF THE "TALES OF MY LANDLORD."
In One Volume, crown octavo, 6s.

Professor Milligan

THE DECALOGUE AND THE LORD'S DAY,
In the Light of the General Relation of the Old and New Testaments ; with a Chapter on Confessions of Faith. By the Rev. WILLIAM MILLIGAN, D.D., Professor of Divinity and Biblical Criticism in the University of Aberdeen. 4s. 6d.

Professor Mitchell.

THE WEDDERBURNS AND THEIR WORK ;
Or, THE SACRED POETRY OF THE SCOTTISH REFORMATION IN ITS HISTORICAL RELATION TO THAT OF GERMANY. By ALEX. F. MITCHELL, D.D., Professor of Hebrew, St Andrews. In small quarto, price 2s. 6d.

SERMONS.
By the late Rev. C. K. WATT, M.A., Assistant-Minister, North Leith. Fcap. octavo, 2s. 6d.

"He could not only master a subject and go to its very root, but he could breathe life and shape into it from the fulness of his own thoughtfulness. These Sermons appear to me to show the same combination of power in a high degree. Each forms a special study on some theological topic. The topic is not only handled with an easy mastery of all its bearings, but touched with freshness of interest. The writer is plainly at home in the traditional theology; its dogmatic notes are familiar to him, and respected by him; but he expands and vivifies them with a new meaning."—*Editor's Preface.*

Count de Montalembert

THE MONKS OF THE WEST,

From St Benedict to St Bernard. By the COUNT DE MONTALEMBERT. Authorised Translation. Five Volumes. Octavo, £2, 12s. 6d.

THE CONVERSION OF ENGLAND BY THE MONKS OF THE WEST.

Three Vols. 31s. 6d. (forming Vols. 3, 4, and 5 of the 'Monks of the West.')

LIFE OF SAINT COLUMBA, THE APOSTLE OF CALEDONIA.

Republished from the Author's 'Monks of the West.' Price 3s. 6d.

"On the whole, the intellectual interest of the Count's 'Monks of the West' rests mainly on this, that it is the work of a brilliant and accomplished layman and man of the world, dealing with a class of characters who have generally been left to the arid professional handling of ecclesiastical writers. Montalembert sees their life as a whole, and a human whole; and, with all his zeal as an amateur hagiographer, he cannot but view them with some of the independence of a mind trained to letters and politics."—*Pall Mall Gazette.*

"Throughout these volumes what especially strikes us is a certain sort of honesty of purpose, quiet impartiality, and plain truthfulness about the author, which lends a charm to all he writes, and makes his work of double value as mere history. . . . No library of English history can be complete without these glowing pictures of the 'Monks of the West.'"—*Examiner.*

Rev. Dr Nicholson.

REST IN JESUS.

By the Rev. MAXWELL NICHOLSON, D.D., Minister of St Stephen's. Third Edition, price 4s. 6d.

"We heartily commend this book to our readers. They will find in it vigorous thinking and true feeling and manly piety without a trace of mawkishness, combined in honest, earnest directions for Christian living, by one who is clearly giving them the results of the experience of his own life."—*Glasgow Herald.*

Professor Pirie.

NATURAL THEOLOGY:

An Inquiry into the Fundamental Principles of Religious, Moral, and Political Science. By W. R. PIRIE, D.D., Professor of Divinity and Church History in the University of Aberdeen. Price 5s.

"Remarkable at once for its vigour and independence, and will make Professor Pirie much more widely known than he ever has been, as one of the deepest and clearest thinkers of our country."—*Morning Journal.*

Dr Park.
LECTURES AND SERMONS.
By the late Rev. JOHN PARK, D.D., Minister of the First Charge, St Andrews. Crown octavo, 9s.

"Specimens of Scotch preaching at its very best."—*A. K. H. B. in Fraser's Magazine.*

Dean Ramsay.
THE CHRISTIAN LIFE, IN ITS ORIGIN, PROGRESS, AND PERFECTION.
By the Very Rev. E. B. RAMSAY, LL.D., F.R.S.E., Dean of the Diocese of Edinburgh. Crown octavo, 9s.

Rev. Dr Andrew Thomson and Principal Candlish.
LOVERS OF PLEASURES MORE THAN LOVERS OF GOD.
Two Discourses. By the late ANDREW THOMSON, D.D., Minister of St George's Church, Edinburgh; with an Introductory Essay by the Rev. PRINCIPAL CANDLISH. 1s. cloth.

Principal Tulloch.
I.
LEADERS OF THE REFORMATION:
LUTHER, CALVIN, LATIMER, and KNOX. By the Rev. JOHN TULLOCH, D.D., Principal, and Primarius Professor of Theology, St Mary's College, St Andrews. Second Edition, crown octavo, 6s. 6d.

II.
ENGLISH PURITANISM AND ITS LEADERS:
CROMWELL, MILTON, BAXTER, and BUNYAN. Uniform with the 'Leaders of the Reformation.' 7s. 6d.

"It is a book which, from its style—firm and interesting, dispassionate and impartial, but yet warm with admiration—will be hailed for fireside reading in the families of the descendants of those Puritan men and their times."—*Eclectic Review.*

III.
THEISM:
The Witness of Reason and Nature to an All-Wise and Beneficent Creator. Octavo, 10s. 6d.

"Dr Tulloch's Essay, in its masterly statement of the real nature and difficulties of the subject, its logical exactness in distinguishing the illustrative from the suggestive, its lucid arrangement of the argument, its simplicity of expression, is quite unequalled by any work we have seen on the subject."—*Christian Remembrancer*, January 1857.

www.ingramcontent.com/pod-product-compliance
Lightning Source LLC
Chambersburg PA
CBHW032137010526
44111CB00035B/596